Blood on their Banner

For Éloi, Jean-Marie, Yéiwene and the other martyrs

Blood on their Banner
Nationalist Struggles in the South Pacific

David Robie

London and New Jersey

Pluto Press Australia

Blood on their Banner was first published in 1989
in the United Kingdom and the United States of America
by
Zed Books Ltd.,
57 Caledonian Road,
London N1 9BY

and

171 First Avenue,
Atlantic Highlands,
New Jersey 07716.

In Australia and New Zealand
Pluto Press Australia,
P O Box 199,
Leichhardt, NSW 2040.

Author's translation of the poem *La rivière pleure*, from the collection
Sous les cendras des conques, published by permission of Déwé Gorode.
© Édipop, Noumea, New Caledonia, 1985.

Book design by Phillip Ridge/Bookmakers, Auckland, New Zealand
Typeset by Sabagraphics, Christchurch, New Zealand.
Cover designed by Waleed Muhsin
Printed and bound in the United Kingdom
by Biddles Ltd, Guildford and King's Lynn

British Library Cataloguing in Publication Data

Robie, David
  Blood on their banner: nationalist struggles in the South Pacific
  I. Pacific Islands. South Pacific islands.
  nationalist movements
  I. Title
  322.4'2'099

  ISBN 0-86232-864-0
  ISBN 0 86232-865-9 pbk

Australian Edition:
ISBN: 0 949138 35 5

New Zealand Distributor:
Allen & Unwin NZ Ltd, Private Bag, Wellington

Library of Congress Cataloging-in-Publication Data

Robie, David.
  Blood on their banner: nationalist struggles in the South
  Pacific/David Robie.
    p. cm.
  Includes bibliographical references.
  ISBN 0-86232-864-0. —ISBN 0-86232-865-9 (pbk.)
    1. Nationalism—Oceania. 2. Oceania—History. I. Title.
  DU28.3.R63 1989
  995—dc20   89-28954
                                               CIP

Contents

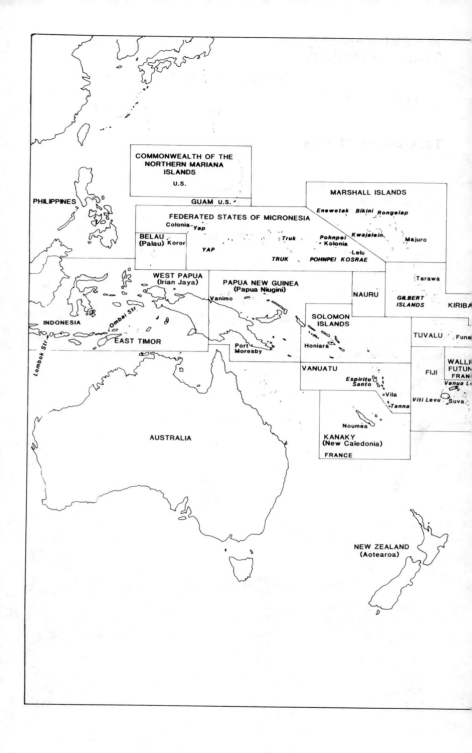

SOUTH PACIFIC

nston

HAWAI'I
U.S.

Christmas

LINE ISLANDS

ENIX ISLANDS

TOKELAU

MARQUESAS ISLANDS

ST AMERICAN
OA SAMOA
Pago Pago
U.S.

TAHITI
(French Polynesia)

TUAMOTU
ARCHIPELAGO   FRANCE

NGA   COOK ISLANDS

SOCIETY Tahiti
ISLANDS

Hao

NIUE

'alofa   Rarotonga

Moruroa
Fangataufa

PITCAIRN Is

AUSTRAL
ISLANDS

GAMBIER
ISLANDS

U.K.

RAPANUI
(Easter Island)
CHILE

The South Pacific Forum, formed at Wellington in 1971, comprises 15 independent and self-governing countries in the region — Australia, Cook Islands, Federated States of Micronesia, Fiji, Kiribati, Marshall Islands, Nauru, New Zealand, Niue, Papua New Guinea, Solomon Islands, Tonga, Tuvalu, Vanuatu and Western Samoa. FSM and Marshall Islands joined at the 1987 Forum meeting in Apia; Belau wishes to join when its continuing constitutional crisis is resolved. The Forum secretariat, SPEC, is based in Suva.

Author's note

Since this book was written, Dr Timoci Bavadra, the deposed Prime Minister of Fiji and a man of great vision in the South Pacific, died on 3 November 1989 after a long struggle with cancer. Ousted in two military *Coups d'etat* in 1987, he had spent much of his life battling courageously for social justice and a multiracial future for his country. Fiji, when he died, was a divided and demoralised republic, founded on racism and treason, and at the point of a gun. But, to the end, Dr Bavadra continued to cherish the ideals for which he had stood throughout his life.

Acknowledgements

My gratitude to all those friends and contacts in the South Pacific who, over the years, have given me valuable insight into nationalism and liberation struggles in the region.

I am particularly indebted to former Stockholm International Peace Research Institute researcher Owen Wilkes. He patiently provided much feedback, guidance and constructive criticism. Marie-Thérèse and Bengt Danielsson have been an inspiration and I warmly thank them for their support. Robbie Robertson and Akosita Tamanisau, co-authors of *Shattered Coups* were a great help with the chapters on Fiji. Alister Barry and Philip Shingler, co-producers of the 1989 Pacific Stories television documentary *Niuklia Fri Pasifik*, provided valuable insight into the South Pacific Nuclear-Free Zone Treaty. Thanks also to my editor, Phillip Ridge, a constant source of advice.

Among many others who have contributed or helped in some way are: *Belau and Micronesia*: Glenn Alcalay, Roman Bedor, Roger Clark, Pheroze Jagose, Giff Johnson and Ed Rampell; *East Timor and West Papua*: Elaine Brière, Carmel Budiardjo, James Dunn, José Ramos-Horta, Liem Soei Liong, Rex Rumakiek, Frank Senge, Pat Walsh and Helen Yensin; *Fiji*: John Cameron, Jone Dakuvula, Nemani Delabaitiki, Richard Naidu, John Richardson, Robert Robertson, Akosita Tamanisau and Reg Sanday; *Kanaky*: Geoff Adlide, Frédéric Bobin, Jean-Pierre Deteix, Helen Fraser, Wales Kotra, James McNeish, Susanna Ounei, David Small, Joseph Tran, Sue Williams and Donna Winslow; *Tahiti*: Téa Hirshon and, of course, the Danielssons; *Vanuatu*: Jonas Cullwick, Hilda Lini, Clarence Marae and Charles Rara; and Sidney Jones of Amnesty International. My thanks also go to Hilary Anderson, Matthew McKee, Phil Esmonde and Phil Twyford for their encouragement and help. My young sons, Lucien and Simeon, cheerfully endured my preoccupation with writing for so many months.

David Robie

Foreword

Many artificial barriers remain in the Pacific that were created by the foreign colonial powers which ruled, or still rule, the islands. The main one separates the people of the colonies governed by France, Indonesia and the United States from the populations of independent countries. While colonised islanders receive directions and impulses only from their 'mother country', liberated islanders have by their own free will established among themselves a network of political, economic and cultural ties.

There also exists among the new island nations, as well as between them and their benevolent protectors, Australia and New Zealand, a free exchange of ideas, news and information. Here again, a sort of iron curtain isolates the dependent territories from the independent island nations.

Having lived most of our lives in French Polynesia, we are, for instance, painfully aware of how thoroughly the local mass media manages to keep us in ignorance of what is happening in other Pacific islands. Except, perhaps, when there has been a particularly bloody tribal feud in the highlands of Papua New Guinea, or a hurricane in Fiji. And every now and then there appears on our television screen a French naval commander who has visited some other Pacific islands in his warship to tell us about the 'terrifying poverty and misery' he has seen there. On the other hand, TV, radio and newspaper journalists regularly inform us about almost every political, cultural and sporting event in France.

With the same vigilance and ruthlessness with which the French colonial administration controls the incoming flow of information, it also ensures that hardly any unfavourable news trickles out. This is actually an easy task because no international news agency has found it worth their while to post a staff correspondent to these remote, supposedly placid islands.

In order to make sure that no unpleasant news appears in foreign newspapers and magazines, a French government official regularly contributes glowing reports of carefully selected local events to Agence France-Presse, one of the world's four big Western news agencies. And these propaganda bulletins are too often accepted by the foreign publications which subscribe to the AFP service as reliable accounts by a bona fide reporter. In addition, the local French administration also employs a bevy of charming Tahitian hostesses and hospitable public relations men to 'guide' visiting journalists.

The situation is, of course, much worse in East Timor and West Papua in western Melanesia, ruled by Indonesian army commanders and closed to outsiders. As for the Micronesian states emerging from the Trust Territory of the Pacific Islands, where admittedly the American democratic system has largely prevailed, there are nevertheless some places, such as Belau, where the colonial masters have clamped down — through, at times, locally-developed proxies — at least as harshly as the French in New Caledonia and Tahiti. On Rapanui (Easter Island), too, the 1800 Polynesian inhabitants have been repressed: there is no assembly, municipal council or other form of institution made up of their locally-elected representatives. All rulers are Chileans, appointed by the colonial government in Santiago. As for information, it comes solely through official channels from Santiago.

New Zealand journalist David Robie managed to break through the Pacific communications barrier in the mid-1970s — simply by travelling widely and investigating. It took much courage to do so, especially in New Caledonia where so-called security agents harassed and hindered him in his quest for the truth; on one occasion he was arrested.

Robie went beyond on-the-spot reporting to produce a series of well-documented analyses and overviews in which he clearly shows how the ultimate cause of the conflicts and revolts occurring in the Pacific is everywhere the same, and has to do with the maintenance and strengthening of the colonial system. This is always done with the help of troops and police forces. Often it is also through the lavish use of money and bribes, and involving the indoctrination of Pacific peoples — starting at an early age in school — and the swamping of some colonies with foreign settlers. In New Caledonia, for instance, the unfortunate Kanaks have already been turned into a minority in their own country.

Part of Robie's first-hand knowledge of Micronesia was acquired in a particularly adventurous manner: he took part as a reporter in the 1985 voyage of the Greenpeace flagship *Rainbow Warrior* when the long-suffering irradiated Rongelap Islanders were evacuated from their atoll. He stayed on board the ship until that fateful day in July when she was sunk by French saboteurs, and his book *Eyes of Fire* remains the best and most vivid account of this tragic event which has so profoundly marked the history of the South Pacific.

It can also be regarded as a tribute to Robie and several other courageous reporters that as soon as a new conservative government came to power in France in 1986 it launched a counter-offensive to polish the French public image, tarnished by the many revealing articles in the Australian and New Zealand press. The strangest manifestation of this new drive was the setting up of an Institut d'Études de la Désinformation (Institute of

Disinformation Studies), under the guidance of the then Minister for Defence, André Giraud, a quite logical arrangement, considering that most of the information in the foreign press about France in the South Pacific concerned the nuclear tests at Moruroa. The well-chosen head of this agency had long experience in the field, for he was none other than the former director of the DGSE *(Directorate Générale de la Sécurité Extérieure)* intelligence service, Admiral Pierre Lacoste, who claimed in 1985 that he and his agents had nothing to do with the sinking of the *Rainbow Warrior*.

But to tell the truth (in accordance with the aim of this 'institute'), its weekly publication, *Désinformation-Hebdo*, has so far made only one major scoop: the quite surprising discovery that all enemies of France in the Pacific region are being manipulated by the Libyans and Russians!

As a necessary complement to this remarkable but little remarked 'truth' crusade, the government of Prime Minister Jacques Chirac had also deemed it necessary to organise occasional special seminars in Tahiti for French ambassadors stationed in the Pacific. At these briefings, high-ranking civilian and military officials explained to the diplomats what to say when the French colonial and nuclear policies came under attack in the countries where they were accredited. This happened, for example, after the 1987 screening in Australia and New Zealand of a British television documentary, *Tahiti Witness*, about the cancer victims of the Moruroa tests. Not all the ambassadors were happy with the way in which the organisers of this seminar advised them to stave off the universal condemnation, for it consisted solely of denouncing the whole programme as a tissue of lies.

Prime Minister Chirac tried a more positive approach by dispatching on a round trip to all Pacific nations, to win friends and influence people, the head of the local puppet government in French Polynesia, Gaston Flosse, who had been accorded the unusual honour of being appointed a member of the French cabinet. The idea was that an easy-going islander in a floral shirt would be more acceptable to other island leaders than a rigid, pale-faced Frenchman in a dark flannel suit.

This was probably the case, but Flosse nevertheless failed, mainly because he was given the impossible task of having to explain in each Pacific country why a government which pretends that the nuclear tests at Moruroa Atoll are 'harmless' does not undertake them in France and, why the indigenous inhabitants of the two Pacific colonies, New Caledonia and French Polynesia, virtually alone among the peoples of the world, should be denied their right to independence.

With the return of the socialists to power in France in mid-1988, Prime Minister Michel Rocard's timid attempt to bring peace to New Caledonia through the Matignon Accord was a long overdue break with the brutal methods used by Chirac, who had labelled Kanak freedom fighters 'terrorists' and dispatched a steadily increasing number of troops to harass them. But the referendum on 6 November put to French voters on the future of

New Caledonia was an ambiguous choice. The voters were not given a straightforward question: *Are you for or against independence for the Kanaks?* Instead, they were asked what they thought of Rocard's vague 'peace plan' that will eventually lead in 1998 to yet another referendum — which the Gaullist RPR party has pledged to cancel, if and when it returns to power.

Since the referendum, which gained an 80 percent yes vote with record low voter participation, skipped over all the real issues, we would like to refer to an opinion poll conducted by the IPSOS Institute only a week before the vote. A representative sample of French people was asked: *Do you accept or reject the idea that the French overseas territories and departments should be granted independence within the next ten-year period?* The answer was a resounding yes in all cases from the Caribbean to the Pacific. For New Caledonia, 47 percent favoured independence and 37 percent were against, while in French Polynesia the figures were 45 percent for and 38 percent against.

We are particularly pleased that Robie's reports of events in the South Pacific have been gathered into a book, which will undoubtedly reach a wide, international reading public. We believe that this will foster greater understanding of the liberation movements in the last Pacific colonies.

Marie-Thérèse and Bengt Danielsson
Papehue, Tahiti
January 1989.

Introduction

*Three Kanak militants guard a barricade across the narrow Thio River bridge
in Kanaky/New Caledonia. One, dressed in a Che Guevara T-shirt, grips
a speargun. Another nurses an ageing shotgun on his hip. The third reads
a* Star Wars *comic, a felling axe nearby. Beyond a barbed wire barrier at
the far end of the bridge, Kanak women stand chatting. One chips away bark
from a niaouli tree with a bushknife. Her letters spell* FLNKS — *Front de
Libération Nationale Kanak et Socialiste (Kanak Socialist National Liberation
Front), the movement which has proclaimed a 'provisional government' of
Kanaky and an end to French rule in the South Pacific territory.*

On a whitewashed building a slogan proclaims Vive Kadafi!, *and scrawled
across the road near the bridge* Freedom or death — we'll win. *Altogether
about 200 Kanak militants gather at seven barricades thrown up around the
small nickel mining township, 130 kilometres from the capital of Nouméa. They
are listless, shocked by the tragedy of the previous night.*

*Since dawn, the radio reports have been disturbing: 'A bloody massacre has
happened near the town of Hienghène . . . details are still sketchy and confused.
At least five bodies have been found so far.'*

*Later news broadcasts fill in the gaps: 'Six Kanaks died in last night's
Hienghène massacre and several others are severely wounded and expected to
die. Dynamite was used in the attack by settlers. Another body, burnt and
riddled with bullets, has been found.'*

*The charred corpse is one of the two brothers of Kanak leader Jean-Marie
Tjibaou who are among the victims . . . Ten unarmed Kanaks are slaughtered
in the ambush on 5 December 1984. And the murders unleash a series of events
which lead to more than 50 deaths and the assassination of peacemaker Tjibaou
himself over the next five years.*

*Seven months later, on 30 June 1985, President Haruo Remeliik of Belau
arrives back at the capital of Koror tired from a day's fishing. It is just after
midnight as he drives up to his hilltop home. His wife and several of their
children are asleep.*

13

*As he steps out of his car, Remeliik is gunned down by unknown assassins
and is shot four times before they flee into the night.*

*The strategic western Pacific nation has already been an international cause
célèbre since 1979 when its 15,000 inhabitants endorsed the world's first nuclear-
free constitution by a 92 percent vote. Remeliik was the 'father' of the constitution
and among its defenders against United States strategic interests. Now he has
become its first martyr.*

*The early official accounts of Remeliik's murder claim he has been killed
by 'crazies'. Other theories blame the drug trade and foreign investors. But
when three men are finally charged it is an alleged political conspiracy which
grips the nation. With the Pentagon needing Belau as a fallback base if the
Philippine government refuses to renew the leases on Subic Bay Naval Base
and Clark Air Base in 1991, it is clear that the United States stands to gain
from President Remeliik's death. Mounting violence in Belau follows his murder
as a series of referenda are held in an attempt to scuttle the constitution.*

*Nearly two years later, on 14 May 1987, Taukei politician Taniela Veitata
makes a provocative speech in the previously tranquil Fiji Parliament: 'Peace
is quite distinct, Mr Speaker,' he says, 'from the political philosophy of Mao
Zedong where he said that political power comes out of the barrel of a gun . . .'*

*Minutes later, at the stroke of ten o'clock, Veitata, a former trade unionist
known for his extremist right-wing views, finishes his address as Fijian troops
storm Parliament.*

*'Sit down everybody . . . this is a takeover,' says coup d'état leader
Lieutenant-Colonel Sitiveni Rabuka, standing up in the public gallery. Ten
masked and armed soldiers burst into the debating chamber. Prime Minister
Timoci Bavadra and 26 members of his Fiji Labour Party-dominated coalition
government are ordered out of the House. Forced at gunpoint into waiting
trucks, they are driven to nearby army barracks.*

*Dr Bavadra, Fiji's first 'commoner' Prime Minister, and his MPs become
hostages as their country is plunged into the greatest political turmoil it has
ever known.*

What do these three apparently unrelated crises in the South Pacific have
in common? The insurrections in New Caledonia, the gangland-style
'execution' of the Belauan President, and the first successful coup in the
region mark a turning point for South Pacific island states. They represent
a loss of geopolitical innocence, a sign that Oceania cannot be taken for
granted in the modern world. Certainly stereotyped images of the Pacific
as a region of untroubled idyllic island paradises have been irreparably
shattered.

Although most Western news coverage of the Pacific islands continues
to give an impression of the region as a tourist dream world of sun-drenched

atolls, sandy beaches and coconut economies where the biggest events are the occasional cyclone or hurricane, the reality is quite different. More than any other issue, nationalist aspirations now define the politics of the South Pacific. And where such nationalism has confronted existing colonial structures within the region, the resulting struggles have had profound and tragic consequences.

The ugly side of Oceania involves genocide, assassination, guerrilla warfare and, most recently, a military takeover and an abortive constitutional coup. Yet these have largely been ignored by the world's media. In some countries the troubles have existed for decades, while in the 'forgotten wars' of East Timor and West Papua, hundreds of thousands of people have died.

The real Pacific

The Pacific Ocean covers nearly a third of the world's surface and is home to more than five million indigenous islanders. And for 400 years, these people have lived under the flag, nominally and otherwise, of various Western nations. At first, Western colonial interests in the scattered islands were largely economic. At the time of Captain James Cook's 'discovery' of New Caledonia in 1774, notes one historian, voyages of exploration in the region were 'motivated as much by scientific curiosity as by the lure of gain'.[1] What was in the 16th century a 'Spanish lake' became a stamping ground in the 19th century for European traders, settlers, planters, whalers, blackbirders and, of course, missionaries. But colonial capitalism gained only a limited foothold in the South Pacific.

The promise of riches in the islands proved illusory. As a result, colonialism tended to be superficial; Britain and France, which superseded Spain as the dominant colonial powers in the region, ruled in an offhand way, with minimal administration. The economic rewards were not great enough to warrant the expense of direct rule over the sparsely populated islands. Apart from New Caledonia, and to some extent Vanuatu, the trappings of colonialism were reasonably easy to dismantle. Yet demands for their removal remained limited.

Thus, while Africa, Asia and the Caribbean were embroiled in intense and often violent liberation struggles after the Second World War, the Pacific colonies enjoyed tranquil or even stagnant relations with their metropolitan overlords. In fact, by the mid-1960s, when the decolonisation process had been virtually completed in most parts of the world, it had barely begun in the South Pacific. Acts of defiance against the colonisers, such as the pacifist Mau uprising in New Zealand-ruled Western Samoa during the 1920s, were rare. Although Western Samoa gained independence in 1962, the 'winds of change' did not really whip through the Pacific until much later.

By the late 1960s a fresh political geography began to emerge in the South Pacific. In a remarkably peaceful decolonisation era, name changes and new nations altered maps, as the last outposts of European empires were cast adrift: Western Samoa was followed into independence by Nauru, a guano-rich island of barely 20 square kilometres, in 1968, and by Fiji in 1970; in the same year the kingdom of Tonga ended its British protectorate status. Five years later Papua New Guinea, by far the largest of the new Pacific nations, with a population of more than three million, gained independence from Australia. It was followed by Tuvalu (previously the Ellice Islands) and the Solomon Islands in 1978, Kiribati (Gilbert Islands) in 1979 and Vanuatu (New Hebrides) in 1980.

Turning Point

The independence of Vanuatu became the turning point in the politics of the region. The only country so far forced to survive a violent struggle to achieve independence, Vanuatu ended the first phase of decolonisation in the region and heralded a new era of growing conflict and uncertainty. In May 1980, two months before the ni-Vanuatu people emerged from a bizarre colonial administration, the Anglo-French condominium, rebels seized control of the largest island of Espiritu Santo and seceded. The rebels called themselves the 'Republic of Vemarana' — rather in the manner that Mayotte became a French island enclave in the Indian Ocean republic of the Comoros. Partly financed by right-wing American business interests and supported by the French colonial administration, the Santo rebellion, was only overcome by the fledgling government of Vanuatu with the help of troops from Papua New Guinea.

Although French commercial interests in the plantation economy had waned several years before, France belatedly decided to sabotage independence in Vanuatu because of its fears of the impact of decolonisation on New Caledonia and French Polynesia. Even the slim hope of a new era after the election of socialist President François Mitterrand in 1981 proved to be an illusion. Vanuatu, under the leadership of Prime Minister Father Walter Lini, absorbed its harsh lesson and became the most outspoken champion of Kanak and other nationalist movements in the region. But it was not an easy role.

Partly this had to do with conflicting imperial responses to independence. Some colonial powers have been happily prepared to sever their colonial strings, particularly where nationalist aspirations posed no threat to the status quo. The British above all have been anxious to abandon unprofitable fragments of empire; none of their remaining colonies have populations of more than 60,000, and Pitcairn — their last Pacific possession — has fewer than 60. New Zealand gave early independence to Western Samoa, and later granted self-government to the Cook Islands and Niue. Australia shed its trusteeship of Nauru, and eventually bowed to Papua New Guinean independence desires.

Both France and the United States, however, have refused to surrender even the smallest part of the South Pacific — except under duress as in Vanuatu. Now, as superpower rivalry threatens to turn South Pacific nations into strategic pawns, the region is being torn by fresh upheavals, a second wind of change increasingly frustrated by the intransigent policies of France, the United States, and also Indonesia.

France claims it wants to retain its South Pacific presence for similar reasons to the United States — a concern about communism and the Soviet Union, the desire for stability and the maintenance of the 'balance of power'. But there are other, more sinister, factors behind the publicly stated reasons. French colonialism in both New Caledonia and Tahiti in the 19th century was largely motivated by the wish to prevent the South Pacific becoming a British lake. Although Britain has virtually withdrawn from the region, France, like the United States, has boosted its economic, military and political presence, and has helped create a Franco-American lake!

France wants to preserve access to its South Pacific nuclear test centre, retain New Caledonia as one of its biggest colonies — a kind of jewel in the the French imperial crown — to which French settlers can still migrate, retain control of the world's second-largest aggregate 200-mile economic zone, and maintain a girdle of French possessions around the globe. Although largely for reasons of pride, prestige and vainglory, the grand imperial design also has practical military significance. The French military has the second-largest global distribution of military bases after the United States — stretching like stepping stones from France to Djibouti to Mayotte to Réunion to New Caledonia to Tahiti to Martinique to Senegal and back to France.

New Caledonia has become the most critical factor in this political equation. When Vanuatu became independent, France's then State Secretary for Overseas Territories, Paul Dijoud, pledged that 'battle must be done to keep New Caledonia French.'[2] The closest Pacific island neighbour to Australia and New Zealand, New Caledonia is the last 'domino' before French Polynesia where the vital nuclear tests for the *force de frappe* are carried out.

'Geography,' noted the Nouméa newspaper *Les Nouvelles Calédoniennes*, 'has turned New Caledonia into an aircraft carrier of 19,000 square kilometres, two-thirds the size of Belgium, situated at the junction of the South Pacific sea lanes between Australia and the United States, and between Asia and South America. It holds a key position, especially in the light of the emerging importance of the Pacific region in the global balance of power.'[3]

The 1984 Kanak revolt against French rule eventually cost 32 lives, most of them Melanesian, with the Hienghène massacre the most devastating clash. Within eight weeks of the start of the rebellion militant Kanak leader Éloi Machoro, who had bloodlessly captured the mining town of Thio, was dead — shot by French police marksmen. From then on nationalist tensions in New Caledonia rapidly became convulsions, spreading throughout the South Pacific.

France sponsored state terrorism in the South Pacific in 1985 when its secret agents bombed the *Rainbow Warrior*, partly in an unsuccessful attempt to scuttle the protest voyage by an anti-nuclear fleet to Moruroa Atoll planned for that year and partly out of paranoia over the more militant pressure for independence spreading from New Caledonia to Tahiti.

After March 1986 the conservative French government of Prime Minister Jacques Chirac turned back the clock and wiped out efforts made by its socialist predecessor to prepare the territory for a form of independence in association with France. A military buildup, harassment of Kanak villages, and provocative political measures pushed the territory to the brink of civil war.

Another insurrection, during the May 1988 French presidential elections, led to 28 more deaths. The uprising climaxed with the Ouvéa massacre in which 19 Kanak militants were killed in a military operation to rescue gendarmes seized as hostages. Chirac was defeated, however, and Mitterrand, safely elected for a futher seven years in office, began addressing some of the worst excesses of *cohabitation* rule. Socialist Prime Minister Michel Rocard introduced the Matignon Accord, a peace plan which would carve up the territory into three autonomous provinces, and prepare for a referendum on self-determination in 1998.

A year later, on the eve of the Ouvéa killings, the Matignon agreement and the independence cause suffered a tragic setback with the assassination of FLNKS president Jean-Marie Tjibaou and his deputy, Yéiwène Yéiwène. They were gunned down by an opponent of the accord, Pastor Djoubelly Wea, at point-blank range; he in turn was killed by one of Tjibaou's bodyguards.

Indigenous conflicts

French colonial rule in the Pacific, obsolete and doomed, deserves to be condemned. But, stresses historian Jean Chesneaux, professor emeritus at the Sorbonne, France should not be singled out as a scapegoat, 'since, in the Pacific region today, there are many other conflicts over the legitimate rights of the indigenous peoples: in colonial Micronesia; in Australia and New Zealand over land rights and political demands on the part of Aborigines and the Maori; while on Easter Island [Rapanui] Polynesians are under Pinochet's fascist rule. These other conflicts and aspirations need to be given the same attention as those which derive from French colonial rule.'[4]

The United States has a more ideological basis for its Pacific presence than France — in the sense that it sees itself as a kind of global ideological police force. Although arguably more subtle, its colonial record is equally disturbing, particularly in Micronesia. Washington, argues a former Stockholm International Peace Research Institute analyst, Owen Wilkes, has during the 1980s encouraged the 'Latin-Americanisation of the South Pacific'. Taking into account the island-and-ocean nature of the region, a more appropriate term might be *Caribbeanisation*. Wilkes is among many who regard the coup in Fiji as the 'first fruits' of this trend: 'The creation of a Caribbean-style military dictatorship which will be more responsive to US needs than a [Bavadra-led] democracy would have been.'[5]

Despite a brief American pullback in Asia following defeat in Vietnam, the Pentagon maintained and is now upgrading its strategic role in the Pacific. Nuclear war in the Pacific has again become 'thinkable' in the minds of American military strategists. Nuclear weaponry is integrated in all aspects of American military activity — as illustrated by United States insistence on free access for nuclear-capable vessels everywhere. The United States does not have a 'non-nuclear navy' for some countries and a 'nuclear navy' for others.

> [Its strategy is] to contain social revolution and to intimidate the Soviet Union. The MX, Trident and anti-ballistic missile tests over the ever-expanding [Kwajalein] Pacific Missile Range and the dangerous new Tomahawk [sea-launched] cruise missile are central components of American striving for nuclear superiority.[6]

American power in the Pacific counts on the support of its regional allies — Australia, New Zealand and island states such as Fiji, as well as France, Japan, Indonesia and the Philippines. A major buildup of military, political and propaganda activity in the region by the United States and its allies over recent years has been preceded and accompanied by a saturation barrage of Western publicity about a so-called Soviet threat to the Pacific, especially the South Pacific.

In reality, the Soviet strategic position in the North Pacific is bleak, and it is negligible in the South Pacific. Even Francis J. West, one of the United States Navy's top analysts, has concluded the Soviet Navy cannot 'perform adequately any but its primary mission of homeland defence'.[7] A major part of the Soviet military effort in the Far East-North Pacific is directed at China. Unlike the United States, the Soviet Union has few forward bases and limited forward capability, and it has no aircraft carrier to match the six American carrier battle groups in the Pacific. To compensate for its weakness in conventional force, however, the Soviet Union has built a huge nuclear arsenal which casts a long shadow over the region.

American and French strategists regard the campaign to make the Pacific 'nuclear-free and independent' as a major threat to their interests. 'The most potentially disruptive development for US relations with the South Pacific is the growing anti-nuclear movement in the region,' warned a former United States Ambassador to Fiji, William Bodde, in 1982. 'The US Government must do everything possible to counter this movement.'[8]

If American possessions become truly independent the United States would lose major military facilities in Guam and American Samoa, its missile and Star Wars testing facilities at Kwajalein Atoll in the republic of the Marshall Islands, and its contingency sites for possible new bases in Belau and elsewhere in Micronesia. If the Philippines becomes truly independent the Pentagon would lose its biggest air, naval, electronic and brothel facilities in the western Pacific.

If French territories become independent, France would lose not only its nuclear testing facilities at Moruroa and its nickel mines and strategic bases in New Caledonia, it would also surrender control over the world's second largest 200-mile offshore economic zone. Conservative French policymakers believe their departure from New Caledonia would risk creating a 'Cuba' in the region.

The third major colonial power, Indonesia, has in the last two decades moved to exert more influence in the South Pacific. Although most recently Jakarta claims to be attempting to check superpower rivalry, it has had difficulty wooing South Pacific nations because of the stain on its own colonial record. In 1962, the same year as Western Samoan independence, Dutch-ruled West Papua (Irian Jaya) was turned over to Jakarta by the United Nations after Indonesian troops landed in the territory; Indonesia later invaded the Portuguese colony of East Timor (in 1975). While Fretilin continues to wage a guerrilla war and seek self-determination in Timor, Amnesty International and other human rights organisations estimate more than 200,000 people — a third of the population — have died in the fighting, or from hunger, or by execution — a level of atrocity regarded by many as comparable with that of the Khmer Rouge in Kampuchea.[9]

José Ramos-Horta, Fretilin's envoy at the United Nations, bitterly criticises the West for having turned its back on his people. 'We Timorese only wished Indonesia were a Vietnam run by communists,' he says. 'Then, our tortured land would be sung about by international stars, Western governments would condemn the violation of our human rights, Christian agencies of mercy would race with each other to help us.'[10]

Just as France has completed the process of outnumbering the Kanaks in New Caledonia, the Melanesians in West Papua (and East Timor) have been subjected to a calculated transmigration programme from Java by the Indonesian government, which threatens to turn them into a minority in their own land by 1990.

Coup d'état

The region's most recent and one of the best publicised political developments, the Fiji coup, sits uncomfortably alongside the struggles for liberation against colonial rulers. Fiji had been independent for more than 16 years when Dr Timoci Bavadra's Labour Party-led coalition was elected to power in April 1987. The coalition had a platform for multi-racial nationhood which would bind ethnic Fijians and Indo-Fijians closer together while protecting indigenous rights.

Bavadra, himself indigenous Fijian and a former trade unionist, pledged far-reaching reforms which would benefit the working classes of both racial groups. The coalition government also declared it would become non-aligned, ban nuclear warships and support nationalist struggles — foreign policies in common with Vanuatu and other Melanesian states.

When the coalition was deposed by Colonel Rabuka a month later, many of the key people in the defeated government of Ratu Sir Kamisese Mara, which had been accused of growing corruption, regained power. Although the coup provoked cries of outrage in neighbouring countries like Australia and New Zealand, and in the Commonwealth, several Pacific nations saw it in simplistic terms as a struggle for indigenous sovereignty and traditional land rights.

A second coup was staged five months after the first, just as the two Fijian leaders, Bavadra and Mara, were on the point of reaching a political consensus for national unity. Rabuka's guns and his illegal declaration of a racially-based republic did more than erase democracy in Fiji. He hijacked the international reputation of the South Pacific Forum, the region's major political organisation, undermining its credibility. At the September 1988 Forum meeting in Nuku'alofa, Tonga, Pacific leaders failed to confront the issue with Ratu Mara present, in spite of the implications for their own countries.

The underlying factors of the Fiji upheaval — growing poverty, uneven development, government corruption, economic exploitation and cultural traditions disintegrating under the influence of Western values — exist in other Pacific countries, particularly Papua New Guinea and Tonga. Scapegoats, such as the Indo-Fijian population of Fiji, can also be found in other Pacific nations. The coup is unlikely to be an isolated event, as was demonstrated in Vanuatu during 1988. A land rights protest in Port Vila during May, followed by anti-government rioting, led to an abortive constitutional coup as rebel cabinet minister Barak Sope tried to seize power. A drawn out leadership struggle ended in a treason trial with Sope — who claimed a promise of support from Rabuka — and the disgraced President, Ati George Sokomanu, being given prison sentences in early 1989. (They were later freed by the Court of Appeal).

The tragedy for the Forum countries is that before the rise of Rabuka they were beginning to develop a united regional voice. The military overthrow of democracy has jeopardised their new-found influence in international forums.

As old leaders have died or lost authority at the ballot box, younger more radical leaders have been emerging to take their place with a new vision for the Pacific. Among national leaders with such an outlook are Vanuatu's Father Walter Lini, President Ieremia Tabai of Kiribati and Fiji's Bavadra. In the nationalist movements there are Tahiti's Oscar Temaru and Jacqui Drollet.

The newcomers have widened the South Pacific's options. They are dynamic, crusading, prepared to challenge the world's damaging, outmoded view of the region as a carefree paradise of coconuts and tourists. They have become an increasingly significant power bloc with an active voice in the United Nations, and a willingness to be blunt. Although Vanuatu is at present the only Pacific nation in the Non-Aligned Movement, others, notably Papua New Guinea, could follow.

'The great ocean surrounding us carries the seeds of life. We must ensure that they don't become the seeds of death,' said Tjibaou in a moving speech before the Rarotonga Treaty to create a South Pacific nuclear-free zone was signed in 1985. 'A nuclear-free Pacific is our responsibility, and we must face the issues to live and protect our lives.'[11] Lini agrees: 'Colonialism and nuclearism in the Pacific are part of the same evil. To eradicate this evil from our region . . . we have to deal with it from its root, which is colonialism itself.'[12]

★   ★   ★

My interest in the South Pacific developed while I was a journalist working for the Agence France-Presse news agency in Paris during the early 1970s. At that time I began reporting developments involving French nuclear tests and colonial policy in the region. Since returning to New Zealand in 1977 I have covered Pacific affairs as a freelance correspondent based in Auckland for *Islands Business* and *Pacific Islands Monthly* news magazines, the *Dominion, New Zealand Times,* Australian *National Times* and several Third World publications.

My first direct contact with the Kanak struggle came in 1981 when I reported on the Nouméa shooting of a French-born *indépendantiste,* Pierre Declercq. Since then I have made eight visits to Kanaky, and covered events such as the 1984 insurrection, the massacre of Hienghène, the assassination of Éloi Machoro and the 1988 Ouvéa uprising. On one assignment in January 1987, I was harassed by French secret agents and arrested at gunpoint by the military. At the time I was reporting on the intimidation and harassment of Kanak villagers by French troops during the leadup to a so-called referendum on independence eight months later.

During the past decade I have also travelled widely throughout the South Pacific, covering the 1983 Nuclear-Free and Independent Pacific conference in Port Vila and several turbulent Pacific events. After reporting the evacuation of the population of Rongelap Atoll in May 1985, who were contaminated by a 15-megaton thermonuclear test by the United States three decades earlier, I remained on board the Greenpeace flagship *Rainbow Warrior* until it reached New Zealand where it was bombed in Auckland harbour. I also travelled to Fiji to cover Dr Timoci Bavadra's electoral victory and the subsequent coup.

This book traces South Pacific liberation struggles of the 1980s amid the escalating conflict, repression and deaths in the region. Frequently such struggles are characterised as simply indigenous struggles. But they are more than this. They represent a quest for national sovereignty that takes into account the legacy of more than two centuries of colonialism.

It was Bavadra who epitomised the new nationalism in a country that had already been independent for 16 years. And it was a chauvinist colonel who — like the French in Tahiti, New Caledonia or Vanuatu, the Americans in Belau, and the Indonesians in East Timor and West Papua — set out to frustrate its realisation, this time under the guise of 'indigenous rights'. Rabuka declared his narrow sectional base an indigenous movement and used military force to strip other ethnic Fijians of their right to carry out far-reaching reforms. The Australian and New Zealand governments, already reeling from internal pressure from the indigenous Aboriginal and Maori people, mounted ambivalent opposition to the military regime, but were embarrassed by activists who supported it for their own sovereignty causes.

Elsewhere other Pacific nationalist leaders have confronted similar misunderstandings, as in New Caledonia. 'Hypocrisy from Canberra and Wellington has helped plunge our country into chaos,' Kanak leader Éloi Machoro told me shortly before he was shot. 'We're a peaceful people, but we have been frustrated in our right to independence for too long. Promises . . . promises . . . promises . . . And in the end nothing!'[13]

Machoro, who some saw as a sort of Che Guevara, had a remarkably simple aim: he was a Kanak who wanted to be citizen of Kanaky. His courage and dedication towards his goal are the inspiration for this book.

The ensign of an independent Kanaky is hung by Kanak villagers from makeshift flagpoles throughout New Caledonia. An image of the sun represents the dawn of hope and a new future. Blue, red and green stripes symbolise the sky, bloodshed and earth. The blood on their banner represents their sacrifice.

Let everyone tear from their hearts
the tree of discord.
Our ancestors used to throw
the tree of mourning
into the water.
We will throw it into the fire;
We want the hatred
to be burned,
and the way of our future
cleared.
And the circle we open
to all other peoples
to be brotherly.
Such is my call.

Jean-Marie Tjibaou in *Kanaké*

Only the struggle counts . . .
death is nothing.

Éloi Machoro as he lay dying
on 12 January 1985.

Part 1
Colonial Aggression

1
Atoll of Great Secrets

The roots of contemporary nationalist struggles in the South Pacific islands lie deep in the colonial past. In French Polynesia, the Second World War fuelled expectations for independence and Pouvanaa articulated them. However, France frustrated Tahitian hopes when it began nuclear testing at Moruroa Atoll for its force de frappe *in 1966. The pro-independence guerrilla force* Te Toto Tupuna *bombed the Papeete telephone exchange and staged the 'execution' of a French businessman in the 1970s. A later nationalist wave emerged in the 1980s with the* Ia Mana Te Nunaa *and* Tavini Huiraatira *parties leading the way.*

Pouvanaa Tetuaapua Oopa, a Tahitian First World War veteran with a chestful of medals, became the champion of the Polynesian nationalist movement after the liberation of France in 1945. In his 50s and with an air of wisdom that earned him the title of *metua*, or father, he became an outspoken critic of colonial injustice. He embarked on a political campaign which led to his being jailed for eight years and exiled; one of the first martyrs to French colonialism in the South Pacific.

But in 1945 Pouvanaa had no way of knowing what the future held in store. Amid post-liberation euphoria, and even after General de Gaulle resigned in January 1946 because he could no longer rule as absolutely as he had during the war, there was little hint of the repression that would crush the wave of nationalism sweeping French Oceania.

Two-thirds of the 300 Tahitian Free-French volunteers — the 'guitar battalion' — who had survived the war returned to Papeete, wiser and more demanding. They had become acutely aware during the year they spent in France that the society and system of government there was more democratic than in the colonies. Although fêted like heroes, they did not want simply to return to their taro patches and fishing grounds. Consequently they became angry when Paris insisted on sending out bureaucrats to Tahiti to fill jobs which they could have done.

Pouvanaa, already a critic of injustices and wrong-doings against the Tahitian people, became their spokesman. (His own son, Marcel, was the most wounded and most decorated soldier of the battalion.) Pouvanaa gave the frustrations of the war veterans a political dimension by convincing the ex-soldiers the colonial system had to change. He advocated 'Polynesia for the Polynesians'.

This 'agitation' was regarded as treason by the French governor. Martial law was proclaimed in July 1947 and troops arrested Pouvanaa and six colleagues in the middle of the night.[1] The 'conspirators' languished in cramped cells at the grim Nuutania jail, on the outskirts of Papeete, for five months while authorities tried to produce evidence against them. Eventually a judge, unable to find any law making it a crime to preach social and political reform, ordered their release.

When, two years later, Pouvanaa contested the French National Assembly elections he won a landslide victory, 9800 votes against 4700 for a pastor heading the Protestant mission. For the first time since the Society Islands were colonised by France in 1842, the Tahitians had found an indigenous leader who could challenge the colonial authorities.

Chief organiser of Pouvanaa's election success was a young *demi* (mixed-race) typographer called Jean-Baptiste Céran-Jérusalémy. He founded Pouvanaa's party, the Tahitian People's Democratic Rally (RDPT), modelling it along European political party lines, with local cells, a manifesto, a newspaper, membership dues and annual congresses. The red-white-red traditional flag of King Pomare, used by Tahitian guerrillas to fight French forces from 1844 to 1846, was hoisted at party meetings.[2]

The result stunned Tahitians. When Pouvanaa faced re-election in 1951, he captured 70 percent of the votes. The Territorial Assembly, the first truly representative local parliament, came into existence two years later and the RDPT won 18 of the 25 seats. Céran was elected speaker.

But Pouvanaa and his supporters were frustrated in their efforts to push through reforms — both in Paris and Papeete. By 1956, the RDPT faced a stalemate. Similar problems were encountered in Algeria and other French colonies in Africa, where nationalist guerrillas began waging liberation struggles. The new socialist government in France led by Guy Mollet, with Francois Mitterrand as Justice Minister and Gaston Deferre as Colonies Minister, broke the deadlock by introducing the *Loi-cadre* (Enabling Act). Passed into law on 23 June 1956, the new legislation granted French-ruled colonies genuine self-government. Mollet's cabinet regarded the move as preparation for eventual independence. A new statute embodying the principles was enacted for Tahiti a year later, renaming the colony French Polynesia instead of Oceania.

Again victorious at the following elections, Pouvanaa headed the new governing council as vice-president while the French governor retained the power of veto. Pouvanaa and his aides immediately began introducing reforms. They halted all land sales as a necessary preliminary step to investigating existing deeds to uncover fraud concerning alienated land. Next, Céran introduced a bill into the Territorial Assembly introducing income tax. French settlers and wealthy *demis* reacted in anger. Led by Papeete mayor Alfred Poroi, they marched through the streets of the capital in April 1958 to the Assembly — the one-time customs building on the Papeete waterfront. The settlers threatened to destroy the decaying building with a bulldozer.

With France on the brink of civil war over the Algerian independence struggle, cabinet ministers did not care for the fate of the besieged assemblymen. But the Papeete police, mainly Polynesians, mounted guard at the entrance, beating back an attack by some of the settler protesters. Street battles followed and the Assembly was stoned. Pouvanaa withdrew the bill, blaming Céran for the bad timing.

Less than a month later, on 28 May 1958, the Fourth French Republic collapsed and de Gaulle was empowered to rule by decree for six months. With such a 'protector' installed in the Elysée Palace, the future looked bright for the Tahitians. After all, just two years before, de Gaulle — regarded as a hero in Tahiti — had made a low-key visit to the islands. On the day he arrived, he told a cheering crowd in Papeete's Tarahoi Park of his wartime debt:

> When France was wallowing in the depths, Tahiti did not lose faith in her. You were on the other side of the world from me, thrown up on the English coast like a shipwrecked survivor, both of us harbouring the same thoughts and purposes at the same time. We both felt that France should not be subservient, humiliated and disgraced — and that it was worthwhile for us to fight for her liberation, victory and greatness.
>
> It was a tremendous consolation to me when . . . [you] decided, by a vote of 5564 against 18, to join the Free French. Thus was formed such a strong bond between you and me, between Tahiti and France, that nothing will ever break it.[3]

Pouvanaa's hope that de Gaulle would return to Tahiti to smooth out the tension was in vain. De Gaulle was too busy preparing for an 'Algerian Algeria' — a policy which three years later provoked an abortive *putsch* in Algiers and a wave of terrorist attacks by the right-wing OAS (Secret Army Organisation). He had decided to push on with the decolonisation programme introduced by the socialists but which they had dropped.

In an empire-wide referendum on 28 September 1958, French colonies were offered two choices. A *yes* vote meant conditional freedom in the form of membership in a sort of French commonwealth, involving generous economic aid and technical assistance. The second choice was immediate and complete independence without aid, 'since you have by voting *no* considered yourselves capable of earning your own bread',[4] as de Gaulle put it.

Although de Gaulle clearly favoured the first option, Pouvanaa, still angry with the hard-line tactics of the French settlers, opted for the second; Céran chose *yes*. Céran explained later that he thought it was easier to gain independence by a two-step process, but he undermined Pouvanaa's stand. Pouvanaa was also denied access to radio, the only effective means of communicating with the outer islands in a colony where the population is spread over 75 islands in an area of ocean the size of Australia. However, Tahitians heard a taped broadcast by de Gaulle repeated for a month before the ballot. Although most Tahitians on the main island supported Pouvanaa, de Gaulle won the referendum overall.

Instead of continuing with a decolonisation programme in Tahiti, de Gaulle took revenge against Pouvanaa for opposing him. On 8 October, by the stroke of a pen under his Algerian emergency powers, he sacked Pouvanaa and his cabinet. Encouraged by the general's action, the anti-tax protesters resumed their demonstrations and threatened the Tahitian leader.

Pouvanaa barricaded himself with a dozen bodyguards in his two-storey house at Manuhoe on the outskirts of Papeete. Supporters gathered around the building to protect him.

Scores of marines, gendarmes and police moved into Manuhoe on 11 October, but instead of breaking up the hostile crowd of French settlers, the security forces surrounded Pouvanaa's house and ordered him to come out. Dressed in a white suit and wearing his parliamentary insignia, Pouvanaa stepped out and was arrested, without explanation, by armed soldiers. According to French law, a deputy or senator cannot be arrested, except when caught *en flagrant délit*, red-handed while committing a crime. An official report made the accusation, branding Pouvanaa an 'arsonist'. Tahiti-based authors and historians Bengt and Marie-Thérèse Danielsson recorded the scene in *Poisoned Reign:*

> We and many other persons had seen with our own eyes that, at the time of his arrest, far from committing any crime, Pouvanaa was willingly and trustingly approaching the police, completely unarmed. Someone in government circles must have realised the mistake by then, for in the next news bulletin it was announced that several 'subversives' had tried to set fire and burn down the town of Papeete. Their clumsiness and ineptitude were striking, as they had thrown four molotov cocktails into empty courtyards and gardens; three of these had immediately gone out, and the fourth produced such an insignificant fire that it could easily be extinguished.
>
> According to this official version, Pouvanaa 'was behind' this 'arson'. Even if this accusation could be proved, it certainly in no way constituted a *flagrant délit* as defined by law.[5]

Detained for a year at the age of 64 in a cramped infantry barracks cell, Pouvanaa was eventually tried and convicted. Without any further evidence, the court sentenced him to eight years' solitary confinement in a French jail, followed by exile, and a 36 Pacific francs fine. His appeal was rejected. The 12 other accused were handed sentences ranging from 18 months to six years.

The 'atomic gangsters'

Why were Pouvanaa and his followers treated so harshly? At the time the reason was unclear. But it emerged later that de Gaulle thought that by 'neutralising' Pouvanaa he would stifle opposition to French plans for nuclear colonialism. France needed an alternative nuclear test site now that war-torn Algeria was about to become independent. (It was indeed obvious by 1960 that an independent Algerian government would expel French nuclear technicians from the Sahara Desert.) Already the northern Marshall Islands in Micronesia, and Christmas Island in the Line Islands, one of the world's two largest atolls, had been devastated by nuclear colonialism. Now it was Polynesia's turn.

Two Micronesian atolls have become notorious — Bikini and Enewetak. Between 1946 and 1958, the United States detonated 66 nuclear bombs (including at least ten extremely powerful thermonuclear devices) on these atolls, causing the irradiation of hundreds of islanders. Six islands were vaporised by the tests. And four decades after the first nuclear blasts at Bikini, many islands remain uninhabitable because of high radiation levels. The Bikinians remain an exiled people; and many islanders report increasing health disorders due to radioactive fallout.[6]

Less well known are the nuclear tests at Johnston Atoll and Christmas Island, both located in relatively uninhabited parts of the mid-Pacific. At Johnston, 1100 kilometres south-west of Hawaii, United States Air Force planes dropped two thermonuclear bombs in 1958, and then used missiles to launch a further ten bombs into space four years later. On Christmas Island, the British triggered their first thermonuclear bomb in May 1957, and during the next 15 months tested eight more nuclear devices. In the year before the 1963 Partial Test Ban Treaty came into force, both the United States and the Soviet Union rushed to complete as many atmospheric tests as they could manage. The United States 'borrowed' Christmas Island in 1962 for a five-month nuclear blitz. During that time 25 bombs, including at least three in the ten-megaton range, were detonated.

By this time, France had triggered six nuclear bombs in the Sahara and was looking for a fresh site. Influenced by the American and British examples in the Pacific, France dispatched a warship to Polynesia with secret orders to find two suitable atolls. Military experts decided on Moruroa — 'the atoll of great secrets'* — and Fangataufa. The Pacific Experiments Centre (CEP) was set up; several companies of French Foreign Legion troops and engineers landed on the atolls to build wharfs, airstrips and two huge watchtowers, which alone required 90,000 tonnes of concrete and 32,000 tonnes of steel.

Both atolls, however, were surrounded to the north, east and west by inhabited islands. Alarmed church, civic and political leaders warned that any nuclear tests in the Tuamotus might harm the health of about 7000 islanders living in the area. But their fears were played down by French cabinet ministers, admirals and generals who claimed the bombs would be exploded only when light northerly winds were present, blowing the fallout across the empty ocean between Polynesia and the Antarctic. On 2 July 1966, France triggered the first atomic bomb at Moruroa. A Tahitian newspaper branded the test a poisoned *poisson cru* (raw fish dish) and Bengt Danielsson described it like this:

> The first bomb was placed on a barge anchored in the lagoon and detonated. The result was a catastrophe — water contained in the shallow reef basin was sucked up into the air and then rained down, covering all islets with heaps of irradiated fish and clams, whose slowly rotting flesh continued to stink for weeks.[7]

Forty further atmospheric tests followed at the two atolls, usually at Moruroa, and usually involving bombs suspended from a balloon at an altitude of 600-700 metres above the atoll. Some bombs were also dropped from high-flying aircraft over the ocean south of Moruroa in 1966, 1969 and 1970. Four tests were of thermonuclear bombs in the megaton range. International protests, particularly from the South Pacific nations and environmental campaigners, forced France to substitute underground tests in 1975.

By the end of 1988, a total of 144 nuclear tests had been detonated at Moruroa and Fangataufa, several of them claimed to be neutron bombs. (Before starting tests in the South Pacific, France detonated four nuclear bombs in the atmosphere and 13 underground in the Sahara.) Since 3 January 1963, the day de Gaulle officially announced the decision to use Polynesia for nuclear testing, the political, economic, cultural and social life of the territory has been dominated — if not paralysed — by *la bombe*.

Two months after the first nuclear test at Moruroa, the father of the *force de frappe*, de Gaulle, visited French Polynesia. On the day of the first test John Teariki, successor to Pouvanaa as leader of the Tahitians, chaired

---

Moru and *roa* are Managarevian dialect words together meaning 'a place of a great secret'. Moruroa was bastardised to Mururoa by a French naval cartographer. Tahitians and most Pacific publications refer to *Moruroa*.

a stormy congress of the RDPT, or as it was now known, *Pupu Here Aia* (Patriots Party). The pastor who opened the meeting called on God to halt the 'satanic' nuclear tests. And when de Gaulle arrived in Papeete, Teariki expected the President to consider solutions for the social and economic woes facing Tahiti as the result of the arrival of nuclear weapons. At an audience in Papeete's government council room, Teariki gave a stunning speech.

Teariki reminded de Gaulle how Polynesians had responded to his appeal as the 'heroic leader of Free France' to fight for freedom. He also stressed the President's role as the 'liberator' who proclaimed for the first time at Brazzaville the right of the inhabitants of the French colonies to equality, freedom and self-government.

'[Now] a widespread uneasiness exists in Polynesia and is worsening from day to day,' continued Teariki. 'It is due to the Fifth Republic's policy since you took over the helm, a policy consisting right from the beginning of a long series of attacks against our liberties, threats and acts of force aimed at reinforcing the colonial system and the military occupation of our islands.' He accused de Gaulle of having only one aim in his policy — 'to freely dispose of our country as a testing ground for your nuclear weapons.'[8]

Turning to the case of Pouvanaa, who had been released shortly before his prison sentence ended but barred from returning to Tahiti or *any* French Pacific territory for 15 years, Teariki said Polynesians had not been deceived. 'On the same day you released Pouvanaa . . . you instructed your minister for overseas territories to issue a decree banishing him . . . because you feared the political power of this old man whom all Polynesians venerate,' he added. 'Is Pouvanaa's crime that he had not spilled any blood?' Teariki appealed to the President to show the same clemency to Pouvanaa as he had to the armed Arab militant Mohammad Ahmed Issa.*

Then Deputy Teariki denounced the 'shameful' decision by France to 'join the atomic gangsters' by installing the nuclear bases in Polynesia without consultation with the Tahitian people. After his message of anguish, Teariki walked up to the President and handed him a copy of the speech. He stepped back and waited for a response. De Gaulle, however, thrust the text into his pocket, shook Teariki's hand in silence and strode out of the room.

Two days later President de Gaulle flew to Moruroa to witness a 120-kiloton nuclear test timed for his visit. He boarded the cruiser *De Grasse* with the intention of watching the explosion from about 30 kilometres away.

---

* While Pouvanaa was condemned to exile on 25 February 1966, in French Somalia, Mohammad Ahmed Issa, leader of the Afar Democratic Union, was released, two days after being arrested while fighting in the streets of Djibouti with a gun. Following years of protest by Polynesian leaders, de Gaulle finally abrogated Pouvanaa's banishment by decree on Armistice Day, 11 November 1968. The *metua* was aged 72 and partially paralysed when he finally returned to Tahiti. He was later elected the islands' senator.

But early next morning, when the test was scheduled, the sky was overcast and the wind was blowing in the wrong direction, from the east. The admiral in charge told de Gaulle that the test would have to be postponed until the following day. (It astonished the President that the device dangling from a helium-filled balloon over Moruroa looked so unlike a bomb. Instead, reported an observer, it had the appearance of 'an iron box the size of a family refrigerator'.)

At dawn on 11 September de Gaulle was back on the cruiser's bridge, demanding that the test go ahead. He had urgent problems in Paris to attend to, he said. It posed a dilemma for the admiral — the easterly was still gusting with a risk of radioactive fallout on inhabited islands to the west. Preferring this to de Gaulle's anger, the admiral began the countdown. The mushroom cloud billowed from the plutonium box and spilled into the sky towards the western Pacific. Noted the Danielssons:

> The radioactive fallout reached all the islands west of Moruroa in a matter of hours or days. For instance in Apia . . . 200 nautical miles downwind, the radioactive content of the rainwater catchment tanks four days later was estimated by the National Radiation Laboratory of New Zealand . . . to be 135,000 picocuries per litre. Almost equally alarming measurements were made in the Cook Islands and Fiji. The exact amount of radioactive fallout received by the inhabitants of French Polynesia, living in the shade of the atomic mushroom, has never been announced by the CEP high command.[9]

In fact, the CEP refused to divulge *any* information about contamination in French Polynesia. Before 1966, health statistics in the territory were made public every month. After the tests began, however, the records became secret and interested people regarded by the authorities with suspicion.

In spite of a claim by the CEP that 'not a single particle of active fallout will ever reach an inhabited island', the agency's own first map of the danger zone prepared for the first test included seven inhabited atolls. The map was hurriedly changed.

News leaked out that the French military was also secretly building nuclear fallout shelters on Mangareva and other islands to the east of Moruroa which lay on the fringe of the vast keyhole-shaped danger zone. In 1968 all 50 islanders living on Tureia were evacuated for a 'holiday' in Tahiti. They were allowed to go back after superficial decontamination of the island. Increasing reports of accidents and the illegal declaration of a 260,000 square kilometre danger zone around Moruroa led to hostile opposition from Pacific nations, and protest voyages to the atoll in the early 1970s.

Piracy on the high seas

David McTaggart, a millionaire Canadian who had lost his construction business fortune, put Moruroa on the international map. He was in New

Zealand on a South Pacific voyage when he decided to protest against French nuclear tests. Aged 40, and with a crew of three, he sailed his 12-metre ketch *Vega* into the danger zone. It was the first protest voyage in the South Pacific by the fledgling Vancouver-based ecology group Greenpeace — although it had already mounted protests against American nuclear tests at Amchitka Island in the North Pacific. Several years later McTaggart would become the organisation's chairman and help turn it into a formidable world environment direct action force.

But in 1972 this was far from his mind. When the *Vega* arrived near Moruroa, the French Navy tried to scare him off by sending a cruiser, minesweepers and tug boats to play 'chicken' with the yacht on the high seas. Finally, on 1 August the *Vega* was rammed and crippled.

The following year, McTaggart and the *Vega* were back again. And, because of the publicity over the ramming of the yacht, a small flotilla of boats — including the peace schooner *Fri* — joined him in protest. New Zealand's Prime Minister, Norman Kirk, who first espoused that country's nuclear-free stance, dispatched the frigates *Otago* and (later) *Canterbury* to gain international sympathy for the cause. 'We are a small nation, but we will not abjectly surrender to injustice,' Kirk declared as the first frigate left for Moruroa.

By the time the *Vega* arrived off the atoll, the frigates had departed and the other small yachts had either left or been seized. This time the French Navy showed no mercy. On 15 August 1973, a Zodiac inflatable with seven commandos was launched from the minesweeper *La Dunkerquoise*. McTaggart described the fury of the next few minutes in his book *Greenpeace III: Journey into the Bomb:*

These were no ordinary French sailors. Their faces were contorted with savagery and I could see that they were struggling to be the first to reach me. I saw the knives sheathed at their sides and I had a brief flicker of relief that they didn't have them in their hands. Then I saw the long black truncheons . . .

The first truncheon came down with a weight and force unlike anything I had ever felt on the back of my head and the second came down across my shoulders and the next blow landed on the back of my neck and the next on my head again and the next one on my spine and the next on my shoulder blade and the next against my kidney and I was suddenly in the air being flipped over the railing and being yanked furiously into the inflatable, unable to catch a single breath or even find a way to make a sound . . . With scarcely a pause, the truncheons were flailing again, each blow rattling my teeth so that it seemed they would be shattered and that my spine and ribs would cave in any second . . .

Something crashed into my right eye with such incredible force that it seemed to come right into the middle of my brain in an explosion so that I thought that half my head had been torn off. And then everything went black.[10]

McTaggart was flown to hospital in Tahiti with permanent damage to his right eye. Crew members New Zealanders Ann-Marie Horne and Mary Lornie photographed the brutal attack on McTaggart and Englishman Nigel Ingram. The commandos, noticing this, angrily tossed a 35mm camera overboard. It was the wrong one. When the *Vega* was towed into Moruroa lagoon, Horne smuggled the telltale film ashore by hiding it in her vagina.

French authorities denied McTaggart's claims that he had been savagely beaten. He had slipped on board and damaged his eye on one of the yacht's cleats, claimed one official. But when the film safely reached Canada and was developed, the 13 photographs of the boarding and attack caused a sensation. They were published worldwide, silencing the French Government.

My first contact with McTaggart's crusade and a focus for my growing interest in the Pacific nuclear-free and independence movements began two years later when his piracy lawsuit seeking $21,000 in damages from the French Navy finally came before the courts. It began at the Tribunal de Grande Instance, a large grey stone building overlooking the Seine, just a block away from the Notre Dame.

Remarkably, McTaggart succeeded in putting the military in the dock in a French court; a Frenchman on board the *Fri* had also filed a writ, but the courts had refused to hear it. At the time, I reported from Paris for the Melbourne *Nation Review:*

> Canadian yachtsman David McTaggart has twice taken on the French Navy in the Pacific Ocean and lost. [Now] he will face it again, but this time it will be in a gloomy Paris courtroom and he has a fair chance of winning. In what has become known here as the 'freedom of the high seas' case, McTaggart, 42, is suing the French government on 24 charges — including one of piracy — arising out of his protests against atmospheric nuclear tests . . .
>
> In the initial court hearing last month, McTaggart's counsel accused the French government and navy of having violated international maritime conventions and of having committed 'unspeakable' acts against the skipper. The counsel asked for reparations for the French government's abuse of the right of free navigation on the high seas and for the violent actions by the navy against McTaggart, his crew and his boat.[11]

When McTaggart finally sat in court on 17 June, several tense hearings later, he was close to physical and emotional exhaustion. The judgement was read out too fast for him to comprehend what was happening. He realised something was afoot when journalists began dashing out of the courtroom.

The judges ruled that the civil court was 'not competent' to deal with the charges over the boarding — including the critical count of armed piracy. Setting the piracy charges aside, however, the judges turned to the actual ramming. They ruled that the minesweeper *La Paimpolaise* had created a 'dangerous situation' at sea and had been guilty of deliberately ramming the *Vega*. The court ordered the French government to pay out 2000 francs, or about $500, to have an independent marine surveyor carry out an inspection to assess damages.

'What's happening?' whispered McTaggart.

'You've won!' replied a French journalist, before running to the telephone.

McTaggart recalled later: 'I wanted to scream after him, "Goddam it, what do you mean I've *won*? They threw out the piracy charge didn't they?" ' But before he had a chance, he was surrounded by supporters and reporters.

Even before this embarrassing court verdict, it had become obvious to President Georges Pompidou and Prime Minister Pierre Messmer that they could not continue to flout international opinion over the atmospheric tests. On 23 June 1973, the International Court of Justice in The Hague, ruling on a case brought by the Australian and New Zealand governments, awarded an interim injunction calling on France to halt further nuclear tests in the Pacific pending a full judgement. France promptly rejected the World Court's competence to deal with matters of national defence. The tribunal, however, declared it was ruling on an issue of international health.

On board the *Fri* had been a retired French general, Jacques Paris de Bollardière, and a group of 'peace commandos' from Paris. Their presence ensured public attention in France. Multi-millionaire French publisher Jean-Jacques Servan-Schreiber, owner of the news magazine *l'Express* and leader of the small Radical Socialist Party, threw his weight behind the anti-nuclear movement. And in Papeete, more than 5000 Tahitians demonstrated against *la bombe*.

Pouvanaa, by now Tahiti's senator in the French Parliament, and Francis Sanford, leader of the 'autonomist' *Te Ea Api* (The New Way) party, who had succeeded Teariki as deputy, declared in an open letter to the French people:

> Since becoming 'French', we Polynesians have twice demonstrated [by sending a battalion to fight in Europe during both the First and Second World Wars] that we are ready to make the greatest sacrifices to save our mother country. In return we demand to be no longer treated as guinea pigs for these lunatic [nuclear] experiments which, if they ever achieve their purpose, will only result in the total destruction of France, through massive retaliation by a far superior atomic power. Your compatriots in the Pacific ask for your help in stopping this madness.[12]

After the sudden death of Pompidou in April 1974, his succesor, Valery Giscard d'Estaing, ordered a halt to atmospheric testing but permitted underground blasts to begin the following year. For the changeover it was announced that Fangataufa, 40 kilometres to the south-east of Moruroa, would be used as the initial site. Fangataufa had not been used for atmospheric tests since it had become heavily contaminated by a 2.5-megaton thermonuclear blast on 24 August 1968. It did not seem to matter that both Britain and the United States had chosen the Nevada Desert for underground tests rather than risk destroying an atoll in the Pacific. Scandals over accidents and pollution would later bedevil the testing site.

Blood of their ancestors

Shortly before midnight on 12 August 1975, while French Overseas Territories Minister Olivier Stirn was visiting Tahiti, an explosion rocked central Papeete. Policemen arrived quickly on the scene and found that a dynamite blast had caused little damage in the telephone exchange opposite the heavily-guarded High Commissioner's residence. A closer search, however, revealed three more charges laid by the outer walls of the building that had failed to detonate. A note in French discovered nearby said, *Take home your flag, your people, Stirn, and go home!*

Police rounded up the most hardline of Tahiti's pro-independence politicians, including Charlie Ching, a part-Chinese nephew of Pouvanaa, and gave them a a tough grilling. They all had alibis.

Two weeks later, French businessman Pierre d'Anglejean, a retired naval officer, was shot dead at home while he slept. The killers entered his luxury villa on the west coast of Tahiti without being noticed.

They also left a note. It said, *We don't want any more Frenchmen in our country!* A signature in Tahitian read *Te Toto Tupuna* (Blood of our Ancestors). But there was no hint why the murdered man had been chosen as a victim. He was apparently uninvolved in politics. It seemed as if he had been chosen at random as a protest against French immigration policies, which were aimed at trying to turn the indigenous population into a minority.

Thirteen young Tahitians, in their teens or early 20s, were arrested and accused of being part of the *Toto Tupuna* movement. Another suspect was extradited from Rarotonga.

Charlie Ching, although he again had an alibi, was charged with being the mastermind behind the 'conspiracy'. Just a few months earlier he had been a candidate in the territorial elections, a surprise nomination after returning from a stay in a French jail where he had served a two-year sentence for stealing munitions from a French army camp in Tahiti in protest against the nuclear tests and the colonial occupation.

Four of the arrested Tahitians confessed to the murder, saying they regarded themselves as 'soldiers' in a Tahitian liberation army. They also revealed plans to sabotage CEP aircraft and ships which ferried supplies to Moruroa. The other ten admitted only to stealing 400 kilos of dynamite. All the accused denied that Ching had any role in their activities. But French authorities refused to drop the charges.

The case eventually came to trial in January 1979, and became an indictment of French colonial justice. Family and supporters of Charlie Ching raised money to hire several leading French civil rights lawyers, including François Roux, who later became involved in cases defending Kanak *indépendantistes*.

The prosecutor sought a life sentence for Ching, without a single witness to support his allegation that the politician had organised the bomb attack and murder. Marcel Tahutini, the self-confessed killer of d'Anglejean, revealed that the French police had tried to coerce him into perjuring himself. He had been promised a lenient sentence as a reward for incriminating Ching. Eventually the prosecutor dropped the 'organiser' charge and alleged instead that Ching had 'consorted with proven criminals'.

Defence lawyers concentrated on the wider issues, accusing French colonial rule of creating the climate responsible for growing crime and violence. They also attacked the French government's refusal to grant independence and its policy of flooding Tahiti with immigrants from France.

Tahutini and his brother Jonas — leader of the *Toto Tupuna* commandos — were both sentenced to 20 years, while three other members were given 18, ten and five years, respectively. Ching was sentenced to ten years. While lawyers prepared an appeal, the prisoners were secretly flown by military aircraft to Hao Atoll, and then on to a jail in France.

Grassroot nationalists

In October 1979, during a South Pacific Commission meeting in Papeete, five small pro-independence parties temporarily buried their differences and held a combined open meeting. I was among a handful of foreign journalists who attended the gathering. Some of the guests made impassioned speeches endorsing independence. But the 'interference' by Papua New Guinea's then Foreign Minister Ebia Olewale particularly riled the French authorities. He warned:

> You must stand together, because these people who govern you are very clever and will try to divide you in order to rule you. They play off one group against another. I am speaking from experience, because I and many other Papua New Guinea leaders have gone through all the stages of decolonisation that will confront you. Remember that you are not alone. We are with you.

Among the parties at the meeting was the fast-rising Tahitian socialist party *Ia Mana Te Nunaa* (Power to the People). Leader Jacqui Drollet, a marine

Bengt Danielsson

Tahitian independence activist Charlie Ching outside Papeete court in 1975.

biologist doing research on atoll fish poisoning at Papeete's Louis Malarde Institute, denounced the nuclear tests. 'The experience of Hiroshima, Nagasaki and Bikini is enough,' he said. 'Nuclear tests have got to stop, and there is only one solution: We must have our independence, and Moruroa and Fangataufa must be returned to us.'[13]

As well as *Ia Mana*, present were Charlie Ching's *Te Taata Tahiti Tiama* (Free Tahiti Party) and *Tavini Huiraatira No Porinetia* (Polynesian Liberation Front), led by customs official Oscar Manutahi Temaru. Then quite small, Tavini emerged as the fastest-growing nationalist group by the mid-1980s, appealing mainly to poor indigenous Tahitians. And the charismatic Temaru revealed some of the *metua* qualities of Pouvanaa.

Another grassroots Polynesian party, led by Tetua Mai, set up a 'provisional *Maohi* government' in 1982. It had some of the trappings of an independent state, such as uniformed gendarmes, official vehicles, a constitution and a 'passport'. Mai became self-styled president and he formed a cabinet. At first the French ignored Mai as an eccentric. But when he and his 'prime minister' began travelling around the South Pacific and got a sympathetic hearing from the Vanuatu and other governments, the attitude changed.

When Mai's followers took a French gendarme hostage, the incident provided the excuse the authorities needed. Police fired teargas on the party headquarters, smashed down the doors and arrested Mai and several of his supporters. Tetua Mai was jailed for a year.

Ia Mana, in contrast, modelled itself along European leftist lines. The founders had all studied at French universities, and adapted socialist ideology to the Tahitian context. Their objective was an 'egalitarian socialist society', implying redistribution of alienated land and introduction of progressive income tax — two prospects which disturbed French settlers.

By preaching a partial return to the traditional Polynesian way of life, *Ia Mana* rapidly gained support among Tahitians, and in the 1982 territorial election, Drollet and two Tahitian candidates won seats in the Assembly. This was the first gain for parties seeking outright independence.

But Tahitian politics became polarised in this election. The autonomist coalition headed by *Ea Api's* Francis Sanford collapsed, and the neo-gaullist party *Tahoeraa Huiraatira* — the only party in Tahiti accepting the nuclear status quo — gained control. The new pro-French government leader Gaston Flosse, a *demi* former schoolteacher turned businessman, immediately set about consolidating his power.

Charlie Ching, released from prison the year before, was barred from contesting the election. His dead uncle, Pouvanaa, now honoured by a memorial outside the Territorial Assembly, would have been aghast at the election result. However, within five years Oscar Temaru's rapidly swelling support and a sudden violent social upheaval in Tahiti would swing the pendulum back in favour of the nationalists.

2

The Forgotten Wars

On the other side of the Pacific from Tahiti, on the fringe of western Melanesia, anti-colonial struggles faced brutal military repression and genocide. Here nationalist movements were not pitted against European colonial powers; instead they faced an Asian country, Indonesia, which, ironically, had itself gained independence only by protracted struggle. But for the peoples of East Timor and West Papua the difference was academic, and their struggles became the 'forgotten wars' as the Western world turned its back, thus seeming to condone the excesses of the Indonesian military.

East Timor

Indonesian forces have been landed in Dili by sea, by sea ... They are flying over Dili dropping out paratroopers ... Aircraft are dropping out more and more paratroopers ... A lot of people have been killed indiscriminately ... Women and children are going to be killed by Indonesian forces ... We are going to be killed! SOS, we call for your help, this is an urgent call ...[1]

Through the crackle of static, the voice was desperate. As a group of journalists huddled around the Red Cross radio in Darwin on 7 December 1975, Alarico Fernandes,* a cabinet minister in the ill-fated Democratic Republic of East Timor, made a last plea for international help.

Indonesian paratroopers and marines began landing in the capital of Dili

---

*Minister of Information Fernandes was responsible for Radio Maubere's broadcasts to the outside world. Three years later he shocked Fretilin by surrendering with a group of guerrillas to Indonesian troops in response to an 'amnesty' offer. All were killed except him; he was imprisoned.

The word *Maubere*, originally a Mambai tribal derogatory term for ignorant peasant, is now used to refer to the people of Timor.

at dawn. Six warships were in the harbour. At about five o'clock Monsignor Martinho da Costa Lopes, the papal representative in the predominantly Catholic country, opened his window and looked out. 'The warships and airplanes fired on Dili with rockets and cluster bombs,' he recalls. 'They burned everything and everybody.' The Indonesian soldiers smashed their way into houses, looting them; shops were ransacked. 'They raped women . . . sometimes even in front of their husbands,' he said. 'It was very bad. That day remained forever engraved in my memory. I will never forget.'[2]

During the next days hundreds of people were massacred by Indonesian troops. Amnesty International and London-based Indonesian human rights group Tapol also reported widespread slaughter in other Timorese towns, including Baucau, Venilale and Maubara.

Eyewitnesses described random executions beside the harbour and near the former Portuguese military police barracks in suburban Vila Verde. Among those killed was Isobel Lobato, wife of the then East Timor Prime Minister, Nicolau Lobato. She was travelling with about 15 other people to safety at the Catholic bishop's *palacio*; they were stopped by soldiers. Ordered to go to public gardens beside the port, Isabel Lobato was singled out from the group by an informer and dragged off by two soldiers. A witness told what happened:

> The soldiers kept pushing her forward with their rifles. She was falling down along the way. She was asking them to forgive her. They took her to the wharf. Two minutes later we heard rifle fire.[3]

Her body was still lying there next day. Chong Kui Yan, a Chinese trader now living in Australia, was in a work party forced to throw corpses into the sea. He recalls how troops began bombarding and shooting at the Toko Lay, a large building in Dili where many Timorese civilians were sheltering.

> People started screaming, saying they were civilians, and not political. One person . . . came out of the house next to the Toko Lay to surrender and was shot dead. His son came out also and was also shot but not fatally. He pretended to be dead and survived.
>
> The Indonesians then broke into the building and told everyone to come out. They took us down to the beach. There were more than ten of them. All of us were taken, including my wife who was pregnant, and my child . . . We were made to sit in line. The Indonesians made as though they were going to shoot at us but did not fire . . .
>
> The next morning . . . we were told to go down to the harbour . . . [There] were many dead bodies. Isabel Lobato's was the only one of them that I recognised. We were told to tie the bodies to iron poles, attach bricks and throw the bodies in the sea.
>
> After we had thrown all the bodies in the sea, about 20 people were brought in, made to face the sea and shot dead . . . There were about 100 Indonesians

there. [Troops wearing] green berets brought [the victims] in; [others wearing] red berets — always two of them — killed them, shooting them in the head with M16s.[4]

Among the other people closely linked with Fretilin (Revolutionary Front of Independent East Timor) who were executed on the day of the invasion were Timor's 'Rosa Luxemburg' — Popular Organisation of Timorese Women secretary Rosa Muki Bonaparte, Timorese poet Borja da Costa, and Australian freelance journalist Roger East, who had established an East Timor news agency with Fretilin encouragement after he arrived in Dili the month before. Many people in Dili had no idea about the fate of relatives who had 'disappeared'. It tooks several weeks for some to find out.

Hundreds of people were executed in Vila Verde. Green-beret troops rounded up the population of the suburb and herded them on to a football field opposite the police barracks. Student Carlos Afonso recalled their fate.

The green berets had found a dead Indonesian by the barracks. They thought that he must have been killed by civilians because he had been killed with a sword and not by a bullet.

The Indonesians brought all the people across to the . . .barracks. They selected about 50 strongly built men who were ordered to enter the barracks. I was one of them. There was nothing [inside] . . .

We were all told to stand, then to sit. Indonesians prepared guns as if to fire. Everyone cried out; some tried to kiss the feet of the Indonesians. Some were carrying Indonesian flags.

'Kill them,' said a sergeant. Everybody stood.

'Fire,' he shouted.

I fell and some others fell on me. I had been shot in my right hand. I put my bleeding hand to my face and pretended to be dead. A car came, I thought that they had come to collect the bodies but they left the bodies and took the Indonesian soldiers.[5]

Only four people survived the Vila Verde massacre.

The tragedy of East Timor is of a people who threw off the suppression of one colonial power only to be invaded by another. After nearly three centuries of Portuguese colonialism and neglect, East Timor's brief experiment as a sovereign state lasted less than three months before being crushed by a no less ruthless colonial power.

Portugal had established a colonial presence in Timor in 1642 when it controlled the Indian Ocean. It found the indigenous people culturally diverse. Once dominant among several ethnic groups were the Melanesian Atoni, akin to the Papuans. But they had been pushed inland by waves of Indo-Malay migrants who landed on the island's central north coast in a region known as Belu and thus became known as Belunese. Although

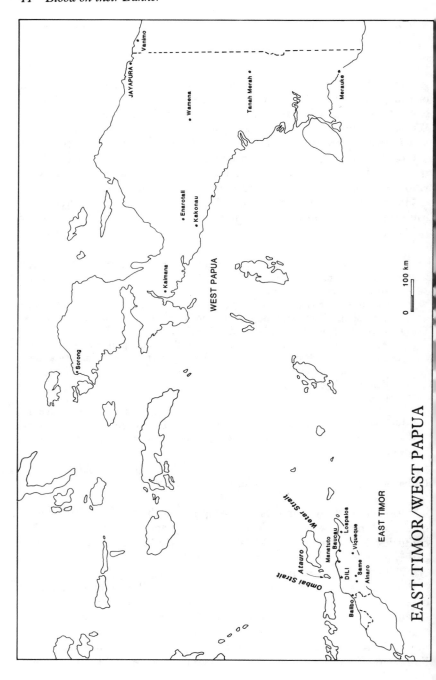

EAST TIMOR/WEST PAPUA

more than 15 languages were spoken on the island, Tetum, spoken by the Belunese, became the *lingua franca* of the Timorese.

Over the next century the Portuguese amassed enormous wealth from trading in slaves, gold, sandalwood and spices from the East. But they never really gained complete control over the Timorese and sporadic warfare dragged on.

In 1859 the Netherlands and Portugal arbitrarily carved up the island between them. The east half, the tiny enclave of Oecusse on the north coast and the offshore islands of Atauro and Jaco were retained by Portugal. The Belunese people in the centre of the island were divided by the new boundary as were other tribal groups.

The Portuguese had a limited impact on traditional social organisation. Most Timorese lived in small isolated villages — perhaps with only three to five houses. The pattern of life was a response to the climate and terrain; a rugged mountain range cleaves the island in half, running east to west. Most of the population were animists worshipping sacred objects called *lulik*, although by the time of the country's short-lived independence in 1975 a third of the population were Roman Catholic. Socially, the Timorese were organised into tiny kingdoms ruled by *liurai*. The traditional leadership was co-opted in indirect rule and for collecting taxes.

In 1910 several of the *liurai* under the leadership of Dom Boaventura rose up against the Portuguese in protest against the imposition of new tax burdens. The Great Rebellion was crushed after thousands of troops were brought to the colony from Angola and Mozambique.

Nevertheless, a small élite of East Timorese became assimilated into Portugal's 'metropolitan' culture: they were educated at Catholic schools, enlisted in the Portuguese colonial army or became minor civil servants. Yet despite such 'tokenism', Portuguese colonial policy largely ignored the interests of the East Timorese. A year before independence, it was estimated that 70 percent of East Timorese adults were illiterate. Like other Portuguese colonies, East Timor was an 'overseas province', but it was regarded as the most neglected territory, remote indeed from the priorities of Lisbon.

During the Second World War, Australian troops were landed on Timor to prevent the island from becoming a stepping-stone for Japanese expansion south to Australia. Those who landed on Dutch Timor failed to survive. The 300 soldiers who landed during 1941 in what was then 'neutral' Portuguese Timor, however, turned it into a major war zone by encouraging the Japanese to invade. Dubbed the 'cloak and dagger gang', the élite commando force tied up 21,000 Japanese troops and killed about 1500 with the loss of only 40 Australians. But at enormous cost to the Timorese — an estimated 40,000 died. As James Dunn, a former Australian consul in Dili, described the 'great catastrophe':

> The war had a devastating effect on the livelihood of the Timorese. Many farms were abandoned, especially in the fighting zones, and most of what little

food production there was went in forced deliveries to the Japanese. In addition to the destruction caused by the war and by the looting of the occupiers, the Timorese had to endure devastating bombing raids by Allied aircraft operating out of Darwin.[6]

After the Japanese surrendered at Kupang in September 1945, Portuguese colonial rule was reimposed 'vigorously and at times ruthlessly', while little attention was paid to development.

In Portugal, dictator Antonio Salazar formed the notorious PIDE* secret police after the war. Within a decade it had spread its tentacles to the colonies, reaching East Timor in 1959 after an abortive revolt by a group of Javanese refugees. Media censorship was imposed to prevent the Timorese becoming aware of the liberation struggles in other Portuguese colonies such as Angola, Guinea and Mozambique.

Marcello Caetano replaced Salazar in 1968 and domestic repression eased slightly — but not the repression in Portugal's colonies. The African wars exerted a growing strain on Lisbon's restricted resources until by 1974 they sapped half the total budget. Caetano became internationally isolated in the wake of allegations of atrocities and massacres by Portuguese troops.

On 25 April 1974, Caetano was ousted in a *coup d'état* which became dubbed the 'flower revolution'. About 200 young army officers led by General Antonio de Spinola seized power and an abrupt change in colonial policy opened the way to independence in Angola and Mozambique.

In East Timor, after the overthrow of the Portuguese military dictatorship, two major political parties were formed: Fretilin and UDT (*Uniao Democratica Timorense,* Timor Democratic Union). Fretilin wanted immediate independence while UDT was content for there to be a period of association with Portugal. Among smaller factions was APODETI (*Associacao Popular Democratica Timorense,* Timor Popular Democratic Association) which favoured integration with Indonesia.

Fretilin was not the hardline socialist party several Western governments depicted. Founded on 20 May 1974, its members ranged from the right to the far left of the political spectrum. The party comprised a loose coalition of Christian liberals, Marxist theoreticians and trade unionists. In fact, at the time of the Indonesian invasion it was still a rather fragmented movement struggling to become unified. But it was by far the strongest and most sophisticated of the Timorese parties.

Indonesia's creeping intervention

As these political changes took shape in East Timor, it became clear that the Indonesian military regime regarded the prospect of an independent

---

* The *Policia Internacional de Defensa do Estado,* International Police for State Defence, became infamous for its torture and ill-treatment of political prisoners. It was empowered to request arbitrarily extended jail sentences.

East Timor with deep apprehension. The regime was extremely sensitive about security. The 'risk' of sharing borders with a potentially democratic, non-aligned country was regarded by Jakarta as a grave threat to that security. This attitude stemmed from the fear that a democratic Timorese state could set a 'subversive' example to people living across the border in West Timor, and to people living in West Papua or in other nearby Indonesian islands.

The concern had arisen a decade earlier when President Sukarno's policy of *Nasakom* (nationalism plus communism) was in serious trouble. In 1965, six generals were murdered in what Western countries labelled a 'communist coup', which spared the pro-American General Suharto while eliminating other senior officers of the Indonesian armed forces who were regarded as opponents of the United States! Suharto then carried out a military coup which lead to the slaughter of more than 500,000 people, mostly landless peasants, and crushed the Communist Party of Indonesia.

With the political opposition destroyed and 750,000 people under arrest — many languishing in jails and concentration camps for more than a decade — Indonesia was welcomed by the West. Since then, most major Western governments have invested and established close economic ties with Indonesia. Military support has also grown substantially. By the time of the invasion of East Timor, the United States was providing 90 percent of Indonesian military supplies on the condition that they were used for 'defence'.[7] Other military suppliers included Australia, Britain, France, the Netherlands, Sweden and West Germany.

Indonesia, the world's fifth most populous country, with more than 150 million people, was under pressure to find room for millions of Javanese settlers. In spite of an increasingly expansionist foreign policy, Indonesia's Foreign Minister, Adam Malik, assured Fretilin in June 1974 that East Timor had a right to independence. However, by September that year, Jakarta was actively intervening in Timor's internal affairs, and Radio Kupang in West Timor was broadcasting frequent commentaries branding Fretilin as 'communist' and UDT as 'neo-fascist'. By December, Malik did an aboutface, declaring there were only two options open to East Timor: union with Indonesia or continued Portuguese control. Independence was 'unrealistic'.

Jakarta's special operations command, led by Major-General Ali Murtopo, launched *Operasi Komodo* (Operation Komodo, named after the giant lizard) in October 1974. The campaign aimed to politically destabilise East Timor through infiltration and intelligence activities. At the same time, preparations were under way for full-scale military intervention.[8]

As part of the campaign, Indonesia supported the UDT when it launched a 'coup' on 11 August 1975 in an attempt to eliminate Fretilin. Two weeks later, amid the chaos resulting from this upheaval, Portuguese civil and military authorities evacuated mainland Timor and fled to the island of Atauro — within sight of Dili. The withdrawal of the colonial administration left a power vacuum in East Timor until the end of September when Fretilin emerged victorious and established a *de facto* government.

Exploiting the civil unrest, Indonesia now mounted a series of border raids against East Timor, under the pretext that it was safeguarding its own national interests and protecting Indonesians living in the territory. During one such raid on the western border town of Balibo on 16 October 1975, five Australian journalists were killed. Refugees and other sources said the reporters had painted an Australian flag and the slogan 'Australia' on the wall of the house where they were sheltering. One or more of the journalists were machine-gunned and the rest were executed with their hands in the air. No full inquiry has ever been held.

The killings by Indonesian troops provoked widespread outrage, yet, curiously, Canberra never made any formal protest. Revelations since then have established that both Australian and American intelligence were closely monitoring events along the border and knew precisely what was going on. As neither the border raids nor the murder of the journalists led to protests by Western powers, Suharto 'could feel confident there would be no international outcry.'[9]

Had the newsmen succeeded in getting out of East Timor with evidence of Indonesia's mounting military intervention, international exposure of the crisis might have changed the whole course of events.

Faced with deepening aggression by its neighbour and a growing death toll, on 28 November 1975 Fretilin unilaterally declared an independent Democratic Republic of East Timor and appealed for international recognition and support. The declaration became the catalyst for invasion, providing a pretext for Indonesia to seize military control.

American officials were told about the invasion of Dili at least a week before it began. Indonesia was asked to delay the attack for a couple of days to ensure President Gerald Ford and State Secretary Dr Henry Kissinger had left Jakarta after their state visit. And five days after the Indonesians landed in Dili, the United States abstained from a United Nations General Assembly resolution (adopted by 72 votes to ten) which strongly deplored the military intervention.

'The American role was thus compliant and accommodating,' recalled former Australian consul James Dunn. 'As a former CIA officer later put it, "we had lots of time to move the Indonesians in a different direction. Instead we got right onto the Indonesian bandwagon".'[10] Central Intelligence Agency reports, monitoring developments in East Timor, show that the United States Government was briefed daily.[11]

The compliance of Australia and the United States highlighted certain of the values of colonial and superpower relations. At stake were not the sovereign rights of people or the ideals of democracy but the perceived necessity to accommodate what was, in Australia's case at least, the expansionist needs of a powerful neighbour and ally. Ironically, the Gough

Whitlam government ignored its own defence advisers, who advocated a policy of accepting eventual independence for the Portuguese colony. Had the Prime Minister followed this advice, Australian pressure on Indonesia might well have averted the catastrophe that followed.

The Governor-General revoked Whitlam's commission a month before the invasion, but the new Prime Minister, Malcolm Fraser, upheld the policy: East Timor was regarded as too unimportant to jeopardise Australia's sensitive relationship with Jakarta. And although the Fraser government protested after the invasion, its opposition was ambivalent and short-lived.

Washington monitored Indonesia's invasion with detachment. In contrast to its bitter denunciation of India's seizure of Goa in the early 1960s, it virtually condoned the far more brutal occupation of East Timor by military force. The American posture also encouraged Jakarta to respond defiantly to other international condemnation.

A vital strategic factor — control of the Ombai Straits — influenced Washington's attitude. One of four waterways linking the Indian Ocean and the Pacific (the others being the Malacca, Lombok and Sunda Straits), the straits are potentially vital to the Pentagon for passage of the Poseidon and Trident nuclear submarines. Along with the Lombok Straits, the Ombai Straits are rated with the Straits of Gibraltar as the most crucial deep-water passages in the world for American defence. The existence of oil fields in the Timor Sea also had an effect on the Australian and United States position.

When Indonesian troops finally landed in Dili on 7 December 1975, officials in Jakarta claimed they were there in support of pro-Indonesian forces in the 'civil war' — a conflict which had ended more than two months earlier! On 18 December, less than two weeks after the invasion, a provisional government was formed, with the presidents of APODETI and UDT leader and deputy, respectively. A 'people's representative assembly' was gathered in Dili on 31 May 1976 to approve a petition seeking integration with Indonesia. Indonesian and foreign journalists covered the event, but were barred from speaking to any of the assembly members. Six weeks later President Suharto signed a Bill of Integration, turning East Timor into Indonesia's '27th province'.

The United Nations refused to accept the annexation and continued to recognise Portugal as the 'government' of East Timor. Western countries, however, largely accepted the brutal invasion and status quo. Dunn analysed their response:

> The forces against [the Timorese people] were not merely a paranoid group of Indonesian generals. The Timorese were unknowns, innocents, in a cynical world in which the fortunes of the weak and unimportant mattered little. In Washington, Tokyo, Canberra [or Wellington], the issue of the rights of the Timorese, it seemed, paled into insignificance when compared with the perceived

aims and aspirations of Indonesia, an important player in the international power game.[12]

•Like the struggle in the other annexed Indonesian colony, Irian Jaya, the resistance in East Timor had become a 'forgotten war'.

Atrocities and genocide

Indonesia's genocidal assault on the Maubere people is believed to have caused the deaths of a third of the population — on a per capita basis that is claimed to be comparable to the holocaust in Kampuchea. According to Amnesty International in its 1985 report *East Timor: Violations of Human Rights*, estimates from a variety of sources put the number of people who have died since the invasion, as a direct result of the armed conflict, as high as 200,000. The victims include those killed during Indonesian bombardments, those killed in battle, and those killed as a result of famine and disease — both in the bush and in concentration camps — as well as many hundreds reportedly executed after surrender or capture.

Comparing Western reaction to the two bloodbaths is revealing. Reported atrocities in Kampuchea were eagerly taken up by the Western media, in many cases embellished with fabrications. Yet the news media showed little interest in examining the atrocities perpetrated by the Indonesians in Timor.

'Since the invasion,' said the Amnesty report, 'Indonesian troops have systematically and persistently violated human rights.' The report cited cases of the 'disappearance and arbitrary killing of non-combatants; of the torture and ill-treatment of people taken into the custody of Indonesian forces, including their detention in cruel and inhuman conditions; and of the imprisonment without charge or trial of people most often held on suspicion of opposing Indonesian occupation.'[13]

There have been four major Indonesian military operations in East Timor. *Operasi Seroja* (Operation Lotus) was launched at the time of the invasion, involved an estimated 32,000 Indonesian troops, and ended in August 1977; *Operasi Keamanan* (Operation Security) ran from September 1977 until mid-August 1983; while *Operasi Persatuan* (Operation Unity), aimed at wiping out Fretilin, began in August 1983 and faltered the following year when the Timorese party's rejuvenated military wing, Falintil, staged daring raids on Indonesian outposts. The fourth operation, *Operasi Kikis* (Operation Eradicate), late in 1986 and early 1987, again failed to gain a military victory over Fretilin.

During Operation Lotus, Fretilin forces withdrew south to Aileu and, when the town fell, to Ainaro in the mountains. Indonesian troops, however, in spite of overwhelming numbers and far greater firepower, were slow to consolidate their control outside of major towns. In fact, by 1977 Indonesia had actually begun to exhaust its military supplies, so President Carter's administration shrugged aside its 'self-acclaim about its devotion to human rights to arrange a large-scale increase in the flow of arms to Indonesia, in the certain knowledge that they would be used to consummate a massacre that was approaching genocidal proportions'.[14]

Heavy aerial bombardment of districts believed to be under Fretilin control during 1977 and 1978 (under Operation Security) led to the surrender of thousands of Maubere, who were often forced out of the bush by hunger. A visiting delegation of foreign diplomats and journalists who visited East Timor in September 1978 was shocked by the evidence of malnutrition among the thousands of Maubere people detained in 'resettlement camps.' By November the following year, Foreign Minister Malik was reluctantly forced by the international outcry to admit the starvation might be 'worse than in Biafra or Kampuchea'.

'Fifty thousand or 80,000 people might have been killed during the war [so far],' he told the *Sydney Morning Herald* two years earlier, before the annihilation operations began. '[But] what is the big fuss? . . . It was war.'[15]

For almost two years, the Timorese were the victims of a campaign of encirclement and annihilation under Operation Security. The campaign had two objectives: to destroy the Fretilin leadership, and to force those living in the mountains to abandon their highland homes for 'resettlement camps'. The traditional system of agriculture was destroyed.

Many guerrillas were captured and executed during the 'mopping up' operations. The Indonesians slaughtered Fretilin Central Committee members and Timorese activists. The death toll in the resettlement camps was extremely high. Radio Maubere reported the use of chemical weapons and napalm to destroy food resources. The Indonesians also employed death squads known as *nanggalas* (knife throwers).

While the flow of information to the outside world virtually dried up, Fretilin was reorganising its 'remnants' and preparing for a counter-offensive. A new Fretilin military commander emerged — Kay Rala Xanana Gusmao, who had been a construction worker under the Portuguese and an Information Ministry official in the independent government. Xanana (pronounced Sha-na-na), who rejuvenated the resistance, recalls 1979:

It was a year of great suffering for the Maubere people, living like captured animals, without agriculture, without clothes, without horses. The famished and diseased people who went to the bush for food were killed when they were seen by Indonesian soldiers on the pretext that they were contacting Fretilin guerrillas. The enemy used the difficult conditions of life that year to establish their system of collaboration.

In some places, large numbers of people were massacred. Disease and famine in 1979 was worse than in the three previous years. In some *desas* [Indonesian-built villages] which had a population of 400 to 600 people, only five to eight families remained alive at the end of the year.[16]

In 1981 Fretilin's resurgence consolidated its new power. Its conference in March of that year demonstrated that lines of communication had been restored; the resistance movement was again operating as a national — though decentralised — movement, with a developing strategy. For the first time Fretilin was united. New tactics contrasted sharply with those of earlier years. The strategy of maintaining permanent bases was abandoned. Guerrilla units were now highly mobile — and a network of underground 'cells' was created — behind enemy lines, inside concentration camps, and in towns and villages under Indonesian control.

The following year, Fretilin's 'year of the strategic counter-offensive', information began to leak out to the world again. After the years of silence, an historical account of the war and a fresh analysis of the nature of Indonesian colonial repression emerged. Xanana sent detailed messages to the United Nations General Assembly outlining the progress of the war and documenting atrocities committed by Indonesian troops. During the year the Australian *National Times* published the 'Timor Papers' — detailed extracts from the daily CIA reports on Indonesian military operations at the time of the invasion.[17]

By far the most important source of information from the Indonesian side has been a set of military manuals smuggled out of Timor during 1983.[18] The nine counter-insurgency manuals include guidelines which allow the use of torture and the ill-treatment of political prisoners. Indonesian officials have repeatedly tried to cast doubt on the authenticity of the documents, but have failed to provide evidence for their claims. Foreign Minister Dr Mochtar Kusumaatmadja dismissed the guidelines as 'fantastic'.

The manuals appear to have been written by officers of the East Timor command for local use. Amnesty cites experts on Indonesia in its human rights report who were satisfied they were genuine on the basis of the military terminology used, the nature of the charts and the diagrams included, the format and style, and the official stamps.

Use of violence and torture, says the document dealing with interrogation of prisoners, will hopefully only accompany interrogation in circumstances 'when the person being interrogated is having difficulty telling the truth (is evasive)'. It adds:

> If it proves necessary to use violence, make sure that there are no [Timorese people] around to see what is happening, so as not to arouse people's antipathy. . . . Avoid taking photographs showing torture in progress (people being photographed at times when they are being subjected to electric current, when they have been stripped naked, etc). Remember not to have such photographic documentation developed outside Denpasar [Bali, where the regional command headquarters is located] which could then be made available to the public by irresponsible elements.
> It is better to make attractive photographs, such as shots taken while eating

Indonesian soldiers displaying the decapitated heads of Fretilin

together with the prisoner, or shaking hands with those who have just come down from the bush, showing them in front of a house, etc. If such photos are circulated in the bush, this is a classic way of assuredly undermining their morale and fighting spirits. And if photos are shown to the priests, this can draw the church into supporting operations to restore security.[19]

Evidence of persistent torture, 'disappearances' and arbitrary executions by Indonesian troops tends to confirm Amnesty International's view that the manuals are authentic. Some reports, supported by photographic evidence, reveal that several executions involved beheading. A Maubere man who worked with Indonesian Intelligence described typical torture methods:

The normal procedure was to interrogate the captives or those who surrendered. People who surrendered and were not soldiers who had engaged in battle with Fretilin would be permitted to go free after the interrogation but only after approval from intelligence headquarters in Dili.

During the interrogation they were normally tortured, especially if the interrogators thought they were Fretilin soldiers or leaders. They would be tortured by hitting them with a blunt instrument, by jabbing lighted cigarettes into their faces around the mouth, or by giving them electric shocks, sometimes on the genitals.

The senior authorities would decide who was to be killed after interrogation. Most of the leaders or more educated ones, those who were talented, were killed.[20]

Frustrated by the failure of the military campaign, the Indonesian command opted for a strategy of negotiation, ruining the credibility of claims that Fretilin was nothing but a 'handful of bandits'. A meeting between military commander Colonel Purwanto and Xanana at a bush hideout in a 'liberated' area near Lari Gatu on 23 March 1983 led to a ceasefire. The guerrillas used the relaxed atmosphere over the next four months to consolidate their support networks and smuggle out information about conditions under the Indonesian occupation. Fretilin's peace plan — later supported by the Angola, Cape Verde, Guinea Bissau and Mozambique leaders at the December 1983 Bissau Summit — called for:

1. Direct negotiations between Portugal, Indonesia and Fretilin under UN supervision to discuss: creation of a UN or multinational peace-keeping force; organisation of a free and democratic consultation of the Maubere people; setting a date for the transfer of sovereignty.
2. Australia having the right to participate as an observer.
3. Provision for further observer nations providing the three negotiating countries agree.

But the negotiations leaked and the truce broke down. As the Timorese clergy denounced the 'process of annihilation and . . . implacable extermination of the people', Indonesia brought in heavy reinforcements for yet another campaign — Operation Unity. General Benny Murdani, the former intelligence head who was now army Commander-in-Chief, warned on 16 August that Indonesia would show 'no mercy' in crushing the resistance.

After the failure of that campaign, the Indonesians launched Operation Eradicate at the end of 1986. The Indonesian military command claimed the offensive was a justified response to a Fretilin attack on Viqueque early in October — the town was occupied for several days and several Indonesian soldiers killed. Diplomatic sources in Jakarta, however, stressed that the operation was primarily designed to create more secure conditions for the legislative 'elections' to be held in April 1987.

For the Timorese, the Catholic Church has become the 'moral fortress'. It has adopted a similar role to that of the churches in Brazil, the Philippines and in Nicaragua during Somoza's dictatorship. Before the invasion, Timor's Catholic population was about 150,000. Now it is more than 400,000. Indonesia's efforts, through bribery and harassment, to win converts to Islam has failed because this is seen as the religion of the enemy.

When Monsignor Lopes finally publicly condemned the Indonesian military for their human rights abuses in 1981 after five years of 'quiet diplomacy', however, he became unpopular with Jakarta. Fortunately, the three Timorese hired to assassinate the prelate burst into tears and confessed when they tried to carry out the killing. But Lopes was forced to resign and he left for Portugal in 1983.

Diplomatic solution?

Many Timorese feel particularly betrayed by Australia. They still speak of the wartime sacrifices their people made to help the Australian commandos in their fight against the Japanese. And they cannot understand why their 'ally' failed to support them against Indonesia.

In the preface to his book *Timor: A People Betrayed*, James Dunn condemns Australian and American acquiescence in the brutal Indonesian annexation. 'It is a shameful story of a cruel conspiracy against a small and vulnerable people,' he wrote, 'an episode marked by deceit, hypocrisy, mendacity, and plain irresponsibility. Many would prefer it not to be told, but the truth must be brought out.'[21]

He accuses former Prime Minister Gough Whitlam of expediency because of American pressure, and of misjudging Australia's responsibility to a small and vulnerable neighbour. But he also blames the Fraser government, in power by the time East Timor was seized militarily, of remaining 'unmoved at the brutal suppression of the Timorese resistance, while loudly assailing the Russians for their intervention in Afghanistan'.

West Australian Labor Senator Gordon McIntosh, then chairman of the Senate Committee on Foreign Affairs and Defence, and one of the five Australian parliamentarians who visited Timor on a fact-finding mission in July 1982, told me: 'We cannot allow the hideous crimes committed in the name of Indonesia's expansion policies to be buried by conservatives and public indifference.

'Unfortunately, the fate of the East Timorese is, to a large extent, in the hands of the politicians.' He called on other South Pacific nations to support East Timor.

McIntosh was distressed to find that at the United Nations not only were countries like Australia 'seeking the destruction of East Timor as a nation, but they were coercing less powerful countries to do so by dangling the carrot of foreign aid'. He claimed Fiji and the Solomon Islands voted against East Timor in 1982 because they were politically pressured by Australia and the United States. McIntosh has campaigned to expose this 'political hooligansim'.

As an Australian, I am not proud of my country's role in the tragic history of East Timor. As a member of the Australian Parliament, I cannot but feel ashamed and outraged by the series of shameful appeasements committed by successive Australian governments. This course of action has resulted in Australia's *de jure* recognition of Indonesia's murderous annexation.[22]

New Zealand aligns itself with Australia in backing Indonesian occupation, in spite of the Portuguese Government's support for Timorese self-determination. Like Australia, New Zealand has voted with Indonesia against every United Nations resolution on East Timor — including 'cowardly and hypocritical' opposition to a 1982 statement expressing concern about human rights violations.

When Australian Foreign Minister Bill Hayden claimed in the *Sydney Morning Herald* that Fretilin had been reduced to pillaging Timorese villages and was losing support from the Maubere people, New Zealand Prime Minister David Lange echoed him.[23] In a December 1984 interview with Radio New Zealand, Lange claimed the annexation was 'irreversible' and it was unrealistic to suggest an alternative government. 'The [Indonesian] government is determined to persist in its amnesty policy,' he said. 'And it seems inevitable that there will be no hope for a successful Fretilin uprising. The strength of the armed resistance has shown a steady decline.'[24]

East Timor's former Foreign Minister José Ramos-Horta, Fretilin envoy at the United Nations until 1988 and now international relations officer, is bitterly disillusioned with Canberra and Wellington. When Horta was granted a brief interview with Hayden in 1984, the concession provoked diplomatic sanctions against Australia by Indonesia. The following year Lange, fearful of a similar response, chose to snub Horta during the envoy's visit to Wellington. The snub defied repeated New Zealand Labour Party resolutions recognising the right of the people of East Timor to independence and citing Fretilin as the legitimate representative of the Timorese people.

Horta described the government's stance as 'pathetic and crude', adding that if the Timorese were not Melanesian but were white Anglo-Saxons, then New Zealand would *care*. He told me:

> Lange takes a courageous stand when it comes to standing up to the United States on the nuclear issue. But when the New Zealand Government faces Indonesia and an issue of human rights it remains silent. No, worse than that, it has either deliberately distorted the tragedy of East Timor or has been utterly misinformed.[25]

Horta concedes that Fretilin cannot win a military victory, but is equally convinced that Indonesia cannot either. He is optimistic of a lasting truce followed by genuine self-determination. A sound basis for this, he believes, is Fretilin's peace plan. The plan was given a boost in 1987 when Fretilin was joined by UDT in a 'nationalist convergence'.

For seven years since 1975 the UN General Assembly has adopted a resolution condemning Indonesia's actions, but support dropped from 72 to ten with 43 abstentions that year to 50 to 46 with 50 abstentions in 1982. The following year the General Assembly deferred debate on East Timor while the Secretary-General was asked to seek a political and diplomatic solution. Negotiations were encouraged between Portugal — still recognised by the United Nations as the administering power — and Indonesia, but Fretilin was excluded. During 1988, a coalition of 50 Australian development agencies launched a campaign for an independent, international commission of inquiry to investigate the fate of East Timor, hoping to focus world attention on the issue.

Towards the end of 1988, there was an upsurge in military and security operations in East Timor in spite of talk of 'opening up' the so-called province. Human rights groups such as Tapol reported at least 3000 arrests coinciding with a November visit to Dili by President Suharto. The following month, Fretilin guerrillas launched two attacks in suburbs of the capital, Lamane and Taibisse. Ali Alatas, the new Indonesian Foreign Minister, warned the European Community 'not to be manipulated' by Portugal over East Timor or it would harm relations between the community and the Association of South-East Asian Nations.

In his book *Funu: The Unfinished Saga of East Timor*, Horta stresses that Fretilin pledges — as it always has — a multiparty parliamentary system and 'a firm guarantee that an independent East Timor would not fall under the influence of any power hostile to Western interests' in the region. In fact, he advocates an effective and constructive role by the West.

> The Indonesian generals, in spite of their loud talk and arrogance, fear any move by the West to bring an end to the Timor problem. They know too well that they could not continue the war in East Timor for long if the West were to suspend weapons shipments to Indonesia. A combined effort by the United States and Britain, with which Australia could be associated, would certainly persuade the Indonesian generals to seriously negotiate an end to the war.[26]

By the end of 1988 Indonesia was under mounting pressure from the West. On 16 September the European Parliament voted 164 votes to 12, with 15 abstentions, in favour of a resolution strongly condemning Indonesia's record in East Timor, and in support of the Maubere people's right to self-determination. In the United States, 229 congressmen signed a letter to the outgoing Secretary of State, George Shultz, expressing their concern at continuing human rights violations in East Timor. But the Australian and Indonesian governments announced an 'interim arrangement' over the demarcation of the undersea boundary of the Timor Gap, which had been long disputed under international law. Portugal threatened to take action against both governments.

After 13 years and 200,000 people dead, says Horta, 'the dream of independence is as alive and strong as ever — Indonesia's brutal occupation has only strengthened our collective will and resolve to continue our *funu* [war of liberation]'.

West Papua

As people of the South Pacific reacted to the invasion of East Timor with disbelief and apprehension, they were reminded of another forgotten war. Seven years earlier, in the name of 'decolonisation' and 'regional stability', West Papua (Irian Jaya)* had been incorporated into Indonesia. The incorporation, cloaked by sham legality and permitted by an indifferent United Nations, was bitterly opposed by most Papuans. Sporadic fighting erupted into a liberation struggle which has raged for more than two decades.

As in East Timor, the history of West Papuan nationalism has been marked by constant betrayal. The interests of the Melanesian population have been sacrificed to those of its larger neighbours, Indonesia and Australia, and also the United States. Even their 'Melanesian brothers' across the border in Australia-dominated Papua New Guinea have tried to buy their security at the expense of West Papua.

At the time of incorporation in 1969 with a growing flow of refugees across the border into Papua New Guinea, a rising leader in South Pacific politics, Michael Somare, accused Australia of establishing 'concentration camps' along the border for fleeing Papuans. 'We often hear the United Nations condemning European colonialism but it never thinks of condemning Asian colonialism,' he told the Territorial Assembly in Port Moresby, 'and this is what is happening now on our border and it is colonialism on the part of Indonesians.'[27]

Several years after independence, however, Somare, as Prime Minister of Papua New Guinea, changed his tune and came to be regarded by Jakarta as a 'good friend'.

Before and during the Second World War, nationalism in West Papua had been characterised by messianic and 'cargo cult' movements. The Netherlands, which had colonised West Papua as part of the Dutch East Indies in 1828, began establishing an educated and politically conscious Papuan elite after the capitulation of the Japanese. Desperately short of administration staff, the Dutch established a Police Training School, a Papuan Battalion of about 400 soldiers and a School of Administration. Almost all the men who later played a role in West Papuan nationalism were trained in these institutions.

Irian: acronym for *Ikut Republik Indonesia Anti-Netherlands* — 'follow Indonesia against Holland', an Indonesian slogan from the campaign to annex the territory. *Jaya:* victorious. Papuan nationalists prefer *Irian Barat*, or *West Papua*, for their country.

President Sukarno pressured the Dutch into abandoning their colony by ordering an Indonesian 'liberation' military force into the jungle swamps of southern West Papua in December 1961. Operation Mandala encountered hostility from the Papuans, but gradually Dutch strongholds fell into the hands of the Indonesian soldiers led by Captain Benny Murdani, later to become Jakarta's supreme military chief.

Five members of the New Guinea Council drafted a manifesto and established a *Komite Nasional*. They convened a congress of educated Papuans at which a flag — the Morning Star, or Venus* — an anthem and a name for the independent country and its people were chosen. They had been assured by the Dutch that their right to self-determination would be honoured. The handover to Indonesia came as a bitter shock.

In the seven years leading to *Pepera*, the Indonesian acronym for *Penentuan Pendapat Rakyat*, a so-called Act of Free Choice, the Jayapura administration removed the nationalist threat by rapidly replacing Papuans with Indonesians in the bureaucracy. In September 1962 three-quarters of the administration was Papuan. One month later, however, when the United Nations Temporary Executive Authority (UNTEA) administration took over, the gaps left by the Dutch exodus were filled by Indonesians, and Indonesian officials quickly outnumbered the United Nations staff. 'Thousands of town people have had to go back to their old villages,' said a Papuan official. 'If you ask Indonesians about government jobs they will tell you there are no vacancies. But that doesn't stop them from bringing in more and more of their people from Java.'

Indonesian troops also brutally suppressed several revolts by the Arfaks and other Papua tribes.

When Indonesia announced its plan for 'free choice', it refused to allow a referendum. Instead *musyawarah* (consultations) were to be carried out by eight representative councils. Suharto himself warned that any Papuan who opposed Indonesian incorporation of the colony as Irian Jaya would be guilty of treason.

Under the headline 'Neo-colonialism', the *Sydney Morning Herald* attacked the 'humiliating' unwillingness of Australia to oppose Indonesia's actions. The newspaper added:

> The alternative to an Indonesian colony is an independent West New Guinea, aided by the UN, by the Netherlands and by Australia, and looking forward ultimately to political association with an independent eastern New Guinea. In realistic terms, by ignoring the fact that New Guinea is ethnically and geographically an entity and that all the *'musyawarah'* in the world cannot turn Melanesian Papuans into Indonesians, we are helping to prepare the ground for a Papuan irrendentist movement and laying up grave trouble in store for

---

*Traditionally, the Morning Star depicted on the Papuan flag is believed to attract supernatural help for the fight against foreign mortals. Now the flag is the symbol of the OPM.

New Guinea and consequently for ourselves. Where else in today's world would the dictum be accepted that a people was too primitive ever to be free?[28]

The *Pepera* ended at Jayapura on 2 August 1969 where potential opponents were detained to keep them silent. Representing Papua's 720,000 population were 1022 delegates in the assembly. Four were ill; none of the others dared speak against incorporation. None of the nationalist groups were allowed to be represented.

Papuans reacted with violent protest. The first uprising was at Enarotali, in the Peniai Lakes central highlands. Another revolt was launched at Waghete after the defection of 85 well-armed Papuan policemen. Villagers dug holes in the Enarotali airstrip and wounded a police inspector when they opened fire on a plane carrying General Sarwo Edhie, military chief in Irian Jaya.

Indonesian troops responded by strafing the rebels with machine-guns from aircraft, and pursuing them into the bush with paratroopers. A later revolt in the same area left scores of Indonesian casualties. The rebels used bows and arrows and deadly, spiked man traps as their main weapons. Resistance was also strong around Manokwari where persistent raids were carried out on Indonesian oil and military installations, and one group tried to seize the town itself.

In spite of an attempt by a critical Ghana, supported by other African nations, which sought a fresh Act of Free Choice five years later, the United Nations General Assembly endorsed the incorporation of West Papua into Indonesia.

OPM *guerrilla struggle*

Indonesian repression forced Papuan dissidents to flee into the jungle and join guerrilla groups. Nationalist groups merged under the umbrella *Organisasi Papua Merdeka* (OPM, Free Papua Movement) and launched a liberation struggle against Indonesian rule. During a general amnesty after the 'consultation', OPM leaders took advantage of the relaxed stance of Indonesian troops to consolidate their resistance.

But the truce failed to last long. Australian journalist Robin Osborne described in *Indonesia's Secret War* how a unit of Indonesian soldiers brutally attacked a group of women in May 1970.

> Before a crowd of 80 women and children, a pregnant villager named Maria Bonsapia was shot dead by soldiers and her baby cut from her [womb] and dissected. Her sister was raped by a group of soldiers and also killed. Papuans then heard news of a massacre of 500 villagers in the Lereh district.[29]

Seth Rumkorem, a 37-year-old Biak islander, formed his own guerrilla force which operated for 12 years until he escaped into exile. A former second lieutenant and intelligence specialist with the Indonesian military, he was embittered by the torture and brutal treatment of Papuans by the soldiers. At the time of the Act of Free Choice he was detained.

The self-styled brigadier-general's OPM faction near the Papua New Guinea border became dubbed *Victoria*, or Victory, the codename of its mobile headquarters. The guerrilla group itself was named *Tentara Pembebasan Nasional* (TPN, National Liberation Army) and its ideology was mainly Christian.

Pemka (Pemulihan Keadilan — Command for the Restoration for Justice), was the other main faction. Jacob Prai, a well-educated border villager, led the military wing, known as *Papenal* (National Liberation Group). Prai, then aged 28, had set up the radical Papuan Youth Movement while a law student at Cendrawasih University, near Jayapura. He was arrested on the campus and jailed without charge. He escaped and joined OPM.

Among other key leaders was political officer Rex Rumakiek, a former bureaucrat who was later to set up an OPM office in Vanuatu. His job was to convince Papuans that the 'free choice' was a fraud. In The Netherlands was OPM's 'elder statesman', Nicolaas Jouwe, who sometimes upset the guerrilla leadership with his extravagant statements.

On 1 July 1971, the Victoria group captured the Waris outpost, about 100 kilometres south of Jayapura, and declared their country's freedom on a shortwave radio. 'To all the Papuan people, from Numbay* to Merauke, from Sorong to Baliem [Star Mountains] and from Biak to the isle of Adi,' said the broadcast in Rumkorem's name, 'with God's help and blessing, we take this opportunity today to announce to you all that . . . the land and people of Papua have been declared to be free and independent.'

With no foreign journalists in Jayapura, little was heard about OPM until 1976. That year, following the invasion of East Timor, the Indonesians launched a drive to crush the liberation movement while publicly claiming it was insignificant. After the campaign, Brigadier Imam Munander announced 20 guerrillas had surrendered, and 50 had fled into Papua New Guinea. He insisted the movement had been reduced to 'scattered remnants' and was no longer a military threat.

In April 1977, however, guerrillas attacked a police post in the Baliem Valley, leaving 15 Indonesians dead. Fighting raged throughout the year in different parts of Irian. Jacob Prai — who had split with Rumkorem over personal and ideological differences — claimed 198 guerrillas and about 2000 villagers had died. Indonesian casualties were undisclosed, but Prai claimed 'several hundred' Indonesian troops had been killed.

A series of explosions on 23 July caused damage estimated at US$11

---

* Local name for the capital, Jayapura (which had been called Hollandia by the Dutch).

million at the United States-owned Freeport copper mine at Mount Ertzberg in the Fak Fak region. The mine's airstrip had been used for bombing several highland villages. Three Papuan villages close to the mine were razed by the Indonesians in reprisals.

About 10,000 Indonesian troops were deployed near the border with Papua New Guinea in an attempt to crush the liberation movement while it was feuding. Bands from Prai's more numerous Pemka faction had attacked the Victoria wing several times and the skirmishes between the two groups sapped OPM's strength until both leaders were in exile.

Prai and his lieutenant Otto Ondowame were arrested in 1978 by Papua New Guinea police while waiting to meet Prime Minister Somare who was attending a cabinet meeting in the border town of Vanimo. Prai was eventually given political asylum by Sweden. In August 1982, Rumkorem and some of his followers set out in a motorised outrigger canoe for Vanuatu. But PNG police illegally boarded the boat off Rabaul and arrested the ten people on board. Vanuatu was prepared to grant Rumkorem asylum provided he would not continue to claim he represented the whole of OPM and would cooperate with others. He refused and was deported to Greece.

The next few years were marked by growing unity in the OPM and a more visible international profile. At dawn on 13 February 1984, a Papuan corporal serving with the Indonesians tried to raise the nationalist Morning Star flag outside the provincial parliament building in Jayapura. It was supposed to signal an uprising. The corporal was shot dead by an Indonesian policeman. But Major Joel Awom and 100 Papuan soldiers later seized an arms cache and deserted. They carried out a series of hit-and-run raids against Indonesian forces around the capital. The Indonesians carried out ruthless reprisals and an estimated 8000 Papuan refugees fled to Papua New Guinea during the next three months.

In March, a 29-year-old Swiss pilot, Werner Wyder, flew to the village of Yuruf with an Indonesian construction manager and doctor, and a Papuan teacher, on board his Cessna 185. When the aircraft landed, armed guerrillas tied up the two Indonesians. As the group were marched through the bush to the hideout of James Nyaro, now the Pemka faction leader, the Indonesians were shot. A photograph of them with arrows and spears plunged into their bodies was sent to the Port Moresby newspapers.

About midnight on 21 April, a Papuan academic and intellectual Arnold Ap — who had been arrested the previous November and accused of supporting the OPM — disappeared from his Jayapura prison cell in a bogus escape. The bodies of Ap and another prisoner were found several days later. Both corpses showed signs of torture; Ap had bayonet wounds in his side and stomach. They were reportedly murdered by elite *Kopassandha* troops.

Although Ap was regarded as a Papuan nationalist, he was not an activist in the guerrilla movement. He was, however, deeply dedicated to preserving Irian culture in the face of 'Malayanisation' and 'Westernisation'.

Problems for Port Moresby

Indonesian border violations in pursuit of the guerrillas posed mounting problems for the Papua New Guinea Government which had become unsympathetic to the liberation movement since independence in 1975, partly because of fear of a fullscale Indonesian invasion and partly to uphold Australian policy. Australian officials working for the PNG National Intelligence Organisation reportedly passed on information about OPM to their Indonesian counterparts.

But Brigadier-General Ted Diro,* then Port Moresby's military commander, wanted his government to take a tougher stand against the guerrillas. Wishing to avoid a possible large-scale Indonesian border 'clean up' which might kill Papua New Guinea citizens, Diro and fellow officers reportedly planned a *coup d'état*, codenamed 'Electric Shock'. According to Osborne, news of the plan reached the Somare government and it became known as the 'coup that never was'.

> The aim was to occupy the Central Government Office in the Port Moresby suburb of Waigani and to hold the leadership captive until it agreed to act decisively against the OPM. Two dress rehearsals of the coup were held, including a core force of 30 officers and 20 enlisted men. Trial runs were done in jeeps and trucks which rumbled through the capital after midnight . . .
>
> Significantly, the army's plan was revealed to Indonesia's ambassador, Brigadier-General Roedjito . . . If [the coup had been] launched, the Indonesian general planned to travel to Jakarta . . . to recommend that the period of turmoil in Port Moresby would be an appropriate time to move into the border zone.[30]

In April 1983, a Papua New Guinea survey helicopter photographed the southern border area. The photographs and an inspection revealed the Indonesian-built Trans-Irian Highway to the capital from Merauke had entered Papua New Guinea territory three times. Jakarta eventually apologised, but the incident angered Port Moresby and further boosted public support for the Papuans.

---

* In November 1987, General Diro was accused in Parliament of receiving almost US$132,000 in election campaign funds from the Commander-in-Chief of Indonesia's armed forces, General Benny Murdani. A one-time foreign minister, he was forced to resign as minister without portfolio. Diro was leader of the People's Action Party at the time and the scandal eroded his standing with the PNG military forces. The funds were alleged to have been delivered to Port Moresby in a diplomatic bag by the defence attache at the Indonesian embassy when the PNG-Indonesian Friendship Treaty was signed earlier in the year. In August 1988, the Barnett Commission of Inquiry into Papua New Guinea's forestry industry, which heard evidence about the campaign funds, found Diro to have been 'disgraceful and dishonest'. The commission recommended criminal prosecutions against him. However, the Supreme Court later ruled that the commission had no power to prefer perjury charges against Diro.

The following month, OPM leader James Nyaro was interviewed by and Australian Broadcasting Corporation *Four Corners* television team. The Port Moresby government insisted the interview had been held on Papua New Guinea soil. Somare demanded that the programme should not be broadcast. After a row within the ABC, the interview was shown and ABC radio correspondent Sean Dorney was refused a work permit extension although he had not conducted the interview.

Shortly before he was talked into seeking political asylum, Nyaro told *Pacific Islands Monthly:* 'We do not want to be ruled by Indonesia and we will fight until we are free.' He appealed to Port Moresby to become 'part of the struggle' to win independence for the 'republic of West Papua New Guinea'. If Papua New Guinea did not help, then 'sooner or later' the country would join West Irian under Indonesian rule.[31]

Where the Somare government had failed, however, new Prime Minister Paias Wingti and Foreign Minister Legu Vago scored a diplomatic coup in 1986 when they persuaded the Indonesian government to allow the United Nations to help with the festering problem of the West Irian refugees, whose numbers had swelled to 10,000. The agreement was for the United Nations High Commissioner for Refugees to determine the status and future homes of Papuans who had fled across the border.

'It is a tremendous breakthrough,' said John Etheridge, the Catholic bishop of Vanimo, who had close contact with the Blackwater camp refugees. 'For the last two years I have been asking and praying for the United Nations to be allowed to get completely involved with these people, so that in a sense they are handed over to a completely neutral body for them to work out who is a genuine refugee and who is not.' But he warned that Wingti's ideas on resettlement might not match the aspirations of the camp people who believed they would all be resettled inside Papua New Guinea.

Etheridge had long been a campaigner for human rights among West Papuans, and often a conduit to the OPM for the Port Moresby government. But his activities earned criticism from some cabinet ministers, leading to an expulsion order by the Somare administration which was overturned under Wingti.

The British magazine *Ecologist* blamed the flood of refugees on Indonesia's transmigration policies which it said was now so associated with human and environmental abuse 'that the continued support provided by Western nations seems almost incomprehensible'.[32] It called on the World Bank to suspend funding for 'the largest colonisation programme in history' until Indonesia observed internationally recognised human rights and sound economic principles. 'The programme dwarfs the controversial and widely criticised programmes for the colonisation of Amazonia with which it has been compared,' the magazine said. The transmigration scheme was attacked on three grounds: its effectiveness in resettling population, its effect on the environment and its 'shattering effect' on the tribal minorities in its path.

The magazine also said transmigration was fuelling the West Papuan nationalist struggle. In mid-1988 Papua New Guinea authorities airlifted West Papuan refugees from Blackwater camp inland to Kiunga following a raid on a transmigration camp. Politicians in Port Moresby condemned the evacuation, claiming it was in response to Indonesian pressure to take OPM supporters safely out of reach of Jayapura. OPM's regional commander in Jayapura, Mathias Wenda, reported heavy fighting in the western districts of Nabire and Panaia with the loss of about 150 lives.

When, in October 1988, PNG Foreign Minister Michael Somare protested to Jakarta over the latest of seven raids across the border by Indonesian troops during that year, Indonesian Foreign Minister Aki Alatas said bluntly that the incursions would continue 'as long as the OPM continues to engage in illegal activities in the border region'.[33] In an editorial, *Pacific Islands Monthly* said Papua New Guinea could not mount an effective deterrent to Indonesia's 'ceaseless violations'. The magazine appealed for a United Nations-sponsored Pacific peacekeeping force — including Papua New Guinea troops — to supervise the troubled border.[34]

In spite of Wingti's move towards greater appeasement with Indonesia through a friendship treaty in 1987, a policy endorsed by his successor Rabbie Namaliu, the future prospect of a free West Papua may yet emerge. It could, however, take several years. But an independent state, or a province with considerably more autonomy than at present, would depend on political pressure on Jakarta rather than any hope of an OPM victory in the 'forgotten war'.

3

Vanuatu: Beyond Pandemonium

East Timor and West Papua were forgotten. For a time it seemed as if the same fate might be in store for the New Hebrides, a condominium ruled by not just one but two colonial powers — Britain and France. But the ni-Vanuatu people survived an attempted secession to achieve independence in 1980, which prompted widespread changes throughout the South Pacific. Prime Minister Walter Lini's government became the lynchpin for other nationalist groups. It developed an independent, non-aligned foreign policy with support for liberation movements and anti-nuclear campaigners.

In the British Paddock in the town of Luganville, on Vanuatu's largest island of Espiritu Santo, groups of Melanesians armed with clubs and bows and arrows were in an angry mood. They chanted abuse and threats at the civil servants cowering in their homes skirting the Paddock. Then many started pelting the houses and offices with stones. A handful of police present fired teargas grenades, but they were soon overwhelmed by the rioters.

Some of the armed men locked the policemen in the Paddock jail. Many of the civil servants fled into the night and the rioters surged through the houses, smashing windows, wrecking furniture, and seizing weapons and official vehicles. Groups of rioters also seized control of the British police station in town, and the post office and British District Agency; the offices of the French administration were left untouched. Ten cases of dynamite and seven cases of ammunition were seized from the police station.

By the morning of 28 May 1980, 13 hostages had been captured, the airstrip barricaded with oil drums and cars, and radio equipment was commandeered. The so-called Santo Rebellion had begun and the island was effectively cut off from the rest of the New Hebrides, just two months before the nation was to become the independent republic of Vanuatu.

Jimmy Stevens, a self-styled chief and leader of the rebel *Nagriamel* movement*, which was backed by the French Government and American businessmen, began broadcasting on his pirate radio:

> This is the voice of freedom and liberty, protected and defended by the *Nagriamel* Federation Independent Government in Tanafo, Santo, New Hebrides. This is the broadcasting service located approximately 25 degrees latitude south and 168 degrees longitude west, Planet Earth or Urantia, on the edge of the Milky Way cluster of stars.
>
> Today Vemarana is born. Santo people [aré in charge]. Come and join Vemarana no matter what race you belong to . . . You must be careful as independent Vanuatu is not the same as independent Vemarana.[1]

Stevens ended his broadcast by declaring that Santo had seceded from Port Vila and that other islands should also break away.

Father Walter Lini, the Anglican priest who was chief minister of the New Hebrides Government, reacted quickly. Within two days of the revolt's beginning, his government suspended all air and sea traffic between Santo and the outside world. It also recalled all civil servants who were not being held hostage and appealed to all loyal residents to leave. Within a week more than 2000 people had been evacuated from the island. The exodus was reported around the world.

After more than three months, the rebellion was finally crushed by Papua New Guinea troops in response to an appeal by Lini's post-independence Vanuatu Government. This episode was seen as an indictment of the colonial administrations of Britain and France, which had jointly ruled the New Hebrides. It was also the first time a South Pacific nation had been torn by violent upheaval while gaining independence. And this became a key factor in Vanuatu developing a more radical foreign policy and a commitment to liberation struggles in the region.

★　　　★　　　★

A double chain of 80 islands, the New Hebrides was culturally diverse when European colonisers arrived. Even today, 110 languages are spoken by the population of about 14,000 — possibly the most linguistically-divided nation in the world. The lingua franca is *Bislama*, a pidgin tongue developed among islanders who had contact with sandalwood traders. But unlike the pidgin variations in Papua New Guinea and the Solomon Islands, it includes a blend of English and French words. The name *Bislama*, also known as *Bichlemar*, is probably derived from *bêche-de-mer*, the name of a tasty sea-slug gathered in lagoons by traders and the islanders.

---

*Nagriamel is named after the taboo leaves *namele* and *nagria*, symbolising respect for traditional custom. It began as a land rights group in the 1960s.

At the start of the 17th century, when the Spanish were seeking a colony in Oceania, Portuguese navigator Pedro Ferdinand de Quiros was commissioned by the King of Spain to raise the Spanish flag in the Solomon Islands. De Quiros, however, missed the Solomons because of a navigational error and in 1606 arrived in the New Hebrides instead. He landed in what is now known as Big Bay, in the north of Espiritu Santo.

During the mid-19th century ruthless European settlers and traders began arriving from Australia and New Caledonia. Vanuatu Government officials Grace Molisa and Nikenike Vurobaravu have described them as: 'Blackbirders* taking slaves by force and deception; traders taking sandalwood and other produce without due regard for indigenous property rights; and planters acquiring land by fair means and foul — in one extreme case introducing smallpox to eliminate the indigenous population.'[2]

Traders supplied the islanders with guns, inflaming tribal disputes. Missionaries — mainly Europeans and Polynesians — also settled, most of the islands having missions by 1885. Most settlers were either British or French who bought or gained large tracts of land from the islanders by trickery. By the early twentieth century there were five times as many French settlers as British.

One of the major land-buyers, John Higginson, was a speculator rather than a settler. A British-born naturalised Frenchman of New Caledonia, he asked France to annex the New Hebrides. Although his request was refused, rivalry between Britain and France eventually led to the farcical condominium. While neither country wanted to annex the islands, each wanted to prevent the other gaining any advantage. Under the Joint Naval Agreement of 1887, the two nations agreed that warships from both navies could together patrol the New Hebridean waters. This pact was consolidated in 1906 when the Anglo-French Condominium was set up in response to growing German interest in the area.

The condominium was so schizophrenic that it became dubbed 'Pandemonium' by English speakers. For the French it was the *'Pot-pourri'*, or mess-up. Wasteful dual institutions were established — two police forces, two education systems, two resident commissioners and their staffs, two district agencies for local government centres, and eventually two post offices. Administration offices and homes frequently clustered around a field known as the British or French 'paddock'. The Union Jack and the Tricolor had to be raised or lowered at the same time. It was as Lini's private secretary, John Beasant, described: 'one of the most bizarre arrangements ever to be incubated in the womb of European imperialism'.[3]

---

*During the height of the blackbird trade, from 1863 to 1904, about 40,000 ni-Vanuatu were abducted and recruited to work in the canefields of Queensland. A further 10,000 went to Fiji and New Caledonia. Conditions were harsh. Australia deported most of the labourers in 1906; many died abroad.

When the first joint court was established in 1910, it consisted of a French judge, a British judge and a president appointed by the King of Spain. The first president, Count de Buena Esperanza, could hardly have been accused of being prejudiced against defendants or witnesses. 'He could not speak English, barely understood French, knew no Melanesian, was bewildered by pidgin and was as deaf as a post.'[4]

Both resident commissioners, the administrative heads of the colony, frequently tried to upstage each other. While the French commissioner chose a bluff with a commanding view of Port Vila for his residency, his rival had to be content with a more modest administration site among a grove of flame trees. The British commissioner, however, built an imposing home on Irriki Island in the harbour.

Following the Second World War, France was regarded as the most progressive colonial power in the South Pacific — certainly in its main colonies of New Caledonia and French Polynesia. By 1957, elected assemblies made the laws and chose ministers who made up the executive. But a 'rebellion' by French business and settler interests in New Caledonia and the return to power in France of General de Gaulle reversed the enlightened policies. Self-government was scrapped, autonomy and indigenous political parties were suppressed and de Gaulle pledged France would remain in the Pacific for ever.

While France braced itself against the 'wind of change', Britain embarked on a policy of decolonisation, shedding its interests east of Suez. By the early 1970s, all the British, Australian and New Zealand colonies had either become or were becoming independent.

Whitehall and the Matignon responded to growing Melanesian nationalism in the 1970s by sending two important civil servants to Port Vila. British Resident Commissioner Andrew Stuart, a tall, aloof Scotsman, considered his priority was to organise an elected government and to lead Britain out of its joint responsibility in the colony. Inspector-General Jean-Jacques Robert, however, a portly former rugby league player from Bordeaux, presided over one of the most unsavoury chapters of French colonialism.

The task entrusted to Robert was blunt: maintain French control in the New Hebrides at any cost. If the French were to lose their grip in Port Vila, argued the policymakers in Paris, it could touch off a 'domino' effect, encouraging agitation for independence in New Caledonia and ultimately in French Polynesia where it could threaten the nuclear tests programme.

Wantoks and cargo cultists

Unlike the other islands of Vanuatu, where a man often becomes a chief by slaughtering a large number of pigs, or through a chiefly blood line, the chiefs on the northern island of Pentecost gain their status by recognition of their character, courage, strength and voice. Walter Lini was such a leader.[5]

Born in 1942 at Agatoa, North Pentecost, he came from a line of chiefs on both sides of his family. His parents were Anglican; his father was noted for his leadership and as a builder of churches. His name appropriately means to 'let loose', 'set free' or 'to heal'. In his autobiography, *Beyond Pandemonium*, Lini revealed that at first he wanted to be a lawyer, 'but at the same time I could not get the idea of becoming a priest out of my mind'.[6] The priesthood won. He studied at St Peter's Technological College at Siota in the Solomon Islands and then continued his studies at St John's Theological College in Auckland.

While a student in New Zealand, Lini launched and edited a newspaper called in pidgin *Wantok*, or Onetalk, which articulated Pacific nationalist sentiments and the emerging philosophy of 'Melanesian socialism'. Published by the Western Pacific Island Students' Association, the paper 'aimed to make Melanesian and other Pacific island students aware of and think seriously about the political and social situations in their own countries and try to come to terms with the problems faced by their own people'.[7] *Wantok* contributed to many political changes in Pacific nations during the following two decades.

Towards the end of 1968, Lini recalls, 'life in Auckland grew frustrating for me because I felt that the Western ways and influence there were almost overwhelming me. I think I got away from New Zealand just in time'.[8] After graduating from St John's, Father Walter Lini worked as a deacon for two years in Honiara, where he met his wife Mary, before returning to Vanuatu and becoming ordained as a priest on Aoba Island.

At the time political opinion among ni-Vanuatu reflected growing impatience. The islanders resented the lack of political representation and the increasing alienation of *kastom* (customary) land. The land laws favoured expatriate planters and settlers. Two teachers, Donald Kalpokas and Peter Taurakoto, met Lini in 1971 and formed the New Hebridean Cultural Association to express these ideas. The group renamed itself the New Hebrides National Party within a year and by 1977 it became the *Vanuaaku Pati* (Our Land Party).

Lini also launched a pro-independence newspaper called *New Hebrides Viewpoints*. While he preached love, peace and justice from the pulpit, he urged the church not to ignore the injustices being inflicted by the Anglo-French administration. After trying to remain involved in both church and politics for three years, he was released from his parish and elected leader of the National Party. Lini wrote later:

> The [party] has consistently struggled and spoken unceasingly against any form of colonialism, and any tendency towards neo-colonialism. In particular, we

have opposed the way in which the British and the French governments in this day and age apply colonial tactics, continue colonial rule and appear to encourage neo-colonialism.[9]

Confidential French residency documents discovered after independence, however, revealed just how much France was determined to sabotage the nationalists. French policy was to stall progress while trying to establish a French-speaking majority within Vanuatu which Paris could manipulate. One of the first moves by France was to extend French education; discrimination against ni-Vanuatu students by the French *lycée* ended in the early 1970s.

France also provided encouragement and backing for the formation of the *colon*-dominated party, *Union des communautes des Nouvelle Hebrides* (UNCH — New Hebrides Union of Communities). The loose coalition of the UNCH and other French-speaking parties opposed to independence, including *Nagriamel,* eventually became known as the *Modérés,* or 'Moderates', a term coined by the French Residency newspaper, *Nabanga.*

Nagriamel had its roots in the 1960s in a campaign to reclaim alienated land. When settlers began felling and bulldozing large tracts of bush and erecting fences on the 13,000 hectare 'Luganville Estate', north of the main town on Santo, they enraged the *kastom* owners. Chief Buluk, one of the custom leaders, pleaded with condominium officials to halt the clearing but he was ignored. He and his followers attempted to hinder the development by removing marker pegs and fences. In the name of 'law and order', Chief Buluk was jailed for six months.

Like Chief Buluk, *Nagriamel's* leader, Jimmy Stevens, insisted traditional land rights should take precedence over registered land title. The flamboyant Stevens, who was born on Santo of Scottish and Tongan descent, identified with ni-Vanuatu more than with the settlers. He joined forces with Chief Buluk on the latter's release from jail in 1964.

Now enjoying more grassroots indigenous support, the *Nagriamel* supporters began occupying the land being settled by the *Société Français des Nouvelles Hebrides* (SFNH — French Company of the New Hebrides), a powerful land-owning and trading corporation established in 1894. Buluk and Stevens built a new village about 30 kilometres north of Luganville which they called Tanafo ('basket of fruit'). The village became the base for land occupation campaigns on the alienated estate. When Buluk and Stevens were jailed for six months for 'persistent trespass', they were seen as martyrs and *Nagriamel* rapidly gained support.

Ironically, it did not take long for the movement to become exploited by foreign business interests, especially when Stevens talked about seceding from the New Hebrides. In 1969 Stevens began dealings with a Hawaii-based American property speculator called Eugene Peacock, who bought large tracts of freehold land, particularly at Santo's Hog Harbour and in other choice areas. High-powered sales methods aimed at Americans living in Hawaii and soldiers serving in the Vietnam War earned him US$5 million.

Condominium officials reacted with characteristic lethargy, although the British were clearly concerned about Santo turning into the 'Florida of the South Pacific'. The British resident commissioner warned his French counterpart: 'In 30 years the Americans will be in the majority in Santo and will lay down the law to the administering powers'.[10]

But the huge scale of Peacock's operations and growing protests from the ni-Vanuatu finally forced the condominium to act. Under retrospective joint relations in 1971, developers were required to seek British and French approval for subdivision schemes and to pay a 50 percent tax. Peacock's plans were crushed.

For three years Peacock fought back unsuccessfully with lawsuits and political pressure. Then in 1974 he sought support from Stevens, who had been fostering a growing relationship with the French to counter the rise of the *Vanuaaku Pati*. Stevens agreed to back Peacock's proposals.

Nagriamel was encouraged by both Peacock and French *colons* on Santo to become a political party. Stevens also developed closer relations with the cargo-cultist John Frum★ movement on the southern island of Tanna. He established links with Antoine Fornelli, a Nouméa-based Indo-China War veteran who had once declared himself 'King of Tanna' and had been deported.

★   ★   ★

A turning point for the nationalist movement in Vanuatu came in 1975 when Paris finally agreed with Britain it was time for the election of a local parliament. It was not because of a change of heart by the French, but rather a belief that their nurturing of the *Modérés* over the previous few years had been successful and they would win. Sweeping victories for the *Modérés* in the Port Vila and Luganville municipal elections appeared to confirm this view.

Both Vila and Luganville, however, were 'French' towns. The majority of French-speaking islanders and settlers lived in the urban areas and any foreign national who had lived there for more than six months could vote. The November 1975 election for the first Representative Assembly showed how wrong the French assumptions were about the rise in nationalism among the ni-Vanuatu. Molisa and Vurobaravu described the result:

★This cargo cult movement became entrenched on Tanna in 1941 after the arrival of American military forces with their material goods. Its followers believed that a figure known as John Frum would deliver them from the influence of missionaries and Europeans. Ironically, they also believed Frum would bring them great wealth in the form of refrigerators, trucks, canned food, cigarettes and so on.

In spite of widespread attempts by the French Residency to 'buy' voters — prior to the election bags of rice, cartons of canned foodstuffs and even motor vehicles were passed out to potential supporters — and the existence of special interest seats in the new House, which were intended to dilute National Party influence, the party came within one seat of winning an absolute majority. Most important, the National Party won 55 percent of the ni-Vanuatu vote.[11]

The National Party won 17 of the 29 'people's' seats, against ten for the UNCH and two for the *Nagriamel*-MANH alliance. Thirteen other seats in the Assembly were filled from the Chamber of Commerce (six seats), cooperative federations (three) and custom chiefs (four). Stunned by their defeat, the French Residency launched a drive to manipulate the election of four chiefs — one from each of four districts elected by separate electoral colleges of custom chiefs. But when the French — with British agreement — succeeded in pressuring for a fresh college of chiefs in the Southern District, the elected *Modéré* chief sided with the *Vanuaaku Pati* in the Assembly.

Just as Peacock had refused to accept the legislation controlling subdivisions, he now refused to accept the election results. *Nagriamel* had won only two seats. Peacock's support for *Nagriamel* had been aimed at creating a national political force which would favour his development plans but Nagriamel won only two seats. The protest and demands for federal government by *Nagriamel* reflected his frustration and bitterness. Eventually Peacock was declared a restricted immigrant and he lost interest.

At the first session of the Assembly, in November 1976, the National Party demanded that six Chamber of Commerce seats, appointed by the resident commissioners, be discarded. When the motion was defeated, the National Party members stormed out of the chamber. The party demanded a new election based on universal suffrage, and presented a five-point demand for the ballot.

1. Only ni-Vanuatu should be allowed to vote and stand as candidates.
2. Eighteen-year-olds should be given the vote.
3. Any future government of Vanuatu must be formed by the party gaining the majority universal suffrage vote in an election, or the majority in Parliament.
4. The two governments should honour their pledge to respect the wishes of the people of Vanuatu over self-determination — by being prepared to hand over to the next legislature self-government powers.
5. A referendum to answer *yes* or *no* to independence should be held before the end of 1977.

Condominium officials refused to agree to any of the conditions — in spite of the first three principles applying to both the British and French electoral processes. The refusal to comply with points four and five which would have committed the colony to independence was further confirmation of French intransigence and British compliance with the status quo.

Members of the National Party faced growing threats and intimidation. In one incident on the island of Malekula, about 300 *Modéré* supporters armed with bush knives and clubs surrounded an aircraft which had landed. It was supposed to be carrying a party official who was organising anti-election rallies. Forewarned of an assassination attempt, the official flew on a different flight. The National Party claimed the plot had the backing of the French administration. It said:

> A [party] supporter who was a passenger on the plane was threatened with his life. His handbag was taken from him, opened, and the contents thrown on the tarmac. The mob of demonstrators threatened to cut him to pieces and put him in a coffin which the demonstrators had brought with them, purportedly intended for the *Vanuaaku Pati* officer who had not gone on the flight. The threatened passenger later recounted that the French gendarmes, who were standing near the demonstrators, made absolutely no move at all to stave off the angry demonstrators.[12]

Although the National Party went ahead with its threat to boycott the election, the condominium refused to budge. On 29 November 1977, the resident commissioners declared the *Modérés* elected in an uncontested ballot. Changing its name to the *Vanuaaku Pati*, the National Party formed a 'people's provisional government' and raised 'independence' flags. During the flag-raising ceremony at the party's office in Port Vila, *Modéré* supporters launched an attack. British police intervened and dispersed the crowd with teargas.

The *Modéré* Government, led by Chief Minister George Kalsakau, had little moral or political authority. The performance of several ministers and scandals made them an embarrassment even to the French authorities. In an attempt to gain credibility, Kalsakau established several ad hoc committees including *Vanuaaku Pati* representatives. At the end of 1978, the Assembly elected a Catholic priest, Father Gerard Leymang, as a 'neutral' chief minister. After several meetings, he and Father Lini announced a government of national unity in which both *Modéré* MPs and *Vanuaaku Pati* members became ministers; Leymang remained chief minister with Lini as his deputy. Lini and his ministers joined the government on the understanding that it was only a transitional step towards independence.

Under the so-called Dijoud Plan, named after the then French Overseas Territories Minister, Paul Dijoud, who set out his government's conditions for independence, a constitutional conference was convened. It included representatives of the *Vanuaaku Pati, Modérés,* the Santo and Tanna secessionist groups, the churches and custom chiefs. Every issue was resolved by consensus and no vote was needed.

After the constitution was approved by the two resident commissioners

Vanuaaku Pati *activists give the 'Seli Hoo' salute after raising an independence flag, 1978.*

and later by the British and French governments, fresh Assembly elections
were held on 14 November 1979 under United Nations supervision. The
Vanuaaku Pati, which campaigned on a platform of immediate independence,
gained a landslide victory. With more than a 90 percent voter turnout,
the party captured 62 percent of the total vote and two-thirds of the 39-
seat Assembly. Significantly, the party also won majorities on *every* island,
including Santo and Tanna, where secessionist sentiments were strongest.

It was a major setback for France which had expected a *Modéré* victory.
The French considered the *Vanuaaku Pati's* policy of returning alienated
land to its custom ownership as a threat to the *colons*. It also feared the
nationalist triumph would encourage the growing demands for independence
in the other French Pacific territories. In the months leading up to
independence, the French Government set about trying to sabotage the
Lini administration by encouraging revolt.

The Santo Rebellion

Jimmy Stevens and his *Nagriamel* movement, which were to play a pivotal
role in his plan, had meanwhile been courted by a right-wing American
organisation, the Phoenix Foundation, led by Michael Oliver. A self-made
man, Oliver was a Lithuanian Jew who had been brought up in Europe
before making his fortune as a property developer in the United States.
He was a millionaire by the age of 30.

Oliver wanted to create a free enterprise state in which American
supporters of capitalist ideology could take refuge from the 'socialist west'.
One aide, Dr John Hospers, a philosophy professor at the University of
Southern California, contested the 1972 United States presidential election
campaign as a candidate for the Libertarian Party. The same year the
Libertarians planted their flag on the partially submerged Minerva Reef
between Tonga and Fiji but the Tongan Government scuttled their scheme
to develop a settlement on stilts by declaring sovereignty over the reef.
A secessionist attempt by the Libertarians on Abaco, an island in the
Bahamas, was also unsuccessful.

About 15 members of the Phoenix Foundation reportedly visited Santo
during 1975 and the following year. Two of the men set up a $6000 short-
wave radio station at Tanafo and trained *Nagriamel* followers to operate
it. Radio Tanafo became an important weapon in the Santo Rebellion.

Oliver and Stevens agreed the secessionist island 'nation' would be
renamed the 'Vemarana Republic'. Oliver financed the printing of passports,
flags and currency for the breakaway state. Four days before the planned
declaration of independence, however, the Phoenix Foundation forced the
condominium into acting against it by going too far. After four associates

of the foundation tried to land illegally on Santo with more radio equipment, the authorities declared Oliver and 13 aides prohibited immigrants. Stevens noted later:

> Mike Oliver came finally to make the passport of the federation. He went, and sent me a full set of [the] constitution after he had studied it well. But since he left I've heard no more news, as the two governments have banned him.[13]

The French Government, however, stepped up support for the secessionist groups on Santo and Tanna as Lini's government prepared for independence. On a visit to Nouméa in early May 1980, Dijoud asked to meet a New Hebrides government delegation to discuss the date for independence and other issues. But Lini had already agreed on 30 July and asked London and Paris for approval. Britain agreed; France set conditions so Lini's government refused to meet Dijoud. The showdown had begun.

Inspector-General Robert, who had earlier claimed to support the Lini government, declared at the Nouméa talks that he did not care if civil war broke out. He indicated that in his view whoever would win the war had the right to rule. In a television and radio broadcast, Dijoud encouraged the French *colons* to continue destabilising Lini's government. But while pledging to safeguard and protect the settlers' rights and interests, he said France had agreed to the date for independence.

Lini blamed the Phoenix Foundation for disrupting French plans, thus triggering the premature rebellion in Luganville. In his autobiography, he explained:

> While both the French and the Phoenix Foundation wanted the island to break away after independence, the *Nagriamel* and Vemarana leaders on Santo forced the breakaway to take place before independence. This was not convenient to the French who wanted Santo to break away from the rest of the New Hebrides after independence so that they could say and prove to the rest of the world that the New Hebridean government and . . . people were not ready for independence. On the eve of independence the French were still panicking over what happened on Santo and disturbed by the issues which erupted on Tanna . . .
>
> The taking over of the police station and the district commissioner's office on Santo by force was not according to the traditional way. The terrorist activities which began in 1976 and are still continuing are not compatible with the Melanesian way.[14]

As news of the revolt spread beyond the South Pacific, foreign editors on newspapers in Europe, Australia and New Zealand recognised the potential for a journalistic feast — a self-styled chief with mixed Scottish-Tongan ancestry and '25 wives', leading a 'stone age army' in a 'bow-

and-arrow rebellion' against the forces of an insensitive central government. This was the simplistic manner in which most journalists portrayed the struggle. Many reports contained more farce than fact. One particularly crass example in the London *Daily Express* said:

> New Hebrides officially renounced cannibalism a long time ago. But one can never be completely certain. Even the first three words of the new national anthem sound sufficiently evocative of a cannibal festivity: *Yumi,* * *Yumi, Yumi.*[15]

Handicapped by the lack of a police force responsible to the government, Lini tried to restore order with little or no help from the British and French authorities. Stevens, however, was being backed by the French administration, the *colons* and the Phoenix Foundation. 'Stick it out: we're on to it in Paris where [we are] going to sabotage Lini's aid agreements with Paris and get recognition for you,' a Vemarana leader was told. 'I'll send an adviser as soon as I [can] . . . Up with Santo!'[16]

But instead of on Santo, as expected, violence erupted again on Tanna. About 300 supporters of the self-proclaimed 'republic of Tafea' surrounded the Isangel government post on the night of 10 June 1980. During gunfire, prisoners burst out of their cells and Alexis Yolou, a *Modéré* firebrand, was fatally shot.

Father Lini's government refused to compromise with either the Tafea or Vemarana rebel leaders. Lini had already appealed in vain for peace-keeping help from the United Nations and now the idea of seeking assistance from a Pacific nation, perhaps Papua New Guinea, was being suggested. As government ministers continued to try to resolve the crisis, preparations went ahead for the independence celebrations: Home Affairs Minister George Kalkoa was elected on 4 July as President-designate of the Republic of Vanuatu with the title Ati George Sokomaru. The next day more than 3000 people marched through Port Vila demonstrating their support for Lini.

Six days before independence, 100 British marines and 100 French paratroopers flew into Luganville under the command of a French colonel. Only a day earlier, Inspector-General Robert had alarmed a crowd on Santo by warning that the troops were coming to avoid 'a massacre' by a South Pacific force.[17]

The colonial troops did nothing to maintain law and order. Looting of shops continued, and then the rebels turned from theft to violence. A pilot described how he was manacled by a mob when he landed at Luganville airport as British and French soldiers stood by, ignoring the incident. The condominium was dying, but not the 'pandemonium'.

Twelve hours after the flag of Vanuatu was raised in a midnight ceremony

---

*The Bislama expression *yumi* literally means 'you-me' — you and I, all of us together.

on 30 July 1980 and the President and Prime Minister had been sworn in, Lini pledged a confident future in a national broadcast:

> Our road to independence has sometimes been exalting and at other [times] it has been depressing. More recently it has been deeply tragic . . . We cannot and we must not waste our talents in internal quarrelling. The spirit of unity . . . can only grow if it is nourished . . . We must work for it and I give you all my solemn assurance today that it will be the principal aim of the government which I lead.[18]

Papua New Guinea agreed to send a peace-keeping force to act for the Vanuatu Government and to train a small Vanuatu defence force. On 17 August British and French troops — believed by Lini's ministers to be actually prolonging the revolt — were ordered to leave Santo. In a drunken binge on the night before leaving, several European soldiers looted the deserted stores in Luganville; they were later court-martialled.

'The troops from Papua New Guinea are entirely ruthless,' warned Radio Vemarana. 'They are used to blood!' But the 90 soldiers of the 'Kumul Force' acted with an efficiency lacking among the British and French troops. Colonel Tony Huai's men quickly set up two machine-gun 'nests' on the roof of the airport control tower, mounted guard over radio and telephone stations, police posts and other strategic points, and established road blocks.

At dawn the next day, the troops and the small Vanuatu Mobile Unit took action. Four supply vessels used to run guns and other goods for the rebellion were seized. Forty people were arrested, seven of them French. As Lini's private secretary, John Beasant, noted, the Kumul Force soldiers achieved more in 36 hours than the condominium troops had in more than a month.

Skirmishes with a French-trained Melanesian *'maquis'*, named after Second World War resistance groups, and other *Nagriamel* supporters continued over the next few days. Sabotage by the rebels included the dynamiting of a copra-crushing plant outside Luganville. But the rebellion was doomed.

Jimmy Stevens was arrested, and his eldest son, Eddie, was killed by a grenade when he tried to run a roadblock. Expatriates involved in the rebellion were given the option of self-exile, or facing trial if they remained residents in Vanuatu. They left, mainly for Nouméa. Stevens was sentenced to 14½ years' imprisonment for his role in the rebellion and is serving his sentence in the old French jail near Port Vila's stadium.

★　　　★　　　★

Documents captured at the Tanafo headquarters implicated several of Inspector-General Robert's senior aides in the revolt; Robert is now persona non grata in Vanuatu. Other documents found in Vila exposed French efforts to sabotage independence.

When the decision was finally made to leave in the last days before the Vanuatu flag was raised, the staff of the French Residency were ill-prepared to depart. As a result chaos reigned as officials furiously burned mountains of paper and documents. As time ran out they dumped a large pile of apparently unimportant files in the residency carport. Among the rubbish, however, was a small collection of monthly confidential reports about New Hebrides affairs sent from the residency to the Overseas Departments and Territories Ministry in Paris.

Summing up the documents, Howard Van Trease, then director of the University of the South Pacific Centre in Vila, wrote: 'One must conclude that the policies followed by French officials in Vanuatu reflect the overall strategy of the French Government — to apply whatever techniques would achieve their goal of maintaining New Caledonia, Wallis-Futuna and Tahiti as colonies of France forever.'[19]

Since independence, however, the Vanuatu Government has been taking a remarkably courageous independent stance for an economically vulnerable nation. It has championed the liberation struggles in Kanaky/New Caledonia, Tahiti, East Timor and West Papua. But although it has provided spirited moral and diplomatic support, it has refrained from allowing provisional governments in exile on its territory — as was considered in 1984 by the FLNKS. Vanuatu is also now the only Non-Aligned Movement member country in the South Pacific. (Prime Minister Paias Wingti of Papua New Guinea pledged late in 1987 that his country would also join.)

Two years after independence, Vanuatu banned two visiting American warships from its territorial waters after Washington refused to breach its 'neither confirm nor deny' policy over nuclear weapons. The following year, in 1983, the Lini administration adopted an anti-nuclear resolution in the Assembly — a year before the New Zealand Labour Government was elected to power with its controversial nuclear ships policy.

'It is a matter of life and death,' Lini declared in a prophetic message to a Nuclear-Free and Independent Pacific conference in Port Vila in 1983, 'that our Pacific Ocean be declared a nuclear-free zone. Testing of any kind must be outlawed, as must the dumping of nuclear waste, the firing of nuclear devices, and the passage of submarine or overflying aircraft carrying them. On this crucial issue there can be no compromise or retreat. If we continue to deny ourselves any decision on this, our children of tomorrow will condemn us, and it will be a condemnation we have deserved.'

But when the nuclear-free Rarotonga Treaty was tabled in 1985, Lini refused to sign it, saying it did not go far enough.

Part 2
Kanaky in Revolt

4

From Atai to Tjibaou

Frustrated in Vanuatu, France was determined not to lose another
South Pacific 'domino' in neighbouring New Caledonia, a vital
nickel producer. After the rebellion led by Chief Atai a century
earlier, modern Kanak nationalism had emerged there with the Red
Scarves militants in the 1970s. As the stakes grew higher, French-
born indépendantiste leader Pierre Declercq was murdered in 1981,
becoming the first 'white martyr'. Three years later the Kanaks
staged an insurrection: 32 people — mainly Kanaks — were killed
and this became the catalyst for an intensified nationalist struggle.

French explorer Captain Bougainville came close to 'discovering' New
Caledonia in 1768. After visiting Tahiti and making several discoveries in
the western Pacifc, he travelled south from the New Hebrides and saw
signs of land without going to investigate. Six years later, however, James
Cook, making his second voyage of discovery on the *Resolution*, followed
up Bougainville's observations. Landing at Balade on the north-east coast
on 4 September 1774, Cook named the island New Caledonia because the
pine-clad ridges reminded him of Scotland. But while Cook was impressed
with the warm welcome from the Kanaks*, describing them as courteous,
good natured and like the people of the Friendly Isles, a French navigator
who landed at the same spot 19 years later was scathing. Hostility and
suspicion marked the relations between d'Entrecasteaux and the Kanaks
from the outset. The conflicting impressions of the explorers have been
a problem for historians ever since.

---

*The word *Kanak*, meaning *homme du pays*, or 'man of the country', came into use in the
late 1960s. The term represents an intimate, spiritual relationship between the Melanesians
of New Caledonia and their land, their soil and their environment. In its original form, *Canaque*,
which had Polynesian origins and was first used by Tahitian and Tongan crewmen on European
ships, it was mainly an expression of racial abuse. For decades it was widely used by *colons*
to describe Melanesians, rather like 'nigger'. Young activists eventually changed the spelling
to Kanak and the word took on an assertive, nationalist meaning, reflecting cultural pride.

Few Europeans visited New Caledonia before 1800. In the first half of the nineteenth century, however, explorers and traders began arriving more frequently. They hunted whales, cut sandalwood and gathered *bêche-de-mer*. Trading posts were established on the coast of the main island, Grande Terre, in spite of frequent resistance from Kanak tribes.

By the middle of the century, Christian missionaries had begun to arrive. Protestant pastors of the London Missionary Society and their Samoan catechists got there first, setting up missions on the Isle of Pines in 1840 and in the Loyalty Islands in the following year. Catholic Marist priests settled at Balade three years later. Both churches were rivals and promoted the interests of the great powers they represented; the customs and values of the Kanak culture were undermined. The Marist missionaries saw their objectives as turning the 'heathens' into Christians, establishing a French presence and taming the 'aggressive cannibalistic instincts of the natives'.[1]

Kanak clans were pressured into accepting alien ideas and institutions, such as private property and monogamous marriage. Their customary nakedness was discouraged — the women were persuaded to adopt the 'missionary robe', while the missionaries regarded the Kanak men as 'indecent' because they wore only penis covers, or *bagayous*.

The Kanak clans varied greatly in size, from 200 people up to 5000. Clans were often isolated from each other; they had little sense of Kanak unity and there was no name for the whole main island. They spoke different dialects, with about 36 different languages being spoken on Grande Terre, as the French dubbed the island.

Food supplies were irregular and nutritionally unbalanced. The clans had no animals and although human flesh occasionally supplemented the Kanak diet, this was usually associated with war and its accompanying rituals. This historical fact has been recently distorted by settlers opposed to independence in denouncing leaders of the Kanak independence movement as 'cannibals'.[2]

Much cultural symbolism was derived from cultivation of the yam and taro. The yam, for example, was regarded as sacred and many rituals marked its cultivation. The yam was considered to give the male his virility and to contain the ancestral spirit which continued the family line. By contrast, the taro was considered a female crop, grown in water instead of dry soil.

The family *case*, or conical beehive-shaped hut, was surmounted by an inverted arrow decorated with seashells — the guardian of the household. This *flèche* eventually became incorporated into the flag of the Kanaky 'republic'.

On 24 September 1853 the French empire of Napoléon III formally annexed New Caledonia, pre-empting a British takeover. France hoped the new colony would become the 'Emporium of the Pacific', a place of great commercial wealth as well as a penal colony like New South Wales. But at that time, the colony was merely two military outposts, one at each

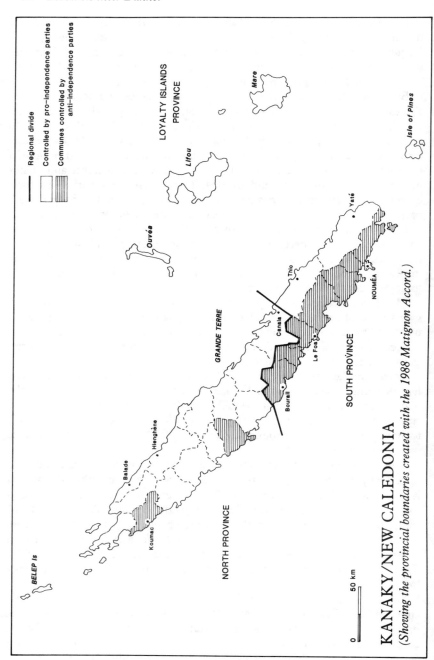

KANAKY/NEW CALEDONIA

(Showing the provincial boundaries created with the 1988 Matignon Accord.)

end of Grande Terre. Settlers began arriving, seizing the ancestral land of the Kanaks, either illegally or under the 'justification' of French law. In just over two decades this expropriation would lead to an indigenous uprising. As New Zealand historian Alan Ward described it:

> The attempt to distinguish between 'occupied' and 'vacant' lands was a classic one among European powers colonising the Pacific, but like the British in New Zealand and the Germans in New Guinea the French soon found that truly vacant land — in the sense of land not subject to any claims by indigenous clans — was practically non-existent. Virtually all land was claimed or controlled by one or more clans and, if not subject to actual cultivation, formed their hunting and gathering zone.[3]

For several decades, France had been considering where to establish penal colonies as an alternative to the notorious prison hulks of Rochefort and Toulon. Early in the nineteenth century, Western Australia was being considered. By 1830, New Zealand had been recommended. But Cayenne and Devil's Island in French Guyana, where many French revolutionaries had been deported, remained most popular.

After the 1848 Parisian workers' insurrection when prisoners swelled the jails, an urgent solution was needed. Three years later Louis-Napoléon seized power in a *coup d'état* and more political prisoners joined the list of potential deportees. Favourable reports of New Caledonia as a possible prison site led to it being incorporated into the empire; it was designated a penal settlement in 1863.

Nouméa became a little white outpost, dominated by the military barracks, the nearby Isle Nou prison, bars and brothels. The sexual imbalance in the population was so marked that the governor's ball of 1864 was attended by sixty men and nine women. The following year, New Caledonia's 'first fleet' of 250 deportees arrived on board the *Iphigénie*. During the next three decades at least 20,000 convicts were deported from France to New Caledonia, although no more than 8000 were detained there at any one time. The prisoners included common criminals, and political deportees, among which were Arab nationalists who had fought against France in North Africa and about 4000 *communards* who had taken part in the 1871 Paris insurrection.

Between 1859 and 1868, the French government promoted cattle raising and by 1878 there were about 80,000 head of cattle in New Caledonia. European stockmen seized extensive landholdings and let their cattle run free, destroying Kanak crops and damaging traditional burial grounds. A decree by Governor Guillain in 1868, followed up by decrees in 1876 and 1897, legalised the wholesale alienation of Kanak land. The French policy of *cantonnement* isolated the Kanaks from their ancestral lands. The decree granted land ownership to a large entity, the tribe, undermining traditional clan authority and creating artificial tribal units. French governors were also empowered to name or depose Kanak chiefs at will.

Frequently, Kanak chiefs campaigning for the interests of their people would be replaced by more pliable leaders, chosen by the colonial authorities. These methods often brought 'disorganisation and tension in the life of the tribes, since the indigenous people continued to only take their orders from the real [traditional] chiefs'.[4]

Kanaks began attacking European settlements in retaliation against the French land-grabbing as early as three years after annexation. French troops responded with punitive expeditions and more land alienation. Some clans chose to collaborate with the French régime. They were rewarded with uniforms and medals. 'Chief Ouatou,' noted British historian Martyn Lyons, 'received a gold [medal] in 1862, as well as brandy, beef and 1000 francs, for turning two rebel chiefs over to the authorities.'[5] One collaborator, Chief Koindo, was assassinated by his own tribe in 1858. The authorities burned the tribe's villages, deported the rebels to Tahiti and gave their children to missionaries.

At Pouébo in 1867, a guillotine was set up on the beach after French gendarmes 'press-ganging' Kanak workers were killed and settlers attacked. Twelve Kanaks were beheaded in reprisal.

Chief Atai's rebellion

The first of three major Kanak revolts against French colonialism erupted in 1878.* Resentment over the alienation of traditional land and the destruction of Kanak culture had been smouldering, but the catalyst for the so-called Great Insurrection was a row over a woman. A *bagnard*, or convict settler, named Chêne had abducted a Kanak woman from her *tribu* (tribal home) near Bouloupari. Lyons records what happened after he went back:

> [When] he returned, accompanied by his *popinée*† . . . the woman's tribe decided on revenge. Chêne, his mistress, and one of their children were assassinated. Local gendarmes arrested several local chiefs . . . [including from Dogny] some innocent tribesmen, and this was a fatal French mistake . . . [On 25 June] they were assailed and massacred by armed Kanaks. The insurrection had begun.[6]

---

*The second major revolt was in 1917 (although there was also an uprising in 1914); the third an election boycott and insurrection in November 1984. Both earlier revolts are regarded by modern Kanak nationalists as part of the struggle against French rule.

†Black Doll, an insulting term used by settlers to describe their Kanak concubines and children.

Several hundred Kanaks marched on Teremba, near La Foa, where they were beaten back by well armed troops and convict warders. Other Kanaks attacked isolated settlements. The following day, the revolt spread to Bouloupari. Kanak rebels freed several chiefs held captive there and massacred their guards. The nearby convict camp was also attacked and more than 30 warders and convicts were killed. The victims numbered 124 over the two days. High Chief Atai, the leader of the revolt, was regarded as a hero. His deeds, preserved by oral tradition, provide 'a model . . . [for] the defence of a social group threatened in its economic, political or religious interests'.[7]

Before the revolt, in response to the expropriation of land near La Foa, Atai had met Governor Olry and showed him two sacks. 'Here is what we used to have,' he said, pouring out the earth from one sack, 'And this is what you are leaving us!' He emptied a sack of stones.[8] His followers had prepared for the revolt by gathering guns, doing systematic reconnaissance of the military outposts and telegraph lines, and in establishing guerrilla camps with gardens to where the rebels could retreat.

The settlers rallied at Teremba and when French military reinforcements arrived, reprisals began. Captain Henri Rivière mounted several 'mobile columns' at La Foa which carried out lightning raids, burning Kanak villages, slaughtering the men and making the women captives.

Helped by pro-French collaborators from some of the Canala clans, one of the mobile columns surprised Chief Atai in his own camp on 1 September. He was executed and his severed head sent to Paris. But the revolt still spread to the area around Bourail and Poya without reaching the east coast, where few settlers lived. The French military continued their 'scorched earth' attacks over the new few months, devastating villages, destroying crops and cutting off water supplies. If an outbreak of typhoid had not broken out among some troops, several tribes would have faced annihilation.

Reinforcements arrived from Saigon and an estimated 5000 troops were deployed against the rebels. More than 1200 Kanaks were slaughtered — including many chiefs — and more than 800 were deported to the Isle of Pines and the remote Belep Islands. And others were sent to Tahiti, never to return. Property was confiscated from the defeated tribes and redistributed. The remaining Kanaks were herded into overcrowded, infertile reserves. Many of the survivors were overcome with despair. One chief, Gario of Nera, demoralised by the decimation of his tribe, hanged himself. Asked by the govenor to report on reasons for the revolt, Captain Rivière said:

> Bitterness has accumulated among the Kanaks, dispossessed of their best land, harassed even on their own reserves by graziers' cattle, subject to labour requisitioning, to which they submitted with repugnance, and which usually fell upon the tribes nearest the local gendarmerie. I think I can assure you

that the arrest of the Dogny chiefs was the signal for this insurrection, which was long premeditated.[9]

Yet while the Kanak people were plunged into a half-century of depression and suffering, the French authorities learned little from their mistakes. There were few changes in attitudes or policies. Governor Paul Feuillet, the first civil governor, arrived in 1894, pledging to 'turn off the dirty water tap' — by abolishing the penal settlement. However, he also encouraged the arrival of more *colons;* the defeat and displacement of the tribes in the west and south-west had left these areas wide open for exploitation by settlers. During his governorship, the first labourers from Japan, Java and Tonkin arrived. Feuillet passed a decree in 1897 which gave French officials the right of 'appropriation of portions of reserve land and the right to relocate the inhabitants on other land of the administration's choice'.[10]

Kanaks were forced on to less fertile lands in valleys or mountain slopes in the interior, depriving them of their subsistence living. The clans were isolated from their ancestral lands, forced by the French authorities to share unfamiliar land with the traditional owners or other displaced tribes. The *cantonnement* policy continued until 1903 when arbitrarily created reservations on Grande Terre reduced Kanak land from 320,000 to 120,000 hectares, or less than one-tenth of the island. The Loyalty Islands escaped this fate; they were declared Kanak reserves in 1899.

Besides alienation of their land, the Kanaks were subjugated by the *indégenat,* a 'native regulations' code common to French colonies before the Second World War. It enforced segregation and restricted movement outside the reservations. Kanaks were deprived of any French common law rights and were faced with arbitrary colonial authority. Kanaks were barred from trespassing on 'private property', or disturbing the peace of the whites. Kanaks could not enter public bars, or carry traditional weapons in European residential areas. They were forbidden to hold *pilou-pilou,* or traditional feasts and festivals, in 'unsocial' hours. Native crimes included 'charlatanism', witchcraft, showing a lack of respect for the authorities and breaches of leprosy regulations. Kanaks could also be fined simply for being naked, and they faced a 9 p.m. curfew except for Wednesday and Saturday nights. Offenders risked up to 15 days in jail and fines.

Kanaks were forced into compulsory labour on roads and other public works. A head tax obliged them also to work for settlers. Refusal to work or 'insubordination' resulted in their being sentenced to an *atelier de discipline* (discipline workshop), or prison.

> The 'prisoners' of a discipline workshop worked from 5 a.m. to 8 p.m. breaking stones for roads — without wages of course. In the case of insubordination they were imprisoned. If they were ill, the time spent in the infirmary was not counted towards their sentence which they continued serving once cured.[11]

Land alienation, the repressive system of the *indégenat,* introduction of new diseases, alcohol and guns, and demoralisation were disastrous for the Kanak people. From a population of 42,500 in 1887, the Kanaks dwindled to 28,000 by the turn of the century. According to some sociologists, there were even signs that the people were in danger of dying out. 'The colonial administration facilitated genocide,' recalls Kanak leader Yann-Célène Uregei. 'Confined on reserves and with their rights abolished, the intention was to totally emasculate the Kanak people.' He added:

> This outrageous law [*indégenat*] was not abolished until 1946, and then not from humanitarian concern, but because of a man-power shortage in the nickel industry. From partial or total slavery, the Kanak people emerged into a proletarian system which is a life of misery and exploitation.

But while Kanak culture and society were in decline, the discovery of minerals and a mining boom drew New Caledonia closer to other countries. Nickel, which was to become the economic mainstay, was first mined in the 1870s. Gold, chrome and cobalt were also discovered in significant quantities. The giant corporation Societé le Nickel (SLN) was founded in the 1880s and by the end of the nineteenth century, New Caledonia had become the world's largest nickel ore supplier. With the mining boom, New Caledonia became a more typical colony with the white oligarchy gaining profits from the exports while the Kanaks were virtually excluded. Trade linked Nouméa closer to Australia, as well as France.

In 1892 the first group of Japanese contract labourers arrived to work for SLN and according to official records 6880 Japanese arrived in New Caledonia between 1892 and 1919 when the immigration stopped. Indonesian (mainly Javanese) labourers were also recruited for the expanding nickel industry as well as for the large agricultural, particularly coffee, plantations. The Javanese, regarded as 'docile, orderly and adaptable', were the most popular labourers. Their numbers peaked at 7602 in 1929. Large numbers of Vietnamese coolies were recruited and by 1929 the 14,535 Asians in New Caledonia outnumbered the Europeans.[12] The 1930s depression ended the labour traffic between Indochina and New Caledonia. Many Vietnamese were repatriated.

While about 1000 Kanaks enlisted for the French forces during the First World War*, another revolt against French rule was brewing. This time the rebellion broke out in the north-east at Hienghène, where 16 whites were killed. Resentment against the *Caldoches,* or settlers, had grown as they expanded their pastures into the northern valleys. The two-month rebellion left more than 200 Kanaks dead and once again the French

---

* About one-third of the Kanak 'volunteers' in the Pacific Battalion were killed — double the death rate of white Caledonians. Many of the Kanak soldiers were coerced into joining up in the same way that village labour was found for road-building and other colonial projects.

authorities carried out brutal reprisals, deporting scores of rebels to the New Hebrides or Wallis Island and alienating more land.

During the Second World War, the New Caledonian administration rallied to the Free French cause of General de Gaulle and in March 1942 American forces arrived to defend the colony against the Japanese. The United States military set up their South Pacific general headquarters in the colony, with thousands of American troops being based there. They treated the Kanaks better than the *Caldoches* had and paid them well for their labour. This contact later played an important role in the development of Melanesian nationalism. Ironically, the *Caldoches* were also influenced by the Americans and during the 1984 insurrection many openly advocated that New Caledonia should become another American state.

'Two colours, one people'

Following the Second World War, the liberal international climate and growing demands from the Kanaks forced many changes in French policy. The newly formed United Nations and its charter espoused many ideals including racial equality and decolonisation. The French colonial empire itself was in retreat; French control was near its end in Morocco and Tunisia, and the 1954 defeat at Dien Bien Phu marked the French withdrawal from Indochina. Kanak soldiers returning home protested strongly for equal rights.

One group of former soldiers from Ouégoa returned home in 1946 to find their plantations abandoned and that many tribes had not received medical treatment in six years. In a petition to the Colonial Ministry, the soldiers said:

> We would like to be paid according to our work, and not according to the colour of our skin. We demand that our chiefs should be elected by us, so that they can be our representatives and our guides, and not instruments of oppression in the hands of the administration . . . We have built all the roads in New Caledonia, and none of them come anywhere near our tribes, which explains the absence of doctors.[13]

Kanak demands drawn up the same year with the backing of High Chief Naisseline on Maré went further. 'Since the Kanaks had shed their blood under the French flag in the Second World War,' historian Lyons explained, 'they demanded the rights of French citizens . . . They claimed equal pension rights with those of white soldiers, and they wanted higher pay for native teachers and nurses.'[14]

After 1946 political life took a new turn in the colony. The Catholic-based Caledonia Native Union for Freedom in Order (UICALO) and the

Protestant-formed Association of Natives of French Caledonia and the Loyalty Islands (AICLF) were founded. This was partly in reaction to the formation of a communist party by a group of settlers led by Tunica y Casas, who was later expelled from New Caledonia. According to Kanak priest Apollinaire Anova Ataba, the objective of both church groups was to 'slow down the decolonisation movement in New Caledonia and to work towards integrating the blacks and whites, a necessary precondition for the continued colonisation of the island'. However, although conservative, both groups helped raise Kanak political awareness.

The post-war period was a time of industrial expansion in New Caledonia. The Doniambo nickel smelter was renovated, the Yaté dam was built, and new mining sites were opened at Poro and Népoui. Nickel production rose sharply.

New Caledonia's economy has long been dominated by the nickel industry. Nickel is removed by open-cast bulldozing from the mountain ranges, which leaves a badly scarred, eroded and polluted landscape. The territory has almost one-half of the nickel resources of the non-communist world; SLN is the largest mining interest and has maintained close links with the French government.

Heavy dependence on nickel has emphasised the growing polarisation in New Caledonia — the separation between the rich, white, export-oriented sector and the poor, rural, subsistence Kanaks. 'Although migration for work in the urban and mining sectors was increasing,' notes Canadian researcher Donna Winslow, 'the majority of Kanaks continued to live on the reserves while the white population in urban centres, particularly Nouméa, continued to grow.'[15]

In 1948 French overseas territories were granted the right of representation in the National Assembly. Three years later a law granted the previously disenfranchised Kanaks the right to vote and in the French parliamentary elections later that year *Caldoche* politician Maurice Lenormand, the only candidate advocating Kanak interests, won overwhelmingly. Lenormand, a chemist from Burgundy, had stayed in New Caledonia after his military service in 1934. He had married a Kanak from the Loyalty Islands. He described himself as a 'left-wing Gaullist'.

After Lenormand was elected deputy, the settlers hit back bitterly, seeing him as a threat to the white oligarchy and their privileges. Accusing the Kanaks of lacking political maturity, the settlers fought a year-long battle in an attempt to introduce a two-tier electoral college and bicameral legislature which would maintain white domination. However, the 1952 decree upheld a single electoral college and created five *arrondissements*, or electoral districts.

By 1953 Kanak aspirations were channelled into a new, and increasingly powerful party, the Caledonian Union (UC). While most of its support came from Kanaks, it saw itself as a multiracial party and had backing from urban liberal *Caldoches*. Rallying under the paternalistic leadership of Lenormand and the slogan *'Deux couleurs, un seul peuple'* ('Two colours, one people'), it won the territorial elections that year, gaining 15 out of 25 seats. Nine of the 15 were Kanaks. 'The social revolution has been consummated in peace and dignity,' noted the left-wing settler newspaper *Le Calédonien,* 'and has been accepted as normal by the population.'[16]

In power, the UC granted Kanak children unlimited access to public schools (they had been barred until 1953), improved health and economic conditions and introduced a progressive land tax. The party's government indexed taxes to world nickel prices. A coalition of Kanaks, church missions, trade unions and *broussards* (small white farmers), the party became the predominant political force for several years in defiance of the powerful business interests that had previously controlled New Caledonia.

One electoral manifesto of the UC denounced the 'conservative and colonialist mafia', and attacked the dominance of 'upper bourgeois racists'. But while Lenormand sought autonomy, he was careful not to demand independence. Nevertheless, the French Government and the powerful *colon* business élite, led by industrialist Henri Lafleur and Nouméa mayor Roger Laroque, became increasingly worried about the political success of Lenormand and the Kanaks.

In 1956, a year after the socialists came to power in France, a new statute for overseas territories was adopted — the *loi cadre,* or the autonomy law. It was introduced in response to demands from several black African colonies for independence. The bill defined the framework of local and central powers, fostered decentralisation in overseas territories and increased local powers granted to the government council, giving it greater responsibility for economic development. The French state, however, retained overall responsibility for finance, defence, foreign affairs, tariff policy and tertiary education. The law also introduced universal suffrage for all citizens over the age of 21 and a single electoral college.

But the increased local powers worried the conservative settlers, many of whom did not really understand the new law. 'We want decentralisation but not disorder,' said one *Caldoche* spokesman. 'Any change that would decrease our links with France must be avoided.'

Although Lenormand campaigned for New Caledonia remaining within the French republic in de Gaulle's independence referendum in September 1958, he became the target for attacks. A thousand settlers demonstrated on 18 June, the date of De Gaulle's historic 'Free French' radio broadcast, for the ousting of Lenormand and his government. Vigilantes dug trenches and threw up barricades in the streets of Nouméa. The protesters also kidnapped 10 UC assemblymen,[17] and mobbed Rural Economy Minister Roch Pidjot, a Kanak chief who later became an *indépendantiste* deputy in Paris. De Gaulle's government mounted an inquiry; the Territorial Assembly was dissolved in October and a new govenor, Laurent Péchoux, appointed, who had a record of repression in the Ivory Coast and Togo.

Fresh elections in December confirmed Lenormand and the UC as the local government with a majority 18 seats in the 30-seat Assembly. Governor Péchoux ignored a vote for the *loi cadre* to be fully applied and began stripping the government council of its powers. Lenormand protested in vain to Paris.

Lenormand could not be ousted at the ballot box, so his powerful settler business opponents were forced to use other means. On 8 March 1962, two days after Lenormand's government refused to grant SLN a tax exemption, a bomb exploded in the Assembly. Although the Assembly was dissolved, the UC was again re-elected. The following month, a bomb exploded at the UC headquarters. Two men were arrested, both apparently having infiltrated the party and they alleged Lenormand was associated with the bombing. One man, a Ciavaldini, was an Indochina War veteran who had joined the party just three months earlier. The other, Gallewcki, was a former member of Irgun, a Jewish terrorist movement. As historian Lyons noted:

> Both seem typical of the extreme rightist thugs and criminal elements (the *barbouzes*), who hovered on the margins of Gaullist politics, without ever being completely disowned.[18]

Lenormand insisted on his innocence and no evidence was produced in court to offer a motive for why he should have been involved. But he was accused of advocating independence 'against European interests'. Even though Ciavaldini withdrew his original testimony and tried to commit suicide, Lenormand was given a one-year suspended prison sentence, disqualified as a parliamentary deputy and stripped of his civil rights for five years. Roch Pidjot took over his parliamentary duties.

In 1964 French Overseas Territories Minister Louis Jacquinot claimed the *loi cadre* was 'unsuited to a territory that is an integral part of France'.[19] He introduced a set of restrictive measures which reduced the executive council to an advisory role, and substituted proportional representation for a majority vote to end the Caledonian Union's monopoly of portfolios. The new statute caused a storm of protest. Assembly vice-president Roch Pidjot denounced it as 'a 20-year step backwards into colonialism'. The *loi Jacquinot* was reinforced by the Billote law in 1969, which stripped the local government of any control over the mining industry or economic investment, and later by the Stirn (1976) and Dijoud (1979) statutes. New Caledonia's experiment with self-government was over.

In spite of Lenormand's political comeback in the early 1970s, the UC was by then in a state of upheaval and he had lost much of his influence. Yann-Célène Uregei defected to form the more radical New Caledonia Multiracial Union (UMNC) and Kanak party supporters of the UC campaigned to move the political agenda from autonomy to independence.

Caldoche supporters seeking a more moderate stand widened the racial split.

Successive French governments had continued vigorously to encourage mass immigration. During the nickel boom between 1969 and 1974, 25,000 immigrants entered the territory. Even as the Kanak people were moving to assert themselves politically, they had been turned into a minority in their homeland. In the early 1960s more than 33,000 French (38.6 percent of the total population) and about 12,000 other immigrants (who were mainly Indonesians, Tahitians, Vietnamese and Wallis Islanders) were living in New Caledonia, compared with about 41,000 Kanaks — only 47.6 percent of the population.[20] By 1974 the Kanak population had dropped to 41.7 percent of the total. The Kanaks still remained excluded from the territory's prosperity.

Rise of the Red Scarves

While several neighbouring South Pacific states, including the Melanesian countries of Fiji, Papua New Guinea and the Solomon Islands, were becoming independent, a radical generation of Kanak leaders emerged. Many political factions were formed, often differing more over personalities than policies.

A major inspiration for the new leaders was the priest Apollinaire Anova Ataba. After studying theology at the Catholic Institute of Paris, he wrote a thesis entitled *Historie et psychologie des Mélanésiens*. Ataba brilliantly articulated the Kanak grievances under French colonialism and expanded his work into a book, but before the manuscript was published he died of leukaemia, aged 36. Although the archbishop of Nouméa banned its publication, Professor Jean Guiart published two chapters in a review in 1969; Francois Burck later published extracts and the book was released by the radical publishing house Éditions Populaires in 1984.[21]

Several Kanak activists had studied in Paris and been influenced by the student uprising of May 1968. Nidoish Naisseline, the charismatic son of High Chief Naisseline of Maré, returned to New Caledonia the following year and formed the *Foulards rouges,* or Red Scarves. Mainly comprising young Kanaks from the Loyalty Islands, the Red Scarves organised demonstrations against the annual 24 September celebrations marking French annexation — denouncing the date as a day of mourning for the indigenous people because of 'colonial crimes committed by the French'. French police brutally suppressed the first protest and Naisseline was jailed for six months because of allegedly 'inciting racial hatred' by publishing nationalist pamphlets.

'We oppose the capitalist killings, the Bible, the land thefts, alcohol and arms, the mass media owned by the bourgeoisie, which represent French imperialism and white prejudices,' wrote Naisseline in *Réveil Canaque*. In another article, he added: 'Our Kanak people have lost their dynamism and they have become fatalistic, but the spirit of the legendary Atai should galvanise them to oppose the common enemy.'[22]

Another more radical group, *1878*, honouring the 1878 insurrection, was formed by Déwé Gorodey and Élie Poigoune. It was the first Kanak group to agitate for unconditional return of Kanak land. While the Red Scarves demanded that alienated land should be handed back to Kanaks, it still favoured cooperation between the ethnic groups. But the group *1878* simply refused to recognise the laws of the French republic.

Still the links between the two groups were close. In fact, *1878* was really a Grande Terre branch of Red Scarves, the latter strategically splitting into the Atai — Ouvéa Island — and two other groups representing Lifou and Maré.

French repression hardened the resolve of young· Kanaks. On 24 September 1974, French police violently dispersed a protest by the *Groupe 1878* and two leaders, Poigoune and Henri Bailly, were arrested for allegedly inciting rebellion. They were convicted and jailed for eight days; 12 supporters, including such notable activists as Gorodey, Susanna Ounei and Gaby Monteapo, were arrested in the courtroom for refusing to leave and were later imprisoned for two months. The same year, two Kanak militants, André Gopea and Edmond Nekirai, who had been expelled from Uregei's UMNC, founded the Melanesian Progressive Union (UPM), seeking a greater economic role for Kanaks, land reforms and eventual independence.

In 1975 the UMNC demanded outright independence. Uregei stood in the Territorial Assembly on 9 September and for the first time officially demanded Kanak independence. Eleven Kanak territorial councillors joined him, declaring that after 122 years of French rule their people were excluded from political administration, from the economy and from education. Rejecting integration and stressing that Kanaks could only develop 'on the ruins of colonialism', the councillors ended by saying:

> We say **no** to the French government and France.
> We say **yes** to Kanak independence and to Free New Caledonia.[23]

By the time Uregei's party had been reformed as the United Kanak Liberation Front (FULK) in 1977, however, it had been outflanked by another radical independence party, PALIKA *(Parti de Libération Kanak)*. Emerging out of the *Groupe 1878* and the three island branches of the *Foulards rouges*, PALIKA had adopted some Marxist concepts and had a more radical political, economic and cultural agenda than any other Kanak party. As Poigoune described the party's objectives: 'We want a Cuban-style socialist party without a small Melanesian bourgeoisie. There will be no capitalist system and the nickel firm SLN will not remain.'

In March 1977 a delegation of Kanak leaders lobbied the United Nations for the first time in an attempt to have New Caledonia relisted with the United Nations Decolonisation Committee (it had been removed in 1947). Support for the Kanaks was also growing in the Melanesian states.

Anti-independence settler political groups, meanwhile, had also been consolidating their power. The most conservative of 'loyalist' parties was the New Caledonia and New Hebrides Democratic Union (UDNCNH, later becoming the Rally for the Republic, RPR), formed in 1968. Its main objectives were to promote private business, agriculture and tourism, and to oppose autonomy and decentralised government. Two years later millionaire industrialists Jacques Lafleur and Roger Laroque formed the Rally for Caledonia (RPC), aligned with the Giscard d'Estaing party in France. In 1977 both parties joined forces again as the Rally for Caledonia in the Republic (RPCR). The party wooed Kanak support by grooming a handful of Kanak leaders such as Dick Ukeiwe — branded as *'Kanaks de service'* (lackey Kanaks) by pro-independence Melanesians.

Intransigent French colonial policy, a right-wing shift among the *Caldoches* and frustrations over seeking land reforms encouraged Kanak demands for independence. In 1977 Kanak activists began harassing and intimidating property-owning settlers after being angered by *Caldoche* encroachments on the reservations and the slow pace of land reforms. The UC, which had been in decline in the face of right-wing extremism, presented a rejuvenated platform with a new generation of Kanak leaders — former Catholic priest Jean-Marie Tjibaou, Éloi Machoro and Yéiwene Yéiwene, along with *Caldoche* Francois Burck and French-born Pierre Declercq. Declercq was elected party secretary-general. The party rejected the ambivalence of Lenormand and declared itself for independence.

★   ★   ★

The 1977 Territorial Assembly elections were the first in which independence was an issue. Independence was opposed by French business interests, by the mining industry, by the *pieds noirs* from Algeria, and by the recent Wallis Island immigrants, who feared being deported back to their home islands. Eleven parties contested the elections with the RPCR and other right-wing or centrist parties winning 19 seats, or 51 percent of the vote, in the 37-seat Assembly. The pro-independence parties gained the support of a third of the total electorate, but more than two-thirds of the Melanesians.

Uregei, the only FULK councillor in the Assembly after the election, and PALIKA's two councillors demanded nationalisation of *Societé le Nickel*. They also pledged employment priority for Kanaks in an independent state, and demanded the return of all traditional land. The French government's response to the Kanak rhetoric was to reinforce its military and paramilitary gendarme forces by deploying *gardes mobiles* riot police and paratroopers.

Right-wing *Caldoche* politicians tightened their grip on New Caledonian institutions. Following an electoral reform, Grande Terre was split into electorates, one corresponding with the 'white' West and Nouméa. In the March 1978 French legislative elections, Jacques Lafleur won the new electorate; veteran Kanak deputy Roch Pidjot retained the other seat. Further gerrymandering guaranteed pro-French parties a majority in the territorial elections.

In 1979 President Giscard d'Estaing's Overseas Territories Minister, Paul Dijoud, proposed a new plan for social and economic development aimed at improving the lot of Kanaks in the hope that agitation for independence would weaken. Kanaks were offered agricultural progress, better educational opportunities, and some recognition of their historical grievances, including land alienation. But the French Government was not prepared to make any political concessions. New Caledonia seemed fated to become just like any other *métropole* department with bureaucratic control from Paris.

When Dijoud tried to buy time by asking the *indépendantistes* to drop their independence claims for ten years, the Kanak parties refused. At Dijoud's behest, the Territorial Assembly was dissolved early and a new 7.5 percent threshold law introduced in the hope that it would reduce the number of seats of the fragmented Kanak parties. In retaliation, the UC, UPM, FULK, PALIKA and the Caledonian Socialist Party (PSC) formed the Independence Front, winning 14 seats. The RPCR, which won 15 seats, and the newly formed centrist party, Federation for a New Caledonian Society (FNSC), with seven seats, were linked up in a governing coalition.

Support for independence increased. In August 1980 the synod of the protestant Evangelical Church unanimously declared itself in favour of independence, the Independence Front sent delegations to the South Pacific Forum, the Nuclear-Free and Independent Pacific conference in Hawaii and to the United Nations. A newly independent Vanuatu under the leadership of Father Walter Lini gave outspoken moral and diplomatic support.

But the following year PALIKA split into two factions. One, led by Nidoish Naisseline and Henri Bailly, took the name Kanak Socialist Liberation (LKS) and continued as part of the Independence Front. The other, more radical faction, retained the party name and quit the front, accusing it of 'lacking coherence and clarity'.

When Francois Mitterrand was elected French President in May 1981, the Independence Front heralded his victory as a major step towards independence. After all, his Socialist Party had close links with Kanak leaders. In 1979 it had written a letter declaring 'full solidarity with the struggle of the Independence Front' and pledging to 'support and guarantee the right of the Kanak people freely to decide their future'.[24]

Assassination of Declercq

Anger exploded in New Caledonia as right-wing *Caldoche* feared losing their economic control over the territory as a result of the socialist policies. Pierre Declercq, aged 43, became the first white martyr for the Kanak cause when he was assassinated on 19 September 1981 in the study of his home in Mont Doré, near Nouméa. Declercq's murder triggered protests and roadblocks across the islands; the Independence Front factions patched up their differences and became more unified than ever before. Journalist Maurice Szafran of the Paris socialist daily *Le Matin* reported:

> White, militant and Catholic, Declercq took up cudgels for the Melanesians. The Nouméa *colons* never forgave him. They regarded him as a 'traitor'. Now the Kanaks have their martyr . . .
> Declercq was killed by blasts from a 12-gauge riot gun*, his chest shattered by 19 pellets. The police found 17 pellets peppering the cupboard door he was opening at the moment he was assassinated. When his wife reached him, he was bathed in a pool of blood.[25]

Detested by right-wing settlers, respected by Kanaks, Declercq had been a gifted strategist and his death was initially a blow to the Caledonian Union and the front. He had first come to New Caledonia as a voluntary technical assistant in 1964. Until the age of 25, he had studied to be a priest. But then he became a trade unionist, finally devoting himself to Kanak socialist independence. 'He understood that colonialism corrupted all the institutions of the islands,' said a Kanak colleague, 'and the Catholic Church was obviously among them. It even plays a leading role.'

Five days after his killing, French police arrested 20-year-old motor mechanic Dominique Canon. He was held in prison for ten months and then released without facing trial; a ni-Vanuatu suspect was also freed for lack of eveidence. It was widely believed the pair had been framed as a cover for the real political killers. Although some theories suggested a *crime passionel*, it is most unlikely that the murder was without a political link. Amnesty International protested over the slow judicial inquiry. Human rights activists established the Pierre Declercq Committee; originally formed to have the killers brought to trial, it later championed justice for Kanak political prisoners and exposed other cases of colonial injustice.†

In July 1982, right-wing protesters demonstrating against land reforms invaded the Territorial Assembly in Nouméa and attacked several pro-independence deputies with clubs and fists. Police used teargas to quell the rioting in the street outside. But in spite of the mounting tension after

---

*An American-designed short-barrelled shotgun developed for hunting Vietcong guerrillas. Rounds do not pass through the body but explode like grapeshot. Weapons such as this are readily available to whites in New Caledonia.

David Robie

Kanak children honour martyr Pierre Declercq at the Church de La Conception, October 1981.

the socialists had come to power in France, the Independence Front was gaining solidarity. Former schoolteacher Éloi Machoro had succeeded Declercq as secretary-general and independence was now on the agenda for the first time in dialogue between the Kanaks and Paris. The centrist FNSC deserted Lafleur's party in 1982 to form a coalition government with the front.

But in spite of the Kanak optimism, the socialists' pre-election promises were not matched by their action. Under pressure from the right wing, the socialists watered down their policies. In 1982, they managed only minor reform proposals, including creating several new agencies such as the Office for Development of the Interior and the Islands, the Kanak Scientific, Cultural and Technical Office and the *Office Foncier* (Land Distribution Office). Established in response to Kanak land occupations, the Land Office was responsible for buying unused land from *Caldoches* and redistributing it among Kanaks. But the scheme, like the similar Dijoud Plan, had limited success.

Kanaks stepped up their agitation. At Koinde in January 1983, the local clan demanded compensation for pollution of their rivers and contamination of their fish by a *Caldoche* sawmill. When the mill owner did not respond, the Kanaks confiscated the sawmill machinery. New High Commissioner Jacques Roynette ordered in the *gardes mobiles* who dispersed the crowd with teargas and force. In the following clash, two gendarmes were shot dead.

Trying to defuse the mounting tension, Overseas Territories Minister Georges Lemoine invited the conservative parties and the Kanaks to a series

---

† Among examples of 'rough justice' in New Caledonia are:

Richard Kamouda. On 27 December 1975, Kamouda, a 21-year-old Kanak, was acting out a mock boxing match with a friend. He was hailed by a French policeman, called Blairet, who shot him dead when he bolted. French lawyers claimed Blairet was acting in 'self defence'. He was given a 15-day suspended jail sentence and then returned to active duty. Ironically, on the day of Blairet's trial, 19 November 1976, PALIKA leaders Naisseline and Gorodey were sentenced respectively to two months (suspended) and 15 days for distributing 'rebellious pamphlets'.

Theodore Daye. In 1981, Police Inspector Ferriau ran into a group of Kanak youths on the way home in Mont Doré. After trading a few insults, Ferriau returned later — drunk and armed. He shot and killed Daye, one of the youths. He was sentenced to five years in prison and went back on duty after being released seven years later.

Emile Kutu. In 1981 in Gomen, in the north-west of New Caledonia, a member of the prominent de St Quentin settler family argued with a group of trespassing Kanaks. When the Kanaks got into their car to leave, de St Quentin fired at it, killing Kutu. The verdict: one year in jail.

Boae Poitchili. In 1983 a group of Kanaks were in the middle of a noisy argument in their house in Temala. A neighbouring settler, Sauvageot, apparently took offence at the noise, walked over to the house, pointed his rifle through the window and killed Poitchili. After three years in investigative detention, Sauvageot is now a free man.

of meetings at Nainville-les-Roches in May 1983. The French Government recognised 'the innate and active right of the Kanak people — as the first inhabitants of the territory — to independence'. The Independence Front expressed preparedness to accept the so-called 'victims of history' — *Caldoches* and other non-Kanak settlers who had been in New Caledonia for several generations — and to include them in the electoral process.

When Lemoine arrived on a visit to Nouméa in November 1983, however, he was boycotted by right-wing parties. And the Independence Front walked out of the Assembly before he addressed it. They were not present for Lemoine's proposal of five years of self-government, followed by a referendum on independence in 1989. Lemoine had defied *Caldoche* anger to outline a path towards possible independence.

The proposal was soon in tatters. Front leaders stressed that it did not meet their demands for electoral reform before any vote and an earlier date for the referendum (to ensure the 1986 legislative election could not jeopardise it). The electoral laws still gave all French citizens who had been in New Caledonia for at least six months the right to vote (government officials and military staff could vote immediately). The front proposed that the right to vote be restricted to Kanaks and those non-Kanaks with at least one parent born in the territory. At first the referendum was advanced to 1985 and then postponed to 1986 (it was eventually held in 1987 by the right-wing Chirac government — *see chapter 14).*

At its congress in January 1984, the front decided to boycott the elections due in November that year unless its prosposals were considered. A call was made for Kanak mobilisation and land occupations were stepped up. In May the French National Assembly debated the Lemoine law. Out of 488 deputies, only 17 bothered to turn up for the debate. The front denounced this as 'a lack of consideration, or even contempt . . . towards the Kanak people'.[26]

Seeking to broaden its popular base, the front reformed itself as the Kanak Socialist National Liberation Front (FLNKS) — including four of the five Independence Front parties, the UC, UPM, FULK and PALIKA, along with the Kanak and Exploited Workers Union (USTKE) and the Kanak and Exploited Women Syndicate (GFKEL). A *bureau politique* was created, comprising two members elected from each group. Only Naisseline's Kanak Socialist Liberation refused to join the FLNKS, preferring to work towards independence within the French political system. The inaugural congress of the FLNKS called for a 'struggle outside the colonial institutions' and a massive 'active boycott' of the November election. Delegates decided on a new name for an independent republic, Kanaky, a flag, and discussed a constitution. Other ethnic groups were invited to join the movement in its struggle for national liberation 'because only solidarity with the liberation struggle will legitimise their citizenship in tomorrow's socialist Kanak independence'.[27] The FLNKS declared in its founding charter:

1. The French government is an accomplice to colonialism and intends to maintain and support it.
2. President Mitterrand has not fulfilled his commitments.
3. The declaration of Nainville-les-Roches, concerning our right to independence, has not been respected or put into practice.
4. The French government has refused all attempts on the part of the Independence Front to prepare for accession to a Kanak socialist independence by imposing on us the Lemoine statute . . . [and] by directly threatening the Kanak people with cultural genocide by making us a minority in our own country.
5. Capitalist and imperialist exploitation by foreign interests continues to profit colonialist France and her allies.
6. The French government follows a policy of immigration which is aimed at preventing the Kanak people from: managing their own economy; realising their right to employment; achieving and maintaining their social, cultural and political integrity.

Elected as first president of the FLNKS was Jean-Marie Tjibaou. His grandmother was shot and killed by a French soldier during the 1917 rebellion and his political consciousness stems from that tragic event. A poet and sociologist, Tjibaou abandoned his Catholic priesthood for a political vision — an independent Kanaky. 'You cannot take up a stand for your brothers,' he explained, 'without questioning the role of the official church.'

His political rise dated from the *Melanesia 2000* festival he organised in 1975. Ironically, he was backed by Nouméa's right-wing mayor, Roger Laroque, and the ultra-conservative business establishment in staging the celebration of Kanak culture.

Tjibaou, recalled a colleague, chose his moment well. 'The mines were booming, immigrants pouring in. The business houses were flush. Jean-Marie wooed the very men he knew were going to be his political enemies and persuaded them to shell out. They gambled that by underwriting Tjibaou's festival they would win him for the French. They realised their mistake too late.'

Tjibaou's political speeches were often difficult to translate. He made frequent use of imagery and poetic symbols drawn from the Kanak's cultural and natural environment — the ancestors, birds, forests, ocean and yam plantations. He believed the French had a serious flaw in their national psyche: 'The precise rationality of their Cartesian mind gives them no room for dreams, or the imaginary. So they cannot understand the South Pacific.'

The first Kanaky independence flag was hoisted on Lifou Island during an official ceremony marking the 44th anniversary of General de Gaulle's call for a Free France; the Independence Front felt betrayed by the adoption of the Lemoine statute. Mayor Edouard Wapae, a front supporter, recalled that De Gaulle's speech in 1940 showed a determination to 'liberate French soil from the Nazi occupiers and to reconquer French independence, the principles of which had made her the home of rights of man and liberties'.

In the next breath, Wapae declared that the children and grandchildren of Kanaks who fought for France then were fed up with vain promises. He made a 'last chance' plea for France to honour 'her declarations condemning colonialism and defending the right of each people to decide their own future'.[28]

Tjibaou went further. He warned Kanaks they faced a tough struggle. And he talked of 'sacrifices' made by Arab peasants during the Algerian war of independence.

Battle of the ballot box

When New Zealand Prime Minister David Lange visited Nouméa on a controversial 'reconnaissance mission' in October 1984, he described the political climate as explosive. He was echoed by Vanuatu's Walter Lini. In fact, Lini had already warned the South Pacific Forum the situation was desperate and that if it did not take the New Caledonia issue to the United Nations it could become disastrous.

In the week before the election Éloi Machoro, despite insisting that the FLNKS was peaceful, declared the *indépendantistes* would use 'every means' to disrupt the election and force France to annul them. Nidoish Naisseline likened New Caledonia to Lebanon. He warned Kanaks they had to choose between, 'independence with cooperation — or by guerrilla struggle'.[29]

The spectre of Libyan-inspired 'terrorism' also hung in the air. Machoro and Uregei had visited Libya in August, and Uregei later returned there with 17 young Kanaks for 'training'. Fiery orator Roger Holeindre, a former French paratrooper and ex-*Paris Match* journalist who was campaigning for the extreme right-wing National Front, warned New Caledonia would be 'bathed in blood'.

On polling day, Sunday 18 November, I visited several towns and villages to cover the boycott. After skirmishes, firebombs and barricades in the days leading up to the election, election day itself erupted in fury. As I reported in a cover story for *Islands Business* magazine:

> 'It's happening everywhere,' said a Nouméa radio news commentator as he breathlessly tried to keep track of the action. The little west coast town of Poya was the hottest spot. Kanak militants threw up barricades and waged running battles with the *gardes mobiles*, who fired teargas repeatedly at them.

A warehouse and grocery store were set on fire, and a shop was looted.

Only two people dared run the gauntlet to get to the town hall to vote and they were stoned in their cars. Seven people voted out of 445 registered voters.[30]

In other communes, ballot boxes and papers were burned, barricades erected to prevent people voting and pro-independence mayors would not open town hall doors. Jean-Marie Tjibaou, also mayor of Hienghène, refused to preside over the the polling staff.

The town hall at Sarraméa, near La Foa, was razed. As I looked at the smouldering ruins, an 80-year-old man said with tears in his eyes, 'It's terrible . . . I built this with my bare hands 10 years ago.'[31] A group of angry *Caldoche* settlers stood by a makeshift polling booth next to a bus under a corrugated iron shelter. One threatened me and warned 'meddling' journalists to keep out of the village. Alleged interference by Australia, New Zealand and South Pacific nations was a key issue in the election campaign.

The 'white city' of Nouméa and the second-largest town, Bourail, were calm with only minor incidents such as firebombs being tossed at buildings in the capital. By the end of the chaotic day at least three Kanak mayors — including Lifou's Edouard Wapae, who was charged with burning ballot papers — and a Kanak government minister had been arrested. Police arrested 30 people and about 20 gendarmes and Kanaks were injured.

When Éloi Machoro raised an axe above his head and cleaved the ballot box in half in the Canala town hall, his gesture became symbolic of the boycott. The ballot papers spilled out and in moments they were a bonfire on the *mairie* floor. A photograph of the protest taken by a Kanak polling official was splashed across the front page of the right-wing newspaper *Les Nouvelles Calédoniennes* next morning and published around the world; some blame the picture for his eventual assassination.

An hour earlier two truckloads of armed *gardes mobiles* with shields and teargas had been guarding the town hall. They knew 200 protesters were about eight kilometres away at Machoro's home village of Nakety, where they had built tree-trunk barricades. The gendarmes probably also suspected an attempt to storm Canala would be made. But for some reason they returned to the Canala gendarme post. When Machoro's 'active boycott' force arrived there was no resistance. The pro-independence mayor and other polling officials stayed sitting while the ballot papers were destroyed.

'The people have spoken,' one Kanak official said later. 'You can see for yourself. That's all there is to say.'

5

The Massacre of Hienghène

The November 1984 election boycott precipitated fast-moving, violent events in New Caledonia. Two weeks later, the slaughter of ten unarmed Kanak militants in an ambush almost provoked civil war. An eventual acquittal by a Nouméa court for the self-confessed killers was condemned as the worst miscarriage of justice in the South Pacific. It was a further stain on France's colonial record.

Moonlight filtered through the coconut palms and bamboo thickets on to the track skirting the Hienghène River. Night had just fallen. Two battered pickup trucks bumped along the rutted earth surface; 17 Kanaks squeezed into the vehicles joked and laughed as the trucks lurched along.

A two-hour meeting of the local *comité de lutte* (struggle committee) at the Hienghène Cultural Centre had ended on a happy note. It had been called that afternoon, Wednesday 5 December 1984, to explain why the FLNKS had decided to lift the barricades and abandon its campaign of destabilisation, a decision announced the day before in Nouméa. About 50 people attended the meeting. At 7.30 the local militants left and headed for home. Fourteen piled into the two pickups; three others hitched a ride along the 14-kilometre track to Tiendanite, home village of the Kanak provisional government leader Jean-Marie Tjibaou. One of Tjibaou's three brothers, Louis, chief of the Tiendanite *tribu*, drove a Mitsubishi. Behind, travelling almost bumper-to-bumper because his headlights were smashed, was a younger brother, Vianney, at the wheel of a Chevrolet.

At Wan'yaat, eight kilometres up the valley, the track is hemmed in between a cliff and the river. Beside the track are a barbed-wire fence and cleared pasture leading to the river 20 metres away. When the Mitsubishi reached a house belonging to Maurice Mitride, a 50-year-old settler of mixed race, it stopped abruptly. A felled coconut palm blocked the way.

'Road block . . . road block,' shouted 17-year-old Joseph Wathea in the back of the truck. Louis Tjibaou, who hadn't seen the tree until five metres away, backed off and bumped into the Chevrolet.

An explosion* ripped open the right-hand side of the Mitsubishi as two sticks of dynamite slung from a wire made contact. Spotlights lit up the track and a deadly crossfire from rifles and shotguns opened up from Mitride's house and from the other side of the track.

'Everybody out,' yelled Vianney Tjibaou, dragging himself through the barbed-wire fence and fleeing towards Tiendanite. Some of the other men also managed to jump out of the trucks and run for cover by the river. Vianney, 38 at the time, and one of two survivors of the ambush who were unhurt, recalls:

> I saw flames coming out of the gunbarrels when the shooting started from Mitride's house and from the river. I opened the car door [and shouted to everybody to get out] and then I jumped. I . . . ran towards the river. Then I followed it upstream and felt a burn on my shoulder. While I was running, [they kept firing] but never hit me.
>
> After a while, I came to a bend where there was a fence and saw another two or three people firing. I stopped about 200 metres from the ambush site to watch and listen, hiding in the coffee bushes.[1]

Louis Tjibaou sat frozen in the Mitsubishi. Beside him, Pascal Couhia ducked under the steering wheel to dodge the shots. As soon as Couhia slid through the door, he was hit by two bullets in the thigh. He crawled along a ditch and hid under a stand of dead bamboo which had fallen into the river, staying there until a doctor arrived after the ambush. Wathea, also wounded, joined him under the bamboo.

Vianney recognised Maurice Mitride, another settler, Henri Garnier, his wife, Rose, and other ambushers among the shadows. He saw Garnier walk towards the body of Louis, who had scrambled past the coconut tree before being shot.

'You bastards, we've got you,' Garnier snarled. Vianney saw Garnier shoot Louis point blank in the head.[2] Slipping away, Vianney ran to a causeway where the Tiendanite track left the river. A horse was tethered there and he rode to the village to warn the women and children of the *tribu*. They hid in the bush.

Mickael Maepas was wounded and dragged himself into the river. He floated in the water until about 10 a.m. next morning, when he was found still alive. (He died a day later, after giving evidence.)

In the back of the Chevrolet, Lucien Couhia, Pascal Mandjia and Tarcisse Tjibaou lay unable to move — shots had shattered their spines. They lay

---

* Several witnesses testified to seeing a dynamite explosion. People living in the valley heard a loud noise about 8p.m. — 'like an airplane crash', one said. Damage to the leading vehicle was consistent with their statements, and a piece of wire, attached to a peach tree, was recovered the next day.

silently in agony until Tarcisse, unable to bear the pain anymore, cried out. Some of the killers returned with spotlights and opened fire from close up.

Lucien Couhia was wounded in the right forearm and chest. He stopped breathing. Mandjia pretended to be dead. Tjibaou was dead. (His body was later incinerated in the truck.) After the killers went off to the river to hunt the wounded, Couhia dragged himself off the truck, escaped to a Kanak family further along the track and was taken to the Hienghène dispensary.

Bernard Maepas, aged 27, in the back of the Chevrolet, had been one of the first to run for his life. He recalls:

> At first it was the people in front of [Mitride's] house doing the shooting, so we ran to the left of the cars. We didn't see the guys below, in the pasture, because they had not begun to shoot. But as we got past the barbed wire fence, they started too. Some were even sitting down and they shot at us point blank.
>
> I was wounded then and got shot in the lower abdomen. At that time, those who were up at the house began to walk down the drive and let the dogs loose. They had flashlights. I hid on the river bank. I was unable to swim but managed to hide under some plants. There were wounded men lying in the grass near me. When the dogs, who followed the scent of blood, found them, the people followed and shot at the men on the ground.
>
> They finished off the wounded, took their bodies and dragged them into the water. All the time, they insulted us. I heard one of the killers shout, 'There's Auguste [Wathea],' and the others screamed, 'kill him, *kill him*'.[3]

Maepas kept hearing shots for about 20 minutes. Then silence. When the dogs barked the ambushers would find another wounded man and finish him off. By the time the assassins thought everybody was dead, they began to talk loudly. Maepas thought there were 15 of them.

Joseph Pei was down at the river too. He had been shot twice in the foot. They could not swim across because the killers were on the river bank, lighting up the water with their spotlights. Maepas recalls:

> I saw one man swim. He was obviously hurt and couldn't swim very well. The killers came with their lights and saw him. Two or three of them started to fire on him. The man was struggling for his life in the water. And they shot at him until he no longer moved.[4]

As the attackers blasted away at the wounded, 14-year-old Jerry Lapetite went to the bank and shone his spotlight over the river. The water was red with blood. He called over his companions, shouting, 'Hot shit, look at all that blood!'

When the killers moved away, Bernard Maepas crawled out from under some patchouli plants. 'I was walking on bodies. They had not yet thrown the bodies into the river,' he recalls. 'I felt I was going mad. Among the bodies was Louis Tjibaou. When they found him the next day, he was [riddled] with at least 30 bullets and [shotgun pellets].' Twenty-year-old Jean-Luc Vayadimoin also escaped, with superficial wounds.

> I came upon Éloi Maepas, who was moaning. I was about to carry him when I saw the spotlights go on [again] and lay down. I took a good look at the people. On the other side, the shooting continued — shot after shot . . . They talked loudly among themselves. Henri Garnier said, 'I'm gonna kill those lousy Kanaks.'
>
> I got up and ran, but didn't make it as far as the canna lilies because the searchlights turned on again and shots came in my direction. I heard a bullet whistle past. I dived into the water and they continued to light up the river. I recognised the voice of Jacky Charles who asked, 'Where is he? Who are you shooting at?'[5]

They shot at the bodies in the river. Vayadimoin heard the bullets hit the swirling water. He stayed hidden in pampas grass for a long time, flat on his belly.

'There's someone in this car,' shouted Jesse Lapetite.

'Kill him, *kill kim*,' replied Henri Garnier. Roger Tein screamed, 'Shoot . . . *shoot*'. Vayadimoin heard three shots. First one, then two together.

★   ★   ★

Six men died that night and a further four died in the next two days from their wounds.* Seven survived, four of them gravely wounded; a fifth suffered superficial wounds. The survivors spent the night by the river or crawled and ran to a nearby village. Mickael Maepas was airlifted by helicopter next day to hospital in Nouméa, when the gendarmes and reinforcements arrived. Five bodies were found within a 50-metre radius of the vehicles; another, that of Tarcisse Tjibaou, was found in the fire-gutted shell of the Chevrolet.

Although alerted within an hour of the start of the massacre, the local gendarmes at Hienghène did not arrive at Wan'yaat until almost midday on 6 December — 16 hours after the slaughter. By Saturday four more victims had died in hospital from their wounds.

When I arrived at Wan'yaat two days later for the traditional burial ceremony at Tiendanite, the only obvious evidence of the massacre were the bullet-scarred and charred pickup trucks. Police recovered 200 cartridge cases which had been fired in the half hour of terror.

---

*The victims were Antoine Couhia, Michel Couhia, Simileon Couhia, Éloi Maepas, Mickael Maepas, Pascal Mandjia, Louis Tjibaou, Tarcisse Tjibaou, Alphonse Wathea and Auguste Wathea.

The bodies of the 1984 Hienghène massacre victims being taken to Tiendanite for burial.

To the outrage of the *Caldoches*, the French Army flew the ten coffins by Puma helicopter to Hienghène Valley where they were transported by military truck to Tiendanite. Heavily armed *gendarmes mobiles*, with armoured personnel carriers and machine-gun-festooned trucks, guarded the track through the valley and the ambush site.

About 600 Kanaks came to the village to bury the dead — but not Tjibaou himself. Tjibaou, mayor of Hienghène, was believed to be in danger and was closely guarded by armed FLNKS militants. After several hours of wailing and custom rites, and a tribute to their martyrdom by Kanaky's Interior Minister Yéiwene Yéiwene, the victims were buried in a line with their caskets draped in the blood-red, blue and green bands and golden orb of the Kanaky flag, and frangipani and hibiscus blooms. Déwé Gorodey wrote a poem dedicated to the victims.

> *The river weeps*
> *tears of blood*
> *The mountain groans*
> *echoes of mourning*
> *The trade winds breathe*
> *soothing words*
> *The forest covers*
> *the gaping wound . . .*[6]

★　　　★　　　★

Senator Dick Ukeiwé, president of the territorial government, flew back from Paris and was welcomed by a mainly European rally of about 6000 people protesting against independence. Though they gave a minute's silence for the tragedy victims, their message was clear: most New Caledonians wanted to remain French while the FLNKS were 'terrorists and rebels' and should be outlawed. The Kanak Socialist Liberation occupied the Territorial Assembly chamber in a symbolic protest against the 'insensitivity' of Ukeiwé's rally in the wake of the killings.

For Edgard Pisani, a former Gaullist cabinet minister with a reputation for giving Third World countries a fairer deal, the events were a baptism of fire. He arrived in Nouméa just two days before the massacre and a few hours after a local French journalist, Frank Depierre, of the right-wing daily *Les Nouvelles Calédoniennes*, and a UTA Airlines staffer had been shot and wounded at a barricade at Saint Louis, near the capital.

★　　　★　　　★

Identified by survivors and other witnesses on the night of the ambush, the killers escaped along a forest track to the west coast European township of Voh after burning down Jean-Marie Tjibaou's home near the Hienghène River. They were helped by other settlers to elude police. After five days, on 10 December 1984, Maurice Mitride gave himself up, saying he 'couldn't live with his conscience'.[7] The following day, bull-necked, stockily built Raoul Lapetite, aged 58, four of his five sons, Jacques, Jean-Claude, José and Jesse, and Robert Sineimene, aged 24, were also arrested, near Voh. Lapetite's fifth son, Jerry, was caught in a Nouméa disco but later released as a minor. At least another eight, mostly white attackers — including a woman — identified as having taken part were never charged.

Several of Mitride's ancestors came from Réunion, a French possession in the Indian Ocean. He is slight and dark-skinned with short, kinky hair. Raoul Lapetite's father was French, but his mother was a Kanak. He is also dark-skinned; his sons could easily be mistaken for Kanaks. Sineimene's mother is a Kanak from Lifou; his father Javanese. Yet all seven fervently consider themselves European. Like other *Caldoches*, they defended the capitalist notion of land ownership. Once Kanak clans began to suggest to Mitride and Lapetite that their land should be shared again with traditional, indigenous owners battle lines were drawn.

The 'no case' scandal

The sordid judicial aftermath of the massacre of Hienghène is certain to go down as one of the greater stains on French colonial history in the South Pacific. Almost two years after the massacre the self-confessed killers were set free by examining magistrate Francois Semur who ruled *non-lieu* — no case to answer. They had been charged with the murder of 10 Kanaks and the attempted murder of seven others.

Citing a rarely used highway robbery law dating back to Napoleonic times, magistrate Semur said the accused had acted in 'self defence'. He referred to the 'exceptional circumstances' at the end of 1984 — the three-week period of unrest and barricades which gripped New Caledonia after the Kanak boycott of the elections on November 18. Yet in the Hienghène and Tiendanite Valleys there was little violence and less trouble than anywhere. Semur ignored this; his decision reflected the settler version of events.

The magistrate neglected to mention the fact that at the time of the ambush the Kanaks who died had been unarmed and were returning from the meeting at which it had been decided to resort to peaceful negotiations with the French authorities.* Semur also did not explain why he shunned

---

* The accused claimed the first shot was fired from the Chevrolet pickup. But the only gun recovered from the trucks was found charred in the Mitsubishi, wedged behind the driver's seat, with one bullet in the chamber. It had not been fired. No trace of a gun was found in the Chevrolet.[8]

the testimony of more than 20 witnesses which showed the attack was an unprovoked slaughter of unarmed Kanaks. Nor did he question or charge other settlers named by the survivors — at least two of them regarded by gendarmes as 'seriously implicated'. Semur rejected a request by lawyer Gustave Tehio, a barrister representing the families of the victims, to carry out a reconstruction of the ambush. Some lawyers claimed the magistrate was acting under pressure from the French government to drop the case.

A young French military doctor, Gustave Savourey, stationed at Hienghène, made an ambulance trip on the night of the ambush. He rescued two wounded survivors and also picked up Rose Garnier, who is alleged to have been one of the attackers. The settlers later claimed that the house belonging to her and husband Henri had been burned in an attack by the Kanak villagers. However, the doctor reported that the house was intact when he passed by. But his testimony was hushed up and he was posted back to France.

Semur appears to have ignored or suppressed almost all evidence indicating a carefully orchestrated and premeditated massacre. 'After 21 months of investigation,' he said, 'I am convinced there is no case for holding these men on murder charges.'

Released from Camp Est prison before dawn on 1 October 1986, the killers were taken to a secret hideout in Nouméa. Photographs of them were splashed across the front page of *Les Nouvelles Calédoniennes*, and they appeared on the state-run television defending the massacre. *Les Nouvelles* greeted their release in triumph as if they were popular war heroes.

France's Association of Magistrates denounced the ruling as a 'mockery of justice'. It added in a statement: 'On the evidence, this provocative ruling is purely political and we fear the consequences for public order in New Caledonia.'[9]

'This is a monumental judicial gaffe,' said New Zealand author James McNeish. 'It is going to have serious consequences in France and is bound to cause an international *cause célèbre*.' McNeish, visiting Nouméa at the time of the *non-lieu*, covered the event for British and New Zealand newspapers. He reported for the *New Zealand Listener:*

> In a 153-page judgement of almost unbelievable colonial bias, [magistrate Semur] described the Tiendanite Kanaks as having a 'bad character'. He spoke of a state of 'insurrection' and 'war' in the valley; of settlers 'abandoned' by the then socialist authorities of Nouméa; of the 'mere certainty' of an impending Kanak 'attack'; of almost daily burning and pillaging by Kanaks; of settlers held hostage by a state of siege, terror and menace.
>
> Far from menacing the settlers, however, the Hienghène Kanaks appear to have helped them — in one case offering shelter to a settler woman whose house it was revealed . . . had been burned by the settlers themselves in provocation on the eve of the ambush.[10]

The Pierre Declercq Committee, a human rights group set up in 1981 to investigate the still unsolved assassination of the French-born leader, denounced the *non-lieu* order as an open invitation for white settlers to kill Kanaks with impunity. New Caledonia's local chapter of the International League of Human Rights said the 'scandalous' move deprived Kanaks of a right to justice. The Declercq committee also attacked the ruling on these points: the examining magistrate only gave credence to European witnesses (Kanak witnesses were ignored); there was no reconstruction at the scene of the massacre (lawyers representing the victims later organised their own reconstruction); the accused had not faced the survivors in a courtroom; no action was taken against other witnesses implicated by witnesses; and the order was not based on judicial grounds, but as a political measure against the FLNKS.[11] The committee also cited other cases where there had been a denial of justice involving Kanaks or the independence movement. Two men charged over Declercq's assassination were freed without ever facing trial and no further arrests were made. Kanak Security Minister Éloi Machoro and his lieutenant, Marcel Nonaro, were shot dead by police sharpshooters and nobody was charged over the killings.

A week after the Hienghène killers were freed, the league and the Declercq committee called a press conference in Nouméa and made public the testimony of the witnesses for the first time. Their evidence was handed to world human rights groups like Amnesty International and the League of Human Rights. In Paris, four leading French lawyers went on television to denounce a miscarriage of justice, political 'manipulation' and appealed to President Mitterrand to intervene. Countering this, a new right-wing settler group calling itself the Patriotic Action Committee (CAP) sent an open letter to Mitterrand and Prime Minister Jacques Chirac urging them to uphold magistrate Semur's ruling.

Ironically, the scandal over the release of the killers broke while Jean-Marie Tjibaou was at the United Nations lobbying to help the South Pacific Forum's case for New Caledonian independence. At the time of the killings, Tjibaou, grieving over the loss of two brothers, declared:

> Since the beginning of colonial times it has always been Kanaks who die. During our present campaign 10 have died on our side with two seriously wounded in hospital — and one white has died. My father's mother was killed by soldiers' bullets and colonialism is still trying to destroy the Kanak people.
>
> This speech [Hienghène] with rifles is the same as existed in the United States, in Australia. And it's in Tasmania — where there are no more blacks — that it worked best.[12]

Tjibaou's moderate stance came under severe pressure as a result of the *non-lieu*. Then the fragile truce collapsed at the eastern mining town of Thio. A pro-independence stronghold and symbol of resistance under the grip of Machoro before his death, the township was chosen by the anti-independence National Front and RPCR for a provocative rally in November 1986 which ended in a shoot-out. *(Caldoche* extremists set fire to a pro-independence bakery on 16 November 1986; shooting broke out with one 14-year-old-white boy dying and 12 people being wounded.) Four days later, cars belonging to barrister Tehio and his brother-in-law, Claude Le Ray, an FLNKS official, were firebombed in an attempt to frighten them into abandoning the case.

The attack coincided with the surprise appeal tribunal ruling on 20 November that the seven Hienghène killers had to stand trial. A three-judge tribunal ruled the slaughter was premeditated and the freed settlers must be put in the dock.[13] But the accused remained at liberty until the trial, almost a year later. 'It's a matter of too little, too late,' complained Jean-Pierre Deteix, a spokesman for the League of Human Rights. 'All those implicated should stand trial.'

★   ★   ★

When the trial began on 19 October 1987 it was not in Nouméa's *Palais de la Justice* because the main wing of the lawcourts had been destroyed in a bomb attack two years earlier by settlers in an attempt to get the accused freed. Instead, the Assize Court heard the case amid tight security in a hilltop cultural centre overlooking the port and the French High Commission.

Three leading French civil rights lawyers and Tehio represented the survivors and the families of the victims. They included Francois Roux, who defended Tahitian independence leaders Pouvanaa a Oopa and Charlie Ching, and French League of Human Rights vice-president Michel Tubiana. 'Public feeling among settlers in this mainly European city is so strong for the accused,' said Deteix, 'it is hard to see how an unbiased jury can be chosen.'[14]

Calling for sentences of nine and seven years for the accused, public prosecutor Henri Lucazeau described the killings as ritual executions — 'a psychosis and collective intoxication for [murder]'. The ambush, he said, was planned and premeditated: 'All the dead were found face down on the ground or in the river and they were riddled with bullets and lead shot.'

In court, the accused denied having told the examining magistrate that they had deployed themselves in 'combat formation'. Or that they had con-fessed to hunting down their victims with dogs and searchlights. They claimed, instead, to have stood and shot without moving. One said, 'We shot at shadows. I couldn't tell the difference between the cows and the people.'[15]

Not unsurprisingly, ten days later the jury of nine (all white except one part-Indonesian woman) acquitted the killers. After considering the evidence for two hours, including time out for dinner, the jurors returned a verdict of 'legitimate self-defence'. The not guilty ruling was greeted by applause, cries of *'Vive la France!'* and singing of *La Marseillaise* from settlers who packed the courtroom. In a cruel contrast, scores of the several hundred Kanaks gathered outside the building wept.

'Kanaks can now be gunned down like dogs,' said Tjibaou. 'There will be no justice in New Caledonia before independence.' The FLNKS branded the acquittal the most 'infamous, abject and unbearable affront possible against Kanaks', which threatened to lead to a 'situation of extreme violence'. It added the verdict had 'inflicted the most extreme humiliation upon the Kanak people' and 'opens the door to barbarism'.

About 1000 Kanaks marched peacefully through Nouméa and staged a peaceful sit-in protest outside the gates of the High Commission. Lawyers for the victims' families prepared appeals to the World Court and the European Court of Justice.

★　　　★　　　★

But who were the real winners and who the losers? The seven killers may have won the legal battle, but their 'war' was irredeemably lost. They and their families could no longer go home, their subsistence farming lifestyle ruined. They were condemned to live in a drab high-rise apartment block outside Nouméa where they existed on a meagre pension and handouts from the National Front.

Ten graves in Tiendanite's cemetery today remind the villagers of the night a massacre cut down most of their menfolk — and their denial of justice. At Wan'yaat, on Mitride's former farm, the ambushed trucks are mounted in concrete as a memorial to their sacrifice. Among the billowing strips of traditional cloth tied to the rusting vehicles is a simple, marble slab inscribed with the epitaph:

> *Give your blood. Give your life. For the beloved land.*
> *Your brothers. Your widows. Your young children weep.*
> *In a supreme gesture, you were offered in a holocaust*
> *And cried liberty.*
> *You have gone. Keep in your memory*
> *That the conquest of Kanaky*
> *Is written in letters of blood forever.*

6

Martyrdom of Machoro

Five weeks after the Hienghène massacre, in January 1985, Kanaky Security Minister Éloi Machoro was assassinated by French police marksmen. His death deprived the Kanaks of arguably their most charismatic and influential leader. Some regarded him as the 'Che Guevara of the South Pacific'; others looked upon him as a 'Robespierre'. The shooting of the 'liberator' of the mining township of Thio broke the back of the post-election insurrection but the tension continued.

'There are many *fachos* [fascists] who dream of getting me,' remarked Éloi Machoro, just a week before he died. 'But if they succeed, there will be ten, a hundred Machoros . . . until the dawn comes when Kanaky is independent.'

Machoro, an engaging former schoolteacher and a territorial councillor who became Security Minister in the provisional government of Kanaky proclaimed on 1 December 1984, had no illusions: from the day of the election boycott he knew he was a marked man. Five minutes before midnight on the eve of the boycott, he declared in what colleagues regard as his last 'testament':

> I will not be imprisoned for nothing and tomorrow I will take part in a boycott action which will be staged at the Canala *mairie* [town hall]. This will be to exploit the events of our struggle, so that our fellow Kanaks will better understand the gravity of our predicament . . . I have confidence in you all. The struggle must never cease through lack of leaders or combatants.[1]

Next day, Sunday 18 November 1984, Machoro led his militants from the village of Nakéty to Canala, chopping open a ballot box and burning the voting papers in a defiant symbolic gesture. A photograph of him splitting the urn in half with his axe earned him instant international notoriety and an epithet in the conservative French press as the 'axe man of Canala'.

Part of this chapter is drawn from sources, cited by Helen Fraser, 'New light on how Machoro died', *Pacific Islands Monthly*, March 1986, pp. 18-19.

David Robie

Éloi Machoro with the axe he used to smash open the ballot box in Canala in 1984.

He and his *machochos** then drove through the rugged Col de Coeur-Brisé (Heartbreak Pass) and 'liberated' the east coast township of Thio, 130 kilometres north-east of Nouméa. Barricades were set up on all roads leading into the mining town and Machoro said they would not be lifted until the election result was annulled, the Lemoine statute rejected and the Kanaky provisional government recognised as the sole legitimate authority in New Caledonia. The three-week siege of Thio was launched. And so began the legend of Machoro.

At one point the flag of Kanaky was flown at the gendarmerie after it had been captured by the FLNKS, the first of several to be seized throughout the territory and then later freed. The FLNKS split the town into sectors, with seven barricades controlling them. Militants commandeered vehicles, boats and fuel and closed the nickel mines. Mayor Roger Gaillot, leader of the National Front, was forced to abandon the town. The name Thio became a household word in France, representing shame for the conservatives while for supporters of Kanak independence it was a source of pride.

When Machoro and a lieutenant, Marcel Nonaro, were eventually shot by French police snipers during a siege of a farmhouse at Dogny, near the western village of La Foa, at dawn on Saturday 12 January 1985, just over a month after the massacre of Hienghène, a furore erupted in the colony. With Kanak militants and settler loyalists on the brink of civil war, High Commissioner Edgard Pisani declared a state of emergency in New Caledonia, with a dusk-to-dawn curfew. It was the first such declaration in any French territory since 1961 when De Gaulle assumed emergency powers in Algeria.

Like his mentor and close friend Pierre Declercq,† Machoro became a martyr for the Kanak people; in the Kanak-run regional government offices photographs of the liberation leader replaced the traditional portraits of the French President, Francois Mitterrand. Yet even two years after his killing, branded by Kanak leaders as a summary execution in cold blood, the circumstances remained unclear.

Amnesty International, which made its first foray into the South Pacific in 1985, investigated the case along with a long list of other alleged injustices in New Caledonia. In its 1986 yearbook — the first one to mention a South Pacific territory — the human rights group said it was concerned about allegations that the two men were the victims of extrajudicial execution

---

* Young militant followers of Machoro. Term borrowed from the Nicaraguan word *muchachos*, youthful guerrillas.

† After Declercq was assassinated in 1981, Machoro refused to attend his funeral; he organised protest barricades. 'He said that it achieved nothing to cry over Declercq's body,' recalls a colleague. 'But the best way to show one's respect for him was to carry on the struggle that he had given his life for.'

by French security forces. Amnesty asked the French Justice Minister on 8 February about the reports and two weeks later 'received assurances from the ministry that the killings would be investigated. Amnesty [is] not aware of the results of any official investigation . . . and a civil suit, brought against persons unknown, [has] reached no conclusion.'[2] Amnesty's 1987 report again criticised the slow investigation into Machoro's killing and the 'no apparent progress' into the death of Declercq.

Other members of Machoro's family have since been jailed and defence lawyers claim they have become 'judicial hostages' of French colonialism.

Every revolution, it seems, produces a notoriety for the international media, and as far as the conservative French press was concerned, Éloi Machoro was their target for hatred. The newspapers branded him 'iron man', 'axe man', 'extremist' and 'the Robespierre of the South Pacific'. It was Machoro whose photograph wielding an axe made front pages around the world; it was Machoro who, with Foreign Minister Yann-Célène Uregei, made a highly publicised visit to Libya to seek support for the independence cause. And it was Machoro who succeeded Declercq as secretary-general of the moderate pro-independence Caledonian Union. In a speech at Canala at the time, Machoro declared:

> The reconquest of Kanaky will begin here. When we have cleaned up this area we will move on to Thio, La Foa and Bouloupari. Each tribe must draw up a list of those [*Caldoche* and *colon*] they want to leave. This is going to be a trial of strength. Everyone should know that we are prepared to use guns if necessary.[3]

Machoro was as good as his word, and surprisingly successful. But his aim was remarkably straightforward: he was a Kanak who wished to be a citizen of Kanaky. He had contempt for being French. His sense of alienation from the land was profound, and it was towards reoccupation of the land that had been expropriated by French *colons* that he dedicated his efforts.

Born on 19 January 1946 at the *tribu* of Nakéty in the traditional region of Xaracûû, Machoro was the second youngest of a poor family of four boys and four girls. He first went to school at the Saint-Tarcisius seminary in Canala, later attended the Saint-Léon seminary at Paita and completed his education at Nouméa's La Pérouse college. He worked for the Treasury, as a mason in a construction company, and a guardian for a minor on a stud farm at Pouembout before becoming a teacher at Canala in 1975. With Francois Burck, he inspired groups of young Kanaks.

His political career began in 1977 when he was elected Caledonian Union's associate secretary-general to assist Declercq. He was also elected a territorial councillor later that year and re-elected in July 1979 on the Independence Front ticket.

★　　　★　　　★

When I first met Machoro, among the headstones at La Conception village cemetery on the outskirts of Nouméa during the first anniversary of Declercq's death, I was impressed by his singlemindedness and his optimism. Both characterised him in future meetings —even at Canala *maire*. But by the last time I saw him at Thio, several days before he died, the stress of the rebellion was taking its toll. He seemed tense and edgy.

A *'colons assassins'* (settler killers) slogan spray-painted on the wall of Nouméa's popular St Hubert brasserie had been changed a few days earlier to *Éloi assassin'*. Machoro had become fatalistic about assassination. Almost any day could be his last. But he did not expect to die at the hands of French police. Reactionary settlers or hit men were his real worry. 'White extremists want me dead. They will do anything to get rid of me,' he said.

As we sat down to a *bougna*-and-taro lunch, cooked with beef 'requisitioned' in a raid on cattle belonging to a nearby farmer regarded as a racist, Machoro revealed a glimpse of his harsher side. One of his militants, drunk, was pestering a Canadian woman academic eating with the group. Ignored, he became more persistent. Machoro suddenly stood up, knocked out the man with one punch and dragged him away from the camp. He gave him a thrashing with a piece of wire.

Leaving the militant under a mango tree to cool off, Machoro strode back to our table and said, 'We have to keep discipline!'

Machoro bitterly attacked Australia, New Zealand and other South Pacific nations such as Fiji over their New Caledonian policies. 'Hypocrisy from Canberra and Wellington has helped plunge our country into chaos,' he said. 'We're a peaceful people, but we have been frustrated in our right to independence for too long. Promises . . . promises . . . promises, and in the end nothing! For five years we pleaded with the South Pacific Forum for our case to be taken up in the United Nations. For five years we got nowhere.

'Instead, when we took action ourselves, all we got was a hypocritical roasting over the Libyan and Moscow "links", which are a load of rubbish. There was no serious attempt to understand our quest for sovereignty. If Canberra and Wellington had followed Vanuatu's lead, the Libyan issue would not have arisen. But when you're desperate you have to seek help where you can.'[4]

In one of the last interviews before he died, Machoro told the left-wing Paris newspaper *Rouge:*

> Australia, as well as New Zealand, are cornerstones of the Forum. They are also two satellites of the United States. There you have the problem — imperialism and control of the Pacific region. That is why over the years we have seen a shift in the position of Australia and other countries in the Forum. At the beginning, they were favourable to independence because they had

designs. They wanted, with the help of the Kanak people, to get France out of here and gain control of the Pacific.

However, as our demands became more well defined, these countries became afraid of removing a power such as France from the Pacific. We think that is because of this fear that today they are supporting the policy of France.

Moreover, we are a native people, and so that [a victory for the Kanak people] would pose the threat of provoking reactions from their own native people. Thus, the last position taken by the Forum was to support the Lemoine statute that we have rejected.

We knocked for a long time on France's door asking for help in decolonising our country. The answer was a document [Lemoine plan] designed for the destruction of the Kanak people. We asked the Forum to support our struggle. They supported the policy of the French government. So, we have been obliged to go looking for help elsewhere and we will seek it wherever it may be found.[5]

Documents and witnesses have surfaced which reveal some of the circumstances of Machoro's death. At the time, the *indépendantistes* claimed it was an 'assassination', while General Deiber, commander of the paramilitary gendarmerie in New Caledonia, confirmed the gendarmes had been ordered to *'neutralise'* Machoro — the identical go-ahead for the sabotage of the *Rainbow Warrior* by French secret agents in New Zealand later that year.

According to the official version, marksmen of the élite GIGN (National Gendarmerie intervention group) fired from a range of 130 metres at Machoro's shoulders, instead of his legs which were obscured by an embankment, and thus 'accidentally' killed him. He died 20 minutes after being hit in the chest, Nonaro was killed outright. The two men were accused of leaving the farmhouse near La Foa — where they were holed up with 37 other Kanak militants — and shooting at the 300 gendarmes surrounding the building. The FLNKS stated neither man fired any shots and added they left the farmhouse carrying a white flag to negotiate with the gendarmes. No evidence was found of cartridges having been fired by the Kanaks.

At the time of Machoro's death, settlers in Nouméa were rioting in protest at the apparent inaction by French authorities following the shooting of a 17-year-old farmer's son. The youth, Yves Tual, was killed the day before on his father's 400-hectare ranch, near where Machoro died. Tual was a nephew of Roger Gaillot, then leader of the extreme right-wing National Front and mayor of Thio. His uncle was the front's only candidate to be elected in the boycotted election.*

The Tual family was in the frontline of the anti-independence movement.

---

* As a result of the boycott, only ten Kanaks and less than a quarter of Thio's 1700 registered voters took part in the election. Not only did Gaillot lose control of his town to Machoro's militants, but he also lost possession of his fishing business when Machoro 'requisitioned' all his boats.

Every night they would take part in vigilante patrols in the La Foa area. Before Yves Tual's death, the French authorities had begun moving cattle (abandoned by panicking *Caldoches* in their haste to flee Thio) to the family ranch for safekeeping. These animals were helping to feed the FLNKS militants, who were slaughtering the 'requisitioned' animals one by one as they were needed.

Tual's death shocked the *Caldoche* community. Demands for vengeance triggered the Nouméa riots. Machoro was rumoured to be responsible for the youth's death. (The rumour was unfounded. A 19-year-old Kanak named Maurice Moindou was later arrested and charged with Tual's killing.)

After the shooting, Machoro and several of his militants left the protection of their Thio stronghold on 11 January and crossed the central mountains, arriving early that afternoon near La Foa. An FLNKS communique said later that Machoro's band had gone to La Foa to attend a political meeting to discuss Pisani's proposals for independence in association with France. 'It seems clear, however, from documents found after his death that Machoro intended to occupy La Foa in the same manner as Thio,' said Montréal University researcher Donna Winslow. 'Whether the takeover was to begin that weekend or not is not known. But by 2 p.m. on 11 January, about 40 people had gathered at a meeting on the Kanak farm of Auguste Bouarato'.[6]

The gathering was reported to French authorities by Bouarato's alarmed *Caldoche* neighbours. At 4 p.m. a helicopter flew over the farm and the pilot reported the presence of 'at least 30 armed men'. It was not 'officially' known at the time whether Machoro was there. Roger Gaillot, however, was certain he was.

'We have given the authorities an ultimatum,' he told journalists. 'Either they go after him — or we will!'

In an investigative report for *Pacific Islands Monthly*, Australian journalist Helen Fraser reconstructed the events. She reported that Machoro and his militants did not guess what was about to happen, in spite of élite GIGN marksmen being flown to the farmhouse by helicopter late in the evening. The unit had been protecting the High Commission while the rioting raged in Nouméa. Machoro sent a messenger to a nearby FLNKS member's house to telephone Pisani, urgently seeking a truce. Explained Fraser:

> Machoro appears to have had good reason to believe that a truce was possible, since on two previous occasions, at the request of the High Commissioner, he had agreed to free captured gendarmes, leaving all guns at the scene. The message was phoned from La Foa to the home of an FLNKS official in Nouméa. He, in turn, gave it to a French public servant to transmit to Pisani since, at the time, it would have been impossible for a Kanak messenger to have got through the rioting in Nouméa and reach the High Commissioner's offices. The French public servant has made a statement saying he gave Pisani the message which said: 'Give us a truce or the FLNKS will move into the third phase [armed insurrection].'[7]

Although a spokesman for Pisani said at the time that no such message was received, the high commissioner revealed to Fraser almost a year later that he received only the second half of the message. 'Certainly,' noted Fraser, 'Pisani had a lot to cope with: heavy rioting, buildings burning opposite his residence, exhausted and wounded riot police, and no let-up in sight at the moment he received the message. A colleague present in the operations room set up in the High Commission during the emergency described Pisani as "a man stunned by the events, who eventually went to bed".'[8] Back at La Foa, Machoro and his militants were awaiting word from Pisani.

5.30 a.m. January 12: Warnings were given by the gendarmes and then teargas and stun grenades were fired at the FLNKS group.

6.30 a.m. Shots were fired by GIGN. Machoro was shot in the sternum; Nonaro in the chest, dying instantly. Machoro had been shot as he stood near a fence on the farm. He staggered across the grass.

'Barre-toi! . . . Save yourselves,' he warned as he collapsed in front of the farmhouse. As he lay dying, he gasped, 'Only the struggle counts — death is nothing.'[9] Shocked by the betrayal of an apparent truce, most of the other militants surrendered to the gendarmes.

(Ironically, Dogny, where Machoro died, was the launching point for Atai's 1878 rebellion.)

In Nouméa the rioters stopped pelting police with stones, and cheered and hooted when they heard news of Machoro's death. Officials reported 26 injured, including several policemen in the rioting — Nouméa's worst. Police used armoured cars and fired teargas and stun grenades. One armoured car, its turret in flames, hurtled out of control into the crowd, seriously injuring a protester. Demonstrators chanted, 'Pisani assassin'. Months later, when much of Nouméa's characteristic wall-to-wall political graffiti had been cleaned up, at least one slogan remained, a crude example of settler racism: *Machoro ordure tu es mort* (Machoro garbage, you're dead).

Kanak leaders reacted bitterly to the assassination. 'The only people fired upon were two leaders,' said FLNKS spokesman Louis Uregei. 'It was a premeditated plan to assassinate our leaders.'[10] A statement by the Kanaky provisional government said:

> As far as Kanaks are concerned the Pisani proposal is jeopardised; it has the smell of blood on its hands . . . It is with regret that France, whether it is governed by the left or by the right, whether it is in Indochina, in Algeria or in New Caledonia, has only been able to discuss decolonisation with the smell of gunpowder and/or corpses.[11]

Mitterrand launched one of the biggest gambles of his political career; a week after Machoro's death he flew to New Caledonia in a desperate bid to salvage Pisani's initiatives. It was a dramatic ten-hour visit on 19 January

1985. In spite of a predictable anti-independence rally of 20,000 people waving the French flag and with banners appealing to Mitterrand 'don't sell the South Pacific to the Russians', the President succeeded in breaking the political deadlock. Tjibaou agreed to meet Mitterrand. They met alone, Tjibaou taking along with him a photograph of Machoro. The FLNKS agreed to resume negotiations and Mitterrand returned to Paris saying, 'The threads that were almost severed have now been restored and the dialogue will continue.'[12]

Thousands of Kanaks mourned their lost gladiator and Machoro became a celebrity for indigenous rights groups across the South Pacific and beyond. As far as they were concerned, Machoro would not die in vain. Among the many tributes, Black Revolution, ni-Vanuatu reggae band, recorded a song dedicated to his life.

> *Long ol life blong yo*
> *From freedom blong yu*
> *From future blong nation yu faet strong*
> *Kasem det blong yu*
> *Akensem white man we i stilim graon think evriting blong hem*
> *Goodbye Machoro, bae yu stap long heart blong mifala*
> *Thank you long big work blong yu bae mifala i complitim*[13]

The judicial aftermath

According to first reports of the killings by French authorities, several FLNKS militants were wounded. A second version claimed Machoro died 'shooting his way out of the house'. The final and 'official' version said the FLNKS had fired shots after the 6.10 a.m. warning and that the two men were killed in an attempt to 'neutralise' them. Later, French officials dropped their insistence that shots were fired by the FLNKS but claimed Machoro had his gun in a firing position when shot. (This conflicts with reports that he actually had his rifle slung from a shoulder.) The other militants who were arrested after surrendering told their lawyers they heard shots as they were being driven away. They alleged the gendarmes fired their guns to 'prove' a shoot-out had actually happened.

On 2 December 1986 a former gendarme present at the siege accused the French Government of having planned Machoro's killing. Facing a hold-up charge at the Aisne lawcourts in north-east France, Lahouari Bouhout, 32, gave evidence saying: 'The gendarmerie were supposed to kill *three* men — but they got only two.' Asked by the prosecutor to repeat his words, Bouhout declared: 'The gendarmerie were supposed to kill three men. We were ordered to keep it secret and to say the killings were an accident.' The courtroom was in an uproar and Judge Valentin called an adjournment, later saying the Machoro affair could not be spoken about again during the case before the court.[14]

Bouhout had earlier been asked to explain the circumstances of his leaving the gendarmerie. He said he had been forced to resign because he had taken graphic photographs of Machoro's corpse and then sold them to *Paris-Match* magazine. A gendarme captain gave collaboratory evidence. On his return to Aisne, Bouhout was unable to find work. He was charged with carrying out a hold-up with an accomplice, Karim Benhamed, at Flavy-le-Martel on 29 May 1985.

Sceptical Kanak lawyers and officials seeking justice in the Machoro affair told me they considered the statement in court 'state-fed disinformation', reminiscent of the deluge of misinformation leaked to French newspapers about the *Rainbow Warrior* sabotage. They regard the witness as unreliable, although they are still investigating.

'There are parallels with our own reconstruction of the killings,' said Jean-Pierre Deteix, a spokesman for the local human rights group, Pierre Declercq Committee. 'But we think the courtroom drama was a ruse planned to discredit our own case.'

According to Kanak investigators, three men *were* supposed to be killed in an attempt to crush the Kanaky rebellion. The targets were Machoro, Nonaro and Francois Burck. Burck, who later became *chef de cabinet* of the Central Region government, was not actually at the farmhouse at the time of the siege; his substitute target, Andre Assao, was shielded from the sniper's sights and escaped, only to be jailed for three months.

Commissioner Pisani, a veteran troubleshooter for France in the Third World, was fascinated by Machoro's image. Nearly three months after the shootings he visited Thio. He was again accused of responsibility for the killing by Kanak militants and members of the Machoro family.

'I salute Éloi Machoro — he died in combat and for that he deserves respect,' Pisani replied. 'We didn't intend to kill him. I bow before his mortal remains.'[15]

Lawyers for Machoro's family allege that transcripts of military radio communications on the night of the shootings show no trace of a request fron the GIGN for permission to shoot, nor any trace of an order being given to shoot to 'neutralise' by senior officers, including Pisani. One early Kanak statement claimed the killings were decided on by the GIGN and other gendarmes under pressure from anti-independence settlers.

However, later accounts indicate a conspiracy within the French Government and intelligence services, hatched at the same time as the operation was being prepared against the *Rainbow Warrior*. It was open season against the enemies of France in the South Pacific and Nouméa had been the base for many former *barbouzes* with powerful connections since the end of the Algerian war.

Several factors cited by journalist Helen Fraser, a long-time resident of New Caledonia, pointed to planned murder, rather than Machoro being shot accidentally: no trace was found of an official order to shoot; French ballistics expert Professor Ceccaldi indicated the weapons used by the marksmen were an FR F1 sniping rifle, 'inappropriate for a neutralisation shot' with an 'inadequate' telescopic sight of 3.85 magnification; the ammunition used (7.5 mm) was designed to kill not neutralise; the shots were not fired from a fixed tripod — as usual — but by marksmen resting their rifles on the shoulders of colleagues.[16]

★　　　★　　　★

After the right-wing coalition government of Jacques Chirac gained power in March 1986, French authorities began to arrest and harass members of the Machoro family. I was at Machoro's home village of Nakéty in January 1987 for a memorial service when his elder brother Albert, aged 57, was arrested for failing to stop at a military roadblock and for 'abusing' gendarmes. Prevented from attending the graveside rites, he was flown by helicopter to Nouméa and sentenced to three months' (two months suspended) imprisonment. In court, the judge asked him: Why did you behave like this?

> *Albert Machoro:* Because it was the anniversary of the death of my brother, Éloi.
> *Judge:* Do you intend to renew the 'rodeo' every year on your brother's anniversary?
> *Defence lawyer Gustave Tehio, interrupting:* Why make an example of this affair? The gendarmes are being repressive all the time.[17]

Machoro's sister, Marie-Francoise, was also arrested, and detained without charge. (She was eventually freed on 17 August 1987.) Tehio, a Tahitian who acts as one of the key lawyers defending Kanaks in political cases, has been the target of death threats by anti-independence extremists. His car was firebombed in November 1986.

More than 120 prisoners at Camp Est (although only 37 were being recognised by international human rights groups as political detainees) went on a hunger strike on 12 January 1987 to mark the deaths of Machoro and Nonaro. In a letter smuggled out of jail, the prisoners said:

> We salute the courage of our two leaders, and show that in spite of being imprisoned, we still struggle for Kanaky. We struggle for a Kanaky purged of the killers of Machoro and Nonaro, for a Kanaky where the judges are no longer members of the extreme right, and for a Kanaky where we are in charge of our own country.[18]

One signature stood out. *Marie-Francoise Machoro.* A protest for her martyred brother.

7

Dien Bien Thio

In spite of the mounting tension, the murder of his brothers and the siege of the 'liberated' town of Thio, Kanak leader Jean-Marie Tjibaou made limited progress towards independence with the socialist government of France during 1985. In fresh territorial elections the Kanaks won control of three out of four regional governments — a result dubbed the 'ballot box monster' by opponents of independence. Mitterrand was seen as the chief villain by Caldoche settlers. But the FLNKS was given little opportunity to take advantage of its 'green revolution'.

The killing of Éloi Machoro and Marcel Nonaro brought into sharper focus differences between the FLNKS leadership and grassroots membership, especially Kanak youth cynical about continued negotiations. President Jean-Marie Tjibaou articulated the dilemma of espousing moderation: 'All this is very unrewarding for our militants, because the leaders talk, talk, talk . . . while the militants still remain in prison. The dead have been buried but no action has been decided.'[1] Clashes pitting young Kanaks against the French settlers and authorities were becoming more frequent. Machoro's death was a major setback for the FLNKS, because he had been able to influence the young radicals and direct their anger and energy into effective action. Machoro was a vital balancing and complementary force to the negotiator Tjibaou.

While the bitterness of the French conservative press was not reserved for Machoro and his *machochos* alone, they took the brunt of it. 'The situation in New Caledonia is explosive,' wrote Thierry Desjardins of the right-wing Paris daily *Le Figaro* in a typical attack over the siege of Thio. 'The French Government is knowingly leaving 40,000 whites and 100,000 other French to the mercy of a handful of savages who are prepared to massacre . . . It's just as if the Kanaks are already warming the cooking pot.' Following a 'reportage' at a Kanak barricade, the journalist said: 'It was like a Stone Age horror film. Everybody was armed to the teeth . . . These nasty looking "rebels", with bloodshot eyes, perhaps a little drunk, approached me. I beat a hasty retreat!'[2]

In the same vein, the right-wing weekly *Minute* speculated that with independence, 'to the distress of the French flag, tribal wars would break out again and the only cement holding the peace between the 300 tribes of the islands is the French presence. Three hundred tribes for less than 50,000 Kanaks: a fine pickle, gentlemen.'[3] Such newspapers and magazines projected the colonial myth that Kanaks were too immature to be allowed to gain independence.

At the same time the *colons* were usually portrayed as the promoters of modern economic development for New Caledonia, always ready to offer a patronising hand to the 'backward' indigenous population to 'show' them the way to independence.

The conservative French press maligned the Kanak revolt and depicted the FLNKS and its leaders as 'criminals'. *Valeurs Actuelles*, for example, dismissed Machoro as an 'apparatchik [puppet] of international communism, identified as such by the Australian secret services, who counts on the high-bidding of left-wing revolutionaries like Jean-Louis Dion* friend of Alain Krivine, who assured contacts with Tripoli.'[4] Even in death, Machoro was abused by the news media. Two days after he was shot *Les Nouvelles Calédoniennes* tried to ridicule the 'myth', saying he was 'no Che [Guevara]. He wasn't a revolutionary ideologue. He gave more an impression of being motivated by hatred for the French and whites'.[5]

But Machoro was not the only one to be maligned. According to *Le Quotidien de Paris:* 'Tjibaou not only claims to be the head of a government that doesn't exist, he makes the claim through violence at the head of armed bands already culpable for murders, rapes and robberies . . . Six bullets would be enough for this half-priest.'[6] It was a virulent attack on the moderate Tjibaou, who had contained the anger of Kanak militants in the face of provocation as severe as the massacre of Hienghène and the assassination of Machoro.

Paramilitary buildup

During the next few weeks right-wing and pro-independence forces became increasingly polarised. Ultra-rightists stepped up their activities in spite of the state of emergency declared after Machoro's death and Mitterrand's dramatic one-day visit to the colony in a gamble to appease both sides.

---

* Dion returned to France in 1986 after living in New Caledonia for more than 12 years. A militant trade unionist, he played a leading role in the 1978 nickel workers' strike and later helped found the Kanak union USTKE. Krivine is a radical French left-wing ideologue in Paris.

David Robie

Kanak militants guarding the road to 'liberated' Thio in early 1985.

But Mitterrand's subsequent announcement to increase substantially the French military presence in New Caledonia revealed his preference for appeasing *Caldoche* fears. High Commissioner Edgard Pisani had already called in a further 1000 paramilitary police to boost French security forces to 6000 — one policeman for every 25 inhabitants in New Caledonia.

On 17 February the fragile truce was shattered and the death toll since the ballot boycott climbed to more than 20, two-thirds of the victims being Kanaks.

The fresh crisis began with a 'picnic' on the beach at Thio — at least that was what the right-wing Caledonian Front claimed. But it ended in teargas and battered bodies, mainly Kanak. The plan for the provocative mass *pique-nique* by white settlers was in defiance of a specific prohibition by Pisani.

For the *Caldoches*, Thio remained a bitter reminder of the FLNKS occupation under Machoro's leadership; for the Kanaks it symbolised resistance and successful political action. Some settlers had dubbed the township Dien Bien Thio — evoking the bitter memory of a protracted siege and then crushing defeat of French military forces at the fortified hamlet of Dien Bien Phu during the Vietnamese nationalist struggle three decades earlier.

Thio had been all but deserted by whites for most of the previous three months. Many of the 500 *Caldoches* and other non-Kanaks had slipped out of the town — many abandoning it for good. Most settlers there were associated in some way with the nickel mining industry.

Only a week before the Thio picnic, the FLNKS had decided at a congress in Canala to resume the militant tactics it had waged for two months since the boycott and disruption of the November elections. Kanak leaders decided cooperation with Paris had been too high a price to pay after what it saw as provocation by right-wing Europeans. They pledged a fresh campaign to 'destabilise colonial interests' — undermine the economic stranglehold of Nouméa, in other words — to back Tjibaou's hand in negotiations with Pisani. However, the plan would not include barricades, now regarded as potentially suicidal.

The FLNKS delegates had also decided to build up grassroots organisation while still negotiating with the French Government. Local groups were reorganised as *comités de lutte*. The committees were given the task of organising self-defence, developing a parallel economy and creating *écoles populaires kanakes* (EPK, people's schools).[7] A relatively large degree of autonomy for the committees was confirmed. This was partly a logistical need: because of the geography of Grande Terre and *Caldoche* control over both print and electronic news media, communication between the central committee in Nouméa and the inland tribes, and among regional committees, was difficult.

Pisani's original brief for working out a New Caledonian solution had included a two-month deadline expiring early in February. But his bold plan for independence in association with France met stiff resistance and tension had remained high with the state of emergency being extended to 30 June. Nevertheless, FLNKS leaders pledged independence would be declared on 1 January 1986 regardless. Right-wing groups claimed a Kanak republic would be 'racist'.

Fears of a new confrontation on the streets of Nouméa were rekindled when the RPCR leader, Jacques Lafleur, called for public defiance of an 11 p.m. curfew ordered by Pisani's administration. Lafleur called on supporters to refuse to 'respect the curfew'. About 1000 carloads of Europeans heeded his call one night and headed, horns honking and *Tricolores* fluttering in the balmy darkness, towards the vast Place des Cocotiers in the heart of Nouméa. The protesters cheered Lafleur and sang the *Marseillaise*. Some large groups faced police cordons guarding the French High Commission four blocks away before the protest broke up. A smaller demonstration was held the following night.

But the so-called picnic at Thio was the first serious trouble since Machoro had been shot. Police turned back most of 500 people travelling in 190 cars and two buses before they got to the town. They let through about 70 carloads — almost 200 people — who could prove they had earlier lived at Thio. FLNKS leaders had held a political meeting in the town the day before.

Kanaks from the St Phillipo *tribu* who were gathered on the side of the road protested to police and shouted abuse at settlers who were allowed past. The police charged the villagers, firing volleys of teargas and invading their tribal grounds. When the Kanaks retaliated by throwing rocks and wielding clubs, the police fired stun grenades. At least 11 people were injured, two seriously. Reported Helen Fraser:

> Women and children were very active in the Thio clash . . . [There has been a] growing prominence of women on the barricades from both Kanak and non-Kanak sides. In some recent demonstrations they have been much more militant than men. After the Thio incident Kanak women warned that they would 'now take the front line' in any future clashes between riot police and villagers.[8]

Kanak leaders accused the settlers of brutality and provocation under police protection. Security Minister Léopold Jorédie declared he had lost confidence in Pisani and urged Kanak militants to mobilise for self-defence. Pisani called for a special inquiry, upheld the provocation complaint and acted swiftly. He issued expulsion orders for Claude Sarran, leader of the right-wing Caledonian Front, three other party officials and a supporter.[9]

'I'm not going and I'll fight for our right to stay,' said Sarran, a 34-year-old Nouméa salesman. And the five defiantly went into hiding. Later, the Thio district police chief was recalled to France.

Thio's picnic had followed several weeks of efforts to re-establish normal life in the town: nickel workers had begun a gradual return to work, shops had opened their doors and people were in the streets again. But after the rioting tension rose again, with daily incidents of rocks being thrown at cars and the burning of several houses.

The Thio clash was also just one of many examples of close co-operation between the security forces and right-wing groups. 'Members of the police forces repeatedly participated in anti-independence demonstrations and have been very hesitant to arrest *Caldoches*, while being quick to jail Kanaks involved in clashes between pro and anti-independence activists,' wrote Austrian researcher Ingrid Kircher. 'As in Algeria, anti-independence forces engaged in a *terre brûlée* [scorched earth] policy, damaging equipment and resources used by Kanaks.'[10]

A member of the extreme right-wing National Front, for example, admitted sabotaging seven heavy trucks and other mining equipment at Camp des Sapins mine near Thio. He claimed to have acted on the orders of party leader Roger Gaillot,* at the time mayor of Thio and a newly elected territorial councillor.

A private militia of Wallis Islanders, noted for their physical strength and hostility to Kanak aspirations, was established to help the RPCR 'fight to the end'. Pretending to be agricultural workers, militants were sent by the party to defend *broussard* farms in the bush. They were reportedly the instigators of several clashes, the most violent of which were riots on 8 May. On that day a group of more than 20 Wallis Islanders, led by extremist Henri Morini,† and several hundred white settlers attacked a small group of FLNKS members who were protesting against the arrival of the French nuclear submarine *Rubis*‡ in Nouméa. The attackers chased the fleeing Kanaks to the Montravel where fighting raged for the rest of the day. One Kanak was killed and more than 100 other people were injured.

The Wallis Islanders were paid US$300 each from the 'territorial unemployment funds' for their role as *agents provocateurs*.[11] Kircher's report noted:

> A former top French intelligence officer, Colonel Charrier, has been working with Morini, chief of 'security' of the RPCR, to train the [party's] militia. Charrier established a sophisticated communication system, enabling the anti-independence forces to monitor the movement of the FLNKS in the bush.

---

* The only *Caldoche* mayor of an east coast town or village, Roger Gaillot had his own private militia. On one occasion, police manning a roadblock on the route to Thio reportedly discovered seven rifles in Gaillot's car but he was not prosecuted.

†Henri Morini, a *pied noir*, was founder of the secret paramilitary group Peace and Order Movement (MOP), modelled on the Algerian OAS.

‡The Nouméa-based *Rubis* was reportedly used after the *Rainbow Warrior* raid to pick up three French secret agents off the yacht *Ouvea*.

The *Caldoches* are well stocked in weapons. At the time of the election boycott, there were some 40,000 rifles registered for a population of 145,000 with a ratio of four guns per *Caldoche* to one rifle for every four Kanaks.[12]

Early in March 1985, when pupils were due to return to school, the FLNKS organised a boycott of many schools. Some villages set up their own EPK people's schools for Kanak children. Front leaders branded the French education system as 'colonialist' and 'ill-adapted to Kanak language and culture'. But Pisani, while readily admitting the education system needed to adapt to teaching Kanak culture and French as a second language, warned that people's schools were not the answer. He said they would become marginal with few means to support them.

Nineteen FLNKS militants detained at Camp Est prison launched a hunger strike in a bid to gain political prisoner status and improvement in jail conditions. Interior Minister Yéiwene Yéiwene appealed to Amnesty International to send an observer to New Caledonia to investigate human rights abuses. To show solidarity with the hunger strikers, the FLNKS called for a mobilisation day on 8 March. More than 3000 Kanaks marched on the prison where a sit-in was staged while at least 1000 people demonstrated in other towns.

At the north-eastern township of Pouébo, a gendarme died after being slashed in the back by a machete. Sergeant-Major Roland Lecompte was killed while gendarmes were climbing into a truck after they had cleared a barricade and dispersed Kanak militants with stun grenades and teargas.

The Fabius Plan

Edgard Pisani, increasingly unpopular with the *Caldoches* who saw him as 'pro-Kanak', was recalled to Paris in mid-May 1985 and appointed minister in charge of New Caledonia. He was succeeded as High Commissioner by Fernand Wibaux, then French ambassador to the Lebanon. Among Wibaux's first gestures on arriving was to take a stroll through the streets of Nouméa and to lift the curfew. He made it plain that his priority would be to restore the day-to-day life of the nervous city to normality.

Shortly before Pisani left Nouméa, Prime Minister Laurent Fabius tabled yet another proposal for the colony. The so-called Fabius Plan incorporated parts of the Lemoine, Pisani and Ukeiwé proposals — but few of the FLNKS demands. Its key points were: a referendum on self-determination by 31 December 1987; the creation of four regions governed by regional councils, to be elected in autumn 1985; economic, social and cultural reforms to alleviate the inequalities between Nouméa and the rest of the territory; and reinforcement of the French military presence in New Caledonia.

The FLNKS condemned the proposal. As political bureau member and UPM president Edmond Nekirai put it, the plan contained 'too much of France and not enough of Kanaky'. While the geographical makeup of the region would probably enhance FLNKS representation, the referendum would not be held until after the French legislative elections in March 1986 — and a conservative government would be less sympathetic.

In early June the RPCR-dominated Territorial Assembly also rejected the plan, with only one of 31 councillors voting in favour. The party claimed the proposal would gerrymander a majority for the FLNKS. The pro-independence LKS, which held six seats, boycotted the chamber.

Later, the FLNKS changed its mind and decided to give the plan a try. President Tjibaou said the front did not like the 'neo-colonial' logic of the regional government scheme but it would go along with the carve-up because it did not want to be accused of being responsible for the breakdown of the process of independence.[13]

Regional governments were to be elected by universal suffrage on a basis of proportional representation. Two Kanak-dominated regions, Northern and Loyalty Islands, would have nine and seven councillors respectively. The Central region, containing the important towns of Bourail and Thio, and with a fairly balanced Kanak and *Caldoche* population, would have nine councillors. The Southern region, based on Nouméa and overwhelmingly comprising French, Asian and Polynesian settlers, would have 18 councillors. It was expected that a new 43-seat territorial Congress (with reduced powers) would swing on whether the Southern region would be FLNKS or European dominated. The agreement of the FLNKS to take part was based on anticipation that it would win three of the regions and enhance progress towards independence. It would also provide the FLNKS with the opportunity to introduce some of its policies.

But the development did not appease the foreign ministers of the so-called Melanesian Spearhead Group — Papua New Guinea, the Solomon Islands and Vanuatu. Meeting on 3 June 1985 in Port Vila, where FLNKS Foreign Minister Yann-Célène Uregei lobbied hard, the ministers reaffirmed the 'legitimate right' of the Kanak people to independence and complained of inaction by the South Pacific Forum. They issued a communiqué that 'refuted the credibility and genuineness of the French Government's effort to bring independence to New Caledonia'. The ministers also pledged to press the Forum at its August meeting in Rarotonga to support putting New Caledonia before the United Nations Decolonisation Committee.

However, after some tough debating among Forum delegates it was decided again not to try to get New Caledonia reinscribed. Instead, as *Pacific Islands Monthly* put it, the United Nations 'will be asked to give a legal, international definition of the territory's status so that Forum countries may be guided on whether they are dealing with a piece of France, or a most suspect chunk of the South Pacific'.

The Fabius Plan finally became law in late August. It had suffered a lengthy delay caused by delaying tactics of the right-wing opposition and a decision by the French Senate to send a special commission to New Caledonia to investigate the proposals. President Mitterrand was forced to call an extraordinary session of the National Assembly. The amended version of the New Caledonia Bill, including an increase from 18 to 21 seats for the Nouméa region out of a total of 46 for the Territorial Assembly (renamed Congress), was finally adopted by the National Assembly on 20 August 1985.

One of the side-effects of delaying the statute was to bring an end to the state of emergency. Under the Fabius Plan it was to have been further extended until April 1986. However, because the new law had not been passed by the expiry date of 30 June, the state of emergency literally ran out.

Although the commission pushed for minor changes to the plan, it agreed with the major proposals. One conservative commissioner, Senator Francois Collett, condemned the Australian news media, saying he believed most Australian journalists presented a sensational pro-FLNKS picture of New Caledonia and painted people against independence as 'white settlers on the rampage'. He said some consideration had been given to sending Territorial Assembly president Dick Ukeiwé to Australia to put the anti-independence case, but the idea was rejected because of the 'aggressive' approach taken by the Australian press. Collet said Ukeiwé was 'a gentle man who speaks from the heart, and to present him to Australian journalists would be like leading a lamb to slaughter'.

Tensions rose again during the lead-up to the elections for the Fabius-created regional governments. The first incident happened early in August when gendarmes moved in to the Thio *tribu* of St Phillipo to arrest Maurice Moindou, a Kanak youth accused of the murder of 17-year-old Yves Tual near La Foa the day before the shooting of Éloi Machoro. FLNKS supporters set up barricades and attacked the gendarmerie headquarters in Thio. The youth escaped.

Two weeks later trouble erupted again when three right-wing politicians from the *métrople*, Roger Chinaud, Jacques Medecin and Francois Léotard, tried to visit St Phillipo to talk with FLNKS members. The three were met at the entrance to the village by about a dozen Kanaks, several wielding machetes and iron bars. 'This is Kanaky — not France,' they yelled. '*Dehors!* (Get out of here).' Sue Williams reported:

> After some minutes of heated argument which threatened to deteriorate into a brawl, Léotard [secretary-general of the RPR, Republican Party] decided to retreat. However, this was prevented by several large trucks carrying nickel ore to the ship-loading facilities and which had moved in behind the cavalcade carrying the visitors and accompanying journalists and officials. This further infuriated the Kanaks.

The party eventually got clear, but on the way back to Thio [it] was virtually ambushed by several Kanaks on the roadside hurling large rocks at the 20-odd cars. There was no way the motorcade could reverse . . . passengers [lay on the floor] and hoped for the best. At least seven vehicles were badly damaged and three people slightly injured . . . [Protesters] chased the party all the way to their helicopters.[14]

The three politicians made the most of the trouble, rousing passions at a public meeting of 5000 settlers in Nouméa the next night. 'Spring comes in six months,' Chinaud told the cheering rally, referring to the expected conservative victory in the March legislative elections. Medecin warned that they would not let 'Moscow gold buy the strategic position in the Pacific that the people of New Caledonia represent'.

On his return to Paris, Léotard proposed that 130 French parliamentarians should be sent to the colony to survey the poll. Although Pisani rejected the idea, he did acknowledge the need for scrutiny at the ballot boxes. He opted for a magistrate being present at each polling station along with the members of four special commissions set up in each of the regions to control the election.

The FLNKS focused on a voter registration drive to get Kanaks on to the electoral rolls. Professor Jean Guiart, a French anthropologist and noted authority on New Caledonia, cited 'irregularities' in the rolls in a protest letter to the president of the National Assembly. Comparing the rolls to census figures, Guiart found the names of several thousand French settlers who had returned to France but had not been struck off, 'while the Kanak population figures remained underestimated, disenfranchising several thousand Kanaks'.[15] About 6500 new voters, mostly Kanaks, registered in the last few weeks before the poll.

After the barricades and boycott of the New Caledonian elections almost a year earlier, the 29 September ballot was almost an anti-climax. But the FLNKS was justified in hailing it as a triumph: a record 80.6 percent of an electorate of 90,000 voters took part. But the peaceful elections probably reflected the maturity and discipline of the FLNKS more than the presence of French police.

Among the poignant images of this ballot was one of a Kanak voter sitting at the feet of a monument to war dead in a Melanesian stronghold village in the north Grande Terre. Painted on the steps was the slogan: *'French colonialism is dying . . . little by little.'*

Under the new electoral system giving the four regional councils wide government powers, the FLNKS was in a strong position and immediately pressed independence demands for a 'state' which had been unofficially dubbed Kanaky less than a year earlier. As expected, the FLNKS wrested control in three of the four new regions — Northern, Central and the Loyalty Islands. In the marginal Centre, it won five out of nine seats.

Only Nouméa remained in anti-independence hands. More than 80 percent of Kanaks voted for the pro-independence parties.

But there was a sobering lesson for the FLNKS over any referendum on independence under the existing franchise. Overall, anti-independence parties gained 60.8 percent of the votes compared with 35.2 percent for pro-independence parties, giving the RPCR and its allies a 12-seat majority in the 46-seat Congress. With its allies, the RPCR controlled a total of 26 seats; the FLNKS won 16 seats, the National Front three and the LKS one. The results in the regions were: Loyalty Islands — FLNKS 5, RPCR 4, LKS 1; Northern — FLNKS 6, RPCR 2, RPC 1; Central — FLNKS 5, RPCR 4; Nouméa RPCR 17, FN 3, FLNKS 1.

The Congress setback, however, did not detract from the FLNKS victory as most of these seats were in Nouméa and the Assembly was seen as a paper tiger, with all major decisions on the territory being made in Paris. The regions wielded greater power than the Congress. Delighted, Jean-Marie Tjibaou called on supporters to work hard to make the regional councils succeed in the lead-up to the referendum due before December 1987. He declared:

> Independence is now an irresistible step in the Caledonian consciousness. The European centres which voted *en masse* to block the FLNKS progress should now question the wisdom of their actions. History has always proved freedom movements right; history will prove right the movement emerging from the belly of Kanaky.[16]

The right-wing settler parties angrily denounced an election result that gained an overall majority yet lost three regional governments. 'The monster of the ballot box,' raged *Les Nouvelles Calédoniennes*. *Caldoche* politicians regarded Mitterrand's socialist government as the chief villain. Jacques Lafleur complained, 'This is the materialisation of a political carve-up designed to give power to the FLNKS, which is the minority.'

While Vanuatu Prime Minister Father Walter Lini praised the ballot result, New Zealand Prime Minister David Lange expressed anxiety about the polarised *Caldoches* and Kanaks, saying that hopes for a 'moderate middle ground' had been dashed.

The moderate pro-independence Kanak Socialist Liberation, previously a powerful force in Kanak politics, was virtually wiped out. It was a bitter blow for its leader, Nidoish Naisseline, who had pioneered radical Kanak politics with the *Foulards rouges* almost two decades earlier. The party had contested the previous election on a platform of multiracial independence, winning six seats.

Yet the FLNKS was not able to bask in its success for long. Barely three weeks after the elections the front was locked in a struggle for the leadership of the new Congress in Nouméa. *Caldoche* politicians staged a mass walkout from the opening session of the Congress in protest against Yéiwene Yéiwene, who began making a speech hailing the election result as a triumph for independence. The pro-independence politicians stormed out of the chamber shortly after Dick Ukeiwé won the Congress presidency ahead of Jean-Marie Tjibaou. Regarded by the *indépendantistes* as the settler-dominated RPCR's 'puppet' Ukeiwé won by 29 votes to 16. Tjibaou was elected president of the Northern region; Léopold Jorédie — Machoro's successor in the Kanaky government — won in Central, and Yéiwene in the Loyalty Islands; and Pierre Frogier headed Nouméa.

Extremist backlash

Three days before the election a bomb wrecked the *Office Foncier*, a government bureau set up in central Nouméa to handle land reform. (Barely had the office moved to new premises when it was again bombed on 21 November 1985.) A petrol bomb was also tossed at the new pro-independence radio station, Radio Djiido, mainly funded by the Australian Teachers' Federation and the West German Green Party, which had begun broadcasting the week before the ballot. The bomb exploded under a car, however, and did not damage the station. But many of its broadcasts were jammed.

Another bomb was defused before it could destroy a luxury motor yacht in Nouméa harbour, and a large bakery was destroyed. Police made no arrests over the incidents and Tjibaou blamed them on *provocateurs* trying to stir up violence before the poll.

Over the next few weeks right-wing extremists stepped up their campaign of intimidation and violence. More than a dozen bombings and other attacks on pro-independence targets and supporters followed the elections. The FLNKS headquarters in Vallée du Tir was ransacked and burned on 29 October and the two-storeyed *Palais de Justice* was completely destroyed on 3 December by a large bomb. A tract found in the smouldering debris of the lawcourts suggested a link with earlier attacks claimed by the *Organisation de l'armee secrète pour la défense de la Nouvelle Calédonie Francaise*. Groups of Europeans and Wallis Islanders have also attacked Kanaks. In some cases, gangs of Wallis Islanders raided Kanak suburbs, threatening people with rifles and iron bars.

Authorities believed the bomb attacks were carried out by vigilante groups which had emerged the previous year, styled on MOP and the OAS. About 2000 *pieds noirs*, settlers from Algeria, were among thousands of French people who considered New Caledonia their last frontier. They pledged to oppose independence by any means. The paramilitary groups seemed highly organised, skilled in explosives and well stocked in arms. 'Yes, we have arms,' admitted Nouméa Mayor Roger Laroque, 'and we will fight.' (Laroque later died of a heart attack.)

When police raided one Nouméa house, making two arrests, they discovered a cache of three bombs, 15 automatic pistols, three rifles and a large supply of ammunition. During 1985, as gun-running to New Caledonia was stepped up, three major arms shipments destined for anti-independence forces were confiscated in Australia and New Zealand; several French nationals were arrested.*

'We aren't dealing with small unorganised groups of the extreme right,' said Norbert Caffa, an FLNKS official, 'but rather with a conscious strategy of the colonial Right which plans its actions seriously.'

One group, the Patriotic Action Committee (CAP) which was founded in November, quickly claimed more than 1200 card-carrying members. Its objectives included mobilisation of *Caldoches* to active resistance and support for 'militants who attempt to neutralise FLNKS action commandos or their sympathisers'. CAP included several well-known extreme right-wing personalities, including deputy Justin Guillemard and RPCR security chief Henri Morini.

One of the most extreme right-wing groups, Free Caledonian Forces (FCL), circulated a 'hit list' of 56 Kanak leaders with details of their private addresses, car numbers and other useful information. The name *Jean-Marie Tjibaou* headed the list. The document called for the establishment of three or four-person cells. It suggested a series of tactics, ranging from threats and house attacks to far more brutal methods.

'Take action against people which can range from *passage à tabac* [beating up] or the full treatment [killing],' it said. 'Ideally, to get the full impact of fear of the unknown make the body disappear without trace: throw the corpse to the sharks.'[17]

The reforms introduced under the Fabius Plan were as much to ensure that Kanaks were incorporated into the modern economy — making them

---

* The arms shipment hauls for anti-independence groups were made in Brisbane (March 1985), Sydney (November) and Auckland (December). New Zealand police seized 25 cases of munitions on board the Nouméa-registered freighter *Ile de Lumière* at Auckland; a 29-year-old cook was arrested and charged with illegal possession of explosives. The police at first suspected the arms were part of a plot to rescue two French secret service agents jailed in Auckland the previous month for their role in the sabotage of the *Rainbow Warrior*. But it was later admitted the munitions, loaded in Sydney, were to supply anti-independence settlers. Plastic-wrapped crates found hidden in the ship's bilges and fuel tanks contained 5500 rounds of ammunition and parts — mainly magazines — for automatic pistols. In Brisbane, weapons worth $44,000 were seized on a Nouméa-bound ship, and 36 rifles and ammunition were discovered on a ship in Sydney heading for the territory. A total of six French nationals were charged in Australia with illegal possession of explosives.

less likely to withdraw into isolation and destabilise the territorial economy — as a genuine wish for Melanesian economic development. By preparing to hand control of primary education, rural development and land reform to the regional councils, the FLNKS was offered the chance to move towards the style of self-reliant society envisaged for independent Kanaky through the EPK schools and the co-operatives. As well, the election results gave the Kanak-dominated councils the more challenging opportunity of demonstrating that independence would not be racist and that development would benefit all ethnic groups.

But the 'green revolution', as Tjibaou coined it, had its own dilemmas. There was a conflict between withdrawing to develop a more distinctly Kanak economy and society, one that was less dependent on the world economy, or taking advantage of the electoral gains in the new councils and the extra finance to play a more active role in New Caledonian society. The FLNKS opted to demonstrate its 'respectability and responsibility' and work within the institutions rather than become more radical and work towards independence by rejecting them. It was not an easy choice and rifts were created within the coalition as a result.

Unfortunately, the FLNKS was given little opportunity to show what it could do. Within months the socialists were ousted from office, Jacques Chirac became the new French prime minister and the conservative government scuttled the Kanak regional powers and sabotaged their economic initiatives.

Part 3
Nuclear Colonialism

8

Niuklia Fri Pasifik

In the colonial history of the Pacific, colonies and nuclear tests go together. Britain, France and the United States all chose island possessions to test their deadliest and dirtiest nuclear weapons. The tests have left a legacy of cultural destruction and radiation-induced illnesses among islanders, particularly in Micronesia. China, the United States and the Soviet Union have used the region for missile testing. Nuclear colonialism has spawned a people's movement for a nuclear-free and independent Pacific and a ten-year campaign for a nuclear-free zone. But the 1985 Rarotonga Treaty failed to adequately meet these aspirations.

The people of the Pacific have borne the brunt of nuclear colonialism — 'nuclearism' as Vanuatu Prime Minster Walter Lini describes it. Within three months of the nuclear devastation wrought on Hiroshima and Nagasaki in August 1945, Washington opted to set up an atomic bomb testing programme on the remote atolls of Micronesia: a move that has had destructive consequences for the islanders for decades.

Situated in a vast expanse of ocean in the central Pacific, the more than 2000 islands of Micronesia have played a vital role in modern strategic history. Japanese aircraft launched their attack on Pearl Harbour from Micronesia, plunging the United States into the Second World War. And it was from Tinian Island in western Micronesia that the *Enola Gay* took off with its deadly weapons for the attacks on Hiroshima and Nagasaki which ended the war and ushered in the nuclear age. The islands of Micronesia have been used by Washington ever since as pawns to enhance its strategic posture.[1]

The Micronesians have also been subjected to more colonial rule than any other Pacific islanders. Spain 'discovered' the islands of Micronesia in the late sixteenth century, and since then the islands have been ruled by three successive colonial powers. Germany seized the Marshall Islands from Spain in 1885 and purchased the remaining islands at the end of the century. Thirteen years later, the United States seized the Philippines and the island of Guam at the end of the Spanish-American War. Being the largest island of Micronesia, Guam has served United States strategic interests well, and was one of the launching pads for B52 bombing sorties during the Indochina War.

At the outbreak of the First World War, Japan captured the Micronesian islands from Germany, and later administered them under a League of Nations mandate. After the war Japanese economic expansion meant rapid changes throughout Micronesia. During the late 1930s, however, Japan violated its mandate by militarily fortifying several Pacific outposts, using Truk lagoon in the Caroline Islands as its Pearl Harbour.

The strategic importance of the islands was demonstrated during the Second World War. The bloody island-hopping battles of Kwajalein, Enewetak, Truk, Tinian, Saipan and Peleliu left more than 6000 Americans dead and a further 22,000 wounded while Japanese casualties were far higher. Caught in a war they wanted no part of, an estimated 5000 Micronesians also lost their lives.[2]

At the end of the war, the US Naval Military Government took possession of the Japanese-mandated islands; in January 1946 it had selected Bikini Atoll in the Marshall Islands for the first series of nuclear tests — known as Operation Crossroads — to demonstrate the destructive capacity of its atomic bomb on a fleet of wartime warships. When the American military governor of the Marshalls, Commodore Ben Wyatt, went to Bikini to explain the action to the islanders, he told them the United States was testing nuclear bombs 'for the good of mankind and to end all world wars'.[3] The islanders were then 'asked' to leave.

The public spectacle was staged on 1 and 25 July 1946 and was monitored by 42,000 military personnel and scientists — all men. Between 1946 and 1958, 66 atomic and hydrogen bombs shattered the Bikini and Enewetak Atolls. Six islands were vaporised by nuclear weapons and the people of Rongelap and other atolls were irradiated. Many islanders claimed they were used as guinea pigs for the experiments. Now, more than 40 years after the first Bikini tests, many islands are still uninhabitable because of the high radiation levels while the Bikinians and Rongelap islanders remain exiled people.

In July 1947 Washington became the administering authority of the United Nations-sanctioned Trust Territory of the Pacific Islands, the only 'strategic' trust of the 11 United Nations-supervised territories created after the war. The territory was divided into three geographical parts — the Marshall Islands, the Carolines (Kosrae, Pohnpei, Truk, Yao and Belau), and the Marianas Islands, including Guam, Saipan and Tinian.

After signing the trusteeship agreement, only the United States military paid any attention to Micronesia. The Marshall Islanders suffered most from the military occupation: a major supply base was set up at Kwajalein with smaller command centres at Bikini and Enewetak for the nuclear tests. Kwajalein also became a vital link in the supply route for American forces during the Korean War and later became a base for missile tests. In 1951 the Central Intelligence Agency set up a camp on Saipan which operated a secret training camp for nationalist guerrillas as part of an unsuccessful plan to invade the China mainland.

Micronesia was neglected during the 1950s: almost no money was provided for development. Roads, usually little more than riverbeds, were frequently impassable; electricity and water supply were erratic; and hospital and other social services were virtually non-existent. The Japanese-built buildings and infrastructure left after the wartime building were deliberately destroyed by United States forces after the war.[4]

With the other ten trusteeships becoming independent, and with an anti-colonial mood sweeping the world, the United States created a Congress of Micronesia in 1965 to silence United Nations criticism of the lack of political development. While the Micronesians now had a forum to air their concerns, the American High Commission frequently vetoed any decision made by their Congress.

Although the loss of Asian bases in the wake of the defeat in Vietnam revived strong Pentagon interest in establishing forward bases in Micronesia, the military policy of 'strategic denial' remained the crucial issue in political status negotiations between the United States and Micronesia. The trusteeship was split into four political entities — Mariana Islands (which opted to become a United States commonwealth) and the republics of Belau, Federated States of Micronesia and the Marshall Islands.

After 14 years of negotiations and four Washington administrations, a compromise between commonwealth and full independence — labelled 'free association' — was agreed to in principle by American and Micronesian negotiators in 1985. The Compact of Free Association is a complex legal document defining economic aid and foreign affairs provisions. It has involved compromises on both sides — but the islanders have been forced to do most of the compromising.

The main provisions include the power of the United States to maintain *permanent* 'strategic denial', or the authority to keep other nations out of Micronesia; 50-year military and nuclear rights in Belau (in spite of the islanders' overwhelming approval of a constitution which bans the entry of nuclear warships and weapons); and 30-year military use of Kwajalein Missile Range for continued testing and development of intercontinental ballistic missiles, anti-ballistic missile systems and space tracking (in spite of Kwajalein landowner demands that the term be limited to 15 years). In return, the Micronesian governments have the authority to run their internal *and* foreign affairs — but with qualifications.

Both the Federated States of Micronesia and the Marshall Islands formally adopted the compact at the end of 1986; Belau remained the only state thwarting the American plans to end the trusteeship while retaining military control. In spite of repeated referenda and a climate of increasing violence, the conflict between the compact's military and nuclear clauses and the nuclear-free constitution remained unresolved. Once the Belau document is constitutionally adopted, notes American researcher and commentator on Micronesian affairs Glenn Alcalay, the United States will have consolidated its western Pacific strategic flank in the 'ingeniously-crafted' compact agreement. But he adds:

> Instead of peace and prosperity, the US has used the picturesque isles of Micronesia for achieving a military escalation in a precarious world. As Ezra Leban from Atirik Atoll said to me a few years ago, 'Now I have to take a pill every day until I die. The US came to our islands and threw bombs at us, and now we are slowly dying.'[5]

★   ★.   ★

Although Britain tested atomic devices in the Pacific in the 1950s and 60s, it later abandoned its nuclear role in the region. France, however, embarked on a policy of nuclear colonialism like the United States. And while the Americans began to absorb some of the lessons from the devastation they had caused in the Marshall Islands, France ignored the Partial Test Ban Treaty and chose two atolls for its own atmospheric tests.

French nuclear involvement in the South Pacific stems from two distinct but closely linked policies — the decision to have an independent nuclear deterrent, and the decision to remain a middle-ranked global military power. But unlike the Americans, France began nuclear tests in the Pacific in 1966 only because it was forced to abandon the Reggane test site in the Sahara as a result of Algerian independence. When France ended atmospheric tests in 1974 after growing protests from South Pacific nations, there was no evidence to indicate it needed to continue underground tests at Moruroa. In fact, had France conducted underground tests from the beginning it would have seriously needed to consider other options within metropolitan France. The Australian government declared in 1986 that it had surveyed possible test sites in France, finding the Guerét area, the Margeride and Corsica all suitable. But France opted to continue testing at Moruroa and Fangataufa Atolls, having already set up the costly test centre in Polynesia.

There are many flaws in the French strategy. Carrying out the tests in the Pacific, for example, does not make France a 'Pacific power' in a full military sense. In reality, France has been using its political grip on Polynesia to serve a defence strategy with its priorities based on the other side of the globe — in Europe, where France regards West Germany as the major potential flashpoint in any conflict with the Soviet Union. As French historian Professor Jean Chesneaux puts it:

France is an outsider in the Pacific. In the military sense, Moruroa is an enclave and not a true military base, as is the US base at Subic Bay in the Philippines. It is very likely that when they realised this situation, French authorities, very late, decided to build in New Caledonia a genuine military base with submarines, aircraft-carriers and Jaguar aircraft.[6]

Also, there is little evidence to suggest that *la bombe* gives France any more diplomatic or political clout internationally. In few world crises — whether Afghanistan, Chad, Lebanon, Nicaragua or Vietnam — has France been able to speak with any more authority than countries such as Australia, Italy or West Germany.

Yet the bomb is a vital symbol of French nationalism, the country's passport to 'independence' from the superpowers. This nationalist appeal is as strong among politicians of the Left as it is for those of the Right. Since 1958, when France decided to develop its own nuclear capability, Gaullism in defence policy has become a key factor in the French political consensus. No French government could rule without the nuclear strategy being a cornerstone of its policy. According to President Mitterrand's first Prime Minister, Pierre Mauroy: 'France's strategic nuclear forces have the capacity, even after an enemy first strike, to retaliate with a very high degree of credibility and to inflict damage in excess of the demographic and economic potential we present.'

Likewise, Moruroa has become a symbol of French determination to assert its independence from superpowers. New Caledonia gained greater nuclear strategic importance in 1985 with the first visit there by a French nuclear attack submarine, the *Rubis*. Other visits could follow if Nouméa's Port Denouel is expanded as a base for aircraft-carriers and nuclear submarines.

The visit and increased port calls by French warships among independent Pacific states is regarded as evidence of growing collaboration between France and the United States in the region — a reversal of de Gaulle's 1967 decision for France to pull out of NATO. With the third largest nuclear force after the United States and the Soviet Union, France has increasingly co-operated with the Americans in recent years. It has made use of American computers, sold to France in 1982, which have been used in developing new nuclear warheads.[8]

The People's Charter

The grassroots Pacific anti-nuclear movement was launched at the first Nuclear-Free Pacific conference at Suva in April 1975, backed by the Against Tests on Moruroa (ATOM) committee which had been formed in 1970.

It consisted of people from the Pacific Theological College, the University of the South Pacific and the Fiji YWCA. The committee was merged into the Pacific People's Action Front in the mid-1970s and then the movement went into decline.[9] It surfaced again as the Fiji Anti-Nuclear Group (FANG) in 1983. Other Pacific anti-nuclear groups existed already but the Suva conference established a Pacific-wide network.

This movement proved to be a major factor in persuading Pacific governments to take a stronger nuclear-free stand and shaping public awareness and opinion throughout the region. A draft People's Charter for a Nuclear-Free Pacific was produced at Suva and influenced the then New Zealand Prime Minister Norman Kirk to call for a nuclear-free zone treaty at the 1975 South Pacific Forum — an ideal that took a decade to be realised. After the draft charter was reaffirmed at a second conference in Pohnpei in 1978, the third meeting two years later at Kailua, Hawaii, expanded the group's identity as the Nuclear-Free and Independent Pacific (NFIP) movement. Resource centres were set up in Honolulu and Port Vila. The fourth — and biggest — congress was held in Port Vila during 1983 in recognition of the Vanuatu Government's support for a *niuklia fri pasifik*, as it is expressed in pidgin.

'Vanuatu is not seeking *only* a nuclear-free Pacific,' Deputy Prime Minister Sethy Regenvanu told delegates at the opening. 'We are seeking a Pacific . . . free of every last remnant of colonialism. But freedom and independence will have no meaning if our very existence is threatened by the constant fear of total destruction.' The People's Charter for a Nuclear-Free and Independent Pacific, adopted in Hawaii and reaffirmed in Vila, declared:

> We, the people of the Pacific, have been victimised too long by foreign powers. The Western imperialistic and colonial powers invaded our defenceless region, they took over our lands and subjugated our people to their whims. This form of alien colonial, political and military domination unfortunately persists as an evil cancer in some of our native territories such as Tahiti-Polynesia, Kanaky, Australia and Aotearoa. Our environment continues to be despoiled by foreign powers developing nuclear weapons for a strategy of warfare that has no winners, no liberators and imperils the survival of all humankind.
>
> We . . . will assert ourselves and wrest control over the destiny of our nations and our environment from foreign powers, including transnational corporations. We note in particular the recent racist roots of the world's nuclear powers and we call for an immediate end to the oppression, exploitation and subordination of the indigenous people of the Pacific.[10]

The nuclear-free zone envisaged in the charter would embrace Micronesia, the Philippines, Japan and Hawaii as well as the original South Pacific Forum nations and would ban nuclear weapons even on board ships. NFIP campaigners support the Kanak struggle; oppose the Indonesian government's policy of transmigration in West Papua; denounce the presence of

United States military bases in the Philippines; endorse a protest against the dumping of nuclear waste in the Pacific; condemn the use of Kwajalein Atoll for the testing of the MX and other missiles; call for an end to the mining of uranium; and support Belau's nuclear-free constitution. 'Critics say the movement demands such a radical change in the security relationships of Pacific countries that it is doomed to irrelevance,' noted historian Stewart Firth. 'But this is to misunderstand the power and status of the nuclear-free idea in the Pacific Islands.'[11]

Grassroots actions have contributed boldly to the NFIP campaign. Several Greenpeace protest voyages to Moruroa climaxed with the French sabotage of the *Rainbow Warrior*. In 1982, a 'sail-in' by more than 1000 island landowners on Kwajalein Atoll forced the United States military to shut down missile testing there for five months. The same year, the Australian-based yacht *Pacific Peacemaker* embarked on a voyage across the Pacific, supporting a Waitangi Day protest by Maori activists in New Zealand; protesting at Moruroa — where it was rammed by a French Navy minesweeper; visiting Kaho'olawe (the US Navy's Hawaiian target island); and taking part in a blockade of the arrival of the Trident submarine at Puget Sound.

The Port Vila NFIP conference ended with a traditional taro planting ceremony, intended to symbolise unity. Mary Lini, wife of the Vanuatu Prime Minister, dug in a plant representing the nation on tribal land while other women delegates planted on behalf of other Pacific countries.

'Unity of the people in our efforts to protect cultural and traditional values is important,' said Roman Bedor of Belau. 'After all, Pacific people have cooperative, not competitive, societies.' But unity was an elusive quality for delegates who were faced by a series of rifts.

Even Bedor, however, was forced to admit the conference became seriously torn by tension as delegates faced several difficult issues. One faction favoured splitting the conference so that only indigenous people were involved, with *pakeha, haole, palagi* and *popa'a* being excluded.[12] Other delegates believed the conference was not radical enough and would not confront the vital sovereignty questions confronting indigenous people in the Pacific rim countries. It was an issue which continued to bedevil the NFIP movement for the next three years and came close to provoking a split after the Fijian coup d'état. A partial solution was worked out by staging an exclusively indigenous caucus before the opening session of the November 1987 conference at Manila.

'Uncle' Harry Mitchell, a 67-year-old indigenous Hawaiian from the *Kaho'olawe 'Ohana* movement, summed up the Port Vila mood: 'We must stop the nuclear evil,' he said. 'It has been forced down our throats by the angels — US, Britain and France — the angels with the dirty faces. The sea is our bread basket . . . and the ocean our ice box.

'The *best* thing we Hawaiians ever did was get rid of Captain Cook.'[13]

David Robie

Anti-nuclear protesters at Independence Park in Port Vila during the fourth Nuclear-Free and Independent Pacific conference, 1983

The Rarotonga Treaty

Although the grassroots movements began the campaign for a nuclear-free Pacific, they found its progress slow. A year after Fiji abruptly decided in July 1983 to scuttle part of its popular anti-nuclear stance and allow American nuclear-armed and powered warships into its ports, United States Ambassador Fred Eckert completed his Suva assignment well satisfied. He could claim that he had successfully wooed Fiji's leaders to adopt a position acceptable to American interests. But just over three years later, his accomplishment seemed under threat. The South Pacific Nuclear-Free Zone Treaty (SPNFZ, or 'Spinfizz' as American officials dubbed it), was formally tabled at the United Nations, and the conservative government of Prime Minister Ratu Sir Kamisese Mara faced a challenge from a rising new anti-nuclear political force. The new Fiji Labour Party was turning the country's politics upside down. It supported New Zealand's stand and planned to reimpose the port ban.

The Soviet Union lost no time in gaining favour with several South Pacific nations by putting its signature to the nuclear-free treaty's protocols; the United States refused. On 11 December 1986, the SPNFZ treaty took effect under international law when Australia became the eighth South Pacific Forum member to ratify it. The Cook Islands, Fiji, Kiribati, New Zealand, Niue, Tuvalu and Western Samoa had already ratified the document. The treaty prohibits nuclear testing, the dumping of nuclear waste and the presence on land of nuclear weapons in an area stretching from the west coast of Australia almost to Easter Island, off Chile, and from north of Kiribati to about 3000 km south of New Zealand. The zone adjoins the boundaries of the Antarctic and Tlatelolco (Latin America) nuclear-free treaties.

Next day a Soviet Embassy official in Canberra telephoned Henry Naisali, director of the South Pacific Bureau for Economic Co-operation (SPEC) in Suva. Moscow had already made it clear several months before that it planned to formally recognise the treaty. Now the question was brief and to the point. Where and when, asked the official, could Dr Evgeny Samoteikin, the Soviet Ambassador to Australia and Fiji, sign the document?

'Here and now,' replied Naisali. Two days later Ambassador Samoteikin flew to Suva and on Monday, December 15, signed two of the three protocols that the Forum had invited the five nuclear powers to accept. 'It's a pleasure and honour to sign them,' said Samoteikin, while noting Moscow still had reservations. Naisali welcomed the signature as evidence of international support for the South Pacific's desire to keep the region free of 'nuclear terror'. He described the treaty as 'perhaps the most noteworthy advance in international nuclear disarmament' in the past decade. But, noted the conservative *Economist* rather cynically: 'The Russians could not resist signing Spinfizz. It has enabled them to make a peace-loving gesture without offering a single rouble.'[14]

The first protocol applies only to nuclear powers with dependencies in the Pacific — Britain, France and the United States. It asks them to refrain from using the Pacific islands colonies as nuclear weapons bases or testing grounds. The two other protocols require the five recognised nuclear weapons states to refrain from using or threatening to use nuclear weapons against any treaty members and to refrain from testing nuclear explosive devices anywhere in the zone. In signing the protocols, though, the Soviet Union can take advantage of an escape clause which allows any signatory to withdraw with three months' notice.

On 10 February 1987, less than two months after the Russians, the Chinese ambassador to Fiji, Ji Chaozhu, also signed the protocols. But he said the South Pacific could be nuclear-free only if the other big powers accepted their 'special responsibility'.

France, predictably, and Britain joined the United States in refusing to sign the protocols; France showed its contempt by triggering a ten-kilotonne test in the South Pacific on 7 December 1986 — the day Australia's Federal Parliament ratified the treaty and four days before it took effect. Shortly afterwards the Reagan administration made it clear it would not sign.

In February France's State Secretary for Pacific Affairs, Gaston Flosse, visited Washington and later boasted about his success. He had met Secretary of State George Shultz, 'whom I persuaded not to sign the Rarotonga Treaty'. Annoyed by his statement, New Zealand Prime Minister David Lange retaliated by cancelling a state visit by Flosse to New Zealand that had been scheduled for the following month. Lange cited the resignation by Flosse the week before from his other job as president of the Tahitian government as the major reason; Flosse had been invited as an elected representative of the Tahitian people.

Flosse, aged 55, is a part-Tahitian and among the wealthiest men of Polynesia. He is the architect of a French Government attempt to regain credibility in the South Pacific through aid and political contact. (His visit to New Zealand would have been the first by a French cabinet minister since the *Rainbow Warrior* bombing.) Flosse also leads the conservative *Tahoeraa Huiraatira* (Rally of the People) party, which was in power at the time.*

Tahoeraa is the Tahitian political party most sympathetic — most are opposed — to French nuclear tests in the Gambiers. 'All precautions are being taken,' he said. 'Moruroa Atoll will not be another Bikini.'

---

* Flosse's party, *Tahoeraa Huiraatira*, was re-elected to office on 16 March 1986 with 22 seats in the 41-seat Territorial Assembly, the first party to gain an outright majority in Tahiti for 30 years. Gaston Flosse was appointed State Secretary for Pacific Affairs three days later, the first Pacific islander to be included in a French cabinet. A $3 million South Pacific fund for aid and co-operation was provided, and it was doubled by the end of 1987.

Both suave and abrasive, Flosse is impatient with Lange's nuclear-free policy and other Pacific nations' criticism of France. 'I don't understand the real reasons for their criticism and opposition to nuclear testing,' he said. 'Let me be precise. We do not manufacture the bomb at Moruroa. Moruroa is a laboratory 500 to 600 metres deep. The military are not the sole beneficiaries. All the engineers are civil, and civil research benefits. What really is the opposition being voiced? It is hazardous to the health of the population? Or is it introducing disorder to this part of the world.'[15]

The most vocal Forum opponents of the treaty — Vanuatu, Papua New Guinea* and the Solomon Islands — argue that it does not make the South Pacific a nuclear weapons-free zone at all since it permits treaty countries to continue to make individual decisions about letting their sea and airports be used for brief periods by nuclear weapons-carrying aircraft and warships. This feature of the treaty was included on the insistence of Australia, which wanted a treaty that would not restrict any nuclear activities by its most important ally and protector, the United States. Besides Australia and Fiji, the other Pacific countries which are prepared to entertain the US Navy are Tonga and Western Samoa.

'In the final analysis,' asked *Pacific Islands Monthly*, 'what good is a nuclear-free zone not recognised by the nuclear powers? Or, for that matter, one that is not recognised by all the Forum countries?' The magazine said that to some critics it was an 'empty gesture' and to others it was an effort by a frustrated minority, a plea to be left alone by larger nations.[16]

On 18 May 1986, just two months before the SPNFZ treaty was approved by the Forum at Suva, Lange made an enthusiastic but qualified endorsement of it while opening the Pacific Trade Union Forum conference at Auckland. 'Embrace it as the start,' he said. 'Let's draw back from the brink and don't let us lose the chance of this move which is a very significant extension of the [Nuclear] Non-Proliferation Treaty. Don't let us see that sabotaged. Some people say they want nirvana at the first port of call, but I'm afraid we're not going to get there.' Delegates warmly applauded Lange, and conference chairman James Raman, of Fiji, told the Prime Minister he had given people of the Pacific great hope.

To many of the more outspoken anti-nuclear unionists present, however, and to some cynical Pacific government officials and peace activists, Lange's words failed to allay the suspicions they had entertained about the treaty long before details had become public. Indeed, since the Norman Kirk proposal was revived by Australia at the Tuvalu meeting of the Forum in 1984 there was good reason to be suspicious: it seemed that the treaty was being promoted by Canberra as a way of deflecting attention from the pro-uranium, pro-nuclear weapon policies of the Hawke government. But the treaty's supporters argued that at least it prevented the nuclear status quo from deteriorating.

---

*In spite of its reservations, Papua New Guinea signed the document.

'All treaties spell mischief for someone,' said the *Economist*. 'But Spinfizz seems less troublesome than most. Its beauty is that signing it amounts to little more than saying you are against nuclear war in the South Pacific.' It had been a 'godsend, if that is the word' for Hawke, added the magazine. 'It enables him to give the nod to the anti-nuclear instincts of his Labor Party without interfering with his defence promises to the Americans.'[17]

The treaty's flaws

Eight of the 13 Forum leaders signed the historic treaty in the Rarotonga Hotel in the Cook Islands on 6 August 1985, the 40th anniversary of the Hiroshima bombing. The signatories were Australia (Prime Minister Bob Hawke), Cook Islands (Prime Minister Sir Thomas Davis), Fiji (Prime Minister Ratu Sir Kamisese Mara), Kiribati (President Ieremia Tabai), New Zealand (Prime Minister David Lange), Niue (Premier Sir Robert Rex), Tuvalu (Prime Minister Dr Tomasi Puapua) and Western Samoa (Prime Minister Tofilau Eti). But the ink was barely dry before dissent within the Forum became public. A day after, the conference spokesman, David Lange, assured journalists that *all* Forum members would sign the document, Vanuatu Prime Minister Walter Lini declared his country would *not* — at least until the treaty was more watertight.

Vanuatu is committed to remaining totally free of all nuclear weapons. It imposed a port ban on United States nuclear ships in 1982, two years before New Zealand. The treaty was 'not comprehensive, it is partial' and not what Pacific Islanders wanted, Lini said. He predicted that the region's churches, academic institutions and peace activists would continue to promote a comprehensive treaty. If governments were seen to be ignoring their true wishes, there would be a loss of 'confidence and credibility in the democratic institutions' of the region. Lini cited Australia's uranium exports and the fact that the treaty would leave foreign nuclear warships free to roam the region at will and enter ports that welcome them as key flaws in the document.

Fiji's Ratu Mara, like Hawke, wanted to preserve good military and trade relations with the United States and was prepared to accept nuclear warships. He stressed that the Australian Prime Minister had clearly argued the case for the treaty. 'No counter argument was heard,' Mara said. 'It satisfies the wishes of the majority of the people of the Pacific, but what happens if a war breaks out? I don't know.'

Like many anti-nuclear activists and campaigners, however, New Zealand peace researcher Owen Wilkes believes the 'partial' treaty with loopholes has not lessened the urgency of establishing a comprehensive nuclear-free zone. 'The Aotearoa Peace Movement has been suspicious of the treaty since well before the details became public,' he argues, 'and, indeed, ever since it was first mooted by Australia at the 1983 Forum meeting in Tuvalu. There were some good reasons to be suspicious.'[18]

Wilkes attacks, in particular, the promotion of the treaty by Australia as a way of deflecting attention from the pro-uranium, pro-nuclear war policies of the Hawke government. Among treaty flaws he cites:

1. *It fails to ban or even restrict the transit of nuclear weapons in any way.* Nuclear powers are still free to cruise anywhere in the zone with submarines loaded with Trident missiles, ships loaded with Tomahawk cruise missiles and so on. Any nation within the zone is free to invite nuclear-armed ships or aircraft to visit its ports and airfields — as long as the ships and aircraft are not 'stationed' there.

2. *It does not ban the testing of ballistic missiles intended to carry nuclear warheads.* By far the biggest contribution the Pacific makes to the arms race is as a testing ground for intercontinental and submarine-launched ballistic missiles (ICBMs and SLBMs). The United States tests its MX from Vandenberg Air Base, California, to Kwajalein Atoll and to various 'broad ocean area' target zones elsewhere. The Soviet Union test-flies its missiles into the North Pacific and occasionally into the South Pacific. The Chinese have also made tests into the South Pacific.

3. *It does not ban facilities which are part of nuclear war systems and networks.* It leaves untouched such nuclear support facilities as the North-West Cape transmitter in western Australia which is used to communicate with missile submarines; the electronic spy satellite base at Pine Gap; and the missile early warning satellite ground station at Nurrungar (all in Australia).

4. *The zone does not cover Micronesia.* The Micronesians are the Pacific people whose lives have been the most affected by nuclear war preparations. They have been forced to play host to United States atmospheric nuclear tests at Bikini and Enewetak, to US missile tests at Kwajalein and elsewhere, to US missile storage, Polaris basing, and B52 operations at Guam. And they have had to yield substantial portions of Belau, Saipan and Tinian for the future requirements of the United States military should it be forced to withdraw from the Philippines. The republic of Belau has been denied a nuclear-free constitution by the United States. The Marshall Islanders live downwind of the mothballed United States atmospheric nuclear test facilities at Johnston Island* — which is also outside the zone. (Both the republics of the Federated States of Micronesia and the Marshall Islands became members of the South Pacific Forum during 1987.)

5. *The treaty fails to prevent Australian uranium being used for weapons production.* Australia is already subject to NPT-IAEA safeguards, so

little is gained by reaffirming these in the treaty. The safeguards make it difficult, but not impossible, for Australian uranium to end up in nuclear warheads. Only a total ban on uranium mining would guarantee that this could not happen.

6. *The treaty will not prevent non-signatories from dumping nuclear waste within the zone.* The treaty partners, however, are prevented from helping them dump (and Protocol II apparently prevents nuclear powers from dumping). Palmyra Island, the most likely possibility for United States long-term, high-level waste storage, has been carefully left just outside the zone.

'After such a dismal catalogue of deficiencies one is left wondering if there are any good things about the treaty at all,' says Wilkes. 'There *are*. The treaty does prevent the spread of nuclear weapons into South Pacifc countries which are currently free of them — let us be thankful for small mercies.' But, adds Wilkes, the treaty would not prevent France deploying nuclear weapons in New Caledonia, since New Caledonia is not free to join the Forum and France has refused to sign Protocol I.

The treaty does ban nuclear tests on the territory of the signatories, and it bans states from testing anywhere else in the zone. It does not, however, hamper French testing at Moruroa. It has also become impossible, in theory at least, to guarantee the secrecy of military installations on the territory of treaty members. Wilkes adds:

[The treaty should not be condemned] as useless or worse than useless. Of course it does much less than we would have hoped for, but on the other hand it is a treaty which is being signed, and it does bring into being some useful bans. It is a useful tool to use in the campaign against French testing. It is an inspiration within the South Pacific to achieve more comprehensive bans . . .

Let us emphasise that it is a partial nuclear-free zone treaty, and always

---

* South-west of Hawaii, Johnston is also probably the most bizarre United States military installation in the Pacific. It is an aircraft carrier-shaped (and not much larger) islet artificially created on the atoll's coral reef. This is where the United States does everything that is 'too dangerous, too secret, or too unpopular to do anywhere else in the Pacific'. It is particularly suited to activities involving hazardous substances because, although less than two hours' flying time from Hawaii, the constant north-east tradewinds ensure that all chemical or radioactive fallout heads away from the United States and towards other places and people — in particular the Marshall Islands.

Eighteen million litres of dioxin-contaminated Agent Orange defoliant left over from the Vietnam War were stored on the atoll. The defoliant was burned there, just offshore, on board the Dutch-owned *Vulcanus I*. The island presently hosts several thousand tonnes of old and leaky nerve gas and mustard gas munitions. The army is building a land-based incinerator plant to dispose of this and plans to bring more old chemical weaponry to the atoll as it becomes too dangerous to store or burn elsewhere.

call it a partial zone, to emphasise that we are still seeking a comprehensive or total zone.[19]

Pacific countries which joined Vanuatu in not signing the treaty at Rarotonga were Nauru, Papua New Guinea, Tonga and the Solomon Islands. Nauru and Papua New Guinea expressed approval of the treaty in principle but said constitutional processes had to be observed before they could formally become party to it. Tonga and the Solomon Islands indicated similar positions. But by the end of 1985, Papua New Guinea's Michael Somare, who was strong on anti-nuclear rhetoric but heavily influenced by Ratu Mara, had been replaced as Prime Minister by his former deputy, Paias Wingti, and both Port Moresby and Honiara joined Port Vila in taking a harder line towards the treaty.

Several Pacific nations tried unsuccessfully against Australian and New Zealand opposition to push through stronger provisions while the treaty was being drafted.[20] The ban on permanent stationing of nuclear weapons was promoted as one of the treaty's strong points, something which would stop any future United States plans to store nuclear weapons on Australian territory or use that country's bases (such as Cockburn Sound) as a home port.

Both Papua New Guinea and Vanuatu sought a definition of permanent stationing that would include limits on the length and frequency of nuclear armed ship visits. They were overruled by Australia and others on the drafting committee. From 1982 to 1984 nuclear-armed submarines were present in Cockburn Sound about a quarter of the time, yet Hawke said this would not be a violation of the permanent stationing provision. It would be possible for the United States to store nuclear weapons on an auxiliary supply ship for most of the year in the Cockburn sound area, and to have nuclear-armed ships calling in repeatedly to be resupplied — without breaking the treaty. However, since 1984 the frequency of visits had slowed and there were no visits during 1987-88.

Nauru, Papua New Guinea, Solomon Islands and Vanuatu tried to persuade Australia to include a ban on nuclear missile testing in Protocol III of the treaty, which covers only nuclear weapons testing. But, says researcher Michael Hamel-Green, this too was rejected by Australia.

Nauru and Vanuatu also sought bans on uranium exports. Again Australia blocked the island nations, claiming that its uranium exports were safeguarded and destined for peaceful purposes only. This argument ignored the weaknesses in existing safeguards and the intimate relationship between the spread of the civilian nuclear industry and the proliferation of nuclear weapons.

Over nuclear waste-dumping, Papua New Guinea tried to strengthen the treaty by including a fourth protocol which would require all potential nuclear waste-dumping countries (such as Britain, Japan, the Soviet Union and the United States) not to dump on land or in the seas in the region. This was overruled on the ground that another treaty was being negotiated under the South Pacific Regional Environmental Programme which could accomplish the same end. (France and the United States endorsed the treaty which includes a ban on dumping radioactive waste within 200-mile offshore zones; Japan did not.) Anti-nuclear campaigners, however, claim France already stores some low-level waste at Moruroa and nothing in the Rarotonga Treaty (or the SPREP convention) prevents this.

Both Papua New Guinea and Vanuatu argued for the nuclear-free zone to be based on the boundary lines of the South Pacific Commission — including the Micronesian nations north of the equator, Belau, Federated States of Micronesia and the Marshall Islands. This was rejected because 'inclusion of the United States trust territory in the zone could complicate current negotiations on the constitutional future of these territories,' especially since nuclear issues were a major element in these negotiations.

But these considerations did not appear to apply in the case of French territories in the South Pacific where the issues facing independence movements were regarded as 'different'.[21] Yet the FLNKS and all the Tahitian parties seeking independence are opposed to French nuclear testing. The FLNKS also mounted protests against the visit of the French nuclear submarine *Rubis* to Nouméa during 1985. And the nuclear concerns of states such as Belau and Federated States of Micronesia seem to specially qualify them for the zone. Treaty critics regard failure to include the Micronesian countries as a gesture to the United States which betrayed the nuclear-free aspirations of many Micronesians.

★　　　★　　　★

Walter Lini was the first Pacific leader to warn that he would not sign the treaty at the 1986 Forum meeting in Suva. Papua New Guinea and the Solomon Islands — the latter having declared a port ban on nuclear ships in 1983, the year before New Zealand — announced they would join Vanuatu in criticising the treaty's weaknesses. Both the Solomon Islands and Vanuatu go further than New Zealand; they also ban nuclear ships from territorial waters.

During July, at a three-day meeting at Goroka, in the Papua New Guinea highlands, the foreign ministers of the three Melanesian countries discussed nuclear and independence issues. They agreed to approach the Suva meeting with a common front over Kanaky, the treaty and other issues. Their meeting was followed by another one, also in Papua New Guinea, of Wingti, Lini and Deputy Prime Minister Ezekiel Alebua of the Solomons (he became prime minister by the end of the year) in which they had endorsed the earlier decisions and heralded the formation of the Melanesian Spearhead Group. At the Forum, the 'troika' reaffirmed their stand that the treaty needed to be completely reviewed to ban *all* nuclear weapons from the region in all circumstances before they would sign it.

Tonga was also hesitant, but for opposite reasons. Although Tonga signed the treaty at Rarotonga and was expected to eventually ratify it, Crown Prince Tupouto'a had remarked at Forum meetings that Tonga wanted to be free to 'host the entire might' of the United States Navy in its ports should it ever wish it as an insurance for its own security. Kiribati, Nauru and Western Samoa were among countries that thought the treaty was at least a beginning.

Melanesian countries were disappointed in New Zealand's stand which they thought to be inconsistent with its own port ban. 'It is hard to understand Lange; to us he is rather hypocritical,' said a senior Vanuatu government official. 'We wonder just what really is behind his nuclear-free rhetoric. Vanuatu is deeply committed to its role as a nuclear-free country. Our country would never sell out on our principles like New Zealand has over the treaty.'

New Zealand came in for bitter criticism from the Fiji Labour Party too. Attacking the treaty as a 'useless document' for preventing nuclear activities in the region, party leader Dr Timoci Bavadra described the protocol's escape clause as a farce.[22] He also rebuked Lange for commenting that France was not disliked in the South Pacific.

'Actually there is *hatred* of France because its policies are bent on genocide of the South Pacific people,' Bavadra said. 'I'm surprised that Lange can say this only a year after the *Rainbow Warrior* was sunk by French agents. We have no intention of compromising our nuclear-free stand. But it weakens our position if New Zealand becomes two-faced.'[23]

Bavadra added that such comments coming from a person of Lange's status would do little to comfort Pacific people who had been looking to the Forum with some hope. 'Apparently, decisions made in the Forum are clearly individual decisions of leaders of the countries and not that of the people.'

The treaty was overshadowed at the Suva Forum by a decision to ask the United Nations Decolonisation Committee to add New Caledonia to the list of colonies kept under scrutiny as candidates for independence. After five years of lobbying by the FLNKS to take such a step, the Forum finally lost patience with France. It declared grave disappointment about the 'significant backward step' in New Caledonia since the conservative government of Prime Minister Jacques Chirac had won power in March 1986. Both the Kanaks and the Forum saw the situation as leading to an inevitable resurgence of political violence.

Forum support for Kanaky was a triumph for Walter Lini who had been a lone voice championing the Kanak cause. Unlike the mostly conservative Polynesian leaders, Walter Lini has a clear grasp of the connection between nuclear testing and colonialism in the Pacific: both 'are part of the same evil', he says. 'To eradicate this evil from our region I believe that we have to deal with it from its root, which is colonialism itself. Unless French Polynesia becomes independent France will continue to use it to test its nuclear bombs . . . The same is true of the Marshall Islands.'[24]

Only one country argued against taking New Caledonia to the United Nations: the Cook Islands. Ironically, though, France bitterly criticised the Cook Islands as well as the Forum for finally petitioning the United Nations. 'It was unfair,' complained Cook Islands Foreign Minister Norman George. He blamed the French Pacific Office in Papeete, headed by State Secretary Flosse, for the criticism. 'They've been off-beam for a long time,' George said. 'If whatever moves they make don't succeed, they don't ask for the facts, they just make [them] up. They know what we faced: it was one against 13.'[25] Flosse was particularly bitter because it was the second year in a row he had been rejected while trying to gain observer status for Tahiti at the Forum.

The maverick Walter Lini called a press conference to proclaim that the Forum should now back Tahitian independence. As well, he called for other Forum nations to join Vanuatu in the Non-aligned Movement; to support independence in East Timor and Wallis and Futuna; and to recognise revolutionary groups such as the Palestine Liberation Organisation (PLO) and the South-West Africa People's Organisation (SWAPO). Lange reacted sharply, saying if the Vanuatu leader succeeded in turning the Forum into a mini-United Nations, then New Zealand, at least, would withdraw.

Most Polynesian nations were unimpressed. 'I'd rather liberate the poor people [of the Pacific],' snapped George. But Lini's views were echoed by the Forum's secretariat which warned in a report that the organisation must take a firmer stand on issues to strengthen its solidarity. If it failed to take the initiative, the report argued, the region would have to accept that in the twenty-first century it would have no more real control over its destiny than it had in the nineteenth. The secretariat reminded everyone that small is not necessarily powerless and that Lini was arguing for the region to stand tall in a new era for the Pacific.[26]

★　　★　　★

The flaws in the Rarotonga Treaty have given the island states some hard lessons. In spite of its symbolism and the nuclear-free consensus portrayed to the rest of the world, the tiny nations have little hope of curbing the expansion of American and French nuclear colonialism. The ambivalent role of Australia — and even New Zealand which wanted to avoid any further confrontation with the United States over its own anti-nuclear legislation — has been an important factor in compromising the treaty. It is not surprising that countries such as Vanuatu should look to the Non-

Aligned Movement and other international forums to seek broad-based Third World support. As *Vanuaaku Pati* secretary-general Barak Sope put it:

> In the past the colonialists wanted our labour, so they kidnapped us. Then they wanted our land, so they stole it from us for their plantations. Now they want our sea for the dumping of nuclear waste, testing of nuclear missiles and passage of submarines. The Trident submarine may be a far cry from a blackbirding vessel, but to us they are both ships from the same fleet. That is why Vanuatu is opposing nuclear colonialism in the Pacific.[27]

Three examples of 'nuclear terrorism' in particular have shown the impotence of the Pacific nations when the chips are down: the subversion of Belau's nuclear-free constitution, the assassination of the country's President, and the sabotage of the *Rainbow Warrior* at Auckland.

9
Belau: Trust Betrayed

United States resistance to nationalist sentiments in Micronesia has been most strikingly reflected by Washington's pressure on Belau to revoke its unique anti-nuclear constitution. The people of Belau have faced ten referenda in a bizarre political struggle over the constitution and a Compact of Free Association with the United States which has been drafted to end the island republic's trusteeship status. That constitution is in conflict with the United States military policy of 'strategic denial' and the issue has dominated negotiations between Micronesia and the United States, which sees Belau's nuclear-free sovereignty as a serious threat to its own strategic interests. In 1985 President Remeliik, the 'father' of the constitution, became the first Pacific Islands leader to be assassinated. Three years later his successor, President Salii, apparently committed suicide. Questions remain over both deaths.

Dressed in a T-shirt and shorts, President Haruo Remeliik of Belau* drove home after spending a relaxed day fishing off the spectacular Rock Islands and visiting a lover. He pulled into the driveway of his hillside home in Topside, near the capital, Koror, just after midnight on 30 June 1985. Parking near a slope covered with tangled tapioca and taro plants, the 51-year-old President climbed out of his car.

His wife and several of his children were asleep. Remeliik switched off the engine and climbed out of the car. Before he could walk to the house, he was forced into the tropical undergrowth by assassins. The first .30 calibre rifle shot him in the left thigh. He tumbled down a steep slope as three more rounds were pumped into his neck, behind his left ear and into his forehead. The assassins then vanished into the night.[1]

The gangland-style murder of the Belauan President was the first

---

Palau is the form preferred by the United States; *Belau* is used by the indigenous people. The country officially became the republic of Belau on 1 January 1981.

assassination of any head of a Pacific islands government. Coming just ten days before the bombing of the *Rainbow Warrior* by French secret service agents in New Zealand, Remeliik's murder traumatised the Micronesian state which had been under legal and political pressure from the United States to abandon its nuclear-free constitution. Since then allegations of secret American involvement in his assassination have persisted although they have always been strongly denied in Washington.

Still the controversy and accusations surrounding the killing remain unresolved. Three men convicted of Remeliik's murder won a Supreme Court appeal on 14 July 1987 and were set free. Several civil rights lawyers and Belauan public officials claimed the accused had been framed. The court acquitted the men on all charges and released them from house arrest.

What actually happened that night? Belauan lawyer and anti-nuclear campaigner Roman Bedor is among many who suspect the Central Intelligence Agency of playing a part in Remeliik's death in an attempt to subvert the constitution. 'The facts surrounding his murder remain suspicious,' he said. 'There is a widespread feeling in Belau that it was a professional job done by an outsider.'

'I'm concerned about two questions,' said American lawyer David Richenthal. 'Who really killed the President? And who is responsible for framing these young men?'[2] The evidence in this case, according to Richenthal, who represented the American Civil Liberties Union, was so 'unconvincing and suspect that it would not have survived scrutiny by a grand jury in any American jurisdiction, much less support a conviction.' He also alleged the death was part of a conspiracy which conveniently fitted United States interests at a time when the future of American bases in the Philippines seemed uncertain.

Assassination aftermath

Murder conspiracies would seem remote from the 15,000 people of Belau, whose republic spreads across a western Pacific archipelago of more than 200 tiny but lush islands, east of Mindanao in the Philippines and south of Guam. Balmy breezes warm the beaches, the turquoise waters teem with fish and crab. Belauan women dance a slow, rhythmic *ngloik* for foreign tourists.

Belau is among the smallest nations of the world. In the Pacific it compares with the Cook Islands and its population would be absorbed among many provincial towns in Papua New Guinea. The main island of Babeldaob was once the headquarters of Japan's colonial administration in Micronesia and the capital of Koror was a reasonably affluent 'Japanese' town. In 1944, however, when American troops captured the island the Japanese settlers were expelled and Koror was razed.

Governed as part of the United States-administered Trust Territory of the Pacific Islands set up after the Second World War, Belau became a backwater for colonial officials in Micronesia. With the country approaching 'decolonisation' like the rest of Micronesia, negotiations began in the 1970s for a Compact of Free Association with the United States which would determine its future status. Probably the greatest disadvantage for the islanders is that Belau lies a mere 800 kilometres to the east of the Philippines, where the two biggest American military bases outside United States territory — Subic Bay Naval Base and Clark Air Base — are possibly in jeopardy beyond their 1991 agreement expiration date. So the Pentagon has developed a contingency plan which has been dubbed the 'fallback arc'. Beginning in Saipan, the arc travels south through Tinian, then to Guam, and ends in Belau.

United States strategic interests in the islands were rebuffed in 1979 when the constitution of Belau was drafted and ratified by 92 percent of its people. Creating the world's first nuclear-free country, the constitution was an 'inspiration and hope from nuclear holocaust'.[3] The nuclear-free clause in the constitution (which could be overturned only by a 75 percent majority in a future referendum) directly conflicted, however, with the United States strategic policy of neither confirming nor denying the existence of nuclear weapons on its warships or aircraft. In an attempt to entice Belau into changing its constitution, the Belauan version of the compact, initialled by Belauan and United States officials in August 1982, promised to grant the republic more than $US430 million in aid and a form of self-government in exchange for granting the Pentagon an option to use about one-third of the island area for military bases, jungle warfare training and the transit of nuclear warships.

So far such attempts have been unsuccessful and the Belauans have been forced to vote ten times on the compact or the nuclear-free clause in the constitution. Remeliik, the 'father' of the constitution, held three unsuccessful referenda over the compact during his presidency but each time he failed to deliver the votes necessary to waive the constitutional ban on nuclear weapons.

Some alleged that Tokyo-based crime and heroin syndicates — believed to have major interests in multimillion-dollar development and resort projects in Belau — were behind the assassination of Remeliik. Belauan parliamentarians and tribal chiefs, however, believed the President was killed because he opposed United States bases and nuclear weapons in Belau.[4] Although he had strongly supported the compact, probably for economic reasons, he had hardened his pro-constitution stand. The *Olbiil Era Kelulau* (Belau National Congress) sent a letter to the United States Interior Department claiming there was a 'CIA-funded' plot to force 'Belau into accepting the compact . . . rather than face international embarrassment over financial default'.[5] Remeliik was reportedly about to 'come clean' on the scandal linked to the compact when he was shot.[6]

'No matter what kind of pressure [Washington] puts on us,' declared House of Delegates Speaker Santos Olikong after the murder, 'whether it's forcing us into economic bankruptcy or killing our President, we will not compromise on our independence or the nuclear issue.'[7]

Belauan police investigated the murder with the help of the Federal Bureau of Investigation. According to Auckland University legal researcher Pheroze Jagose, FBI agents made a mysterious visit to Belau at the time of the shooting. Jagose also cited a contingency plan by United States business and military interests to 'assassinate the President and install . . . a puppet regime under martial law':

> [Belauan sources assert] that two FBI investigators, both frequent visitors to Micronesia as part of police training programmes, and friends and acquaintances of several Belauans, flew into Belau only three hours before the assassination and left again early the next morning for Majuro in the Marshall Islands without contacting or seeing any of those friends or acquaintances.[8]

Three weeks after the shooting, four suspects were arrested and accused of the murder. Two of the men, Melwert Tmetuchl and Leslie Tewid, were the son and nephew, respectively, of Governor Tmetuchl (pronounced *meh-tool*). A central figure in opposing and defeating the pro-nuclear compact, the governor had run second to Remeliik in the presidential elections of 1980 and 1984. He was also a leading candidate for a special presidential election planned for 28 August 1985 to choose Remeliik's successor when his relatives were charged.

Governor Tmetuchl pulled out of the ballot, leaving the contest between Belau's roving ambassador, Lazarus Salii, and Vice-President Alfonso Oiterong. Athough Salii and Oiterong were political colleagues of Remeliik they were both regarded as stronger supporters of United States interests in Belau and cooler on the nuclear-free constitution. Salii was elected President.

During the murder investigation no gun was ever recovered, no fingerprints or other physical evidence discovered, no eyewitnesses found, and no strong motive uncovered. Yet the suspects — Tmetuchl, Tewid, Anghenio Sabino and Francisco Gibbons — were charged with conspiracy to commit assassination and murder. The only significant evidence was the testimony of 29-year-old Mistyca Maidesil, a former girlfriend of Tmetuchl and Tewid. But she was a troubled young woman, a self-confessed liar and heroin user. She gave several conflicting stories and three times failed lie-detector tests. She first told the police shortly after the assassination she believed another person — a convict from Guam who was being deported home by Remeliik — had shot the President.

At the trial, Maidesil testified that she had overheard Melwert Tmetuchl, Tewid and Sabino agree that Remeliik should be killed. 'This is a bad President,' she quoted Tmetuchl as saying. 'We'll kill him!'

Damage in the Belau capital of Koror caused by pro-compact militants in 1987.

Ed Rampell

But it was never clear from her evidence why they might have wanted to murder Remeliik. The prosecutors, however, suggested the assassination might have been linked to Melwert Tmetuchl's wish to promote the presidential chances of his father. 'I thought my father was better,' Tmetuchl admitted. He insisted, however, this would not have led him to murder.[9]

The charges were dismissed through lack of evidence. For a further four months the FBI and local police continued to investigate the killing. No significant new leads were found. Maidesil, however, revived her story that the four suspects had killed Remeliik. In spite of twice more failing lie-detector tests, her testimony led to the murder charges being reinstated against Tmetuchl, Tewid and Sabino on 6 December. Curiously, there was no charge against Gibbons, the purported triggerman, who was by now in Guam. (Lack of evidence the prosecutor said.)

Only two prosecution witnesses gave evidence at the trial, which began on 24 February 1986 and lasted two weeks. Mistyca Maidesil testified to the same story she had previously given the FBI, although she admitted not having seen any guns. Under cross-examination, she was asked if she had twice renounced her entire story to the FBI and she falsely replied she had not.

The other witness, Namiko Ngiraikelau, had also given contradictory statements to the police. In court she claimed she had seen two of the defendants about a kilometre from the murder spot, near a pickup truck. But a defence witness, Oliver Delbert, who was with Ngiraikelau at the time of her 'sighting', testified there was one man — not one of the defendants — and there was no pickup truck nearby. He also alleged he had been tortured by the police in an attempt to force him to corroborate Ngiraikelau's testimony.

In spite of the flimsy case, the three men were sentenced to between 25 years and 35 years in jail. However, they were eventually released to house arrest while the appeal was filed.

Later, in an eight-page appeal judgement, the Belau Supreme Court referred to the 'inherently incredible' witnesses in the case. 'Maidesil frequently used marijuana and heroin during the weeks prior to the murder,' it said. 'Testimony by a drug user, particularly where uncorroborated, should be weighed with caution.' The trial court was ordered to acquit the men.[10]

The Ipseco power plant scandal

Although the prosecution failed to resolve many questions about President Remeliik's assassination, one in particular stood out: why the rush to bring in a judgement in spite of the lack of evidence? No certain conclusions have yet emerged, but according to American lawyer David Richenthal 'some answers may yet be discovered by examining the motives and transactions of those who benefited most from the assassination'. And that inquiry led to a power station scandal which was linked to the compact-constitution conflict.

In a remote part of Belau is a 16-megawatt diesel power plant built by the since-liquidated British company International Power Systems Inc (Ipseco). Belau agreed to pay, through agreements authorised by President Remeliik in 1982 and 1983, US$32 million for the plant. But the burden of the debt was, from the beginning, far in excess of the nation's financial resources — at least double the country's annual budget. And its power capacity was several times larger than the needs of the population. Belau defaulted on its first payment to British banks one month before Remeliik was shot.

The ill-conceived project was condoned by senior American officials at the same time that the inspector-general of the United States Interior Department warned that the plant was illegal and likely to bankrupt Belau. Other critics of the scheme claimed the price of the plant would have been halved by normal competitive bidding requirements, but special legislation exempted Ipseco from all Belau laws.

Was the Belau government lured into the deal by the American administration to force it into accepting the compact to avoid bankruptcy? Richenthal suggested as much in a controversial briefing paper on the Remeliik case. 'For possibly related reasons,' he said, 'Belau's first president was assassinated, his chief political rival was effectively neutralised, the islands' dependency on the United States has grown and [American] military interests have been advanced.'[11]

Another lawyer, Martin Wolff, then legislative adviser to the Belauan Senate, claimed he was told hours after the murder that the President had been shot to prevent him exposing details of the affair in a television address and repudiating the loan. Wolff's car was firebombed after he made the allegation and he was forced to move to Hawaii to live.[12]

'Every aspect of the story of this power plant suggests the likelihood of widespread corruption,' said Richenthal. He alleged that Carlos Salii, then Speaker of the House of Delegates, was being paid a $1.5 million retainer over ten years to act as Ipseco's attorney. He also claimed both Carlos Salii and his brother, President Lazarus Salii, were deeply involved in promoting the project. The Belauan chief justice began investigating the allegations late in 1986 and the inquiry continued for several years.

Shortly after the deal was signed in June 1984, one of Belau's two traditional paramount chiefs, *Ibedul* Yutaka Gibbons, filed a lawsuit against Remeliik alleging the contract was illegal and procured by bribery. The high chief's lawyer, Patrick Smith, said the plant would have cost no more than $15 million if competitive bidding had been enforced. Soon after the lawsuit was filed the lawyer's house was firebombed and he left the island; the case was abandoned.[13]

Ironically, the *San Jose Mercury News* revealed late in 1987 that Gibbons had received a $100,000 'political contribution' from Ipseco. The high chief said he used it for political campaigns and Ipseco executives were keen for him to run for the presidency. The same report cited an Ipseco liquidator's report showing President Salii had received $100,000 which had been deposited in a Bank of America account in Hong Kong, and Carlos Salii had been paid $250,000, deposited in a Hong Kong and Shanghai Banking Corporation account.[14]

American officials reject the power plant scenario. Howard Hills, legal adviser in the United States Office for Micronesian Status Negotiations, said no evidence linked the assassination with the Ipseco affair and dismissed the allegations as an attempt to 'politicise' the Remeliik case.[15] But the *Marshall Islands Journal* stressed the under-used power plant was sited next to land conditionally designated for United States military purposes. The *Journal* suggested the United States could be using the surrogate pressure of international capital to get what it had failed to gain by the democratic process of a referendum.

Constitution under siege

Belau has experienced two 'mini revolutions' and been forced by American pressure to undergo ten referenda over its nuclear-free constitution. 'For Belau, a special brand of "democracy" is obviously applied by the United States — repeat a vote until you get the desired result,' says anti-nuclear lawyer Roman Bedor. 'That's what is happening with the vote on the compact, as it happened before with the nuclear-free constitution.'[16]

The constitution must be seen in the context of a history of Belauan actions to prevent outside control of their islands. When United States military proposals for the use of a third of the Belauan Islands were first announced in 1972, traditional and elected leaders immediately opposed the plans. During the mid-1970s, the Belauan people mustered local and international support to halt a huge oil port and industrial centre planned for the territory. Port Pacific, a crude oil transshipment port with related petro-chemical processing possibilities, was backed by the United States military, and supported by Japanese industrialists and the Shah of Iran's government. Opposition to the proposal was led by *Ibedul* Gibbons, the nationalist *Tia Belau* (This Is Our Nation) coalition, village groups and foreign environmental movements.

In an attempt to allay Belauan fears, United States officials said there were no current military plans for Belau: it only wanted 'options' to use the land for jungle warfare training, weapons storage and transit and overflight of nuclear vessels and aircraft.[17] Many of the islanders, however, believe the United States military will bring another war to Belau.

'The Americans look to us as if we're a bunch of animals,' said a village elder on the main island of Babeldaob, where two-thirds of the land is tagged for jungle warfare training. 'We don't want their soldiers to come here; they will take away the land from us — and this is our soul and our life.'[18]

In 1979 Remeliik chaired Belau's constitutional convention, which produced a document regarded by some to be as radical as the United States constitution had been two centuries earlier. The Belauan constitution was the first to declare a nation a nuclear-free zone. Any change to the ban on storage, testing and disposal of nuclear material within its territory was required to have the approval of 75 percent of votes cast in a referendum. Two of the constitution's clauses provide the crucial nuclear bans. Article XIII, Section 6, says:

> Harmful substances such as nuclear, chemical, gas or biological weapons intended for use in warfare, nuclear power plants, and waste materials therefrom shall not be used, tested, or stored, or disposed of within the territorial jurisdiction of Belau without the express approval of not less than three-fourths of the votes cast in a referendum submitted on this specific question.[19]

On 9 July 1979 the constitution was approved by 92 percent of votes cast in a referendum. The Trust Territory High Commissioner, however, refused to certify the result. A revised draft constitution complying with United States objections was defeated on 23 October 1979 by 70 percent of the voters. Later, a third ballot, on the original constitution, gained 78 percent of votes. Since then the United States State Department has repeatedly declared that the Belau constitution is 'incompatible' with the compact.

According to an American author and former American aerospace engineer, Robert Aldridge, who has worked for 27 years designing and researching nuclear weapons, the republic is earmarked as a forward base for Trident submarines. 'For almost a decade I have warned that Malakal harbour . . . is coveted by the US Navy,' he said. 'Carefully worded disclaimers by those in the know, and categoric denials by the less-informed, have rebutted my prognosis.'[20]

The overriding justification for Trident missiles has been their ability to reach targets from a greater distance than other missiles, which gives their best submarines a corresponding wider range, 'It is certain that the planned fleet of ten submarines to be home-ported at Bangor, Washington, aren't going to be concentrated in the north-east Pacific,' Aldridge says. 'When they do patrol the far reaches of the [Pacific], it does not make sense to return to home port every 70 days just to change crews and replenish supplies.'

Aldridge points out that Belau is in line with the deep water Sundra and Lombok Straits of Indonesia, through which Tridents could pass submerged into the Indian Ocean.[21] The Straits of Malacca, although wider, are too shallow for submerged Trident submarines. However, some military researchers, including Owen Wilkes, say Aldridge has little evidence to support his forward base argument.

Alienation of land for proposed bases and for airport runway extensions is a sensitive topic. There is no sale and exchange of real estate in Belau. Neither is a tax, or rent, allowed on property. The land belongs to the clans which trace their ancestry back as far as 3000 years. The land, ocean and water are sacred to the islanders.

★　　　★　　　★

On 8 September 1981 Belau was rocked by its first 'mini-revolution', as Belauans called it. Anti-nuclear campaigners claimed this was an orchestrated attempt to force the imposition of martial law and undermine the nation's constitution. On the day before, a Labour Day holiday, about 300 government workers had met in Koror and voted to stage a strike, demanding a 100 percent wage increase. An all-night party followed the meeting.

Before dawn the Belauan flag in front of President Remeliik's office was torn down and burned — curiously, a nearby Stars and Stripes was left untouched. An eyewitness described dynamite being passed out. At 7.07 a.m. a bomb blew out the front door of the president's office building and five minutes later another bomb blasted open the back door. The debris from the explosions was carried into the offices and the building set ablaze. An hour later, the main office of the local radio station was also bombed — allegedly by a policeman.[22]

The police, apparently co-operating with the strikers, prevented government employees from going to work and encouraged others to take part in the strike. Fifty prisoners were released although 14 refused to leave jail. Some of the prisoners drove around Koror shouting, 'There is no law!' One was shot dead for trying to loot a store.

After the bombings, and reportedly at the urging of Governor Tmetuchl, the protesting strikers demanded to see President Remeliik. 'We want his head,' shouted some demonstrators and several officials feared for the President's life. But Remeliik walked calmly through the crowd and made a short, moving speech. He rejected pressure to call in the United States military and declared nobody would be prosecuted, saying: 'Let's forget this and work for the betterment of our new nation.' Many protestors began cheering.

A government official investigating the strike and the bombings said there seemed to be an unusually high number of Americans in Belau at the time. He did not think they were all 'tourists' because they did not follow the usual tourist pattern of going to bars, visiting the stunningly beautiful Rock Islands and other tourist activities. However, he could not link this with the political disturbances.

Just six months earlier, on 12 November 1980, there had been the '*Galaxy* affair'. A 30-metre, Panama-registered ship called the *Galaxy 10* had arrived in Belau just a week after the presidential election. The crew of six were American, except for an Indonesian woman cook. They claimed the ship was a supply vessel for a salvage operation near Borneo.[23] The crew were friendly, and bought supplies and equipment, including a six-metre fibreglass boat and an outboard motor.

Many Belauans were invited on board for parties and trips to the reef. They later described the ship as being well equipped with about $500,000 worth of sophisticated electronics equipment. It had a computerised navigation system, a dual radar unit, three radios, a radio scrambler to prevent eavesdroppers, and a computerised weather map information system. The ship left two weeks later.

Three months later, on 16 February 1981, the *Galaxy 10* returned. Tipped off by local fishermen who suspected the ship of drug-running, police raided the ship while the crew slept. Although no drugs were found, the police seized 80 cases of M16 rifles, 47 cases of ammunition, hand grenades and $1 million in cash. One witness also saw a variety of rifles, sawn-off shotguns and pistols being taken ashore.

Later that day, Coast Guard, FBI and Micronesia Bureau of Investigation agents flew to Belau, impounded the *Galaxy* and flew out with the arrested crew. The ship vanished overnight without obtaining port clearance.[24]

'Since the crew had already been arrested, there was no need for US officials to fly in on a special plane the same day,' noted Robert Aldridge and Ched Myers in a report on the affair, 'and even less reason for them to remove the ship and crew before the next morning and without the usual clearances — unless they wanted to get them out fast before local people could learn more.'[25] The district attorney refused to release results of the investigation.

The *Galaxy* was first taken to Guam where newspaper reporters were told it had been involved in smuggling marijuana from South America to the US West Coast. No mention was made of the cargo of munitions and money. Later, the *Galaxy* was taken to Hawaii and sold to the US Navy for $50,000; naval authorities handed it over to the University of Hawaii as a research vessel.

Many Belauans believe that had the *Galaxy* gun-running episode succeeded, the 'mini-revolution' could have ended more violently. But others point out there was no evidence that arms were being smuggled into Belau; instead the behaviour of the crew, the references to Borneo and the three-month interval between the visits suggest the crew were more likely to be gun-running to Moluccan guerrillas.

On 22 September, two weeks after the bombing of the Belau President's offices, 28-year-old Baltazar Kitalong was murdered. He was shot with a handgun held to his head as he opened his car door after leaving a nightclub party for a visiting United States admiral. Kitalong was a leading member of a group called *Kltalreng* (pronounced 'tall ring'), which means solidarity, unity and brother-sisterhood. It is a non-violent, apolitical movement which has campaigned strongly against the proposed military bases in Belau.

★   ★   ★

Belauans were the first people of the trust territory to vote on the Compact of Free Association. In a split ballot on 10 February 1983 voters were asked whether they approved of Section 314 which allowed the United States to store nuclear weapons in Belau and the presence of nuclear-powered ships or materials. The 53 percent 'yes' vote fell far short of the 75 percent approval required by the constitution. The other part of the ballot asked voters to accept the compact overall and 62 percent of the poll supported it. Since Section 314 failed to gain the requisite approval, the Senate two weeks later passed Resolution 87 which declared the citizens of Belau had rejected the compact and called on the President to renegotiate the political status of the islands.

Ibedul Gibbons and the traditional Council of Chiefs labelled the compact as 'dead'. But the US State Department declared the nuclear issue merely an 'internal referendum question'. It said: 'The Belau authorities must now devise an acceptable method of reconciling their constitutional provisions to comply with the mandate of the Belauan electorate for free association with the United States.'

An international law specialist, New Zealander Dr Roger Clark, of Rutgers University, disagreed. 'I believe this to be a serious distortion of the results of the vote,' he said, adding that 'the United States, having acquiesced in, or perhaps even insisted upon, the way in which the issue was presented to the voters, is surely bound by the results.' He accused the United States of continuing to subvert the constitution's anti-nuclear provisions.[26]

Although United States officials frequently insisted they took no part in the referendum process, the United States was actually involved in all stages. US Ambassador Fred Zeder ordered the Belau government to change the referendum wording — which was later declared misleading and illegal by the Belau Supreme Court just ten days before the vote. More than $440,000 was appropriated for a 'voter education' programme which degenerated into a pro-compact campaign. For example, 'people's fact sheets' in Belauan and English listed all the advantages of the compact without describing its drawbacks. The money spent can be compared with the $400,000 spent the same year by the electoral commission in El Salvador of which $240,000 was a direct allocation from the United States. El Salvador has a population of five million; Belau has 15,000. Under Belauan law, spending on the referendum was supposed to be restricted to $250,000.

Four more times over the next four years Belauans were forced to vote on whether or not to accept the compact. Each time, they also voted on whether they wanted to suspend the nuclear-free clauses in the constitution. Millions of dollars were spent on the ballots in United States efforts to entice, persuade and confuse Belau's voters into suspending the clauses. The one-sided 'education' programmes funded by Washington continued.

In the 1984 referendum, the only one not observed by a United Nations team, Ambassador Zeder actively campaigned for the passage of the compact and repeal of the nuclear ban. Recorded radio and television messages from President Reagan were broadcast. In each ballot the compact was approved by rising majorities, but never with the 75 percent required to repeal the nuclear sovereignty clause. Each time they were sent to the polls again.

After the assassination of Remeliik, President Salii, who as ambassador had been the architect of Belau's negotiations with Washington over the compact, tried to force the measure through. But even his high-powered support failed to gain the 75 percent vote needed to overturn the anti-nuclear clause.

In fact, by the eighth referendum, on 30 June 1987, compact support had dropped to 67 percent. Within a week a second 'mini-revolution' broke out. The Belau government suspended 900 of its 1300 workers without pay, claiming the nation was in a financial crisis because funds expected to become available under the approved compact were blocked. Pro-compact protesters camped for a week outside the House of Delegates, blaming the legislature for the crisis. House spokesman Belheim Sakuma defended democracy in a radio speech, defying threats. His house was firebombed; two other firebomb attempts were also made. Faced with growing tension and threats of violence against anti-nuclear supporters, the House of Delegates on 19 July approved a further referendum on a proposed amendment to the constitution which would allow the transit of nuclear weapons.

'We had no choice,' said Speaker Olikong, 'our homes and families are in danger.' *Ibedul* Gibbons, denouncing the 'climate of fear', said, 'This makes a joke of the democratic ideals the United States has taught us to believe in.'[27] Both leaders accused President Salii, who favours suspension of the nuclear-free clauses, of being responsible for the crisis. In an address to the US Congress Interior Affairs Committee, Olikong declared:

> Our fundamental freedoms such as freedom of expression, freedom of speech and freedom to dissent are under blistering attack . . . Rather than allowing the political process to naturally forge an accommodation between [the opposed groups over the nuclear-free clauses], the Belauan people are being force-fed only one point of view. It is the combination of these two events — fiscal responsibility on the one hand, and anti-democratic strong-arm tactics — that brings us to this point of near catastrophe . . .
>
> The financial crisis has been brought about by the mismanagement and corruption of President Lazarus Salii . . . Perhaps as part of his effort to ensure

compact approval, he squandered and misused government funds, thus fulfilling his own prophecy . . . Civil unrest and the threat of violence are the result . . . Forcing another vote on the compact now threatens the fabric of the relationship between Belau and the United States. Does the United States want another Philippines? Another South Korea? Another Fiji?[28]

President Salii called a snap referendum on 4 August 1987 to try to amend the constitution. With the lowest voter turnout to date, Salii gained 71 percent approval for overturning the nuclear-free clause. According to the constitution, however, an amendment can only be adopted during a general election — and one is not scheduled until November 1988. In the tenth referendum, on 21 August 1987 under the terms of the disputed constitutional change, 73 percent of voters approved the compact. But the validity of the vote remained in doubt because of legal challenges.

When, under pressure and threats of violence, *Ibedul* Gibbons dropped a lawsuit challenging the ballot, 50 Belauan women elders, led by his sister Gloria Gibbons and Gabriela Ngirmang, arrived at the courthouse in busloads to refile the case. 'We must protect our constitution and our land,' said Ngirmang. 'It is the only place on earth we can express our right to be Belauan.'

'We are under siege,' said Roman Bedor, legal adviser for the women elders. Bedor had contributed to the drafting of the original nuclear-free constitution and was one of its staunchest defenders. 'The Americans will not rest until they have us in their military pocket,' he added. Shortly afterwards, Bedor and his sister, Bernie Keldermans, received several death threats.

On 7 September 1987, the evening before the lawsuit was due to be heard, gunmen drove up to Bedor's Pacific Centre office under cover of the government-imposed blackout. Seeing somebody in the office, they opened fire, fatally wounding Bins Bedor, Roman's elderly father who was in his 70s. Clan leader Bedor had called at the office to pick up a torch and check that the building was safe; he died next morning.

Although the killers' car was identified, nobody was arrested or charged. 'It's like a military coup,' said Roman Bedor, who believes he was the real target. 'My life is in danger. There is no law and order. Anybody could be killed.'

In tears, the women elders filed papers in the Supreme Court to drop their lawsuit. Two of the litigants also cited acts of 'terrorism' against them. But although the legal obstacles against the enactment of the Compact of Free Association had apparently been brushed aside, the US Congress did not agree. Shaken by the events, chairman Ron de Lugo of the interior subcommittee pledged to block ratification of the compact until the constitutional issue was clearly resolved.

Nuclear stalemate

Six months later, on 31 March 1988, the elders again filed their legal challenge against President Salii. Within three weeks the court ruled in their favour: the constitution's nuclear-free clause was reinstated and the compact was again at a stalemate.

'The nuclear control provisions [of the constitution] read together provide the sole mode for approving compacts or any other arrangements dealing with matters nuclear,' stressed Professor Clark in a legal opinion for the US Senate. 'No other approval procedure, whether at a general election or otherwise, will do — only a 75 percent majority meets the constitutional mandate . . . This, I believe, is what the drafters and the voters who ratified the constitution had in mind.'[29]

On 20 August President Salii was found shot dead in his home. Although a police spokesman at first said an unknown gunman had fired the shot, the Belau government later indicated the shooting had been suicide. Salii was alone inside the house at the time of the shooting, while his wife, a driver and a maid ate lunch outside. When his wife went inside the home she found the President slumped in his chair with a gunshot wound to the head and a .357 Magnum pistol nearby. Salii was under growing pressure: the compact stalemate frustrated him, he faced further investigation over corruption allegations and the US Federal Court had ruled his government must repay US$44 million to the consortium of international banks which guaranteed the Ipseco power plant.[30]

According to an official government report the following month which was based on FBI ballistics tests, an autopsy and other testimony, Salii's death was 'self-inflicted'. There remain several intriguing parallels between the Remeliik and Salii deaths: both supported the compact, both died the day before making a national address, and a policy academy was in session in Koror with visiting FBI instructors when each was shot. (The same Americans reportedly headed the FBI both times.)[31]

Wealthy businessman Ngiratkel Etpison, aged 63, governor of Ngatpang state and a strong supporter of the compact, survived allegations of voting irregularities to win the presidency in November 1988. He defeated his closest rival, Governor Tmetuchl, by 31 votes and gained a mere 27 percent of the total ballot in an election contest between seven candidates.

The people of Belau have now voted ten times on the issue of their nuclear-free constitution: three times in 1979 and 1980, when the United States was opposed to it as a basis for self-government; and then again in 1983, 1984, twice in 1986 and three times in 1987 over the Compact of Free Association. Four times the Supreme Court of Belau has ruled that the nuclear compact is in violation of the constitution unless it gets 75 percent of the vote. President Remeliik, the leader who shepherded the constitution into law, has been assassinated; his successor, Lazarus Salii, has committed suicide — and both have been replaced as head of government by another man determined to throw out the nuclear safeguard.

Yet, in remarkable contempt of democracy, the United States has used the financial carrot of the compact to push the Belauans into voting again and again until they finally say *yes* to nuclear access to their islands.

10

Barbouzes and Bombs

*Like the United States, France was also undermining the opponents
of its nuclear interests in the Pacific. In July 1985, it introduced
state terrorism into the region for the first time when its secret
agents sabotaged the protest ship* Rainbow Warrior *in a bizarre
operation in a New Zealand port. As the South Pacific became
more vulnerable, Western intelligence sources also created illusory
Libyan and Soviet threats.*

The night was chilly as the Greenpeace flagship *Rainbow Warrior* lay moored
at Auckland's Marsden Wharf on Wednesday, 10 July 1985. It had arrived
in New Zealand from Vanuatu three days earlier — a week after President
Remeliik had been assassinated in Belau. Greenpeace campaigners were
preparing the former North Sea trawler for the environmental group's
biggest-ever protest voyage to Moruroa Atoll, one which they hoped would
embarrass France over nuclear testing even more than the many brave
forays of the *Vega*. On board, supporters celebrated the 29th birthday of
Steve Sawyer, the American co-ordinator of the Pacific Peace Voyage.

Unknown to the Greenpeace activists, two frogmen, French secret agents
Jacques Camurier and Alain Tonel, had set off in an inflatable dinghy
across the two-kilometre stretch of the misty harbour from Mechanics Bay.
It was ironic that the saboteurs were using a French-made Zodiac — the
craft used by marine commandos to chase the *Vega* in 1973 (when they
bludgeoned David McTaggart), and later adopted by the Greenpeace
'commandos of conservation' in dramatic campaigns against nuclear waste
dumpers and whalers.

Camurier and Tonel crouched low into the icy breeze as they motored
slowly across the harbour. It was bitterly cold, even in their waterproof
jackets and wetsuits. Stowed on board the grey-and-black craft were two
explosive packs wrapped in plastic, a clamp, rope, and the rest of their
scuba gear — including two rebreather oxygen tanks, which did not release
telltale bubbles underwater.

It was about 8.30 p.m. when they were close enough to switch off the little four-horsepower Yamaha motor and paddle towards the *Rainbow Warrior's* berth. They moored the Zodiac to a sheltered wharf pile. So far, so good. It was just as they had rehearsed this phase of the so-called Operation Satanic at their Aspretto base in Corsica.*

Donning their flippers, oxygen tanks and masks, Camurier and Tonel slipped into the inky water. Then they reached over the side of the inflatable to grab the bombs, the heavier of which weighed 15 kilos. They both swam underwater with the bombs, clamp and rope to the stern of the *Rainbow Warrior*. Tonel attached the smaller, ten-kilo bomb to the propeller shaft; Camurier fixed the clamp on to the keel and ran out the rope to pinpoint a spot to attach the larger bomb next to the engineroom. The hull explosive would sink the ship, the propeller mine would cripple it. Both bombs were timed to explode in just over three hours, at 11.50 p.m. The explosives laid, the frogmen headed back to their hidden Zodiac. The hardest part of their mission was over.

The first blast ripped a hole the size of a garage door in the engineroom. The force of the explosion was so powerful that a freighter on the other side of Marsden Wharf was thrown five metres sideways. As the *Rainbow Warrior* rapidly sank until the keel touched the harbour floor, the shocked crew scrambled on to the wharf. But Portuguese-born photographer Fernando Pereira dashed down a narrow stairway to one of the stern cabins to rescue his expensive cameras. The second explosion probably stunned him and he drowned with his camera straps tangled around his legs.

The Rongelap evacuation

I had been on the *Rainbow Warrior* for 11 weeks, among six journalists accompanying the Greenpeace campaigners to the Marshall Islands to report on the evacuation of the stricken islanders of Rongelap Atoll. The Rongelap people had been contaminated by radioactive fallout, or *baigin* (poison) as the islanders call it, three decades earlier in the most tragic disaster of American atmospheric tests of the 1950s.

The H-bomb codenamed Bravo exploded on Bikini Atoll on 1 March 1954 was a 15-megaton giant, about 1000 times as powerful as the bomb which had devastated Hiroshima. The date, dubbed Bikini Day by anti-nuclear activists, opened a terrifying new chapter in the arms race. Hundreds

---

* The *Centre d'Instruction des Naquers de Combat* (CINC), a French Navy training centre for combat frogmen which was also used by the *Direction Générale des Services Extérieurs* (DGSE — French external secret service). The centre was shut by the French government after the sabotage scandal.

of people living downwind on the nearby atolls of Rongelap, 150 kilometres to the east, and Rongerik and Utirik, were exposed to the massive fallout. Tonnes of pulverised coral and debris were sucked up into a fireball 40 kilometres above Bikini and dumped on other islands.

On Rongelap, 64 people were contaminated, as were a further 18 Rongelapese on nearby Ailinginae where they were cutting copra and catching fish. Also hit downwind by the fallout were 23 men on board the Japanese fishing boat *Lucky Dragon*, and 28 United States Air Force technicians who were monitoring Bravo from Rongerik Atoll. Rongelap mayor John Anjain recalled the deadly 'snowstorm':

> Something began falling from the sky upon our island. It looked like ash from a fire. It fell on me, my wife and our infant son, Lekoj. It fell on the trees, and on the roofs of our houses . . . Some people put it in their mouths and tasted it . . . People walked in it, and the children played with it . . .
>
> Later on, in the early evening, it rained. The rain fell on the roofs of our houses. It washed away the ash. The water mixed with the ash which fell into our catchments. Men, women and children *drank* [it]. It didn't taste like rainwater and it was dark yellow, sometimes black. But people drank it anyway . . . [the next day] many vomited and felt weak. Later, the hair of men, women and children began to fall out. A lot of people had burns on their skin.
>
> On the third day some ships came. Americans came on our island. They explained that we were in great danger because of the ash. They said. 'If you don't leave, you will all die.'[1]

The Rongelap Islanders were evacuated to Kwajalein Atoll, 160 kilometres south-east, for 'decontamination'. They were allowed to return to Rongelap three years later without any clean-up operation being carried out on the atoll. Lekoj Anjain was barely a year old when the fallout rained on Rongelap; he died on 15 November 1972 at a National Institute of Health clinic at Bethesda, Maryland, from acute myelogenous leukemia — the first death blamed on radiation from the Bravo test.

Although the US Atomic Energy Commission described Bravo as a 'routine atomic test' in a communiqué designed to calm growing fears over the fallout, US scientists had calculated that each exposed islander had received a 'whole body external radiation dose' of 190 rads — 380 times the current *annual* limit for American citizens. Of the Marshall Islanders and American servicemen, the statement merely noted that they were 'unexpectedly exposed' to some radioactivity. 'There were no burns. All were reported well.'

Besides the burns and hair loss, worse was to come for the islanders. In the four years after Bravo, exposed women from Rongelap suffered miscarriage and stillbirth rates more than double those of unexposed women. By 1985 77 percent of the children on Rongelap who were aged under ten when exposed to the Bravo fallout had undergone surgery to remove thyroid tumours. A smaller number developed other forms of cancer. The people began to realise their contamination was not a chance happening. As I reported:

> The Rongelapese have for years accused United States Government scientists of using them as guineas pigs. They claim that their exposure to Bravo was not an accident but part of an experiment to test the effects of radiation on human beings. The US government has consistently claimed that the fallout was 'accidental' and caused by an 'unprecedented shift in winds'. However, in 1982 a declassified Defense Nuclear Agency report surfaced confirming that the fallout was in fact *not* an accident. The report said that six hours before the blast, weather briefings showed winds at 7000 metres were heading for Rongelap.[2]

In 1978, more than two decades after the atoll had been declared safe, an aerial survey of the northern Marshall Islands revealed that parts of Rongelap were as radioactive as — or even more so than — Bikini, which had been predicted to be contaminated for a century. The following year, islanders were warned not to eat from their traditional food-gathering northern islands.

'While we might understand the quarantine,' said Senator Jeton Anjain, brother of the former mayor and a leader of the Rongelap Islanders. 'I'm afraid the lagoon fish, sea turtles and coconut crabs in our diet don't understand it as they move around freely and end up in our dinner!'

By 1983 the atoll's elders reluctantly reached a consensus: they would have to abandon Rongelap if their people — especially their children — and their culture were to survive. They sought help from the *Nitijela*, the Marshall Islands parliament. Although they won a unanimous vote of approval for their move, they failed to get any financial or logistical help. No help came from the United States Government either, probably to avoid acknowledging the problem it had created.

A belated congressional vote, however, pledged US$500,000 for an independent radiological survey,* long sought by the islanders, and $3.2 million for resettlement of the population of more than 300 to Mejato Island on Kwajalein, providing the study proved the move was justified.

---

* An 11-member panel of international experts released a preliminary report in April 1988 to a Congress appropriations subcommittee concluding that returning to Rongelap is 'permissible' for adults given certain geographic and dietary restraints. But the panel withheld judgement for children until further review. Canadian radiobiologist Dr Rosalie Bertell, author of *No Immediate Danger* and a researcher for the Toronto-based International Institute of Concern for Public Health, and West German Bernd Franke, of Heidelberg's Institute of Energy, dissented. Bertell's institute in 1987 sent a physician to examine 270 Rongelap children, as old as 15, whose parents or grandparents were living on the atoll during or after the Bravo fallout: 40 percent have serious congenital or acquired diseases and the rate of disease was ten times higher than institute physicians have seen in other Third World nations.

The Rainbow Warrior evacuates irradiated islanders from Rongelap Atoll, Marshall Islands, May 1985.

But there was a hitch. The grants were dependent on the Republic of the Marshall Islands accepting the Compact of Free Association with the United States which would allow the Pentagon to continue to use the Kwajalein missile base for a further 30 years and retain strategic military control of the country. It was accepted by the government, but opposed by the people of Rongelap and Kwajalein. Although the treaty's espousal clause provided a $150 million trust fund to compensate Marshall Islanders for the health and environmental damage from the nuclear testing, the people were stripped of their right to sue the United States Government.

Determined to move, Senator Anjain appealed late in 1984 to Greenpeace, which was already planning a visit to the Marshall Islands by the *Rainbow Warrior* the following year. Greenpeace agreed. Within six months the environmental group's flagship, with an international crew, would be at Rongelap to deliver the nuclear refugees.

But this humanitarian role would be an unusual and traumatic challenge for the Greenpeace campaigners, who were more comfortable with high-profile, non-violent 'guerrilla' operations by the *Rainbow Warrior*.*

In June 1980, the *Rainbow Warrior* was seized by the Spanish Navy while on an anti-whaling campaign and held under arrest in the military harbour of El Ferrol. Parts of the propulsion system were confiscated to prevent any escape. Greenpeace activists, however, smuggled replacement parts on board and the ship dashed to freedom. Off Siberia in July 1983, Soviet troops arrested seven crew members while the *Rainbow Warrior* gave a Russian destroyer the slip to escape to Alaska.

In mid-May 1985, after two days of meetings with the Rongelap Islanders, the *Rainbow Warrior* crew helped dismantle the plywood and corrugated aluminium homes and loaded the ship. About 20 tonnes of building materials, two power generators, wooden trunks, furniture, kerosene lamps, tools and sleeping mats were ferried out to the ship in two *bum bums* (small runabouts) and two Zodiacs. Just before dusk, about 75 mainly elderly people, pregnant women and mothers with young children squeezed into whatever space they could on the *Rainbow Warrior* for the first 14-hour voyage to Mejato.[3] It took three more round trips for the entire population of 320 people and their possessions to be moved to the uninhabited island, across the lagoon from the United States missile splashdown zone.

'Blunderwatergate'

News media reports of the exodus were an embarrassment to the United States Government, reinforcing its view of the *Rainbow Warrior* as a threat

---

* By 1987, Greenpeace had 1.3 million members in 16 countries, more than 30 offices, and a budget of $20 million. Yet only one office was in a Third World country, and indigenous people were rarely among its activists.

to its military and nuclear policies in the Pacific. The French had long recognised that fact and the progress of the ship's voyage through the region was closely monitored by the DGSE. A plot had been hatched to sabotage the ship before it led a protest fleet from New Zealand to Moruroa.

While the *Rainbow Warrior* was evacuating the Rongelap Islanders, a 33-year-old DGSE agent, Christine Cabon, flew to New Zealand and infiltrated the Auckland office of Greenpeace. Calling herself Frédérique Bonlieu, she fed information about the Moruroa plans back to her headquarters in Paris. She was a lesbian and a tough former commando who was invalided out of her unit after a parachute accident. Giving the impression that she was writing 'essays' for the French press, she stayed with several Greenpeace and peace movement activists. Among her hosts was *New Zealand Herald* reporter Karen Mangnall. On board the ship were two French journalists, Philippe Chatenay of *Le Point* news magazine and Walter Guerin of Parfrance Television. Curiously, the pair showed little interest in the Moruroa leg of the voyage while they gathered information.

Greenpeace was planning its most sophisticated operation so far at Moruroa. But the plans were far from complete. According to one possible scenario, the *Rainbow Warrior* and other protest yachts from New Zealand would launch Zodiacs from just outside the 12-mile territorial zone. They would attempt to avoid the French security screen and land on the atoll. French military authorities would be forced to arrest many protesters of different nationalities and deport them to their homeland, triggering an embarrassing series of news reports around the world. A medical team would also land at Mangareva in an attempt to carry out health research. Another embarrassment.

Bonlieu also heard speculation about Tahitian pro-independence activists landing at Moruroa. The idea had been floated by *indépendantiste* Charlie Ching* while on a visit to New Zealand during February (and this was one of the reasons why the DGSE went ahead with the sabotage plan). But Bonlieu had confused this idea — never seriously considered by Greenpeace, a non-political movement — with a planned boycott by

---

* Two days after returning to Tahiti from Auckland, Ching was arrested and jailed. At the time he was walking towards Papeete's Tarahoi Park, where a Bikini Day anti-nuclear and pro-independence rally was being held on 2 March 1986. Angered by his arrest, Ching's followers, now led by Guy Taero, tried to burn down the High Commissioner's country residence and a commercial building in Papeete. On 27 August 1985, Ching was jailed for two and a half years for organising an 'illegal' demonstration; Taero was sentenced to five years. Ching was charged under a 1935 French law directed against economic crimes. His sentence was later reduced to two years and he was freed early in December 1986. 'The French government has always wanted to get rid of me,' he told *Les Nouvelles de Tahiti* after his release. 'They found a pretext to do this through the fire. Out of the hundred or so people who took part in the demonstration they found six to accuse me. Only one of them was near me. He claimed I had said. "We must arm ourselves and attack the *popa'a* [settlers]".'[4]

participants of the Pacific Arts Festival due in Tahiti at the end of June. Greenpeace never planned to be involved in the boycott. Nevertheless Bonlieu fed her information back to the DGSE.

Greenpeace International chairman David McTaggart gave an order that the *Rainbow Warrior* should not breach the 12-mile zone around Moruroa. 'If she is taken inside, the shit is going to hit the fan,' he said.

But the DGSE had already made up its mind to stop the protest ship at any cost. Top-level meetings in Paris had set in motion the sabotage plan. A team of combat divers trained at Aspretto had prepared for the operation. One agent, Gerald Andries, purchased the Zodiac and a Yamaha outboard motor in London. Another, Chief Petty Officer Roland Verge, flew to Nouméa — the South Pacific capital of *barbouzes*, or spies — to organise the hire of an 11-metre yacht, the *Ouvéa*.

The plot was absurdly complicated: the Zodiac and outboard were flown to New Caledonia. The bombs and diving equipment were obtained in Nouméa and hidden on board the *Ouvéa*. Verge, Andries, another petty officer, Jean-Michel Barcelo, and 'freelance physician' Dr Xavier Maniguet, a naval reservist who specialised in diving medicine, posed as tourists on a mid-winter diving voyage to New Zealand.

On 22 June, the day the *Ouvéa* entered New Zealand illegally at Parengarenga Harbour in the country's Far North, a second team of agents flew into Auckland from London posing as Swiss tourists on a honeymoon. They were Major Alain Mafart, deputy commander of the Aspretto base, and Captain Dominique Prieur; their 'married' name was Turenge. The next day, Operation Satanic's chief, Colonel Louis-Pierre Dillais (alias Jean-Louise Dormand), arrived in Auckland from Los Angeles. During the next two weeks, the *Ouvéa* crew played out a Jacques Tati-like farce, seducing women and leaving obvious clues to their presence from Whangarei to Auckland. But they eventually linked up with the Turenges, and the bombs and sabotage gear were handed over.

The third team, Camurier and Tonel* flew into New Zealand on 7 July a few hours before the *Rainbow Warrior* arrived in Auckland harbour from Vanuatu. Both men had false passports and claimed to be physical education instructors at the Paofai girls' college in Papeete. Their task was to mine the ship.

After planting the bombs, Camurier was seen in Okahu Bay by yachtsmen vigilantes on the lookout for petty thieves. He was loading bags into the Turenges' rented campervan. The car number plate, LB8945, was jotted

---

* The names were aliases. No real men of these names and occupations were traced in Papeete. The French investigative magazine *VSD* published a detailed account alleging the men were the actual saboteurs. The magazine identified the men with military authorities from a photograph of the pair at a South Island ski resort which was published in the *Auckland Star*.[5] A French book, *Mission Oxygène*, by Patrick Amory (Filipacchi, Paris, 1987) also describes the two frogmen's role.

down and two days after the *Rainbow Warrior* was sabotaged the fake honeymooners were detained by police on false passport charges. Evidence quickly pointed to French responsibility for the sabotage. Police flew to Norfolk Island to question the *Ouvéa* crew on their return voyage to Nouméa. Although they had strong suspicions, the police did not have enough evidence to be confident of arrests.

By the time the police got their act together, the *Ouvéa* had vanished. It had apparently been scuttled in the Coral Sea and the crew (apart from Maniguet, who had earlier flown through Sydney) were reportedly picked up by the nuclear-powered submarine *Rubis* which took them to Tahiti. Dillais, Camurier and Tonel posed as tourists in the South Island before quietly slipping out of New Zealand two weeks later.

Meanwhile, the French government denounced the sabotage and strongly denied any involvement. French press reports claimed the saboteurs were South African mercenaries or British agents — anything to cloud the issue and divert attention away from French involvement. Stories began circulating that the *Rainbow Warrior* had been bombed because Greenpeace was being manipulated by 'communist states'. The dead photographer, Pereira, was claimed to be a KGB agent and the ship was said to be carrying secret espionage equipment — claims which I found laughable after having lived on board for 11 weeks.

As with many secret service agencies, it is a common practice for the DGSE to use journalists as 'honourable correspondents' to gather intelligence and to spread disinformation.

Some French reports alleged that the Australian, British and New Zealand secret services knew of the operation and allowed the bombing to take place to discredit France. (New Zealand's Secret Intelligence Service admitted knowing about the presence of several of the agents.) Other versions claimed the British M16, the CIA or the South African DONS had carried out the bombing to frame the French government.

Several misleading reports were also published by the *New Zealand Herald* and other local papers. *Herald* reporter Karen Mangnall, for example, claimed the saboteurs 'may be French mercenaries — former soldiers from an agency like the Foreign Legion who are available, for big money, for sabotage assignments'.[6] In a later report, apparently influenced by *Le Point*, she said:

A French mercenary has told *Herald* contacts in France he helped the New Zealand preparations for the *Rainbow Warrior* sabotage. The mercenary — known only by his current alias of 'Chabnes' — made brief contact yesterday with *Herald* intermediaries in Paris and the south of France. He confirmed his participation in the preparation [in early July] . . . but he said he left New Zealand before the sabotage took place . . . Earlier inquiries in Paris revealed that the man was one of ten mercenaries recruited earlier this year for a Pacific job reportedly on behalf of right-wing New Caledonian settlers.[7]

The *Herald* had already published distorted reports about Pacific indigenous liberation groups. A few months earlier, for example, the paper carried on its front page a story claiming *Kanaks 'led by whites'*. The story, filed by a right-wing correspondent in Nouméa, said 'about 150 foreign soldiers led by white officers may be supporting Kanak forces' in the Thio area. It added:

> Witnesses living in the area had seen masked white men, who could not speak French, leading Melanesians speaking Pidgin — a language of Papua New Guinea and Vanuatu. The foreign force is believed to account for the arrival in Nouméa . . . of French paratroopers . . . It is also believed that four fishing boats blown up near Thio may have been targets because the Kanaks had planned to use them to bring more foreign soldiers in from ships off the coast.[8]

I was reporting in the Thio area at the time and there was no evidence to substantiate this claim. In fact, FLNKS leaders ridiculed the report. The story was also discredited in Pacific publications, yet the *Herald* never bothered to publish a denial.

The *Rainbow Warrior* misinformation from Paris, however, was unconvincing. After all, the New Zealand police were holding two French secret agents.

When the facts began to leak the French press, sensing a political scandal comparable to Watergate, began to investigate the affair more seriously. A government-ordered official inquiry headed by leading civil servant Bernard Tricot was made public on 20 August — but this 'whitewash' was widely rejected. It appeared to be part of an attempt at an orchestrated cover-up. While admitting the detained Turenges and the *Ouvéa* crew were French agents, the Tricot report made no mention of the 'third team' and cleared the government of ordering the sabotage.

After fresh revelations by *Le Monde* on 19 September, however, events moved dramatically. The next day Prime Minister Laurent Fabius proposed to President Mitterrand that the DGSE chief, Admiral Pierre Lacoste, be sacked and Defence Minister Charles Hernu be asked to resign. Mitterrand agreed. Fabius later appeared on television to admit the DGSE had sunk the *Rainbow Warrior* under orders, and that there had been a cover-up of the operation.

Although Fabius had declared that 'the guilty, whoever they may be, must pay for this crime' and Mitterrand promised 'justice at the highest level' it became clear they were empty words. The whole affair, dubbed at first 'Underwatergate', soon became 'Blunderwatergate'.

While the scandal ran its course, Greenpeace dispatched its larger Antarctic protest ship *Greenpeace* to Moruroa to join the protest flotilla of small boats from New Zealand — including the veteran yacht *Vega* which was seized and its crew deported.

Newspapers throughout the world condemned France for its terrorist 'act of war' in the port of an ally, although both the British and United States governments significantly avoided any clear denunciation of the sabotage. France was pilloried by a wave of international condemnation that would have been unlikely to happen if the *Rainbow Warrior* had been left in peace.

Now charged with murder and arson, Mafart and Prieur faced the preliminary hearing on 4 November. Their wait in Mt Eden Prison had already been eventful; following rumours that mercenaries or the French military were planning to spring the couple, Mafart had been transferred to Paremoremo maximum security jail and Prieur became the only prisoner in Ardmore military camp, both near Auckland. But in a surprise development, Mafart and Prieur pleaded guilty to the lesser charges of manslaughter and wilful damage. Three weeks later, they were both sentenced to ten years' jail for their role in the bombing. Sentencing them, New Zealand's Chief Justice, Sir Ronald Davison, said:

> The sentence imposed must give a clear warning to such as the defendants and their masters that terrorist-type activities will be met with stern reaction and severe punishment. People who come to this country and commit terrorist activities cannot expect to have a short holiday at the expense of the government and return home as heroes.[9]

But a 'holiday' it *would* become. And already they were regarded as patriots and heroes in France.

★   ★   ★

Faced with steadily deteriorating relations with France since the sabotage of the *Rainbow Warrior* and growing threats to the country's trade future, the New Zealand government decided on international mediation as the solution. After an abortive attempt to persuade former Canadian Prime Minister Pierre Trudeau to take on the task, United Nations Secretary-General Javier Perez de Cuellar became mediator on 17 June 1986. He ruled that in return for the deportation of Mafart and Prieur to Hao Atoll for three years France must:

1. Make a formal and unqualified apology for the attack.
2. Pay New Zealand $13 million (US$7 million) as compensation. (The money was used for an anti-nuclear projects fund and a special Pacific trust.)
3. Not oppose imports of New Zealand butter into Britain during 1987 or 1988 at the levels set by the European Economic Commission; not take measures which might impair agreements between New Zealand and the EEC on trading mutton, lamb and goatmeat.

Barely eight months after they were imprisoned — and in spite of a pledge by Prime Minister David Lange that New Zealand's 'system of justice was not for sale' — Alain Mafart and Dominique Prieur were transferred to French Polynesia. The agents were flown by an RNZAF Orion before dawn on 23 July to Uvéa Island in the territory of Wallis and Futuna. After being given leis and embraces from French Pacific Affairs Secretary Gaston Flosse, they were taken by a French military aircraft to Hao Atoll.

The development provided political cartoonists and columnists with an entertaining theme: a tropical holiday for spies in the South Pacific. In one cartoon, the two agents were depicted carvorting along an atoll beach. They were equipped with dark glasses, surfboards, flippers and *'le sun tan'*. Trundling in the opposite direction beyond a *No Mans Land* checkpoint was a bemused-looking character representing New Zealand who dangled a butter sales placard from his finger.

'It mightn't be Club Med, but from the perspective of this dark political winter, it looks embarrassingly attractive,' mocked William Reeves, columnist for the *Dominion*. 'Coral sands and trade winds, beckoning palms and limpid waters, warm days and starry nights — an environment calculated to erase our stoical French spies' worst memories and soothe the hurt of their incarceration in an alien land.'[10]

But the exile of the agents was unpopular with most New Zealanders, who regarded the United Nations Secretary-General's ruling with cynicism. 'The United Nations doesn't favour small countries,' said one commentator. 'If that can happen to New Zealand, what hope do smaller countries have in the South Pacific?'

Rubbing salt in the wounds for New Zealand and the independent Pacific nations was the fact that Hao was the rear military base for the nuclear tests operation at Moruroa. A slap in the face for Lange's anti-nuclear policies. And a similar slap for the South Pacific countries which signed the Rarotonga Treaty. Cynics asked how long would it take for New Zealand to buckle over its port ban on nuclear warships if the United States were to seriously apply an economic squeeze?

Branding the arrangement 'blood money', the *Auckland Star* asked: 'Is the internal deficit so sick, is the balance of payments so astray, that the government is prepared to sell our soul for $13 million? The selling of the justice system is more than contemptible. It is an act of political hypocrisy of the lowest order.'

The move also upset many Tahitians, who took the opportunity to embarrass France by renewing demands that Charlie Ching be freed from jail. Ten European parliamentary deputies had already drawn attention to Ching's case the previous month by condemning French 'colonial justice' and alleging that he was being held in 'inhuman conditions' in Nuutania Prison.[11]

Territorial councillors Oscar Temaru and James Salmon were among a dozen Tahitians who staged a hunger strike outside the Assembly, calling for Ching's release. Temaru, leader of *Tavini Huiraatira* (Polynesian Liberation Front) and mayor of Faaa, also sent an angry protest letter to the United Nations Secretary-General complaining about Mafart and Prieur. And in an open message to High Commissioner Pierre Angeli he warned that if the agents were not immediately removed from Tahitian territory there would be a serious threat to public order.

'Ching isn't a criminal — he is just a Tahitian who has tried to protest for independence and against the nuclear tests,' Temaru said. 'How can they liberate criminals [Mafart and Prieur] and keep him in jail? The French government is always using our land as a rubbish dump. Hao Atoll is like Waikiki Beach in Hawaii — it *isn't* a prison.'

Bengt Danielsson suggested in an article in the *New Zealand Times* that Ching be exchanged for Mafart and Prieur. 'During their numerous trials, Charlie Ching and Guy Taero have always declared themselves to be soldiers in the Tahitian army of liberation,' he wrote. 'The French government can thus hardly object on formal grounds against the proposal to swap them for their own soldiers, Prieur and Mafart, who were also captured while fighting for their country.'[12]

After being awarded $8.2 million in compensation from France by the International Arbitration Tribunal, Greenpeace finally towed the *Rainbow Warrior* to New Zealand's Matauri Bay and 'buried' it off Motutapere in the Cavalli Islands on 12 December 1987. But the affair did not end there. The same day the French Government told New Zealand Mafart had a serious stomach complaint and repatriated him to Paris in defiance of the terms of the United Nations agreement and protests from the Lange government.

It was later claimed by a Tahitian newspaper, *Les Nouvelles*, that Mafart was smuggled out of Tahiti on a fake passport hours before New Zealand was even told of the 'illness'. Mafart reportedly assumed the identity of a carpenter, Serge Quillan.[13] Prieur was also repratriated back to France in May 1988 because she was pregnant. France ignored the protests by New Zealand and the blatant breach of the agreement was referred to the United Nations for mediation.

'Libyan devils' and submarines

The *Rainbow Warrior* affair posed many questions for the South Pacific. How widespread were the activities of Western — or indeed any — secret service agents? How co-operative were intelligence agencies based in countries like Australia, New Zealand, Fiji and Papua New Guinea? What was the nature of disinformation and destabilisation tactics against Pacific nationalist movements and governments such as non-aligned Vanuatu?

A former Central Intelligence Agency officer, Ralph McGehee, author of *Deadly Deceits*, a book exposing the agency's destabilisation methods, warned in Suva of the 'telltale' climate of hysteria then emerging in the South Pacific. He said New Zealand faced a growing campaign of disinformation and 'dirty tricks' designed to undermine the anti-nuclear Labour government. He also predicted — nine months before the *coup d'état* — that Fiji and Vanuatu would face a similar fate. He spelled out the broad outlines of the CIA's likely methods in the South Pacific.[14]

One of the typical scenarios is to focus attention on what is projected as a major threat from terrorism or communism. An example is a campaign of disinformation about the 'Soviet menace' which has been used to discredit Pacific countries regarded as being too independent. Among the targets were Kiribati because of its 1985 fisheries agreement with the Soviet Union (it lapsed after a year) and Vanuatu, which also negotiated a similar deal in January 1987 (it also lapsed). Another example is the anti-Libyan hysteria directed against Vanuatu because it established diplomatic links with Tripoli. Previously it had been disinformation about alleged Cuban influence in Vila.

News media in the region, particularly Australian, frequently fell into the pattern of distorted reports and disinformation. Vanuatu was singled out for attacks over its 'radicalism' — especially the so-called Libyan connection. An image was created of the Vanuatu ruling élite having become almost paranoid with its efforts to assert the country's independence. The FLNKS also faced 'Libyan-bashing'.

Yann-Célène Uregei insisted that the West 'might regard Libya as the devil, but for the people of New Caledonia it is France that is the *real* devil'.[15] Walter Lini agreed, stressing that it was France, not Libya, which had carried out an act of terrorism in the region by sabotaging the *Rainbow Warrior*. Noted *Islands Business*:

> Non-aligned, anti-nuclear, anti-colonial Vanuatu diligently ploughs the fields of many causes with an undergraduate enthusiasm that now frankly exasperates other Pacific island [Polynesian, not Melanesian] leaders when they encounter it at such times as the annual South Pacific Forum meeting. [Yet] diplomatic relations with Cuba, formed two years ago, have not produced an encampment of Fidel Castro's revolutionary [soldiers] on any of Vanuatu's 80 islands . . . A country so hypersensitive to the thought of foreign interference in its affairs is not likely to allow a Libyan or two to make much headway in turning Vanuatu into a Trojan horse for the subversion of the Pacific.[16]

Many of the negative reactions to Vanuatu's foreign policy initiatives have been hysterical, believes political analyst and historian Robert Robertson, of the University of the South Pacific, 'but it has been a hysteria of a specific kind, tempered by wider global concerns and without regard to the realities of Vanuatu's actions or its objectives'. Vanuatu's ministers have often claimed to be 'non-partisan', and the Vanuatu government and ruling *Vanuaaku Pati* do not follow any ideology as part of their policy initiatives.

Vanuatu officials frequently voice suspicions over the motives of Australia and New Zealand, countries they regard as surrogates of big power Western interests. Both Canberra and Wellington, said Robertson, find it convenient to support United States objectives in order to 'maintain their own hegemonic interest' in the South Pacific and their increasingly threatened economic relations with the West. New Zealand, in trying to deflect US criticism of its own anti-nuclear policies, has 'become the United States' strongest "friend" in pushing the concept of a Soviet threat and the false premise that the Soviets are an aggressive military power willing to seize resources or political control in the South Pacific.'[17] Lini was condemning Australia and New Zealand when he told me:

> Some countries, even in the South Pacific, have deliberately misrepresented Vanuatu's aims and objectives in its foreign policy. I think those countries feel that in geopolitical terms, the South Pacific belongs to them, so that when a country like Vanuatu maintains a foreign policy posture which is inconsistent with the 'normal' trend in the region as these countries would expect, then they become rather disturbed. It's like trying to keep people under toe and in line. This we cannot accept. We are an independent and sovereign state. We decide for ourselves and we shall not let others decide for us.[18]

★   ★   ★

Fiji had, at least until the coups, the most highly developed trade union system of South Pacific nations. From 1982 the United States has been 'actively penetrating and subverting' Fijian unions and trying to undermine Pacific Trade Union Community (previously Forum) support for a 'nuclear-free and independent Pacific'.[19]

A 'Labour Committee on Pacific Affairs' was set up by the right-wing United States trade union confederation AFL-CIO originally involving American, Australian and New Zealand unionists. Fiji and Papua New Guinea delegates were invited to its first full meeting in Sydney in December 1983. The committee was described in the *Australian* as the 'vehicle by which the right of the union movement in both Australia and the United States will attempt to influence union movements, not just in developing Pacific nations such as Papua New Guinea, but also in New Zealand.'[20]

Its most obvious activities were arranging trips to the United States for indoctrination on the Soviet threat and briefings at right-wing think tanks. Many Fijian and Papua New Guinea delegates complained about pro-United States and anti-Soviet bias. The *New Zealand Times* exposed the New Zealand activities of the committee, alleging it to have close links with CIA front organisations and individuals — including a labour attache at the embassy in Wellington.[21]

The labour committee was inactive in 1984, presumably because of the bad publicity. But many of its activists were resurfacing in the Asia-America Free Labour Institute (AAFLI which is claimed to have similar CIA connections). Although AAFLI had already been operating in Fiji since the 1970s — wooing the union movement with small grants and free travel — it now opened an office. The manager was Valentine Suazo, an expert in subverting Latin American trade unionists. He was alleged to have strong CIA links.

Fiji activities of the labour committee were exposed by the *Sydney Morning Herald*.[22] Documents obtained under the US Freedom of Information Act showed the Suva office had spent $1 million in the previous two years, and had claimed responsibility for defeat of a nuclear-free Pacific resolution of the PTUC. After the exposé, the office closed in September 1986. But its mission had been completed — an infrastructure had been set up to control Fiji's unions.

★   ★   ★

Two bizarre events focused attention on Western disinformation campaigns: one, in February 1986, involved a mystery submarine which was apparently supposed to be mistaken for a Russian vessel off the Cook Islands. But instead of provoking a 'Soviet scare' the incident backfired and became an embarrassment for the United States. The other event, in January 1987, involved an article about a fabricated Libyan 'dirty tricks' team, which was apparently leaked to the news media by the Australian Security Intelligence Organisation. It was used in an attempt to discredit the Fiji Labour Party and to help provide anti-Libyan hysteria, conveniently timed to coincide with the Fiji elections — and then the coup.

Researcher Owen Wilkes accused the Cook Islands and New Zealand governments, and the military, of a cover-up of the real identity of the the submarine. He claimed in *NZ Monthly Review* that the facts indicated a special operations submarine deployed by the US Navy.

'The entire submarine affair has all the hallmarks of a United States covert action — a covert action that went wrong,' Wilkes said. An abridged version of his documented article was reprinted in the *Dominion*, prompting denials by Prime Minister David Lange and United States officials who rejected the claims as being 'patently untrue'. But they appeared unconvincing in the face of the evidence.

Wilkes revealed that among the spotters of the submarine's conning tower on its second 'showing' on Thursday, 20 February, was a Tahitian policeman who had done military service. He was out fishing with a Tahitian colleague, who also had military experience, in a boat borrowed from Charlie Tetevano, protocol officer in the Queen's Representative Office. They were about five kilometres off shore near Ngatangiia, a village in the south-west of

Rarotonga. And they reported to Cook Islands police that the submarine came within 30 metres of them, almost bumping into their boat. They sketched a silhouette of the conning tower and gave a detailed description.

The previous 'showing' had been three days earlier, on Monday, 17 February, when two Cook Islanders who were on an Air Rarotonga flight from Aitutaki to Rarotonga saw a periscope off Ngatangiia. The submarine was going fast enough to make a bow wave and the periscope was watched for five minutes in clear visibility from less than 600 metres.

After the sighting by the Tahitians, an RNZAF Orion, already in Rarotonga, made a search in response to a request by Cook Islands Foreign Minister Norman George. Sonar contact with the submarine was made soon after arriving off Ngatangiia. New Zealand was informed immediately and a second Orion, which had been standing by, departed for the Cook Islands. Wilkes recounted:

> The submarine was determined to be within territorial waters, and was classified as nuclear and probably American by narrow-band analysis of passive sonobuoy recordings. Contact with the sub was lost early on Friday, despite sowing a large expanse of ocean with sonobuoys [floating devices which monitor submarine noises and relay them by radio to search aircraft].[23]

After initial attempts to hush up the story in both the Cook Islands and New Zealand, it was admitted the Orions had not only detected the submarine, but had detected its nationality beyond reasonable doubt. New Zealand's Chief of Defence Staff, Air Marshal Sir Ewan Jamieson, refused to disclose its nationality, which led to speculation that it must have been an American submarine on a covert opertion. (New Zealand has always been prompt to disclose details of Soviet naval vessels sighted in the region.)

Later, there were 'leaks' from military sources to journalists claiming that it was 'Soviet', and Lange was misrepresented as saying it was Russian. Then it was said the submarine's nationality could not be determined, while United States and Soviet officials denied that it belonged to either country. Finally, it was claimed there was probably no submarine at all — in one account it became a 'flatulent whale'.

Wilkes, however, cited a senior Cook Islands government source as saying the Prime Minister Sir Thomas Davis' office was advised by New Zealand that the submarine was 'probably American'. Opposition Leader Geoffrey Henry and rebel Democrat leader Vincent Ingram were both told the submarine was American.

'Choosing the Cook Islands for the submarine scare was a stroke of genius,' said Wilkes. 'Surfacing a submarine around the New Zealand coastline would have been a bit crass, and would have strained credulousness, but the New Zealand public could hardly fail to be impressed by a submarine appearing "up there" in the Cooks — it is a far enough way to be believable, near enough to be disturbing.'

At the same time, claimed Wilkes, the United States could assume that Davis,* who was a strong supporter of American, French and nuclear interests in the South Pacific, would effectively publicise the simulated Soviet presence. On the other hand, he could also be relied on to cover up if anything went wrong.

After the new twist in the 'Soviet threat' fell flat, it was time for a revival of the Libyan scaremongering. A beat-up came in the form of a six-page article in the January 1987 issue of Australian *Penthouse* — just as the election campaign in Fiji was about to begin. It claimed a Libyan agent operating in the South Pacific had been executed on orders of the Libyan leader, Colonel Muammar Gaddafi, because plans had gone awry.[24]

Apparently culled from information leaked from ASIO sources, which may have been responsible for much of the past disinformation, the *Penthouse* article said the 'failed' agent had been sent to influence the outcome of Fiji's 1982 general election. Members of the then ruling Alliance Party and its two rivals, the Indian-dominated National Federation Party and the Fijian dissident party Western United Front, were claimed to have received a total of $300,000 — mostly American dollars — that were 'spread around' in a scheme with which Gaddafi allegedly hoped to curry favour with the Russians by achieving the defeat of the Prime Minister, Ratu Sir Kamisese Mara. But the 'plot' collapsed.

Writer James Crown, former Brisbane *Courier-Mail* foreign editor and the author of a book about international terrorism, *The Terrorist Connection*, claimed he would reveal more details, and possibly the names of well-known Pacific islands politicians, in an account of the prospects of the spread of terrorism in the region that he was preparing. His information came from an interview given to him in Singapore by a man who claimed he was one of two agents sent to the South Pacific by the Libyan leader.

'I was put on to the man in Singapore by some friends in ASIO who helped me with research for an article I did on the terrorist threat in Australia,' Crown said. Although his claims about the Libyan involvement in Fiji and New Caledonia lacked evidence, they were widely reported in the region.

★   ★   ★

The growing media hysteria over Libya centred on Vanuatu. On 27 April 1987 the United States Ambassador to the United Nations, General Vernon

---

* Sir Thomas Davis was ousted from office in a no-confidence vote on 29 July 1987. Wilkes investigated the 19 years Davis spent in the United States before becoming Prime Minister and checked allegations that he was an agent for the United States and French governments. He concluded for *NZ Monthly Review:* 'Regardless of whether or not Davis did mindbending research for the CIA, whether [agent] Ed Kelly recruited Davis for the CIA, and whether InterAir was intended to be a CIA airline, Davis has consistently acted to support United States, French and nuclear interests in the South Pacific.'[25]

Walters, made a one-night stopover during a tour of the South Pacific. The general and his entourage claimed to have 'discovered' two Libyan agents staying in the same hotel, the Intercontinental Island Inn. These two 'spies' were exposed when Walters's bodyguard, secret serviceman Lee Martiny, gained unofficial access to the guest register after he was denied access by hotel staff.

Melbourne Herald journalist Geoff Easdown alleged they were Libyan government agents working under cover as businessmen. He named them as Taher Marwan and Fathi Farhat. Their presence in Vanuatu was also claimed to be the cause of a dramatic predawn trip to New Zealand on 30 April by Australian Foreign Minister Bill Hayden for talks with Prime Minister David Lange at Ohakea air force base.[26] But the circumstances suggest Hayden was fooled by ASIO, and his 'secret' flight was arranged to create as much speculation and paranoia about Libya as possible.

Some accounts claimed the Libyans were officials of the Libyan Foreign Liaison Bureau, and they had come to Vanuatu to initiate negotiations for setting up a Libyan diplomatic post in Vanuatu. Yet the pair were in Vila for 19 days and spent all the time in their hotel room, rarely answering the door. On 7 May — a week before the Fiji coup — they were expelled by the Vanuatu Government for breaching protocol.

But they had served their purpose. Their 'discovery' could not have been more convenient. Played up by the Australian and New Zealand news media, the Libyan hysteria reached a new peak, the Vanuatu government's credibility was undermined; and now the stage was set for ousting the non-aligned Bavadra government in Fiji.

Part 4
Coup d'État

11

The Rise of Bavadra

In Fiji, growing autocracy and corruption heralded a change of political consciousness. The colonial legacy had left largely racially based parties representing the indigenous Fijians and the Indo-Fijians, descendants of indentured labourers. This was challenged in 1985 by a fast-rising new political movement, the Fiji Labour Party, which genuinely bridged racial barriers for the first time. Committed to multiracialism, social justice and non-alignment, the party swept Dr Timoci Bavadra to power two years later on a popular mandate of reform. His 'new nationalism' became a driving force for a post-independence generation of educated, indigenous politicians and trade unionists. But it also drew into sharp focus traditional tribal rivalries of three confederacies from the previous century and unleased a reactionary backlash.

Viti, or Fiji, means 'notions of spirits'.[1] The 320 islands comprising Fiji are at the cultural crossroads of the South Pacific where the Polynesian and Melanesian peoples and cultures have been blended into a merged identity.

Originally inhabited about 3500 years ago by people with the same culture as those who went on to Tonga and Samoa to become the ancestral Polynesians, Fiji was colonised much later by groups of Melanesians. 'The physical, linguistic and cultural base to Fijian culture was one shared with ancestral Polynesians and different from that of the Melanesians,' wrote anthropologist Everett Frost. 'If one must classify Fiji at all, it seems most logical to group it with West Polynesia.'[2]

Thus, while the many dialects of the Fijian language reflect both strands, the traditional system of *ratus*, or hereditary chiefs, is more Polynesian than Melanesian. Among the stronger early chiefly confederacies was the Kubuna, which became centred on a kingdom based on the little island of Bau. By 1830, the Kubuna was the most powerful tribal alliance in Fiji. Inter-marriage between Bauan chiefs and the chiefly families of neighbouring *vanua*, or clans, especially Rewa and Cakaudrove, strengthened *vasu*⋆ links to the Kubuna. Led in the early nineteenth century by the *Vunivalu*†, Ratu Banuve, and later his son, Ratu Naulivou, the Kubuna influence spread as Bau's war canoes raided the northern and western coasts of Viti Levu.

By the time Naulivou's nephew, Ratu Seru, who took the names Cakobau (pronounced Thakombau, 'Bau despoiled') and Cikinovu (the 'centipede', which strikes without warning), crushed a rebellion and took control in 1837, he planned to become 'King of Fiji'.[3] His skill with European firearms rivalled that of a gunsmith and was unusual among Fijians. Waging war against his neighbouring rivals of Rewa and Verata, however, Cakobau only succeeded in creating an alliance of enemies. But his real threat came from Tonga.

Tongan links with the Fijian political processes had been growing for decades — and they would later play a vital role in modern Fiji politics. Some Tongan warriors and canoe-builders had supported the sea-going chiefdom of Bau. Carpenters and fishermen allied themselves with the Tui Cakau. Many had married into chiefly families. The closest links, however, were with the eastern Lau islands. Tongan blood ties with the Lauan people existed at the highest levels.

Tongan influence led to the spread of Christianity in the eastern Fiji islands and a series of 'religious wars'. The unconverted Fiji chiefs were won over by the Tongans with their claims of divine authority.

> The missionaries preached a doctrine of the equality of all men in the face of God and the existence of a set of rules to be obeyed by all. The Wesleyans had come with Tongan protection. Might they also not have made some sort of bargain whereby Fijians were all to be levelled in the sight of the Tongans as well as in the sight of God?[4]

Taufa'ahau Tupou I, or 'King George', of Tonga dispatched an expedition to the Lauan island of Vanuablavu in 1847 to investigate the killing of a European preacher. With the king's warriors was the King' cousin, Ma'afutu'itonga, who soon became powerful.

In 1853, when he became governor of the Tongans in Fiji, Ma'afu established his power base in Lau, setting himself up as the protector of

---

⋆ *Vasu* was a kinship system whereby a man's sister's son had special privileges of support and access to property. Multiple marriages and the creation of ties beyond the second generation eventually produced such a tangled situation that political allegiances broke down, opening the way for foreign intervention.

† Literally 'warlord', one of the three traditional Fijian chiefly titles most commonly regarded as paramount which have continued until the present. They are currently the *Vunivalu* (Ratu Sir George Cakobau, paramount chief of Kubana confederacy), *Tui Cakau* (Ratu Sir Penaia Ganilau, of Tovata) and *Roko Tui Drekeki* (Adi Mara, of Burebesaga, who is the wife of Ratu Sir Kamisese Mara, the *Tui Nayau* of Tovata).

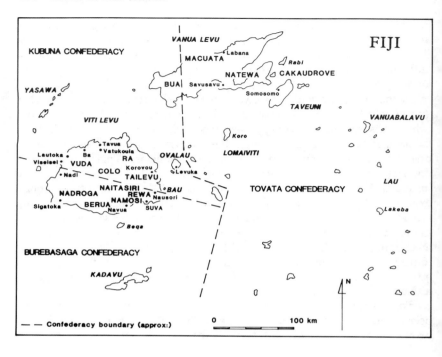

the Wesleyan missionaries and gaining direct influence over the Tui Nayau. The following year he invaded Vanuabalavu after the massacre of 17 Wesleyans there. Challenging Cakobau, Ma'afu extended his influence to Beqa and Kadavu where the chiefs accepted Christianity and his protection. Soon Ma'afu's power spread from Lakeba to the Yasawas. The chiefdom of Lau, with the Tui Lau Ma'afu as a new chief in the Fijian hierarchy, began evolving. Already Lauan chiefs regarded Ma'afu, rather than Cakobau, as their overlord.

Troubled by poor health and wars, Cakobau accepted Christianity in 1854 and alienated many of his allies who rebelled. The battle of Kaba against the rebels was won by the unorthodox tactics of Cakobau's Tongan allies. Regarded as a victory for Christianity over the heathens, the battle led to mass conversions. Cakobau's Kubuna became the leading kingdom in Fiji, but in spite of his claim to be the paramount Tui Viti he was unable to challenge the growing power of Ma'afu.

Cakobau had already faced problems with the Americans as more European settlers arrived in Fiji. In 1849 the Nukulau Island house of the first United States representative, John Williams, was accidentally burned during

American Independence Day celebrations. But the home was also looted and Williams claimed US$5000 in compensation. When the house was again burned down six years later the *USS John Adams* was dispatched to Fiji. Commander Boutwell ordered the Fijians to rebuild the house and pay compensation, which had been unjustly increased to $43,531. Cakobau was taken hostage on board the frigate and forced to sign a pledge to pay the sum within two years.

Faced with growing fears over the spread of Ma'afu's power, and unable to pay the compensation, Cakobau approached the British consul with an offer to cede Fiji to Britain. He made two conditions — that he remain the Tui Viti and the British government pay the debt to the Americans in exchange for 80,000 hectares of land. Consul Pritchard opposed Tongan expansion in Fiji and was worried about the growing activity of German traders in the South Pacific. He travelled to Britain to urge the British government to accept the offer, stressing the possibility of growing cotton on the land.

But the British government was a reluctant coloniser. It did not want a repetition of the troubles between land-grabbing settlers and the Maori in New Zealand which would later lead to a full-scale war. After a negative report on cotton-growing in Fiji and the usefulness of the islands as a port of call between Australia and Panama, Britain rejected the offer of cession.

Fiji was thrown into political turmoil. Local wars broke out and Ma'afu became a greater threat to Cakobau. Lawlessness became more widespread and could only be controlled by visiting warships. Clearly some form of government was needed.

After an attempt at confederation between Cakobau, Ma'afu and their allies failed in 1867, two new governments sprang up. Ma'afu formed the Tovata (north-eastern confederation) with himself as the Tui Lau, or paramount chief. He dreamed of uniting all of Fiji under his leadership, of ruling Tonga after King Taufa'ahau's death, and of extending Tongan influence as far as the New Hebrides. But Taufa'ahau renounced Tonga's interest in Fiji, fearing responsibility for the American debt.

The constitution of the second government, the kingdom of Kubuna (Bau), declared that Cakobau was king of all parts of Fiji not included in the Tovata. He could make his own laws, levy his own taxes and call meetings of chiefs when he wished. Although Cakobau's prestige diminished with the increasing number of European settlers, one problem was solved when an Australian group calling itself the Polynesian Company agreed to pay the American debt in return for a grant of land the same size as that offered to Britain.

★　　　★　　　★

A new trade had emerged in the South Pacific — the labour trade, which was to have far-reaching effects throughout the region, including Fiji. Islanders were recruited for labour contracts on copra and cotton plantations in a system which was little better than slavery. The trade was branded 'blackbirding'.

The demand for labour grew sharply as the cotton industry expanded in the Pacific in response to the American Civil War which disrupted the world's main cotton-producing area, the southern states. Fiji had a large enough population to provide plentiful and cheap labour, but the indigenous Fijians had little enthusiasm for 'regular and continuous employment'. Moreover, the chiefs refused to release men from their village plantations.

Although regarded as 'Polynesian' because the first people recruited had been living in Polynesian islands, by 1870 most of the blackbird trade labourers were actually Melanesian. As the need for labour grew, the masters of ships recruiting islanders took greater risks to fill their ships and boost their profits.

> Soon recruiting turned to kidnapping, natives being lured on board ships by various cunning means, only to find the ship sailing with them still on board. A favourite trick of the blackbirders was to dress up as missionaries so that the natives would think they had come on a peaceable mission . . . the most common method of kidnapping was to sink the canoes which came out to meet the ships, and pick up the survivors.[5]

'The perpetrators of the misdeeds in this trade were generally unscrupulous and callous captains of the various "hell ships" involved,' wrote sociologist Vijay Naidu, 'whose chief concern seemed to be to get as many "Kanakas" under the hatch of the ship as it would carry — and sometimes even more.'[6] Housing conditions in the plantations, poor sanitation, bad food, long hours and rough treatment led to the deaths of many labourers. Bitterness over the blackbirding trade apparently prompted the murders at Santa Cruz, in the Solomon Islands, of Bishop Patterson in 1871 and Commodore Goodenough, Britain's senior naval officer in the South Pacific in 1875.

British public opinion became disturbed over the blackbirding, and the colonial governments in Australia and New Zealand pressured the Colonial Office to annex Fiji. Cakobau's government appeared close to collapse and Fiji was in danger of a civil war. A cession request by Cakobau — his third — finally persuaded a reluctant Britain to take action. When Cakobau withdrew his conditions, the Deed of Cession was signed at Levuka on 10 October 1874.

But the handing over of sovereignty to the British was never universally accepted by Fijians, as is now widely taught and believed. The people of western and central Viti Levu were the first to rebel against colonialism, believing that it implied domination by the Tongan-influenced eastern chiefs who signed the deed. In 1876 their resistance collapsed when expeditionary forces of eastern Fijians led by British officers attacked their villages. Rebellion, however, festered over the following decades — and a century later westerners would find their 'messiah' in Timoci Bavadra.

'Whores of capitalism'

In 1875 Sir Arthur Gordon arrived from Mauritius for a five-year term as governor of the New British colony. A high-minded and strong-willed aristocrat, he had battled with the French planters in Mauritius to give more protection to the indentured Indian labour force and he was determined to protect the rights of Fijians in Fiji's developing sugar industry where planters were pressing for Fijian labour. Their mouthpiece, the *Fiji Times* declared, 'the all-absorbing question of the hour . . . is that of labour supply'.

But Gordon identified with the chiefs — in fact he regarded himself as the paramount chief among chiefs. He believed the pressure for land and labour would undermine the chiefs, and thus also the colonial administration system exerted through them. (Local government was through district and regional councils in which chiefs had the main voice. Chiefly privileges included the custom of *lala* whereby commoners were required to provide goods and services to their chief without payment.)

Events in New Zealand had a profound effect on the way Fiji was administered as a crown colony. After watching a prolonged guerrilla war in New Zealand against a Maori population of only 58,000, the Colonial Office ruled out taking land by a war of conquest against a Fijian population of 200,000. (The Fijians have the Maori people to thank for the fact that they still own 83 percent of their land.) The colonial strategy used in Fiji to exploit the land had to be more subtle than that used in New Zealand and Gordon decided on bringing in Indian immigrants — to ensure that Fiji developed economically while protecting Fijians from the changes it would cause.

Fiji is one of several 'sugar colonies' whose modern history has been shaped by indentured plantation labourers from India. The consequence of this policy has been a segmented society where the descendants of Indian labourers live alongside indigenous people — with little mixing. In Mauritius, the Indians today form 70 percent of the total; in Guyana, 51 percent; and in Fiji, 49 percent. In Surinam, the 35 percent of Indians form the largest group in a mixed population, while in Trinidad their 40 percent comprise the second-largest group (43 percent being Creoles).

Slavery had been abolished in the British Empire in 1833. From then on Indians were recruited in various ways — usually foul — to work in the very colonial plantations that the free slaves had been released from. In an attempt to control the so-called indenture system of migrants recruited by the sugar colonies, the colonial government of India passed an act in 1837. The 'whores of capitalism', as one historian described the labourers, were required to appear before a government official who would also inspect the labour contract, or *girmit* (agreement).[6] They were signed up for five years, renewable for further five-year terms. The migrant ships were required to conform to standards of space, diet and so on, and to carry a doctor.

The first 'cargo' of 464 indentured Indian labourers for Fiji arrived on the *Leonidas* on 14 May 1879. Thirty-two other migrants who had been on board died of cholera, dysentery and smallpox contracted during the voyage.

Indians went to Fiji for a variety of reasons — usually poverty and the chance to make a fresh start, while some went to escape family feuds or trouble with the colonial authorities. Few went to Fiji just to emigrate. Upon completion of their five-year contracts they were freed. They could return to India by paying their own fares, stay in Fiji and work on their farms, or sign up on another plantation. After ten years as indentured labourers they were entitled to a free passage back to India.

After completing their initial contract, however, most Indian migrants chose to work as independent farmers, usually cultivating land leased from the Fijians, the government or settlers. They made Fiji their home.

Although the indenture system had been in existence for almost half a century before the labourers began flowing to Fiji, the abuses that had crept in remained unchecked despite attempts to eliminate them. The labourers' cramped barracks in sugar plantations are remembered in Fijian folklore as *Narak*, or 'Hell'. The huge imbalance between the sexes led to a high rate of sexual violence and other brutality, disrupted family life, and large numbers of children died from congenital syphilis. Labour conditions were harsh, as one man recalled:

> *Kulumbars* [overseers with whips] were bad — the Australians were especially bad, while the New Zealanders were good as they took pity . . . We woke up at four when the mill whistle blew. At six we started to work, cutting grass in the larger cane field and dug drains. Some — those who knew the work — finished their tasks early. But most of the others would carry on and, depending on their relative skill and strength, complete their tasks [by sunset].[7]

Sugar cultivation in Fiji was largely the monopoly of the Colonial Sugar Refining Company of Australia, which controlled the industry from 1882 to 1973. The company established its first large mill in 1881 on the east bank of the Rewa River where the town of Nausori sprang up. From 1883 sugar became Fiji's main export. 'Over half Fiji hangs the shadow of the company,' wrote a governor to the Colonial Secretary in London in 1920, just as the indenture system was abolished. 'In its relations with Indians already settled in the colony the company has mistimed resistance and concession alike.'[8]

The national economy was built on what political analyst William Sutherland, of the University of the South Pacific, characterised as the 'unholy trinity' of European capital, Fijian land and Indian labour. (In 1987, Sutherland became permanent secretary in the office of Fiji's second Prime Minister, Dr Timoci Bavadra, before he was deposed.)

As Indo-Fijian labourers ended their *girmit* contracts, the sugar plantations were eventually carved up into plots leased by Indo-Fijian small planters. But they remained dependent as they were forced to sell their cane to the CSRC on company terms. Strikes to improve their existence were suppressed by the company and the colonial government. Their claims, however, gradually led to slow improvements, while the indigenous Fijians clung to their communal pattern of life.

Initially Fiji was ruled by a governor until a legislative council was set up in 1904. From the outset the political structure was moulded by racial considerations. The council comprised seven Europeans, one appointed Indo-Fijian and two ethnic Fijians. The Fijian members were chosen by the Great Council of Chiefs — established by the colonial government to control the Fijian people — using traditional criteria of hereditary rank. Unlike in New Zealand, where the settlers refused to recognise a chiefly council, the governor could not have ruled Fiji without the co-operation of the Great Council of Chiefs. Their approval was needed to acquire land to lease to cane planters.

The land-holding group recognised as most common by the British colonial authorities in Fiji was the *mataqali* (clan). In traditional Fijian political language, 'land' also means 'people': 'The people are the land, the land is the people,' says a proverb. The village economy of the *mataqali* was based on subsistence cultivation of *dalo*, yams and fishing.

But the chiefs made no effort to use the existing village structure as an economic unit in response to colonialism. Instead, in more recent times, some chiefs have sought to use their traditional relationships as a way of gaining personal advantage. Some have turned land that was previously communally owned into private property through leases, or have monopolised the funds derived from the use of communal property. Many of the problems which would come to a head in the mid-1980s arose from the disproportionate level of land rents which went to the chiefs rather than to their people, although most chiefs rarely had enough to meet their customary obligations to their people.

The Viti Kabani

Some of these problems were already apparent when the first popular commoner Fijian movement, the Viti Kabani — or Fiji Company — emerged just before the First World War. Led by commoner Apolosi Ranawai, this show of political dissent was an attempt to stop the exploitation of ordinary villagers by chiefs and European middlemen who bought the goods produced by Fijians. It accused the chiefs of collaborating with the colonial oppressors. Apolosi also represented another western rebellion against eastern chiefly dominance.

'I alone am the only chief of Fiji: it is the will of God,' declared Apolosi. 'These other chiefs look only to their own interest; they don't spare a thought for you or your welfare . . . Really it is they who are the scum of the earth.'[9]

Besides tackling the economic supremacy of the traders, Apolosi advocated an administrative system which challenged the colonial Fijian system. He pledged that one day the 'sun would rise in the west': westerners would have their own government and a capital in the west. The movement rapidly gained popularity during the war.

If European traders resented the challenge to their control by the Viti Kabani movement, it was nothing to how the high chiefs, like Ratu Sir Lala Sukuna, reacted. On the suggestion of Sukuna, the colonial government declared the movement seditious and banned it. (Ironically, Apolosi had once invited Sukuna to lead his movement.) Apolosi was twice exiled to Rotuma, from 1917 to 1924 and again in 1930. After the Second World War broke out and the colonial authorities feared that dissident Fijians and Indians might link up, Apolosi was exiled to New Zealand where he died in prison in 1940.

Although Apolosi's *Gauna Vou*, or 'new era', for the Fijian commoners collapsed before it had a chance to become established, the movement did not die out.[10] As a result the chiefs were able to convince the British that they were indispensable for the maintenance of order within Fijian society. 'There are no interests,' said Ratu Sukuna, 'other than the interests of the rulers.'[11] (Sukuna's efforts to safeguard traditional chiefly privileges 60 years later would inspire another Fijian soldier, with less tolerance and wisdom, to try to restore a Fijian ascendency he believed to be endangered.)

During his long rise in the Fiji civil service, eventually becoming Secretary of Fijian Affairs, Sukuna was the man to whom the Fijian élite looked for guidance and leadership. He took leave of absence to join the British Army in the First World War. Unwanted, he joined the French Foreign Legion and was wounded and decorated for bravery under fire. He preached that Fiji was a 'three-legged stool' — dependent for its stability on harmony and tolerance among Fijians, Indians and Europeans.

In 1929 the first Indo-Fijians were elected to the Legislative Council and two years later Indian immigration to Fiji was stopped. 'The Fijian . . . until he was spoilt, was one of nature's gentlemen,' remarked the Bishop of Polynesia. 'But he would not work . . . it was very sad and deplorable, but there it was.' Fijians did not see any point in working for Europeans for a pittance when they could earn a month's wage cutting copra in a few days on their own plantations. The official empathy for Fijians was not extended to Indians. As one patronising British official noted in 1942:

> The Indian is disliked and feared by Europeans principally because he is politically conscious and is aiming at placing himself on a level with Europeans. The Fijians are superficially a much more attractive people . . . and the position of Europeans towards them is roughly that of the guardians of attractive, promising, but not yet quite fully developed children.[12]

Under the pressure of the Second World War, these stereotypes were reinforced. Fijians responded eagerly to the British call to arms; one Fijian male in three became a soldier. Indo-Fijians also offered to enlist — but only if the pay and conditions were the same as for Europeans. When this was turned down, few Indians volunteered. Indian sugar workers, affected by high wartime prices, demanded higher pay. When the CSRC and government refused in 1943, the confrontation caused the sugar crop to rot in the canefields. The following year, the Indo-Fijians accepted the old rates. They gained nothing except the label of being 'disloyal' — an image that was to hound Indo-Fijians when the Fiji military seized power four decades later.

The European-Fijian alliance prospered. The chiefs won a permanent place within a Fiji administration and tried to consolidate their monopoly on education. Europeans, likewise, prospered, diverting much of the colonial development aid towards infrastructural developments linked with their tourism investments.

Yet the alliance did not have it all its own way. By the mid-1950s urban developments had resulted in the growth of a substantial Indo-Fijian and ethnic Fijian wage-earning class that had begun to organise industrially. The development of the trade union movement was opposed by some chiefs who feared it would reduce their control over commoners. Europeans also looked warily upon unions because of the impact upon their own profits. Racially divided unions were considered by both sides in the alliance to be the best way of undermining the perceived union threat. Consequently, when a major multiracial strike broke out in 1959, the colonial state crushed the new union movement with the aid of businessmen and chiefs, and set up key racially divided unions. Among the strike leaders were two people who would figure after the *coup d'état* — on opposing sides, Apisai Tora and Jim Anthony.

Indigenous rights enshrined

With the union movement weakened, European businesses were in a strong position. Their hold on the tourist industry, however, slipped with the penetration of transnational tourism companies. In spite of this setback, the Europeans (as so-called general electors) constituted the second arm of the Alliance Party as Fiji approached independence. The major wing, of course, was the Fijian Association, led by chiefs and bureaucrats who had decided to use their positions within the colonial administration to consolidate state power. Although power was not intentionally handed over to the partnership of 'chiefs and general electors' in the Alliance, after Britain withdrew from Fiji this group became an oligarchy.

Foremost among the leaders was Ratu Kamisese Mara (he was later knighted), a Lauan chief with lineage stretching back to Ma'afu and Tonga's influence in eastern Fiji. He was the first Fijian to take a masters degree at Oxford. Although Mara did not join the civil service until 1950, politics gave him the opportunity to build on the foundations of chiefly-led nationhood that Ratu Sukuna had laid. He founded the Alliance Party in 1966 and became Chief Minister the following year, leading Fiji to independence in 1970. Promoting racial cooperation as the key to a happy and prosperous Fiji, he also recognised that a strong economy was vital. He played a key role in negotiations with the European Economic Community to safeguard a market for Fiji sugar, which helped bring the country prosperity and industrial stability.

Ratu Mara also campaigned to have the major powers recognise the potential and needs of Pacific island nations. Dominating the formation of the South Pacific Forum in 1971, he argued strongly that the islands needed trade before aid if they were to survive economically. He also played an important role in establishing the region's role and reputation abroad through his eloquence. But as Fijian society evolved and changed he became increasingly autocratic, aloof and unresponsive to his people.

In 1970 his Fijian Association had recognised what it seemed to forget 17 years later — that Indian support was essential if the sugar earnings were to be used to help Fijians as businessmen. In any case, the strategy was never successful, if only because Fijians found it difficult to penetrate sectors already dominated by Europeans, transnationals or Gujeratis. Also the banks were reluctant to lend money to other than established European and Indian businesses. Instead, according to University of the South Pacific historian Robert Robertson:

> [Fijian leaders] increasingly used access to the state to enrich themselves or relied upon traditional relationships to gain access to the finances of state-run Fijian corporations. In spite of this, Indian support was forthcoming, and many Indian businessmen [joined] a third wing of the Alliance known as the Indian Alliance. The ideological basis for this cooperation was called 'multiracialism', and it seemed to suggest that the days when it had been necessary to highlight racial divisions were over.[13]

In 1966, two years after a constitutional conference, Britain introduced a new constitution preparing the way for independence. It provided for a ministerial form of government, an almost completely elected legislative council, and the introduction of universal adult franchise. The electoral system did not have a common roll of voters and a general election that year exposed a deepening ethnic polarisation. Indigenous Fijians in the Alliance Party campaigned on a declared need to protect ethnic interests in the face of the Indian population dominance (Indians comprised 51 percent; indigenious Fijians 42 percent that year.) They regarded the electoral system of separate communal electorates for the different ethnic groups, with an indigenous advantage, as vital.

The Indo-Fijians, however, were mainly represented by the National Federation Party which, opposing discrimination against Indians, demanded the democratic principle of one man, one vote, with a common roll for all, irrespective of race. This party was led mainly by new Indian immigrants from India — such as lawyer A. D. Patel — who were strongly influenced by Gandhi and the independence movement against the British. They called for another conference the following year and their legislative councillors resigned in protest over the indigenous political domination entrenched in the political system. In the byelections for the Indian communal seats held in 1968, tension and racial polarisation was heightened by a growing Indian militancy over what was perceived as injustice.

Yet another constitutional conference was convened in London and an independence arrangement agreed on which also defined the role of 'general electors'. A political term unique to Fiji, general electors means the minorities — Europeans, part-Europeans, Chinese and Eurasians. Under the 1970 constitution, the country was divided into 52 electorates in a complex two-tiered system of national and communal constituencies. Each voter had four votes — one for a communal electorate of his ethnic group plus one in each of national Fijian, Indian and general seats. Twelve Fijian MPs were elected in communal seats and ten by cross-voting; the same applied to the Indians. General voters had a disproportionately high representation of three communal seats and five national.

Researcher Naresha Duraiswamy, of the London-based Minority Rights Group, explained the NFP compromise at the conference:

> The Indians, who were very active in the movement for independence, settled for the communal rolls and weighted representation favouring the natives in return for stability and a chance to protect their interests through Westminster-style politics. The native Fijians, anxious to avoid the fate that befell many other indigenous people of the Pacific and the New World, were satisfied at the constitutional arrangements which safeguarded their interests in the electoral system and in the ownership of land.[14]

The legislative council was renamed the House of Representatives and a second parliamentary chamber, a nominated Senate, was created. Eighty-three percent of the land was owned by ethnic Fijians and the existing law prohibited the sale of land by the indigenous citizens. Land was not given individual titles but was held in common by the *mataqali*, and it was classified into two categories — reserved and unreserved. Reserved land was prohibited from being either sold or leased to any non-Fijian while unreserved land could be leased to anybody, irrespective of race. Tenure for cultivation would be for a minimum of ten years (extended to 30 years in 1977). The law, therefore, explicitly denied more than half the Fijian nationals the right to own most of the available land.

In the Senate, indigenous Fijians were guaranteed a majority, giving them the power of veto over any proposed change. The Indo-Fijians realised that the dominant position of the ethnic Fijian establishment would block any change in the status quo and that discrimination was entrenched in the political system.

Under Ratu Mara's leadership, the Alliance Party led the way to independence. It was well organised and had a wide party base. For these reasons it managed to defeat the NFP in spite of that party's record among Indian cane farmers in the 1960s in their struggle against colonialism and the CSRC.

Partly because of the nature of the constitution, the NFP found it necessary to stress its Indian character in order to survive. But its gradual domination by business and professional men did not serve well its predominantly poor, rural supporters. Here was a potential source of conflict that racialism also obscured. However, the NFP narrowly defeated the Alliance in a general election in early 1977. It owed its victory to a split in the Fijian vote between the Alliance and the anti-Indian Fijian Nationalist Party, which had been formed two years earlier. Calling for the repatriation of Indo-Fijians, the Nationalists campaigned with the slogan 'Fiji for Fijians'.

The NFP euphoria was short-lived. Personality problems and class divisions caused deep rifts in the party and it was unable to form a government. The divisions provided the pretext for the then Governor-General, Ratu Sir George Cakobau, to ask Ratu Mara to form a minority government instead. A vote of no-confidence passed in the first parliamentary session led Mara to ask the Governor-General to call fresh elections in September 1977. This time the indigenous Fijian consensus was restored and Mara's Alliance Party regained power.

Recovering surprisingly well under new leadership, the NFP rallied briefly to perform strongly in the 1982 elections, when new economic pressures and a coalition with a splinter Western United Front Party of western Fijians provided opportunites for broader support. Shortly after, however, it was again divided and became politically impotent.

Nevertheless, the emergence of the WUF focused attention on growing disillusionment among western Fijians over the eastern-dominated Mara government. Just before the elections Ratu Napoliono Dawai, an Alliance backbencher and the Tui Nadi, made a dramatic speech in Parliament bitterly attacking the lack of development in the west. He then defected to the Opposition.

By 1985 the Alliance had been in power for 15 years and its leaders had come to accept their status as almost divine rulers. As Robertson described the political climate:

> [Many of the leaders] had also become corrupt. Their inability to create a Fijian bourgeoisie had resulted in the creation of a wealthy political clique allied with Gujerati, European and transnational interests, but the Fijian members of this clique depended more for its survival upon access to state perks and the abuse of land rentals . . . [They] were adept at defending their interests in the name of Fijian tradition, often arguing that privileges were necessary because of the 'backwardness' of Fijian people in economic spheres.[15]

The Alliance Party leadership, faced with growing criticism over its inability to confront economic and social problems, resorted to a sophisticated propaganda campaign to defend itself in power. Transnational corporation advisers with previous Central Intelligence Agency links were hired to plan the 1982 election strategy for the party. During the campaign Mara alleged that the NFP had received a $1 million donation from the Soviet Union. The only piece of 'evidence' was a photocopy purporting to be a letter attributed to then Opposition Leader Siddiq Koya. In fact, the letter was forged. Leonard (now Sir Leonard) Usher, former mayor of Suva, publisher of the *Fiji Times* and an Alliance Party strategist, and lawyer Sir John Falvey, were sued by Koya for defamation. Although Koya apparently had a watertight case, he settled on modest terms which were never disclosed. If the case had gone to court it could have proved embarrassing for Mara.

A Royal Commission of Inquiry was set up after the election to investigate Mara's allegation. It also examined claims by the NFP about foreign involvement in the Alliance's election campaign. Mara withdrew his allegation during the commission's hearings, so its main role was to document the Opposition claims.

The commission, headed by retired New Zealand High Court judge Sir John White, produced a report that was criticised for not going far enough. The original exposé by Australian Broadcasting Corporation's television current affairs programme *Four Corners* was actually more informative. What *was* exposed was that Mara's election strategy had been mapped out by a United States consultancy firm, Business International. With offices throughout the world, Business International was described by the *New York Times* as having done contract work for the CIA.[16]

Business International went to Fiji under the wing of a wealthy Indian businessman and friend of Mara's, Motibhai (Mac) Patel. He had engaged the consultants supposedly to advise his business. But they were 'lent' to the Alliance Party, with Patel claiming to have paid the bill. Business International had previously been active in Australia, especially in helping Prime Minister Bob Hawke into the leadership of the Australian Labor Party. For the Fiji contract, the company sent an Australian, Alan Carroll, a graduate of Georgetown's School of Foreign Service. He was joined by an American CIA employee, Dr Jeffrey Race, who operated under a business cover called Asian Strategy, based in Bangkok. The aptly named Dr Race was a specialist in Malaysian politics, which had a racial bias similar to those promoted by the advisers for Fiji.

Among scenarios proposed by Race was one called 'Malaysian replay' because of the 'uncanny likeness' between the political situations facing Mara and Tunku Abdul Rahman in Malaysia. 'Strategies' proposed included one aimed at nationalist leader Sakeasi Butadroka — 'either buy him off or take him out of the running'. Another, against Western United Front leader Ratu Osea Gavidi, said: 'Since he is going to jail anyway, best to pile all effort on and accelerate prosecution so he cannot run [for election]'.[17]

Carroll held a public opinion survey to identify the issues most suitable for exploitation in Fiji. He chose an Australian journalist to generate election propaganda for Mara. The job involved reporting back to Business International on campaign progress from a supposedly non-political position in Fiji's Ministry of Information. The White Commission report subsequently described the Business International recommendations as 'morally repugnant'.

But the relationship between the United States and Mara had begun earlier. For several years Fiji had been the Pacific island nation which most worried the Americans. It had pressed for a nuclear-free zone at the United Nations; it also barred nuclear-armed or powered vessels from Fijian ports in 1982, saying that a refusal to confirm or deny the presence of nuclear weapons on board would be regarded as an admission they were being carried. Since later that year, however, Washington had been energetically wooing the Fiji government.

The pressure on Fiji began after the vocal and vigorous Fred Eckert was appointed United States ambassador in Suva. Eckert was the alleged mastermind behind the Koya forged letter affair. After that year's election, Eckert accompanied Mara on a celebrated 'confidential' visit to CINCPAC in Hawaii. Mara was appointed to the standing committee of the US-sponsored and dominated Pacific Islands Development Programme (PIDP) and later became its chairman. Set up as an alternative to less cooperative organisations such as the South Pacific Forum and South Pacific Commission, PIDP is located at the East-West Centre in Honolulu. This in turn is said to be financed by USIA and the Asia Foundation, the latter at least formerly a CIA front.

Mara responded to the overtures the following year by dropping the port visits ban without consulting his cabinet, or Parliament. The gesture earned an accolade for Mara from President Reagan for having shown 'a high degree of political courage'.[18] In November 1984, Mara was hosted at the White House on the personal invitation of Reagan. He was the first Pacific head of government to be so. He was then taken to New York to be honoured as 'Pacific Man of the Year' by the USAID-financed Foundation for the Peoples of the South Pacific.

While Mara was in Washington, the United States announced that Fiji would become the first South Pacific country to get American military bilateral aid. This aid was launched with about $300,000 a year for Fiji under the Weapon Standardisation Programme — mainly for buying small arms. Justifying the grants to a United States congressional committee in 1986, Defence Department official Paul Wolfowitz described Fiji as one of Washington's staunchest allies in the region because it had 'reopened its ports to all our US Navy ships' and 'gives the United States particularly strong support on a number of international issues, including Grenada, the KAL [shot down over the the Soviet Union on an apparent spying mission] incident, and Afghanistan'.[19] The grants were to be followed by about $2.5 million a year in non-military aid, so that Fiji, already the most economically-advanced country in the South Pacific (apart from Australia and New Zealand), was getting far more United States funding than any other country in the region.

Labour poll victory

But the drift away from Mara and the Alliance had already begun. There was a growing mood for social and economic reform and back towards a nuclear-free stance. When the United States nuclear-attack submarine *Portsmouth* visited Suva in Janaury 1986 the Fiji Government tried to forestall opposition by keeping the visit secret until the submarine had arrived and by refusing protesters a police permit for a march through the streets of the capital. Instead, some protesters boarded a boat and circled the submarine — tailed by US Navy officers in a small inflatable who photographed them.

In July 1985 the Fiji Labour Party was founded in response to this new mood and also as a result of the government-imposed wages freeze and growing pressure on the unions. Fiji's first *real* multicultural political party, it adopted a social democratic manifesto for change and a non-aligned and nuclear-free foreign policy. The party also had the support of the trade unions. An ethnic Fijian trade unionist and general physician, Dr Timoci Bavadra, emerged to become party leader. In his inaugural address he declared that Alliance government rule had been characterised by social neglect and he pledged social justice for Fijians of all races.

Political and racial bickering is often heard in Parliament and not among the common people. We should drive home the message that the party was not only formed to win elections and gain political power, but also to change the society and uplift moral and material life to make Fiji a better place . . . Our aim is the creation of true democracy in this country, and to put an end to the many undemocratic features that dominate the political life of Fiji.[20]

Although Labour was frequently branded communist or socialist, its leadership was far from radical. 'The policies they raised were always couched in terms which reflected the party's major preoccupations,' noted journalist Akosita Tamanisau and historian Robertson in their book *Fiji: Shattered Coups,* 'the need to foster true multiracialism, to distribute more evenly the benefits of development, and to introduce a government that was more open and responsive to popular needs. . . . The party's leadership was clearly reformist.'[21]

By 1986 the Alliance was in deep trouble. The Fiji economy was under severe pressure after a slump in sugar prices and a series of devastating hurricanes. Government mismanagement contributed also to the growing domestic problems, particularly in urban towns where unemployment was rapidly rising and contributing to a soaring crime rate. Hospital services were under pressure, roads were deteriorating, and housing funds earmarked for those on low incomes were being diverted for high cost housing. Scandals were also rocking the government.

Although the Alliance ridiculed the FLP, the fledgling party's multiracial character was troubling. So too was Labour's sudden popularity — and its local elections victory in Suva. It appeared as if the chiefs were again facing commoner dissent as they had in the 1920s with the Viti Kabani movement, and in 1959 with the general strike. These fears eased, however, in two by-elections when the Alliance realised that in a three-way race it could always play Labour off against the NFP.

But in late 1986, Labour and the NFP suddenly joined forces as a coalition. 'It will be a chance to install an efficient, responsive government in place of one that has become arrogant and corrupt through its two-decade rule,' said Bavadra, promising a spring-clean of the administration. Faced with a general election in April 1987, the Alliance was stunned. It campaigned for the election amid an unprecedented series of scandals — and lost. The campaign was long and bitter, but it was fought on social and economic issues, not on racial grounds.

Foreign policy was not a key issue in the campaign, but it dominated news media interest in neighbouring countries. Satendra Nandan, a spokesman on foreign affairs and later a cabinet minister, disclosed two days before polling ended in the week-long election the coalition would put top priority on introducing a ban on nuclear-armed and powered warships.

'New Zealand has inspired us over what small nations can do,' he said, 'and we want to join it in having a moral voice in the South Pacific.' Nandan also criticised a series of newspaper advertisements which branded the two parties a 'communist coalition' and accused them of having a secret plan to align Fiji with Cuba. 'The Alliance is clutching at straws by making such preposterous and outrageous allegations,' he said.[22]

In spite of the smear campaign, the coalition won the election with 28 seats, a majority of four in the 52-seat Parliament. Significantly, the coalition captured the crucial Suva Fijian and Indian national seats as well as the south-eastern Fijian and Indian national seats. Nearly 20 percent of ethnic Fijians did not vote. More worrying for the Alliance, however, was the realisation that ten percent of Fijians who did take part voted for the coalition. And the swing was not just among urban Fijians, but also among rural westerners who saw Bavadra as their new messiah.

★   ★   ★

After celebrating the election victory in a *yaqona* ceremony in the Labour Party headquarters and after Bavadra had been sworn in as Prime Minister, I reported for the *Sunday Times:*

> 'Timoci who?' asked many of the political advertisements during the Fiji election campaign. 'Family planning: Eleven kids . . . where?' was another persistent theme. But Dr Timoci Uluivuda Bavadra, the 52-year-old kindly, compassionate Fiji Labour Party leader, shrugged off these attacks on his credibility to become Fiji's second prime minister.
>
> Known affectionately as 'Doc' to his friends, colleagues and party stalwarts, Bavadra showed Fijians that despite the bitter mud-slinging of the country's most hard-fought general election he had greater credibility than the man he ousted. Ratu Sir Kamisese Mara, who had led Fiji for 17 years with an increasingly aloof and autocratic style founded on his chiefly rank, was finally replaced . . . by a 'commoner'★ who convinced many ethnic Fijians and Indo-Fijians that he could usher in a new era of 'clean, caring and open government'.[23]

The Taukei Movement

Bavadra adopted the role of Prime Minister with ease and aproached his task not unlike a physician with a kindly bedside manner. Some now say too kindly. Labour dominated the 15-member coalition cabinet which

---

★   Although often labelled a 'commoner' by the media, Dr Bavadra is in fact a western chief. He is the head of one of three *tokatoka* of Vuda — the Tui Vuda is another. Bavadra's title is Taukei Werenitotoge. He does not use the ratu title that he is entitled to because he regards it an an 'eastern affectation'.

Bavadra carefully balanced between Fijians and Indians (seven ministers each and one mixed-race). Harish Sharma, leader of the Indian-dominated NFP, was appointed deputy prime minister.

But as the Alliance abandoned any pretence to 'multiracialism' and began to openly whip up anti-Indian feelings among indigenous Fijians in an attempt to upset the government, one cabinet choice by Bavadra in particular fanned the tension: former Opposition Leader Jai Ram Reddy, a lawyer who did not contest the election but is widely credited with having persuaded NFP to enter the Coalition in the move that won the election. Reddy was appointed a member of the Senate and given the portfolios of Justice Minister and Attorney-General. Bavadra was bitterly attacked as an Indian 'puppet'.

Within a week of the election, a militant Fijian movement, known as the Taukei Movement (from the term *taukei* for indigenous Fijian), with several key Alliance leaders involved, launched a campaign of destabilisation. The Taukei Movement encouraged fears that Fijians would be reduced to a powerless people in their own land. The chiefly elite had seized on racism as a desperate means of retaining their political domination, which was threatened by the new partnership between poorer Fijians and Indo-Fijians.

In fact, the Taukei claims of being genuine nationalist movement were dubious. The leadership was shared between right-wing trade unionists, virulent racists, Methodist clergymen with an Old Testament concept of the Fijian as God's 'chosen people' and defeated ministers who feared exposure for corruption. At least two leaders had criminal records, former Dockers Union chief Taniela 'Big Dan' Veitata and Apisai Tora. Nationalist leader Sakeasi Butadroka, who later allied himself with the Taukei, had been jailed in 1977 for six months for racial incitement. Once a member of the Alliance government, Butadroka rebelled after he decided Mara had sold out the Fijian birthright during the 1970 constitution negotiations. Behind their rhetoric, the Taukei were less concerned with Fijian rights than using the chiefs as a prop to seize power for themselves.

Fijian villagers set up barricades near the northern Viti Levu township of Tavua at Easter, demanding that the coalition government be ousted. A meeting of about 600 Fijians in Viseisei, Bavadra's home village in western Viti Levu, also protested against the government. Tora, a former Lands Minister in the Alliance government and an ex-trade unionist, accused the new government of 'dispossessing Fijians in their own country'. He also attacked the assigning of key commerce, finance, foreign affairs and justice portfolios to Indians. The meeting called for a freeze on land leases to non-Fijians.

On 24 April about 4000 Fijians in Suva staged an anti-government protest rally in Suva, the second-largest demonstration in Fijian history. Racist slogans included: *'Fiji for the Fijians'*, *'Fiji now little India — Say no!'*, and *'Out with foreign puppets'*. The protesters petitioned the Governor-

General, Ratu Sir Penaia Ganilau, with a demand that the constitution be changed to guarantee Fijian control in the country. Bavadra warned Fijians in a national radio broadcast not to allow a 'disgruntled few' to sabotage the country.[24]

'Let us not yield,' he said, 'let us not tarnish the image of tolerance and goodwill for which Fiji is renowned.'

A week later Bavadra ordered the police and military forces on alert after a molotov cocktail exploded in the Lautoka law offices of Justice Minister Reddy. Four nearby Indo-Fijian businesses were firebombed at the same time. Shortly after the fires the police detained Senator Jona Qio, one of the Taukei organisers of the Suva protest, later charging him with arson; Tora was charged with incitement and sedition.

In spite of a Taukei claim that at least 30,000 Fijians would blockade the opening of Parliament, the government refused a permit for a legal protest and only about 1000 people picketed the opposition Alliance lobby rooms. The Bavadra government was gaining in popularity and it appeared to have weathered the storm.

But then came the coup.

12

'Out of the Barrel of a Gun'

Agitation by the extremist Taukei Movement provided an ambitious third-ranked Fiji army officer, Lieutenant-Colonel Sitiveni Rabuka, with the pretext he needed to seize military power. Although the coup d'état was claimed to be a reassertion of 'indigenous sovereignty', in reality Indo-Fijians were used as a racial scapegoat for the illegal return of an oligarchy.

'Our chiefs,' said Taniela Veitata, now an Opposition MP, 'are really the guardians of the peace in Fiji.' A day after he and his Taukei colleagues had been plotting the next stage in the plan to depose Prime Minister Timoci Bavadra, Veitata was laying down the law in Parliament about racism.

'Peace is quite distinct, Mr Speaker, from the political philosophy of Mao Zedong where he said that political power comes out of the barrel of a gun. In Fiji, there is no gun. But our chiefs are there; we respect them . . .'[1]

Seven minutes later, at the stroke of ten o'clock, ten soldiers wearing gasmasks burst into the chamber.

'Sit down everybody, sit down,' barked the squad leader, Captain Isireli Dugu* disguised by a balaclava and brandishing a 9 mm pistol. 'This is a takeover. Ladies and gentlemen, this is a military takeover. We apologise for any inconvenience caused. You are requested to stay cool, stay down and listen to what we are going to tell you.'

Lieutenant-Colonel Sitiveni Ligamamada Rabuka, dressed in a suit and *sulu* stood up in the public gallery. He strode towards the Speaker — his uncle, Militoni Leweniqila.

'Please stay calm, ladies and gentlemen.' Rabuka said. 'Mr Prime Minister, please lead your team down the right,' the colonel said. 'Policemen, keep the passage clear. Stay down, remain calm. Mr Prime Minister, sir, will you lead your team now.'

---

* In his biography, *Rabuka: No Other Way* (Doubleday, Sydney, 1988), Rabuka declined to reveal the identity of his squad leader, referring simply to 'Captain X'.

Outside in the corridor, Ratu Finau Mara, son of the former Prime Minister, stood making sure the passage was clear. A back-up team of about 12 soldiers in full combat gear and armed with M16 assault rifles waited there. Moments earlier Finau Mara had been making room in the passage for the soldiers to enter Parliament.

Shocked, Bavadra, his cabinet ministers and MPs were led outside at gunpoint to two waiting military trucks and ordered to get in.

Education Minister Dr Tupeni Baba, noticing uncertainty on the face of a soldier near him, made a gesture of resistance. 'We're *not* going on the trucks,' he said.

Dou raici koya, sa lako yani oqori,' snapped Dugu. 'Watch out for that one heading your way.' Rabuka grabbed a loaded M16 from a nearby soldier and cocked it at Baba's head.[2] Baba, the most outspoken of any of the indigenous Fijian ministers, moved but still protested defiantly.

As the 27 kidnapped government members (one other MP, lawyer Rishi Shankar, was in court at the time and escaped to New Zealand in a vain attempt to seek help) climbed onto the trucks, the opposition MPs were allowed to leave the chamber.

A reporter walked up to one truck driver and asked, 'Where are you taking them?'

The driver shrugged.

'Who is behind this?' the reporter said.

'That's the question I want to ask,' added Baba, who had been forced into the front of a truck. 'We are just following their orders to see what is going on.'

As the trucks pulled away from Parliament, Bavadra turned to Baba. 'Is this really happening? A *coup d'état* in Fiji?'

The captives were driven to the Royal Fiji Military Forces headquarters, at the Queen Elizabeth barracks in suburban Nabua. They were imprisoned in the guardhouse. Heavily armed soldiers wearing military fatigues and gasmasks or balaclavas kept watch.

Democracy in Fiji had ended at 10.04 a.m. when the government was abducted. It was 14 May 1987 — 108 years to the day when the first shipload of indentured labourers from India arrived in Fiji for a new life of hope.

★   ★   ★

Colonel Rabuka, aged 38, a frustrated and ambitious third-ranked officer in the Royal Fiji Military Forces,* drove to Government House less than

---

* Apart from Papua New Guinea, Fiji is unique among South Pacific island states in having a relatively large military force. At the time of the coup, the Royal Fiji Military Forces totalled 2000 regulars with a further 5000 reserves. The army was made up of three infantry battalions (one reserve), an engineer company and support units. The majority of the force was on overseas service — one battalion serving with UNIFIL in the Lebanon, and the other in Egypt with the United States-backed Sinai MFO.

an hour later. Reporting his act of treason to the Governor-General, Ratu Sir Penaia Ganilau, he declared: 'Sir, I have done it! I have just neutralised the government and am taking over control.' Bavadra's team had been detained, Rabuka added.

Rabuka's superior, military acting chief-of-staff Colonel Jim Sanday, was with the Governor-General at the time. Unbeknown to Sanday, Rabuka had already warned Ganilau of the coup, later codenamed Operation *Kidacala* — 'surprise'. Speaker Leweniqila had also telephoned Government House earlier to report the takeover — before he was himself arrested. And while Rabuka was making his explanation, a statement was being broadcast on Radio Fiji at 11 a.m. that the military had seized political control to prevent 'any further disturbance and bloodshed' in the country.

Indeed, in spite of Colonel Rabuka's insistence that he had acted alone in carrying out the coup, later revelations suggested that the Governor-General, Ratu Mara and the Taukei extremists led by former Alliance Education Minister Filipe Bole were linked to the plot, or at least were aware of it in advance. As Rabuka himself admitted six months later in his first post-coup interview with an Indian journalist, Saeed Naqvi, of *India Today:*

> [After the Alliance lost] the Taukei Movement emerged — with all its plans for violence, demonstrations and arson. It was at that point that I went to the Governor-General, Ratu Penaia, and asked him if there was something we could do. This was particularly after the Taukei had submitted their petition to him expressing displeasure at an Indian-dominated government and urging him to intervene and seek an immediate review of the constitution. I told him that if he did not stage a political coup, I would stage a military coup. I then left.[3]

Bavadra insisted the Governor-General never warned him; neither was the military commander, Brigadier Ratu Epeli Nailatikau, nor his deputy, Colonel Sanday, told about the conversation. Was Sanday abruptly called to Government House on the morning of the coup to get him out of the way?

As the news of the coup spread rapidly around Suva, by noon a run on savings in the banks and a buying spree in supermarkets had begun. Sam Thompson, the young news editor of the commercial radio station FM96, had witnessed the kidnappings and flashed a bulletin immediately after the coup.

Nationalist leader Sakeasi Butadroka, wearing his characteristic red bowtie, harangued a crowd outside Parliament. 'Where is Kamisese Mara?' he shouted. 'Don't blame Bavadra, blame Mara who sold Fiji. Where is he now? Mara, the bloody Judas Iscariot!'

The Australian and New Zealand governments ordered their high commissioners, John Piper and Rod Gates, to boycott a briefing the colonel gave to foreign diplomats. At 2.45 p.m., Rabuka summoned newspaper and radio station executives to the cabinet room and gave a frustratingly vague explanation for the coup. Describing it as an 'interim measure' before electing a council of ministers to run the country, he said he had been monitoring the destabilisation by the Taukei in Fiji since the election and 'I see how these events could lead to serious situations and threaten law and order and property'. He did not explain why he simply did not act against the Taukei saboteurs.

Of the Bavadra government hostages, Rabuka said, 'I intend to release them under house arrest . . . they have not done anything wrong. It is my responsibility to see they are made comfortable.'

Colonel Rabuka announced that Brigadier Nailatikau, Colonel Sanday, Police Commissioner Premesh Raman and his deputy, Ratu Mosese Tuisawau, had been suspended. Fijian hardliner Josefa Lewaicei, a cousin of Rabuka, was named police chief. Rabuka also assured the news media executives that they could rely on censorship-free press, but he warned against inflammatory reporting. He was to regret this pledge. Late that night, after the coup leader had suspended the 1970 constitution, a smuggled statement recorded by the Governor-General denouncing the coup was broadcast. Ganilau recorded the message for Radio Fiji while under house arrest, but when the military prevented it being aired a tape was slipped to FM96 which broadcast it at 9.30 p.m. The message was also leaked to the newspapers. In the message, Ganilau said:

People of Fiji:

I am deeply disturbed by the events of this morning . . . The unlawful seizure of members of my government and some members of Parliament has created an unprecedented situation which must not be allowed to continue. The executive power under the constitution of Fiji is vested in Her Majesty the Queen, which by law and convention I exercise on her behalf on the advice of the cabinet. In the temporary absence of ministers of the crown, I have assumed that authority.

I have accordingly issued a proclamation that a state of public emergency exists and I am taking immediate steps to restore the lawful situation . . . As commander-in-chief in Fiji I now call upon all officers and men of the Royal Military Forces, the Royal Fiji Police and members of the public service to return to their lawful allegiance in accordance with the oaths of office and their duty of obedience without delay. For the sake of the peace and prosperity of our beloved country, I command the people of Fiji to respect and obey the constitution.'[4]

Both the *Fiji Times* and the *Fiji Sun* bitterly condemned Colonel Rabuka and the coup in editorials next morning. 'What of the blow to the national psyche?' asked the 118-year-old *Times*, the South Pacific's longest-established newspaper (now owned by Rupert Murdoch's Australian media group News Ltd). 'We plead with Colonel Rabuka to stop this coup that is tearing out the heart of this nation.' The *Sun*, jointly owned by the Sally Aw publishing empire and New Zealand publisher Philip Harkness, was even harsher. It ridiculed Rabuka's claim that he carried out the takeover to pre-empt the possibility of Bavadra calling on the military forces to quell civil unrest.* The editorial, entitled 'Dictatorship or democracy?', declared:

> This is a specious excuse and one that just will not bear critical examination because, when asked for specific evidence which would justify his action, Colonel Rabuka could offer no more than unconvincing generalisations. He had no tangible evidence to offer. . . . What right has a third-ranking officer to attack the sacred institutions of Parliament? What right has he to presume he knows how best this country shall be governed for the good of all? The answer is *none . . .*
>
> During the Second World War, the Fiji military forces fought valiantly and with honour against totalitarian forces to ensure the preservation of parliamentary democracy. Now, in one ill-conceived action the military has besmirched its proud record, each member has broken his oath of allegiance to our sovereign Queen, and collectively descended to the level of a banana republic guerrilla force.[5]

Rabuka reacted angrily to the press attacks. The new military government ordered the two newspapers to stop publishing indefinitely while armed troops and police occupied the two offices. The next day, 16 May, became the first time (apart from once during a hurricane in Janaury 1986) in more than a century that the *Times* was not published.

The military régime began a purge of political critics and opponents by arresting them without charge. Among them were Fiji Anti-Nuclear Group activist Amelia Rokotuivuna, detained at a prayer vigil, and two defeated coalition candidates, unionists Emma Druavesi and Jokapeci Koroi. The arrest of the three women coincided with harassment of foreign journalists. Masked soldiers with drawn guns launched a dawn raid on three radio newsmen whose reports on shortwave radio served as the major source of information following the military crackdown on the media. One of them, Radio Australia's Trevor Watson, was later expelled.

---

* In an open letter to *Islands Business*,[6] headed 'Truths Rabuka Left Out', Colonel Sanday later rejected Rabuka's justification for the coup: 'Rabuka purposefully withheld . . . important information from his military superiors for use in promoting his own political agenda. 'It was never the intention of the military at the time to order soldiers to shoot civilian demonstrators as Rabuka and his apologists claim. In a civilised society, citizens are not summarily shot exercising their constitutional right to demonstrate! Up until 14 May, public demonstrations by the Taukei Movement were peaceful and there was no justification for the military to have contemplated the brutal "counter-action" that Rabuka felt compelled to protect demonstrators from.'

Still detained, Bavadra smuggled out a scribbled note in his son's sock: it was an appeal to Australia and New Zealand for help. He suggested that ousted Brigadier Nailatikau — who was in Australia at the time of the coup — be linked up with two battalions of loyalist troops on peacekeeping duty with the United Nations in Lebanon and with United States forces in Sinai. (More than 70 percent of the soldiers had voted for the Labour-led Bavadra coalition in the elections.) Although Australian Prime Minister Bob Hawke and New Zealand Prime Minister David Lange ruled out intervention, both gave Bavadra's plea serious consideration. There was a vain expectation in Fiji among most Fijians that Australia, New Zealand and all the other South Pacific nations would go quickly to the rescue of Fiji's democracy.

The Tovata conspiracy

Colonel Rabuka appeared in his first international press conference flanked by two unpopular ousted Alliance ministers — former Economic Development Minister Peter Stinson, a local European and failed businessman who was the main target of corruption allegations, and ex-Information Minister Dr Ahmed Ali, an Indo-Fijian regarded by many as chief propagandist for the Alliance. (Ali later became 'education officer' for the military before being appointed general manager of Radio Fiji.) Speaking to journalists, the colonel made a false allegation that two members of Bavadra's cabinet had strong pro-Soviet and Libyan sympathies. The presence of the two former Alliance ministers, and the inclusion of Ratu Mara as Foreign Minister in the military regime, confirmed for many observers their suspicions that the coup was carried out on behalf of the Alliance Party.

In New Zealand, Lange bitterly accused Mara of acts tantamount to treachery, and he also singled out Stinson for attack. He claimed corruption by Mara's cabinet members was the real reason behind the coup. The military takeover, he said, was not because of Fiji land rights or bids to protect the Fijian way of life but simply to prevent alleged corruption by previous government MPs from coming to light.

'I have no fear about any investigation into corruption,' retorted Rabuka. 'I am not concerned about corruption.' (But privately the colonel *was* worried and he eventually launched 'Operation Yavato' as an ill-fated attempt to investigate allegations of corruption by the former Alliance government.)

Mara, said Lange, had pledged allegiance to the Queen but had been instrumental in bringing about a rebellion in one of her countries. 'It is perfectly plain from the reporting that [Mara and Rabuka] are very closely allied in this attempt to change the constitutional structure of Fiji,' Lange told reporters. 'The irony of it was that [the constitution] was actually Ratu Mara's creation.' Asked if Mara's role in taking a place in Rabuka's council of ministers were treason, he replied: 'In terms of the Fiji constitution, it is treachery, yes.'

> He has allied himself with a person who purported to dismiss the Govenor-General, to suspend the constitution and announce they would have a new constitution, which will be a republic if necessary. You can't actually do much more than that ... Why should Fiji flagellate itself, beat itself about, haemorrhage, go economically down the tubes, have civil disorder, simply because a few people have something to worry about and a few other people have something to hide?[7]

Besides Lange's bold assertions, there was growing speculation about Mara's active complicity in the coup — but no hard evidence. Although Mara and Rabuka had played golf together along with Suva tyre merchant Falo Keil, a Fiji-resident Samoan with close associations with the Alliance Party, at Pacific Harbour resort, outside Suva, on the Sunday before the coup, both men later denied the takeover was discussed.

Mara responded to Lange's attack by protesting his innocence. On the day of the coup, Mara was co-chairing a three-day Pacific Democratic Union meeting at the Fijian resort hotel near Sigatoka. A United States-sponsored group of conservative political parties, financed by the National Endowment for Democracy, which in turns get funds from USAID. Mara has had close links with this organisation. (Another vehicle for United States penetration of Fiji is the NED-funded Pacific basin Democratic Development project, run by the National Republican Institute for International Affairs.) Among those present with Mara were former Australian Prime Minister Malcolm Fraser, former New Zealand Foreign Minister Brian Talboys, ex-National Party president Sue Wood, and Australian Liberal Party deputy leader Neil Brown.

Certainly, the PDU meeting provided a kind of alibi for Mara, and both Talboys and Brown back Mara's claim that he was not involved in the coup. Brown also caused a minor political storm in Australia by offering support for the military takeover. Yet Mara admitted to *Islands Business* publisher Robert Keith-Reid that he had first heard of the coup about 9 a.m. on 14 May — or about an hour before it happened.[8] Also, his son Ratu Finau Mara apparently knew in advance. At 3 p.m., Rabuka phoned Ratu Sir Kamisese to say, 'I'm sending security. I understand your life is being threatened.'

Ratu Finau was Rabuka's link to Parliament House. On the morning of the coup it was Ratu Finau who did a 'head count' of MPs present and phoned Rabuka to tell him. So Rabuka entered Parliament knowing Bavadra was there. Many believed Ratu Finau represented the interests of his father in the hatching of the coup conspiracy. This helps to explain why Ratu Mara so enthusiastically supported the granting of 'pardons' to everybody implicated in the coup — Mara could not have been reasonably expected to allow his heir to the Tui Lau title to be smeared with allegations of treason.

Immediately after the coup, Rabuka commissioned Ratu Finau as a captain in the Army, even though the novice had had no formal army officer training and no military credibility in the eyes of Fijian soldiers.

Ratu Mara's failure to condemn the coup and his decisions to endorse it by promptly joining the Rabuka régime were seen by many Fiji citizens as further evidence of a plot. Among indigenous Fijians this was the first sign that the struggle was really between a chiefly elite of the eastern Tovata confederacy and the west (if not the rest of Fiji). According to one report, at the first council of ministers meeting 'Mara sat in the red, velvet-covered prime minister's chair while Rabuka stood nearby and called Mara "Sir" '.[9] Mara told veteran Pacific affairs writer Stuart Inder: 'I must take off my hat to the courage of this man. I would never have done it myelf if I were a soldier . . . What I am attempting to do now is hold the fire so my country is not burned to the ground.'

According to an elder from Ratu Mara's island, Lakeba, when Mara was a young boy he prided himself on being one of the best cricketers. (He captained the Fiji cricket team on an overseas tour in the early 1950s.) They played cricket almost every day at Tubou village and whenever Ratu Mara was bowled out before he scored enough runs, he would just pull up the wickets and take them home. No one would dare question him because he was a chief. And, said the elder, he had not changed.[10]

In his final Radio Fiji broadcast before being defeated in the April election, Ratu Mara had defiantly declared:

> I have not finished the job I started and until I can ensure that unshakeable foundations have been firmly laid and the cornerstones set in place, I will not yield to the vaulting ambitions of a power-crazy gang of amateurs — none of whom has run anything — not even a bingo party! . . . I will keep the faith. Fear not, Ratu Mara will *stay*.[11]

At the Great Council of Chiefs meeting the week after the coup, Mara again denied any involvement. 'But,' he added later, 'I suppose the suspicion will always be there.' The *Sydney Morning Herald* reported that the Australian government had received information suggesting prior knowledge by both the Governor-General and former Prime Minister.[12] It was also one of several newspapers which reported allegations of CIA involvement.

The Sydney *Times on Sunday* noted that while initial intelligence advice indicated a narrowly based military coup, within a few days evidence was available to Canberra showing the coup was 'backed by the entire Fiji power élite.'[13] But there was a growing belief in some Fijian circles that a tribal-based group of conspirators orchestrated the military takeover — the so-called Tovata conspiracy. According to this view, the Alliance Party and the establishment it represented, which is very much the eastern chiefly Tovata confederacy clique, felt that their right to rule had been challenged by Bavadra and his Labour-led coalition. The leaders of the establishment wanted to reassert their privileged position.[14]

Briefly, it was argued that there was a conflict between the traditional rulers and the new, younger, better-educated, progressive group of ethnic Fijians who were prepared to change their vote and bring in a government which not only sought a more equitable distribution of the wealth, but which bridged the ethnic divide between Fijians and Indians. At the same time, those who planned the coup blamed Ratu Mara for the Alliance's electoral defeat — one reason why they accorded the former Prime Minister a less elevated position after the coup was carried out.

How convincing are these claims? The Governor-General had been held in high esteem both in Fiji and abroad. A popular personality who saw military service with the Fiji Battalion during the Malaysian Emergency, Ganilau was widely seen as a man who took his constitutional responsibilities with great seriousness. From the start, he sought to portray himself as an opponent of the coup because he was advised that it was his constitutional responsibility to do so. He called on the Army to return to the barracks and ordered Colonel Rabuka to surrender authority to him. The international media and the Australian and New Zealand governments, although initially hostile in their reactions to the coup, helped promote the image of the Governor-General as an honest broker seeking to find a way out of the crisis.

In Fiji, however, there were some who took a more jaundiced view of the Governor-General's role. One argument was that Ratu Ganilau never had any intention of restoring the Bavadra government to office. The Governor-General, this argument runs, is a former Alliance deputy prime minister and has a close association with key members of the Taukei Movement. His support is for Rabuka and his objectives. Even if Ganilau was initially opposed to the actions of Rabuka — a military protegé of his — he had now effectively thrown his support behind the colonel and the Alliance Party in their attempts to win backing for the coup, 'not least by putting his imprimatur on a draft constitution which almost exactly reflects the aims and aspirations of Rabuka and the Taukei Movement'.

Rabuka, the 'Messiah'

Still something of an enigma, Rabuka began to give some insight into motivation and his vain, simplistic views by granting a series of 'exclusive' interviews in his barracks home with five women journalists. All pandered to his egotistical portrayal of himself. He was idolised for his good looks, charm, sporting prowess (he had represented Fiji in rugby) and wit; the dark side of his character was obscured. Among the eulogists for Rabuka was the *Melbourne Herald's* Lynne Cossar, who wrote:

> He sits comfortably in an armchair, cradling his sleeping son [Sitiveni jnr]. He has spent most of the evening with his soldiers in the barracks. Since planning and staging the coup he was worked 15 hours a day. But with the sharp wit that has not been presented to the outside world he jokes about the long hours of the job.
>
> 'If I had known it would be this difficult I wouldn't have done it,' he says with a smile that is dazzling. A smile he says which left one American tourist pleading for him to stage the next coup in her backyard. Rabuka says he, and he alone, planned and executed the military takeover of Fiji.
>
> 'I belive it was what God wanted me to do,' he says. 'It's very hard to swallow but that's what I believe. He has put me in the right position to do it.'[15]

No mention was made of Ganilau's fondness for Rabuka and how the Governor-General personally backed his promotion through the ranks because the colonel was also from Cakaudrove province. Nor of how Rabuka regarded his two superior officers — Brigadier Nailatikau and Lieutenant-Colonel Sanday — as obstacles: they stood in the way of his ambition to become commander. Rabuka resented Nailatikau's appointment in command merely because he was a chief and Mara's son-in-law. He believed he was better educated and better qualified professionally than Nailatikau. Sanday, however, was widely respected as the most professional soldier in the military hierarchy. He had much higher educational and professional qualifications than both Nailatikau and Rabuka, but being part-Fijian lacked the 'racial' qualification.

In 1985 Nailatikau planned to court-martial Colonel Rabuka for allowing, in defiance of orders, a major under his command to quit his post in the Sinai peace-keeping force and return to Fiji for the funeral of his father. Ganilau intervened to have the charge dropped even though Rabuka had clearly defied the orders of his military superior. Some years earlier, Rabuka had been disciplined over the disappearance of funds from the officers' mess while he was treasurer.

Rabuka was born in the village of Drekeniwai, Natewa Bay, in Cakaudrove province, on the island of Vanua Levu. Ganilau was his high chief before becoming paramount chief. Operations commander at the time of the coup, Rabuka had joined the RFMF in 1968. Like many Fijian officers he was trained in New Zealand. He served as a company officer with the Sixth Gurkha Rifles in Hong Kong, and in 1979 was awarded a dubious MSc 'degree' by the University of Madras for having completed a ten-month course at the Indian Defence Services Staff College at Wellington, in the southern state of Tamil Nadu. There he wrote a paper on the role of the military in the socio-economic development of developing countries. The paper was said to be heavily plagiarised from other writings on military coups.

Rabuka's flaunting of his 'degree' as evidence of his academic prowess — he used it on his calling card without identifying the university — was a frequent topic of bar jokes by his civilian and military colleagues. The colonel had previously twice failed New Zealand's University Entrance examination.

In 1980 Rabuka joined the headquarters staff of the United Nations Interim Force in Lebanon (UNIFIL), where he missed most of the heavy action that the Fiji Battalion had been involved in. Sanday had been in command then and Rabuka was envious of Sanday's better record as battalion commander.

Rabuka was among a select group of soldiers cultivated by the United States Army at the Pacific Armies Management Seminars organised by the Western Command from Fort Shafter, Hawaii. Then a lieutenant-colonel, Rabuka attended a PAMS in Manila in 1981. Among the more interesting speakers at that seminar was General Fabian Ver, the Philippines chief-of-staff, later found responsible for the assassination of opposition leader Benigno Aquino, and a sponsor of the aborted July 1986 coup against President Corazon Aquino.

Rabuka claimed in his biography, *Rabuka: No Other Way*, to have prepared a squad of ten soldiers trained by the New Zealand SAS for the military takeover — drilling his men in two scenarios: the first involved breaking up the Taukei Movement and arresting their Fijian countrymen. The second was abducting the Bavadra government.[16] In fact, military sources reveal there was 'nothing extraordinary' about their training: while the soldiers may have taken commando training in New Zealand, they were *not* trained by the SAS.[17]

Major Isireli Dugu, one of the colonel's henchmen, gave the orders for the coup squad to don gas masks and kidnap the Prime Minister and his government. A captain with only third-form secondary education, he was promoted to major immediately after the coup. He is married to the daughter of the late Tui Cakau, Ratu Ganilau's predecessor as paramount chief of Cakaudrove.

Lieutenant-Colonel Pio Wong was also promoted from major by Rabuka after the coup. An extremely ambitious man with fiercely nationalist Fijian attitudes, Wong is the part-Fijian son of a Chinese shopkeeper. He was regarded as the school bully at Marist Brothers High School in Suva. Like Colonel Rabuka, Wong is said to have twice failed the New Zealand University Entrance exam. And, also like Rabuka, he was disciplined over irregularities concerning the officers' mess.

Wong was put in charge of operations. As such, he was the man responsible for ordering the arrests and harassment of Bavadra supporters. But he later fell out of favour and was demoted to officer in charge of the military auxiliary unit which provided a labour force to help rescue the economy. At one point he was touted as the regime's ambassador in Wellington, but New Zealand made it clear he was not welcome.

The Governor-General not only granted Rabuka an amnesty for treason (which carries the death penalty) but also promoted him to full colonel. Rabuka was later promoted to brigadier after his second coup, on 25 September. A year after the coup he became major-general.

Rabuka claimed to have the entire support of the military. But as time passed there were persistent stories amid the glut of rumours spawned by the news blackout that several officers did not know about the coup, and were opposed to it or had grave doubts about it. Some soldiers were reportedly detained because of their refusal to follow Rabuka's leadership.

Many soldiers believed that had Nailatikau returned immediately from Australia after the coup, they would have rallied to his leadership. But Nailatikau chose to dither in Sydney.

The role of the judiciary

The arrested government was now moved from the military barracks to Prime Minister Bavadra's official residence at Veiuto, four kilometres from the city centre. On 17 May, just four days after the coup, military guards forcibly separated Indian MPs from their Fijian colleagues and transported them to Borron House, the official VIP guest house on a hilltop on the other side of Suva. This was done apparently to reduce the multiracial image of protests against the detentions. Bavadra's MPs — Fijians, Indians and mixed-race alike — linked arms and tried to resist being pulled apart. 'In microcosm,' noted one observer, 'the incident crystallised the forces now tearing apart the nation.'[18] Two days later they were freed.

After secretly swearing in Colonel Rabuka amid the post-coup chaos, Ganilau changed his mind. He had been receiving advice to support the Rabuka régime from Sir John Falvey, a former attorney-general, and Isikeli Mataitoga, a Justice Ministry legal officer who also happened to be an army territorials captain. However, Ganilau was persuaded by the Chief Justice, Sir Timoci Tuivaga, and the six other Supreme court judges to withhold recognition from Rabuka and to assume executive authority. In a letter, the judges said the suspension of the constitution and usurpation of power was 'illegal and invalid', and they pledged to uphold their oaths of office.

The judges prepared a statement for the Governor-General condemning the coup, declaring a state of emergency and ordering the troops back to their barracks. Their action was critical in withholding the cloak of legitimacy that Colonel Rabuka now desperately sought. Over the days that followed they continued to frustrate attempts to legitimise the regime. (When a republic was declared six months later the judges refused to co-operate. Tuivaga, however, eventually agreed to become the republican Chief Justice in spite of there being no constitution.)

As the Great Council of Chiefs discussed the military coup — a generally favourable one — at the Suva Civic Centre, young Fijians milled about a city in which the Indians sheltered in their closed and shuttered shops and homes.

'For the country's minority communities,' noted Suva-based *Islands Business,* 'the image of the friendly, smiling, easy-going, open-faced Fijian also seemed to have been lost. It had been replaced by a menacing military figure shrouded in a mask or balaclava headpiece, and pointing an automatic rifle in their direction.'

An Indian worker at Nadi Airport, Amjad Ali, demonstrated his defiance of the régime six days after the coup by boarding an Air New Zealand airliner with dynamite strapped to his waist. Announcing a hijack he let passengers disembark, demanded the release of the detained government and asked for the Boeing 747 to be topped up with fuel. It was also widely reported at the time that he demanded to be flown to Libya — a claim that turned out to be false. After a six-hour siege, one of the flight crew knocked Ali unconscious with a full bottle of duty-free whisky.

Two days later, however, it seemed as if the immediate crisis and the threat of bloodshed between Fijians and Indians was subsiding. Outwardly business life was returning to normal, the newspapers were publishing again and some of the armed troops were back in their barracks. It appeared as if the Govenor-General, backed by the judiciary, had done the trick. Rabuka's short-lived council of ministers had been replaced by a council of advisers appointed by Ganilau under the terms of the revoked 1970 constitution.

'*Sa noda na qaqa* — We have won!' declared Colonel Rabuka on Thursday, 21 May, his arms raised in a victory salute to a delighted Taukei crowd outside the Great Council of Chiefs. Whatever happened, he promised, he would '*not* agree to anything that will destroy the aims of the coup'. Ganilau was little more than a figurehead.

In an emotional speech to the Great Council next day, Ganilau announced he had dissolved Parliament, and he had terminated the appointments of Dr Bavadra and Ratu Mara as Prime Minister and Opposition Leader, respectively. He said he would manage Fiji's affairs as chief executive with the help of the advisory council until a fresh election could be held in about six months. It was also disclosed that an eight-member subcommittee of the council would review the constitution and make recommendations

Matthew McKee

Bavadra's supporters of all races welcome him after his release from detention by the Fiji military on 19 May 1987.

to the Governor-General so that 'changes will be in place' before the next general election. Initial reaction in Fiji to the development was of relief; the country had turned back from the brink of racial strife and economic ruin.

But then Bavadra, who with the rest of the detained government had been freed about 11 p.m. on Wednesday, 20 May, began to protest. Immediately after his release, he had cried 'treason' to foreign journalists covering the coup. Then, however, he had agreed to co-operate with the Governor-General's plan in the interests of maintaining and restoring peace and democracy. He and his deposed cabinet ministers reacted bitterly after the council was appointed. Only two of the 21 members were drawn from the deposed government — Bavadra and his Deputy Prime Minister Harish Sharma. Only two could be regarded as independents — and one, former Methodist Church president Rev Daniel Mustapha, quickly resigned rather than be compromised. The rest were linked to the Alliance and the Taukei Movement.

After a coalition meeting at Ba, in northern Viti Levu, on 24 May, Bavadra and Sharma announced they would boycott the first meeting of the advisory council due the next day. A statement was issued, condemning the dissolution of Parliament as

'unconstitutional in that it was not done on the advice of the Prime Minister as required by the constitution. The Governor-General's emergency powers do not allow him to dissolve Parliament. The purported agreement between the Govenor-General and those who seized power unlawfully is without any legal or moral basis'.

The coalition also complained that Ganilau had made a deal with Rabuka and the Great Council without consulting Bavadra.

Ganilau, however, was already in the middle of another constitutional crisis. He had apparently overlooked the fact that the 1970 constitution stated that constitutional reforms needed to be approved by a 75 percent majority in the House of Representatives and the Senate. This meant that technically the next election could not be held under the constitution rejected by the military and the Great Council of Chiefs. In order to change the constitution, Parliament would have to be called, and *that* Parliament would be like the dissolved one, with 22 Fijian members, 22 Indian members and eight 'general' members. As *Islands Business* pointed out: 'An election for a Parliament like that would quite possibly return to power Dr Bavadra's deposed government. But Fiji would be back to square one, with the Army, presumably, ready to do its thing all over again.'[19]

Outside Fiji other Pacific states were preparing for the South Pacific Forum meeting in Apia at the end of May. Most member nations accepted the coup as an internal affair and endorsed the principle of indigenous

Fijian paramountcy. Although Vanuatu's Walter Lini had denounced the coup as having damaging implications for regional solidarity, other leaders reacted more to the spectre of foreign intervention — particularly by Australia and New Zealand. Papua New Guinea's Foreign Minister, Ted Diro, managed to convince Rabuka that he had the weight of Pacific islands opinion behind him. He was probably right, at the time.

When Melanesian leaders met at Rabaul on 21 May they warned Australia and New Zealand against reckless military adventurism. Lini, already upset over Canberra's attitude to links with Libya, later accused Australia of neocolonialism and bias towards Western interests.

At the Forum meeting most island leaders tried to keep Fiji off the agenda. Fiji had earlier proposed to send a delegation, including Mara, but Australian Prime Minister Bob Hawke had said he would not participate if that eventuated. It did not and a Hawke-sponsored move for the Forum to send an advisory mission was adopted reluctantly. Ganilau's refusal to receive it was greeted with relief by most nations.

Perhaps inspired by these developments, Bavadra now sought to widen the basis for his support by appealing to the international community. He embarked on what was to prove a futile journey to London to see the Queen, who refused to see him, and to the United States and New Zealand, where he received only lukewarm receptions.

During his absence from the country the Governor-General's constitutional review committee had begun to hear submissions. Headed by Sir John Falvey, one of the architects of the 1970 constitution and a former Alliance Party MP, the committee received both written and oral submissions from throughout the country. Not surprisingly, its composition was heavily weighted in favour of the Taukei. The Alliance, coalition, Great Council of Chiefs and Governor-General each nominated four members; Falvey, who had strong pro-Alliance views, was the 'impartial' chairman.

Among the proposals that were leaked was a Taukei Movement master plan for a 'Fijianised Fiji' which was claimed to have the Governor-General's support. During a visit to New Zealand in mid-August, one Taukei leader, Alliance Party secretary-general Jone Veisamasama, likened his movement to the Nazis. He said his movement's dedication to the cause of the indigenous Fijians was similar to the Nazis' dedication to the German people. 'The difference was that the Nazis were misguided, but the Taukei Movement was not.' Taniela Veitata had already admitted that the Taukei had planned to burn down Suva and kill Indians if the coup had not taken place.[20] And now their draft constitution sought to have the 'foreign values of democracy' replaced by traditional law.

The Taukei submission, backed by Sakeasi Butadroka's Fijian Nationalist Party which wanted Indo-Fijians repatriated to India, urged that Fiji become a republic to ensure there were no legal means to challenge the new constitution in any external law court. This clause referred to a Supreme

Court action begun by Dr Bavadra to declare the suspension of Parliament illegal and which was expected to go to the Privy Council in London, Fiji's final court of appeal. The Taukei submission continued:

> As a concept of government, a *democracy* [Taukei emphasis] does not guarantee the paramountcy of Fijian interests, rights and aspirations. It, however, provides this guarantee to the interests, rights and aspirations of non-Fijians. This situation has arisen in Fiji because the two principal ideals of democracy — *liberty* (or freedom) and *equality* are foreign values, and are indeed contrary to the Fijian way of life where liberty exists only within one's own social rank and equality is strictly constrained by a fully developed social hierarchy.
>
> The contrast between democracy and the values of the Fijian way of life is much too strong for the former to be the basis of government in Fiji. In practice, democracy has meant the subservience of Fijian indigenous values, customs and tradition to the foreign values of democracy.[21]

The republican proposals were supported by the small Fijian Nationalist Party, whose leader, Sakeasi Butadroka, was, like Rabuka, a Methodist lay preacher. He had called for the repatriation of all Indians and wanted Britain to compensate the Indians for assets they would lose. In a signed editorial, *Fiji Sun* publisher Philip Harkness branded the submission as 'madness' and said it would set the nation back decades.

Submissions by the coalition, the Back to Early May Movement which sought restoration of the ousted Parliament and a bipartisan government, and several other groups favouring a genuine multiracial future for Fiji were disregarded. The constitutional review committee's report virtually rubber-stamped the proposals of the Great Council of Chiefs, including

1. A 71-member, single-chamber Parliament. It would be composed of 41 indigenous Fijians [an increase of 19 members from the present 22], 22 Indians and eight general electors as at present. Twenty-eight of the Fijian MPs would be elected by the 14 provincial councils, eight by the Great Council of Chiefs, one nominated by the Polynesian dependency of Rotuma, and four nominated by the Prime Minister.
2. The offices of Prime Minister and the ministers of foreign affairs, finance and home affairs should be restricted to Fijians.
3. The Prime Minister's four nominees, who would be experts in their particular field rather than politicians, would have no voting rights.
4. The Governor-General would be nominated by the Great Council of Chiefs for a five-year fixed term.

This, in effect, meant that indigenous Fijians would not be able to participate in general elections as at present but would go through their *Tikina* (district) councils for final selection of MPs by the provincial councils. The cross voting system under the 1970 constitution would be abolished, and the 22 Indian and eight general elector seats would be contested on a communal system of voting. The constituencies would be redefined.

The Taukei Movement reacted bitterly. 'We had asked for 100 percent,' said spokesman Ratu Meli Vesikula, 'and look what we ended up with.' Vesikula had spent 24 years in the British Army, retiring as regimental sergeant major. He added the Taukei were unhappy because 'our aim is the total abolition of the present constitution as it has proved harmful to the Fijians over the past 17 years'.

Bavadra's deposed Education Minister, Dr Tupeni Baba, however, mocked the proposals as the 'selling out' of the Fijian people. 'Under the proposals put forward by the chiefs the Fijian people will be disenfranchised because Fijian members of Parliament will be selected through the traditional process of consensus by the provincial councils.' He warned many educated, progressive Fijians would not live under the system. He said there would be a massive flight of educated and professional Fijians from Fiji. The proposals were a 'regressive step' designed to keep the ordinary Fijian 'backward and segregate him from society and modern forces which he cannot get away from'.

13

The Rabuka Regime

As assaults on civil rights and censorship worsened in Fiji, and the country slipped deeper into economic chaos, Rabuka finally removed any pretence that his was not a totalitarian regime with the introduction of the draconian Internal Security Decree in mid-1988. The new law, imposed after the seizure of arms smuggled into the country, gave the military and police retrospective and unlimited powers for repression. Any early return to democracy appeared unlikely as military control over the country became entrenched.

By the end of June 1987, Fiji was lurching towards an economic catastrophe. It threatened to aggravate the racial and political unrest that divided the country. 'Fiji is bleeding to death with savage suddenness,' said New Zealand's *Sunday Star*. 'Thousands are now out of work, industry and commerce is at a standstill and the nation is daily edging closer to bankruptcy.'

Ratu Ganilau's shaky administration was officially in control of the country yet was unable to halt army and police raids, arrests and harassment of the largely peaceful opponents of the coup. Deposed Foreign Minister Krishna Datt and Sugar Growers Council chief executive Sir Vijay Singh were among the scores detained without charge; Baba and Bavadra's new press secretary, Richard Naidu, a former *Fiji Times* journalist, were brutally assaulted. Yet the Governor-General implored the nation to support his path of 'national conciliation' back to democracy. As Ganilau and Mara warned that Fiji's Indians must accept Fijian political supremacy as the price for restoring national stability, sugar became a vital factor in the crisis.

The F$200 million sugar industry normally earns more than 60 percent of Fiji's export income. Fiji's Reserve Bank governor, Savenaca Siwatibau, had been expecting a boom year. After six years in the job, he was presiding over the South Pacific's most robust economy. The currency was firm, overseas investment was healthy, and inflation was running at less than two percent. With a record sugar harvest and thriving tourism, a growth rate of five percent was predicted. But when Siwatibau was told the Bavadra government had been kidnapped at gunpoint, he was said to have put his head in his hands and wept.

Later, determined to try to save his country, Siwatibau agreed to join the Governor-General's administration as economic adviser. In a series of tough measures, he devalued the currency by 17.75 percent, removed the interest rate ceiling and froze capital exports. He predicted a negative growth rate of ten percent during the next year and inflation at ten percent.

'I used to go to the Caribbean, South America and the African countries,' said the former International Monetary Fund economist. 'I know what bitter pills the IMF can make you swallow and I am determined that Fiji will never, *never* get into the arms of the IMF.' (Disillusioned with the coup, Siwatibau later resigned from his post and became the UNESCO representative for the Pacific in Port Vila.)

Six weeks after the coup, the four million tonne sugarcane crop was virtually untouched as most of the 22,000 angry Indian cane growers, backed up by 26,000 cutters, mill workers and drivers, refused to harvest. Two of the four Fiji Sugar Corporation mills operated in brief spurts, fed by a trickle of cane cut by small groups of Fijian growers. 'Their harvest boycott was their counter-attack against the army firepower,' said *Islands Business*. 'It was one that, if carried through, would ultimately deprive the army of its bullets since there would be no money left in the national treasury to buy them.'[1]

While the interim government adopted emergency regulations to empower the army to commandeer and harvest the cane crop, it was reluctant to enforce the drastic move in case the provocation forced an uprising among the growers. Sir Vijay Singh said the delay and a local drought had reduced the harvest potential to three million tonnes. After milling, he expected sugar production to be 325,000 tonnes — about two-thirds of the 1986 record of 501,000. He was also confident Fiji would meet its 170,000-tonne EEC contract while smaller contracts with New Zealand and Malaysia would be rescheduled.

Before the coup, 35 investment projects worth more than $200 million involving Australian firms had been planned; only five went ahead. The tourism industry was in chaos. With a turnover of $4 million a week before the coup, it grossed only $1.2 million during late May and June. Air New Zealand and Qantas abandoned flights to Fiji; cheap airfares and accommodation packages were introduced through the Fiji airline Air Pacific in a desperate attempt to fill the country's 4000 mostly empty hotel rooms.

Within two weeks of the coup, almost 1300 citizens had fled the country, most of them skilled and professional people. Twenty doctors and 92 teachers were among those who left their posts. Others filed applications to migrate — 27,000 registered at the Australian High Commission in the first three months alone. In New Zealand, an unprecedented 5000 Fiji students applied for 142 places in secondary schools.

By early August, however, with the Labour-led coalition agreeing to take part in the constitutional review, tension eased briefly and the economy showed short-lived signs of recovering. Indian cane farmers agreed to start the critical cane harvest, so avoiding the risk of general economic collapse. Australian and New Zealand trade unions lifted bans on Fiji cargo imposed by them as a protest against the coup.

'The Taukei vision of Fijians reverting to an 18th century economy in tribal villages betrays a limited grasp of reality,' said *Pacific Islands Monthly*. 'Taukei's dream of a "racially pure" Fiji purged of Indian influence and industry, without Western trade and defence pacts, and with press, judiciary and trade unions muzzled by military muscle is a recipe for ruin. So weakened, so chaotic, so friendless, would such a Fiji be that it would be ripe for the plucking by a predatory power.'[2]

A compromised media

While Fiji wallowed in economic chaos, Colonel Rabuka now embarked on a massive — for a small South Pacific nation — military buildup. With only 2200 soldiers (almost half of them in Lebanon and the Sinai) and 3000 territorials, the military rapidly recruited more troops. The target was to almost triple the military to 6000 soldiers.

'I put it over the radio Kitchener style,' said Rabuka. 'I twisted my moustache up and said, "Your country needs you". And the response was overwhelming.'[3] In late July, he told reporters that the expanded military, new helicopter surveillance divisions and crack anti-terrorist units would be around for a '15-year calming period'. Four officers visited Indonesia, Malaysia, South Korea and Taiwan to shop for new weapons and helicopters. By August, arms and ammunition worth $1 million were on order, five soldiers were being trained as helicopter pilots, and negotiations had begun to buy NB109 helicopters from Indonesia.

Fiji's naval squadron also wanted to expand. Two patrol boats were bought for almost $2 million from an American company; six other boats armed with rockets or missiles, and three landing craft were wanted. When French Pacific Affairs Minister Gaston Flosse visited Fiji in mid-August to present the Legion of Honour to a Lebanon veteran, he reportedly discussed with Rabuka a proposal for French aid to build a new naval base — a move that alienated Kanak and Tahitian nationalists.

A French Polynesia-based frigate, the *Balny*, later paid a lavish goodwill visit to Suva in what one journalist described as 'the best thing for Franco-Fiji relations since Dior produced the perfume *Fidji*'.[4] In October, Rabuka asked France to provide a team from the elite 'ready reaction' unit of the French gendarmerie to train Fijian troops in security measures. The regime also requested the supply of unspecified military vehicles and training for Fiji Army officers at French military academies.[5] In April 1988, France signed an agreement to provide $18 million in soft-loan development aid and Bavadra supporters claimed some of the money was being diverted to the military.

It is indicative of just how complete was Rabuka's control and manipulation of the news media that these developments passed generally without comment or criticism. The Fijian news media, particularly Radio Fiji and the vernacular newspaper *Nai Lalakai*, justified the military build-up as a measure to counter supposed internal and external threats.[6] In one *Nai Lalakai* article prepared by the military, democracy was dismissed as 'trickery of the devil' and Fijians were urged to ignore the educated élite.

> Colonel Rabuka had to carry out the coup because the Bavadra government would have allowed the Libyans and the communists to take over. We would have been turned into a laughing stock in our country . . . Whatever we do we must believe in God. Whatever Colonel Rabuka is doing is the will of God . . . We must not believe in idols, worldly possessions and witchcraft. Do not listen to those Fijians who are educated and cultured.[7]

The newspaper campaign echoed earlier Fiji-language broadcasts and reports that Libyan soldiers and Libyan-supplied weapons had been found in Fiji after the coup. Such unfounded claims were never broadcast in English. But the claims were used as a pretext to search cargo arriving in Fiji. In one case, Fiji troops seized the coffin of an Indo-Fijian who had died in Australia and been flown to Nadi. The soldiers opened the coffin and searched the body bag in what many regarded as a provocative act of disrespect for the Hindu religion. No guns were found.

Several Fiji journalists, reporting for international news services, were criticised as alleged propagandists for the Taukei Movement. Reuter correspondent Stan Ritova was engaged to help prepare Colonel Rabuka's official biography *Rabuka: No Other Way*; Jale Moala, the NZ Press Association stringer, was reportedly forced to resign from the *Fiji Sun* for his partisan views. Moala later became writer on Fiji affairs for the once independent *Islands Business* which faced criticism as an apologist for the Rabuka régime. *New Zealand Herald* reporter Karen Mangnall and former Television New Zealand reporter Derek Fox were also widely criticised as partisan journalists favouring Rabuka and the Taukei Movement.

One newspaper, *Fiji Sun,* remained defiant, championing democracy and the freedom of the press, New Zealand publisher Philip Harkness refused to be intimidated and would not agree to publish after the coup until total freedom was restored. 'To produce censored newspapers without editorials allowing criticism is unthinkable,' he told deputy publisher Jim Carney in a telex message. 'We would simply be turning the newspapers into propaganda organs for a totalitarian régime.'

Carney, also a New Zealander, penned many tough editorials with fellow director Miles Johnson. When the *Sun* was closed after the second coup, Carney and Johnson were detained without charge; Carney was later deported.

The paper's new editor, Nemani Delaibatiki, aged 34, a former president of the Fiji Journalists' Association, emerged as a vigorous journalist defending a free press while the most outspoken editorials were written by the publishers to protect him. A Mormon bishop, Delaibatiki had already run foul of the Mara government the previous year. He had become the first journalist to be charged under the country's 66-year-old Official Secrets Act because of an exposé about the Fiji military, but he was acquitted. The chief magistrate ruled that the prosecution had failed to prove Delaibatiki knew when receiving a leaked confidential report that it was in contravention of the act. The *Sun* had published a series of articles by Delaibatiki quoting the report which was critical of the command structure of the military and revealed low morale among the troops. Delaibatiki did not know that the leaked report had been written by a Tovata faction in the Home Affairs Ministry. The leak was aimed at undermining the leadership of Nailatikau, a Kubuna chief, and helping prepare the way for Rabuka to take command. Later Delaibatiki confided:

> In the past the Fiji news media has enjoyed a good measure of press freedom compared with other Third World countries where there has been turmoil. We have faced threats. The [Mara] government has wanted to exert some control . . . The Official Secrets Act is outdated — it has been on the statute books since 1920 — and it was the first time it had been invoked by the government. But the case raised the awareness of the government over how far the Fiji press can go in reporting events of public interest. Home Affairs security was tightened, special locks put on doors and screening introduced.
>
> During the election campaign, Ratu Mara made a veiled threat at a Lami meeting against the press. But, of course [Bavadra's] coalition won and everybody looked forward to open government. Then the Army took over by force. Colonel Rabuka met publishers and editors after the coup and said we could continue publishing as long as we didn't 'inflame racial tension'. We ran the strongest editorial we have published in condemning the coup. They closed us for five days. Now we have been forced into self-censorship. I have had anonymous phone calls and other threats against me. And I had been harassed. I am also on a 'hit list' of [Taukei] extremists.[8]

But in spite of the 'self-censorship', the *Sun* earned widespread respect for its incisive journalism. The régime tried to silence it through harassment and a series of lawsuits totalling several million dollars in damages claims. 'But,' declared the paper after one of its reporters had been attacked by Taukei supporters, 'let it be said loud and clear: reporters and newspapers will not be silenced. Where tyranny raises its ugly head we will report the facts.'

When the *Fiji Times* and the *Sun* were sent identical 'warning' letters from Information Adviser Rev Tomasi Raikivi, publisher Harkness reproduced the letter and said the *Sun* would not be intimidated. 'The claim by Raikivi, of all people, that both newspapers are guilty of publishing material "of a racist nature contrary to the Public Order Act" is the epitome of hypocrisy,' he said. 'We let the public be the judge of that.' The Commonwealth Press Union's Lord Ardwick also condemned Raikivi's threats.

In contrast, *Islands Business*, which had established a reputation for its independence over the previous five years, became criticised as an apologist for Rabuka. The magazine named him 'Pacific Man of the Year' in its 1987 end-of-year edition which featured a biased cover story on him, yet another eulogy.* In spite of the magazine's tame reportage of events in Fiji, publisher Keith-Reid was detained by the régime for four days. Keith-Reid wrote a series of articles for New Zealand's *Sunday Star* which were remarkably defensive about the régime. Among items about the interim government, he wrote:

> The semi-civilian government is the best sort of management pragmatic Fiji islanders can hope for . . . If you read different anywhere else don't believe it . . .
>
> Outside of Fiji there's been a lot said [by Amnesty International and other human rights organisations] about torture and beatings being handed out by the army to its opponents. What's the real situation? Actually the torture stories are almost all exaggerated. There have been some incidents of troopers overstepping the mark in pushing people around. In jail some people were bashed up. But Fiji under the régime of Rabuka continues to be a rather orderly place.[9]

The second coup

By September 1987 it appeared that Bavadra's coalition, Ratu Mara and Ratu Ganilau had finally reached a bipartisan compromise agreement for a caretaker government of national unity in the so-called Deuba accord. Two days later, on 25 September, Rabuka acted. Prompted by the Taukei Movement, Rabuka this time seized total control.

---

* The magazine's coverage of other Pacific nations, New Caledonia for example, also became rather questionable. In January 1988 Keith-Reid engaged a right-wing apologist as 'main correspondent' in Nouméa to cover New Caledonian affairs. Unknown to the magazine's readers, British-born David Los had close links with extremist right-wing French politicians. In 1978 Los had been convicted and sentenced to jail for the theft of NZ$60,000 worth of rare books from the New Zealand Parliamentary Library. He later set up the Nouméa School of English and began 'poison pen' attacks on journalists regarded as sympathetic to the Kanaks.

The takeover in 'Coup II' was followed by the revocation of the 1970 constitution, Rabuka's proclamation that he was now 'head of state', further devaluation of the Fijian dollar, replacement of the independent judiciary with military tribunals, the declaration of a republic and the announcement of a new hardline Taukei-dominated cabinet. He proclaimed his republic with theatrical timing at midnight on 6 October, well aware that international opinion had condemned his second military intervention and that economic consequences would be severe.

The security forces arrested about 80 politicians, civil servants, judges, journalists and others. Most were released within three or four days. The *Fiji Times* and *Fiji Sun* were closed again; the *Times* reopening again in November under terms of self-censorship while the *Sun* remained defiant — and shut down. A bomb exploded in a car in Suva, killing one man. In subsequent weeks bombs injured a policeman at Nadi and shoppers outside a Suva supermarket. Reports circulated alleging widespread torture and other abuses of human rights.

A series of draconian decrees gave the military wide-ranging powers of detention without trial. Under the Fundamental Freedoms Decree 1987, members of the security forces were made exempt from murder charges if they killed somebody while 'making a lawful arrest or preventing escape, to suppress a riot, or to prevent a criminal offence'. The freedom of political expression was suspended. In early January 1988 troops shot dead a Nadi nightclub bouncer suspected of being a thief in an incident the Taukei branded 'legalised murder'. In an earlier incident — ignored by the foreign news media — a drunken soldier clubbed an Indian to death with his pistol.

The 'freedoms' decree also declared it was the duty of the military government to 'protect and foster' Christianity. 'It can only be wondered,' said the *New Zealand Herald*, 'how Christ might have regarded the fostering of Christianity by a military dictatorship, but the Indian community in Fiji will doubtless fear what this provision could mean for them.'

Sunday activities were prohibited apart from going to church, a move clearly discriminating against Indians. 'Most of the new military council are devout Methodists, and there is a distinct methodism in their madness,' observed one journalist. 'The new rules for Sunday are simple and put you in mind of the old song "Never on a Sunday". Apart from going to church, and eating, pretty well everything is banned.'

Almost a week after the coup, offices of the Fiji Trades Union Congress and the Fiji Public Service Association, the country's largest union, were raided and shut down by the military. An industrial officer with the FPSA, Rakesh Maharaj, was at work when the troops burst in. He recalls:

> I was typing out a personal account of my detention the previous week. On my desk were details of personal accounts of other detainees. My task that

day was to dispatch all of these to Amnesty International in New Zealand. In fact, I had been doing that since the first coup. There was no time to hide anything as we were herded outside while the soldiers searched the offices . . . 'Where are you sending this?' an officer said after finding the statement in my typewriter. I told him nowhere, it was for our files. Later, we were allowed to leave and go home.[10]

At the time, the FPSA and other public service unions were taking Supreme Court action to block Rabuka's arbitrary 15 percent pay cuts. The trade unions were stripped of their rights. A régime-backed Viti Civil Service Association was illegally registered. Rabuka insisted the Fiji trade unions should operate like the government-run unions in Singapore.

Internationally, these developments found a focus when the Commonwealth Heads of Government, meeting in Vancouver in mid-October, decided after hurried consultations to expel Fiji from their ranks; at the same time Queen Elizabeth announced that the Governor-General, Ratu Ganilau, was stepping aside. The declaration of the Fiji republic was accepted as a *fait accompli* despite expressions of regret from Buckingham Palace. Commonwealth leaders had clearly tried to avoid a confrontation with the new régime in Fiji.

Attention now turned to the role of the Governor-General during the crisis. Although his stance after the first coup had been seen initially as courageous, now he was being openly criticised for what was perceived to be his heavily compromised role. New Zealand lawyer Dr John Cameron, a former Fiji magistrate and Bavadra's senior legal counsel, now denounced Ganilau's role throughout the crisis, challenging his neutrality in an open letter to the *Bulletin*. In retaliation, the regime cancelled Cameron's work permit. His appeal against the move was rejected in Janaury 1988 and he was ordered to leave the country. Cameron had served writs of *habeas corpus* which freed Bavadra and his government after the first coup. His letter, written two months earlier but not published by the *Bulletin* until after the second coup, said:

The Governor-General of Fiji, Ratu Sir Penaia Ganilau, is bound by his oath of office and constitutional convention to remain strictly neutral and claims to have acted so. Since the military coup on 14 May he has:

1. Declared a state of emergency in response to a coup led by his protegé Lieutenant-Colonel Sitiveni Rabuka;
2. Assumed executive authority many lawyers would say was in breach of the Fiji constitution;
3. Dissolved Parliament;
4. Dismissed the democratically elected Bavadra ministry;
5. Granted Colonel Rabuka and others implicated in the coup an amnesty expressed in extraordinarily fulsome terms;
6. Promoted the leader of the coup to full colonel;

7. Validated his seizure of that post by appointing him to Commander of the Royal Fiji Military Forces;

8. Sworn the leader of the coup in as chairman of a council of ministers destined to run the government of Fiji;

9. Appointed the leader of the coup adviser on security on his own lopsided council of advisers, granting him not only effective control of the Royal Fiji Military Forces — *de facto* control of which had allowed him to seize power in the first instance — but also of the Royal Fiji Police and the Fiji Prisons Service;

10. Enacted emergency regulations which have been widely abused by the security forces to suppress criticism of the regime and support for the deposed coalition government;

11. Appointed the leader of the coup chairman of the committee of the council of advisers which would recommend changes to the constitution further to enhance the rights of indigenous Fijians;

12. Rejected a mission proposed by the South Pacific Forum countries to be headed by Australian Prime Minister Bob Hawke;

13. Authorised the recruitment of further personnel to the Royal Fiji Military Forces;

14. Authorised an overseas mission to purchase additional military equipment, thus further entrenching the position of those who executed the coup;

15. Refused to issue the writs of election as required by the constitution, justifying that refusal on the basis of the existence of a state emergency;

16. Rigged the terms of reference of the constitutional review committee and stacked its membership so as to render inevitable a recommendation of changes to the constitution in line with the avowed aims of the coup leader;

17. Rigged the composition of the council of national reconciliation in a similar manner so as to ensure that the constitutional changes recommended will be passed into law, thus effectively rigging the result of the next general election and all subsequent elections for all time;

18. Denied entry to Fiji of the distinguished delegate of internationally respected LAWASIA, sent to monitor reported human rights abuses;

19. Claimed by his counsel in legal proceedings brought by the deposed prime minister not to be amenable to the judgement of the Supreme Court in constitutional matters.

If this is neutrality, God help democracy and non-Fijians if he ever decides to take sides with the Fijians.[11]

Foreign involvement

Speculation about CIA involvement had been present since the first coup but was revived after the 25 September coup when Australian journalist Wendy Bacon produced an SBS *Dateline* television documentary on Fiji which exposed the activities of several foreigners linked to the coup leaders.[12]

Right-wing Australian trade unionist Rod Kelly and New Zealand businessman Paul Freeman, who heads the Suva-based External Trade Organisation with links throughout the Pacific, were alleged to have connections with foreign intelligence services — including American and French. A 'handout on Fiji' by the United States Information Service was released in Wellington, apparently as a pre-emptive attack on the Bacon programme. It accused Western news media of poor reporting and repeating Soviet disinformation. No daily newspapers reported the Bacon allegations and Emperor Gold Mines manager Jeffrey Reid, Freeman and Kelly filed defamation lawsuits over the programme.

'One of our aims,' said Bacon, 'was to test the idea that the explanation for the coups was to be found in internal racial tensions and the fears of Fiji's indigenous people that they would lose control of their land.' What she found was not that these factors played no part but that for a struggle fought in the name of Fijian indigenous rights, 'there were some pretty strange characters lurking on the sidelines. All of these characters were white, all of them have played a role in recent Fijian politics and none was happy when . . . the Bavadra coalition government came to power'.[13]

The documentary also focused on the activities of William Paupe. A close friend of Taukei leader Apisai Tora, Paupe went to Fiji in 1982 as director of the Agency for International Development (USAID) South Pacific regional office. Bavadra accused Paupe, on the basis of Fiji security service reports, of encouraging the Taukei Movement to organise anti-government demonstrations and race riots after the elections; others have accused Paupe of being a CIA agent. United States authorities predictably denied all charges, but refuted only some of them.

Strong suspicions remained. Paupe was described by one critic as a 'barefoot Ollie North' after Lieutenant-Colonel Oliver North, a White House aide at the centre of the 1987 Irangate scandal in which arms were secretly supplied to *contra* guerrillas in Nicaragua. Paupe served with USAID in Vietnam from 1966 to 1975, when the agency trained Vietnamese intelligence and police forces and operated alongside or in concert with the CIA. From 1977 to 1981 he was stationed in South Korea, where USAID, through its bankrolling of the Asian-American Free Labor Institute (AAFLI), played a supporting role in the repression of labour and obstruction of democratic opposition. His arrival in Fiji coincided with increased United States efforts to stifle anti-nuclear and pro-independence sentiment in the Pacific Trade Union Forum.

According to New Zealand military researcher Owen Wilkes, the circumstantial evidence for United States involvement in at least the first coup was convincing. Describing the coup as 'the first fruits of the Caribbeanisation' of the Pacific, he said in a research paper that US intervention in Fiji over the six years before Bavadra was elected was well documented and incontestable. 'The one exception is the alleged funding of the Taukei Movement, which may well prove to be true. But at present there is not enough known to document conclusively the extent to which the United States was responsible for the coup.'[14]

While the accusations against Paupe and Tora over assistance for the Taukei have never been proven, there is evidence that money did change hands. But the sum was for less than the US$200,000 figure at the centre of the allegations, and the timing was before the coup. The *Sydney Morning Herald* obtained documents under the US Freedom of Information Act which showed that a USAID grant of US$25,000, supposedly for building a 'multicraft and training centre' in Tora's village, Natalau, was actually used to build a house for Tora himself in 1984.[15]

For the United States, the main issue in the Fiji election was the Labour Party's nuclear-free and non-aligned policy. Originally Fiji had been one of the leaders in the movement to make the Pacific nuclear-free. It had co-sponsored with New Zealand a United Nations resolution for a South Pacific zone in 1975, and banned nuclear warships long before New Zealand did. Then in 1983 the United States persuaded Ratu Mara to drop the ban. This factor contributed to the founding of the Fiji Labour Party two years later.

A week after the election, Mara made a trip to Honolulu, accompanied by Paupe, to attend a Pacific Islands Development Programme standing committee meeting at the East West Centre. A few days after Mara was in Honolulu and two weeks before the coup, the United States ambassador to the United Nations, General Vernon Walters, arrived in Suva. Walters has been described by the *New Statesman* as 'having been involved in overthrowing more governments than any other official still serving the United States Government.'* Just before arriving in Fiji, Walters visited Vanuatu where secret service men in his entourage discovered two 'Libyan spies' at their hotel.

Wilkes suggested that Walters was in Fiji to assess the situation, provide a diversion, and perhaps give a final go-ahead for United States involvement. There were a number of events, 'apparently orchestrated to accompany the coup', which suggested that the United States did much more than just provide a few of the stagehands. Wilkes cited a warning by United States Pacific fleet commander-in-chief, Admiral James Lyons, in Sydney two weeks before the coup in which he threatened to use naval forces against any Libyan activity in the South Pacific; Australian Foreign Minister Bill Hayden's dramatic flight to Ohakea air base to discuss the Libyan 'threat'

---

* Walters' career is described in detail in the summer 1986 issue of *Covert Action* magazine which alleged he was a 'crypto-diplomat and terrorist'. The general admits to being involved in the 1953 coup against Mossedagh which led to the Shah taking over power in Iran. In 1964 he was reportedly the 'lynchpin' in General Branco's bloody coup against Goulart in Brazil. Between 1972 and 1976 Walters was deputy director of the CIA and helped the agency through Watergate and the Pinochet coup against Allende in Chile.

with Lange; British Foreign Secretary Sir Geoffrey Howe's Libyan-bashing visit to New Zealand; the 'discovery' of Libyans in Vanuatu; the allegations of CIA or World Anti-Communist League support for the Taukei marches and firebombings; and the PDU meeting — Mara's alibi.[16] According to journalist Karen Mangnall, Rabuka actually dusted off a 'plan on how to stage a coup' which had been brought back to Fiji in July 1986 by a Captain Mataikabara, whom she claimed had returned from 'special training' in the United States. (In fact, according to Fiji military sources the captain had never been there and no such plan was brought back by him to Rabuka).[17] However, Ratu Mara had begun building up 'Fijian institutions, particularly the military', on the assumption they would be needed for a coup as far back as 1979.

'On balance,' claims Wilkes, 'the United States saw that a coup was possible: it monitored its progress, it helped provide favourable conditions for a coup, and, where possible, it steered the coup in directions favourable to the United States. Rabuka was probably identified by a United States talent scout as a suitable coup-maker. Mara had ample connections with the United States Government for him to make requests of assistance, or for the United States to make offers of assistance. By all accounts Paupe had the background and skills to head, or at least front for, the United States task force.'[18] Later, Wilkes modified his view, believing that American support was more for the Taukei than for Rabuka, and that the coup was actually counter-productive to United States interests.

However, although the evidence for CIA involvement in the coup remains largely circumstantial, there are too many coincidences for the possibility to be dismissed out of hand. Some involvement would not have been inconsistent with a CIA agenda. Only nine months earlier Ralph McGehee, a former CIA agent of 25 years' standing and author of the book *Deadly Deceits,* raised the possibility of CIA intervention in Fiji. He said in a Suva interview that Fiji could become a target because of the 'electoral threat to the pro-Washington stance of the present government'.[19] The *Sydney Morning Herald* alleged that five CIA agents had been active in Fiji just before Rabuka's takeover and that one had actually been in Parliament when the coup took place.[20] Even in 1982 the consultants Business International, known to do contract work for the CIA, had helped with Mara's election campaign.

The influence of certain Australian and New Zealand businessmen, however, is probably even more crucial. While Fiji had been a former British colony, economically it became a colony of Australia and New Zealand — which it has continued to be. It is symptomatic of the neo-colonial relationship that Emperor Mines manager Jeffrey Reid should enjoy a closer relationship with both Ratu Ganilau and Ratu Mara than did either the Australian or New Zealand high commissioners. The Fiji Labour Party's threat to nationalise the mine, later withdrawn, no doubt played a much larger role in the events of 14 May 1987 than did the stated intention to introduce a non-nuclear policy similar to that of New Zealand.

Former magistrate Cameron, who is researching a book about the constitutional issues of the coup, believes that the Australasian multinationals have been well served by the focus on the alleged activities of the CIA. The speculation has been 'diverting attention from the larger, more fundamental, and so far as Australia and New Zealand are concerned, embarrassing issues'.[21] The activities of Reid and other businessmen were of far more significance than those of any representative of United States intelligence. The relationship between the fortunes of Emperor Mines and continued rule by the eastern chiefly élite have been and remain strongly connected.

Counter-rebellion?

By early December 1987 Ratu Ganilau had finally abandoned any claim to 'neutrality'. Rabuka, by now promoted to brigadier (he almost as quickly became major-general), sacked his Taukeist government, 'abdicating' his head of state role in favour of Ganilau as President and Ratu Mara as Prime Minister. But as Home Minister in the military-backed interim government, Rabuka still held tightly to the reins of power. Rabuka's decision to bring back the political old guard, noted the *Australian*, 'is an extraordinary admission that he is ill-suited to the demands of statecraft . . . He has reached the end of his tether with feuding [Taukei] cabinet members.'[22]

With most of the key Taukei ministers excluded from the new cabinet, the Taukei Movement split with the hardline faction lead by Ratu Melí Vesikula joining forces with Sakeasi Butadroka's nationalists. They announced plans to form a new political group — the Fijian United Front.

On 22 January 1988, three spear and club-wielding Taukeists raided the Suva offices of Radio Fiji in an abortive coup attempt which failed to gain the support which had been expected from a disenchanted faction of the military. The crude plot, dubbed Operation Iron Eagle, involved a bizarre scheme to kidnap President Ganilau and replace him with the ailing former Governor-General, Ratu Sir George Cakobau. At the heart of the plan were the chauvinistic tribal loyalties and the deep-seated rivalries that had been inflamed by Rabuka's military takeover.

Ironically, as disillusionment set in over the failure of the coup to achieve its objectives, some Taukei leaders sought dialogue with Bavadra's coalition. They wanted a common front in opposition to Mara's military-backed regime. But the coalition refused to talk. Its bottom line remained unchanged: a genuine multiracial democracy for Fiji with a 'fair and equitable' constitution. The coalition resurrected its Operation Sunrise campaign of village education and prepared to consolidate itself under a single party banner — the Fiji Labour Party. The party's symbol was the *vara*, a sprouting coconut, particularly appropriate for the planned 'rebirth' of a Bavadra government in Fiji.

By June 1988 claims by Rabuka's supporters that his two coups were a virtual bloodless seizure of power appeared under threat. On 31 May Australian customs officers uncovered a huge illegal cache of arms — 'enough to start a small war', as one official described it — bound for Fiji. Sixteen tonnes of Czech-made AK47 rifles, submachine-guns, hand grenades, mortars and anti-tank mines were found in a container about to be loaded on to the Nouméa-based freighter *Capitaine Cook 3*. Consignment papers described the cargo as 'used machinery' shipped from the North Yemen port of Hodeidah and bound for Lautoka, Bavadra's stronghold. But the deposed Prime Minister denied any connection between the arms and the coalition. He also reaffirmed his commitment to a non-violent political solution.

'The deposed government cannot get a typewriter into Fiji . . . let alone 16 tonnes of arms,' laughed a spokesman, suggesting a dissident Fiji military faction was involved. Within a week, the Fiji military and police claimed to have seized three tonnes of weapons hidden near Ba, Lautoka and Nadi and said this was one-third of a shipment smuggled into the country during April. Three former coalition ministers — including ex-Foreign Minister Khrishna Datt — were arrested and later released without charge. After 43 people were detained in raids, 21 suspects were finally charged with arms offences, including Ratu Mosese Tuisawau, a half-brother of Adi Lala, wife of Prime Minister Ratu Mara. He was one of two accused facing the most serious charges — conspiracy to import arms and ammunition. Judge Sadal released him on bail, saying the charge was 'not serious'.

Yet for some the affair appeared to have the hallmarks of a classic case of faking a 'threat' to justify the emergence of a totalitarian state. It was reminiscent of an incident in 1963 when a junk-load of Chinese weaponry was planted by the CIA off the South Vietnam coast to 'prove' to journalists that North Vietnam was aiding the Viet Cong. Other more recent CIA-planted arsenals have been exposed in Central America.

The Fiji arms case centred on a London-based conman and criminal, Mohammed Rafiq 'Ralph' Kahan. He fled Fiji in the mid-1970s with shareholders' funds, leaving a trail of fake cheques. Caught in Canada, he jumped bail when he was returned to Fiji. He was later arrested in the Bahamas and returned to Canada where he served a jail term. Although Australian and Fiji police claim he is a Fiji citizen, his real nationality is uncertain and he uses many aliases.

Kahan made several contacts before the arms seizure, apparently trying to set up people with coalition sympathies and link them to the weapons. However, evidence pointed to either Taukei or military involvement — or even both. Kahan himself had military contacts — in April while in Fiji he had been photographed in a sergeant's uniform inside the Queen Elizabeth Barracks. In one photo he was carrying a gun and was accompanied by two soldiers. Also, while in Fiji Kahan developed close ties with several leading Alliance politicians, including Apisai Tora, Taniela Veitata and Ahmed Ali. The former two are now key right-wing ministers in the Mara interim government; former minister Ali was one of the few Indo-Fijians taken into the Army, with the role of education officer and the rank of captain.

The Rabuka régime reacted in apparent panic over the arms find. Rabuka lashed out at 'foreign government involvement', implying that India was behind the gun-running. A draconian new Internal Security Decree 1988 was signed giving the Army and police retrospective and apparently unlimited powers to combat 'subversion'. The decree empowered Rabuka to detain anybody for up to two years without charge and extend it for further two-year periods indefinitely; to declare any area of Fiji a 'security zone'; for troops to take any necessary action, including shooting to kill, to stop people entering or remaining in such zones; for any soldier above the rank of sergeant to impose curfews, and for any documents believed to be subversive to be seized.

Canadian-born criminal lawyer Christopher Harder was detained for a week by Rabuka because he took on the defence of men accused over the arms. Harder was also among lawyers acting for Kahan in an attempt to prevent his extradition to Fiji. According to Harder's scenario outlined in *The Guns of Lautoka*, senior Fiji military officers, businessmen and politicians had taken part in a plot to topple the military-backed regime.[23] With the fall of Rabuka, Bavadra would return to his rightful role as prime minister, or, alternatively, a government of national unity would play a caretaker role. The latter style of administration, under Ratu Mara, would supposedly restore democracy and seek Fiji's return to the Commonwealth.

During March 1989 the London chief magistrate, Sir David Hopkin, rejected the régime's request for the extradition of Kahan. Sir David freed him on the ground that the alleged offence was primarily political: 'The importation of arms in the circumstances of the present régime in Fiji could not have been done if there was no complicity. There must have been substantial support to enable the arms to get in.'

Meanwhile, on 22 July 1988 a leading Taukei activist, Jone Veisamasama, who had been Rural Development Minister in the post-coup Taukei-dominated regime, died in hospital from a gunshot wound from a small-calibre Lebanese-made pistol designed to look like a pen. Although the mysterious case was officially treated as an accident and three men, including a former Alliance MP, were prosecuted for arms offences as a result, there was widespread speculation about his death being an assassination.

★   ★   ★

The Internal Security Decree was similar to powers adopted by the military after the coups but later toned down by the interim civilian administration. Claims that strong military action was needed to 'safeguard the pace towards restoration of democracy' were rejected by Bavadra and foreign opponents of the régime. The relative lack of death and destruction could not disguise the fact the régime owed its position to armed violence in which a democratically-elected government had been overthrown by the Army. Fijian politics, lamented New Zealand's *Dominion*, had become a sinister mixture of tragedy and farce.

> [Rabuka], making good use of the emergency powers he [has given] himself, has arrested an academic who wrote a critical review of his book. The sensitive author has also given a public blessing to Fijian rugby tours of South Africa, and unblushingly described his own regime as a species of apartheid. He would be merely ridiculous if he were not able to impose his racist and reactionary prejudices on the people of Fiji. As it is, he is an increasingly dangerous buffoon, and what he is doing to his country is no joke at all.[24]

But Brigadier Rabuka had long turned his back on international opinion. 'We don't care about the modern world,' he said. 'We don't have to abide by what the modern world wants. It is right for the Fijians,' What the régime was concerned about more than the world view was the consequences of their decisions for the indigenous Fijian people.

The Taukei Movement's 'legitimacy' had been strong only so long as it presented itself as the champion of the revival of the traditional chiefly system. By sabotaging the Deuba accord decision of the two most prominent chiefs, the second coup partly 'exposed to the Fijian people the hypocrisy of some of the commoners and lesser chiefs in the Taukei Movement (people like Tora, Veitata and Ratu Meli Vesikula) and the military who are merely using nationalism as an ideological cover to promote their own ambitions'.[25]

As traditional chiefs themselves, Ganilau and Mara could only resolve the contradiction between their allegiance to the autocratic elements of Fijian politics and the principles of democratic multiracialism by choosing in favour of autocracy. The widespread opposition to the draft constitution* towards the end of 1988 underlined this contradiction. In December Bavadra made a personal submission to the constitutional inquiry, warning that the undemocratic document could allow a government to be formed with less

---

* Under the draft constitution, the 71-seat Parliament would contain no Senate, or Upper House, as existed in the 1970 constitution. It would have 59 elected MPs, eight MPs appointed by the Bose Levu Vakaturaga through the President, plus four MPs appointed by the Prime Minister. Of the elected MPs, all would represent racially exclusive communal electorates — 28 Fijian, 22 Indo-Fijian, eight general electors and one Rotuman. Of the appointed MPs, at least one through the President must be Commander of the Armed Forces (who would also be Defence Minister regardless of the party winning office). Any MP who is no longer a member of his party is expelled from Parliament.

than 20 percent of the popular vote. He said that a combination of a massive gerrymander and appointed MPs could enable such a minority to gain a majority of 24 elected and 12 appointed MPs in the proposed 71-seat House. As submissions opposed to the racially-based draft continued to be presented, Rabuka threatened he would stage a third coup if the document was rejected.

Although President Ganilau declared the constitution would have to be accepted by the majority of people in Fiji, he made no provision for the majority to express their wish through any sort of referendum, or for a broadly based commission to draw up an acceptable document. Under the draft document, Fiji is established as a republic that upholds 'the teaching of the Lord Jesus Christ' although nominal Christians comprise only 53 percent of the population; indigenous Fijians are granted special privileges, particularly the chiefs who are shielded from public and news media scrutiny; the 'fundamental freedoms' provision is reintroduced, granting the right to kill under certain security clauses; capital punishment is reintroduced; and the state is granted the right to seize property belonging to an undefined 'enemy'. The President, chosen by a small group (the Bose Levu Vukaturaga) of aristocratic nominees from the three Fijian confederacies for five years, must be Fijian and retains full executive power. He nominates both the Prime Minister and the opposition leader.

The way to interpret the coups and their aftermath, according to Professor Yash Ghai, a constitutional adviser on South Pacific affairs, is not in terms of race but in terms of the Fijian chiefly élite versus Fijian workers.[26] This is the argument adopted by former University of the South Pacific academic Robert Robertson and Fijian journalist Akosita Tamanisau in their book *Fiji: Shattered Coups*.[27] The racial emphasis by Rabuka and the Taukei was intended to restore politics to racial polarities and thus strengthen the élite. Most of the chiefs feared they were beginning to lose their traditional hold over their people. Many were also alarmed by the revelations of corruption that were threatened by the Bavadra government and the possibility that they might have to distribute more of their land rental income to commoner Fijians.

Race had been exploited during the colonial era by Europeans and chiefs alike, and successfully tapped by Mara's Alliance in its election campaigns since independence. But the tactics of the Alliance had finally failed to achieve their usual success.

In reality, the 1987 elections were not exclusively an Indo-Fijian victory, nor was the resulting government Indian dominated. It was a non-racial government; the Indo-Fijians held only half the cabinet seats, and were in a minority of the House of Representatives. The Prime Minister was Fijian, and he and his Fijian colleagues held the balance of power. The truth is there was no threat to any specific Fijian interests.

The *real* threat, in fact, was that Bavadra and his Labour Party-led coalition had shown a way out of the racial straitjacket of the constitution.

They had changed the political emphasis from race to the issues of economic class, social justice and common interest. This the Fijian oligarchy refused to accept. Ironically, it is the indigenous Fijian commoners, as well as the poor Indo-Fijians, who are the biggest losers from the coups.

Part 5
Dilemmas of Nationalism

14

'Nomads' and Delusions

While Fiji was effectively a police state in the control of its own army, Kanaks were under French military occupation with a 'nomadisation' strategy reminiscent of the Algerian War. Tension had grown again in New Caledonia as a so-called referendum on independence loomed late in 1987.

Maurice Lenormand burst angrily into the meeting room at the Kanak headquarters in a firebomb-damaged bungalow in the Nouméa suburb of Vallée du Tir. It was early May 1986. Brandishing a tattered copy of the *Revue Militaire d'Information*, the man who became dubbed the 'first Kanak deputy' by *Caldoches* opposed to independence thrust it in front of his colleagues.[1]

'Do you see *this*?' he asked. 'Here is what the bastards are up to.'

Lenormand told the members of the Kanak Socialist National Liberation Front political bureau that he had discovered in a January 1957 issue of the magazine an article explaining the nomadisation military strategy used in the Algerian war of independence. It noted how 'nomad' mobile units, led by élite troops in action against the Algerian 'rebels', countered the 'Marxist-Leninist doctrine of revolutionary war' and prepared 'pacification'. Once established in controlling strategic points, the soldiers divided and 'mastered' the local population.

> This control could be achieved in different ways. The most efficient is to set up a network of small active posts so the garrisons are able to get to know the local population. But it is not always possible to use this system: it is a serious mistake, in effect, to establish posts too weak which can quickly become encircled and threatened. It is better that the quality of the troops makes ['nomadisation'] work; this has the advantage of keeping the rebels guessing about the activity of our detachments or setting up big camps far too strong to attack . . . Experience proves that the only way to control the population is to live close by all the time.[2]

Lenormand discovered the article in May 1986. The previous month the French military had embarked on a new strategy in the territory involving the setting up of small mobile camps. By January 1987, when I toured villages around the main island of Grand Terre, the east coast and northern tip were under the yoke of an army of occupation. More than twenty 'nomad' camps of élite French troops had been established in strategic villages known to have strong FLNKS support.

Already New Caledonia's neighbours in the Pacific were interpreting the victory of the centre-right goverment of French Prime Minister Jacques Chirac in March as a serious setback for independence as the new leader hastily set about scrapping the reforms initiated by the socialists. Visiting Nouméa at the end of April, Overseas Territories Minister Bernard Pons disclosed plans to stifle the authority of the four regional governments — three of them controlled by the FLNKS. Former Prime Minister Laurent Fabius had intended the local governments to accelerate the transfer of power to local hands as a prelude to full self-government and possible independence. Pons also pledged a referendum 'within a year' but it was clear it would be stage-managed to ensure a vote for continuing French rule.

In Polynesia, Chirac's ally Gaston Flosse and his ruling *Tahoeraa Huiraatira* party were further entrenched with 21 of the 41 seats in the Territorial Assembly. He was rewarded by becoming appointed State Secretary for Pacific Affairs — the first Pacific Islander to be included in a French cabinet. His role was to enhance the damaged French image in the region. But he had a 'hands off' brief on the New Caledonian issue. The election changes were a severe setback for the *indépendanistes* throughout the region. But nowhere was the reverse more clearly illustrated than in the military buildup and the provocative 'nomadisation' policy.

By May, French authorities conceded there were 6000 troops (reliable sources put the real figure closer to 8000) gendarmes and riot police in the territory — one for every 24 civilians in a population of 145,000. The military claimed only about 1100 'nomad' soldiers on the mainly Kanak east coast, but during my tour I estimated considerably more. The 8th Marine Infantry Paratrooper Regiment was among the first units deployed in the mobile camps. Less than a year earlier the regiment had intervened against Libyan-backed rebels in Chad. A year before it had been based in Beirut. (The 8th was succeeded by the black-beret 3rd Marine Infantry Regiment and the red-beret 6th Marine Infantry Paratrooper Regiment.)

'It's just like Algeria all over again — France never learns from its colonial history,' said Jean-Jacques Bourdinat, aged 51, a Sydney-educated, fourth-generation *Caldoche*. A human rights campaigner and an FLNKS official, he spoke after having heard a report of the military occupation of the north-western Belep Islands by paratroopers during 1987.

'This is crazy,' he said. 'We are in the powder keg of the Pacific and the military carry on as if they are already at war. They are determined to crush us; if not by intimidation, then by provocation.'

But General Michel Franceschi, then Commander-in-Chief of French forces in New Caledonia, rejected comparisons with Algeria. He claimed the military had restored law and order and earned respect from Kanaks by providing them with aid and protecting them from attack from heavily-armed, white anti-independence vigilantes.

'We could have had a problem with revolution here,' he said. 'The context here has been a little explosive. What we are doing is a matter of security. If we hadn't acted I believe there would have been violence in the tribal areas. We are reassuring the people. It's an old military principle — nothing new.'[3]

Franceschi, aged 56, a two-star general, took command in New Caledonia three months before the November 1984 election insurrection. At the time, the military took no direct role in law and order apart from guarding key communications and strategic installations and providing transport for squads of *gendarmes mobiles*. In fact, under the French system the military usually can act only against an external enemy. The task of maintaining law and order is the responsibility of the gendarmes and gendarmes mobiles — but the distinction between police and military roles has now become blurred in New Caledonia. A change of policy began less than a month after Prime Minister Jacques Chirac's conservative government replaced the socialists in the March 1986 election. As 'nomad' camps were set up in the *brousse,* fewer paramilitary police were needed.

The FLNKS claimed the strategy to 'win the hearts and minds' of the people was a cover for intimidating Kanak villagers and gathering intelligence on local independence leaders and any fresh Kanak campaign tactics. Franceschi denied the claim: 'The army is not political. Political problems are the *government's* problems. We are not there to say to the Kanaks, "You must vote in the referendum". It is merely a matter of security. Our soldiers perform useful tasks locally, like carrying out road works and providing transport.'

Franceschi claimed there had been few incidents of tension between soldiers and Kanaks, a view that was not shared by either the villagers I talked to or the FLNKS leadership. Among the sources of tension were:

The Poupeyron affair: On 6 September 1986, 17-year-old Jean-Christophe Poupeyron was shot and wounded by a lieutenant in the village of Nakéty, near Canala. An inquiry was hushed up and the soldier posted back to France without facing any disciplinary action.

Accounts of what happened differ sharply between the official military version and the villagers. According to the military, they had gone to Nakéty to speak to the chief about a football match with the villagers. On the way in, a group of youths who had been drinking threw stones at two soldiers in a jeep. After the stone-throwing, the lieutenant fired into the air and wounded Poupeyron accidentally because he was standing on the rise of a hill.

Villagers reject this version. Witnesses described how the group of youths had cynically offered the soldiers a beer as they drove into the village to speak to the chief. As the jeep left, Poupeyron gave an abusive gesture to the soldiers with his forearm. The lieutenant swung around in his seat, aimed the pistol, shot Poupeyron in the stomach and then drove off. The eyewitnesses pointed out there was no hill, as the military claimed, and there were no stones on the road. Investigators were aware of the conflict in the military account, but they dropped the inquiry.

Draft dodgers: Kanaks in several villages on the east coast have accused soldiers of entering and searching houses on the pretext of hunting for Kanaks dodging the military draft, or of looking for stolen firearms.

Harassment: Troops in the Houailou area are among the many units that have been involved in harassment raids. On 8 January 1987, a company of 60 *gendarmes mobiles* raided and occupied the agricultural college of Doneva which belongs to the pro-independence Evangelical Church. Schoolteacher Ismet Kurtovitch was arrested and held for 48 hours before being released.

The Beleps 'invasion': On 16 January 1987, 104 paratroopers and other soldiers, and 20 *gendarmes mobiles* occupied the Belep Islands, off the northwestern tip of Grande Terre, to 'nomadise' the area. The islands are among the most peaceful districts of New Caledonia and have a population of 900, mainly women and children. The Kanaks set up barricades on the road from the airstrip and refused to allow the troops into the main village of Wala.

Mayor Aymard Bouanaoue, who had just been elected Kanaky Security Minister, was in Nouméa at the time for a political bureau meeting. He and other FLNKS officials immediately put pressure on French High Commissioner Jean Montpezat to order the troops to withdraw. Montpezat said it was 'technically impossible' to pull back the troops. The military commander demanded that his soldiers be allowed passage through the village to 'conduct exercises'. The villagers refused to dismantle their barricades.

About 30 *gendarmes mobiles* were then airlifted to the Beleps at dawn on 18 January. The men camped on the plateau overlooking the village. Bouanaoue was abused by a lieutenant when soldiers tried to enter the village. When the unarmed villagers refused to abandon their barricades, the officer threatened them.

'I'll enter the village, I will kill everybody . . . the houses will be burned,' he said. 'I'm not afraid of you bastards. I'll shut you up!'

But as tension grew, the troops were ordered to withdraw and they left the next day — three days after they had arrived. Bouanaoue claimed the French military were trying to terrorise the local people with 'nomadisation', by using battle-hardened troops from Lebanon and Chad.

> In some villages they try to win the confidence of our people — play football with the kids and that sort of thing. And then . . . *wham!* . . . they hit with a harassment raid. In one case, at a village near Thio, a house was surrounded at 5 a.m. They smashed the windows and threw a teargas grenade inside. The terrified women and children inside tried to defend themselves with what they had — stones. But against armed soldiers, what's that?[4]

Military authorities were reluctant to talk to foreign journalists about operations in the bush. In October 1986, however, a small group of hand-picked journalists was given a briefing and taken on tour. Kanak leaders accused the military of staging a public relations 'whitewash' because the journalists were shepherded away from troubled villages. According to one account of the tour in the *International Herald Tribune*, paratroopers were now pruning coffee trees, hauling road metal and 'studying' the 13,000 Kanaks in the 75 *tribus* under their jurisdiction. The paper's correspondent reported the soldiers were brought in to Goyetta, near the east coast nickel plant of Poro, for a 'totally novel mission for the regiment'.

> 'When we first arrived they said we would rape the women, kill the men and bring AIDS to the country,' said Captain Philippe Beny, aged 30, head of one of the [commanding] colonel's three 140-member detachments deployed in the area. 'They described us as the killers of Indochina . . . There was little left here when we arrived,' the colonel said. 'No butcher, no food, spare parts or repair facilities. Now the tension has eased. Our presence has reassured both sides and people come to us for help in all sorts of problems.'[5]

But almost all Kanaks that I spoke to were anxious about the presence of troops. A sculptor from Canala, called Alphonse,* bitterly attacked the soldiers. 'Sending them here is an excuse to hound us and oppress us,' he said. 'They claim they are helping us. But actually they are spying on us; gathering information ready for the day they want to waste us. They are mapping our bush tracks, searching for guns so we will be defenceless, smashing their way into homes at night and chasing our young women.'

Instead of making contact with villagers, said Alphonse, the soldiers remained aloof and were usually racist. The troops were on three-month tours of duty and were rotated between 'nomad' camps frequently so that they had little time to form friendships with villagers. 'They do this so

---

* Alphonse was not his real name although Kanaks are forced by law to have French first names; some families give their children Australian names in defiance.

that when the times comes for them to move against us it will be easy,' he said.'And they will know how to track down our leaders in the resistance.'

When I visited New Caledonia to report on the 'nomadisation' policy the attitude of French authorities and *Caldoches* towards foreign journalists was particularly bitter. After five years of waiting and watching over French policy towards the territory, the South Pacific Forum countries had finally lost patience. At the Suva meeting in mid-August 1986, the Forum declared its grave disappointment about a 'significant backward step' that had happened in the territory since the previous year. It finally agreed to back the Kanaks in taking the issue to the United Nations. A few days later, Fiji, the only Forum member country on the United Nations Decolonisation Committee, asked the committee to add New Caledonia to the list of colonies kept under scrutiny as candidates for independence.

On 3 December, in an historic General Assembly debate, a majority of 89 countries voted for the 'inalienable right of the New Caledonian people for self-determination and independence'. Twenty-four countries voted against and 34 abstained. It was a remarkable morale boost for the FLNKS.

In an angry backlash by France following the vote, a group of 38 New Zealand trade unionists, church activists, teachers and peace campaigners was denied visas to visit New Caledonia. Radio New Zealand journalist Fraser Folster was barred entry while I faced severe harassment by authorities and secret agents. In a report for *Islands Business* on the two weeks of harassment and my eventual arrest by the military I wrote:

> It began like something out of a B-grade police comedy. As the French say in New Caledonia, *'c'est le cinema'*. But the funny side quickly turned sour.
>
> At first the French authorities gave me a two-hour grilling at Tontouta international airport. A police 'welcome squad' awaited me at the arrival lounge when I flew in to cover political developments . . . leading up to [the] referendum on independence and the military 'nomadisation' of Kanak villages in the *brousse* . . .
>
> Then I was tailed constantly and kept under surveillance by security police in Nouméa. Later, I was actually arrested by soldiers armed with automatic rifles, submachine-guns and bayonets near the eastern township of Canala and interrogated incommunicado for four hours . . . The deputy commander of [Canala *gendarmerie*] . . . accused me of taking unauthorised photographs of military installations, loosely using the word 'espionage' . . . Although calm, at one point [during the interrogation] I snapped, 'Is this democracy?'
>
> The officer replied, 'No this is France . . .'
>
> *'Non . . . non ici c'est Kanaky!* [this is *Kanaky*]' interrupted Edmond Kawa [an FLNKS official with me]. The gendarme gave him a warning.[6]

Clearly the authorities were trying to 'discourage' me from reporting the truth about the 'nomadisation' strategy. Several villages protested or filed petitions against the presence of French troops — in vain. One protest letter signed by several villagers from Ponerihouen said: 'The important activities of the troops include preparing maps of our tracks, showing a pornographic film (in a church in the presence of women, children and elderly people) and spying on us.'[7]

'They claim they are here to help us and respect us and respect our traditions — but the soldiers just do what they like,' said Joseph Bouarate, deputy mayor of Hienghène. 'It is arrogant colonialism. (His grandfather, a great chief, was exiled for seven years for defying French authority.)

A 'nomad' post was established about 30 kilometres up a rugged mountain track in the valley of Hienghène. According to the military, the soldiers were there to help build an all-weather road from Hienghène to Kaala-Gomen to improve communications between the east and west coasts. The FLNKS, however, claimed the real purpose for the road was for faster deployment of troops and *gendarmes mobiles* on the east coast against Kanaks.

'France is using the same tactics as in Algeria and Indochina against us,' said FLNKS leader Jean-Marie Tjibaou.'It is provocation all the time. They hope our people will react in a violent manner so they can justify the presence of their troops. But,' added Tjibaou, who lost two brothers in the Hienghène massacre, 'we will not rise to their bait.'

The Pons plan

When Overseas Territories Minister Bernard Pons visited New Caledonia in February 1987 he was fêted by most *Caldoche* settlers. The message he brought was just what they wanted to hear. In contrast, Pons was snubbed by the Kanaks who regard him as a foe who could not be negotiated with. As Pons put it: 'We've decided almost by mutual agreement that we have nothing more to say to each other.'

Even before the Pons plan for the referendum was presented to the National Assembly on 18 February the broad outline was already apparent: the ballot later in the year would ensure French control and the territory's four regions would be gerrymandered to the disadvantage of the Kanaks. Three days before he arrived a congress of the FLNKS was held at the northern village of Arama. Although it established guidelines for FLNKS strategy to be adopted towards Paris, it refrained from announcing the expected boycott of the referendum. Instead, the Kanaks decided to expose the Pons plan as a farce and seek United Nations and South Pacific Forum help in achieving a referendum formula which would be more favourable to independence.

Kanak leaders claimed that France was seeking revenge for the United Nations vote favouring self-determination by strangling the regional economic and political structure set up by the socialist government. The

David Robie

Anti-independence rally in 'white' Noumea, 1985.

'nomadisation' strategy, they insisted, was an attempt at undermining FLNKS international credibility by portraying it as a 'terrorist' movement.

The Chirac government also directed its anger against the South Pacific Forum, singling out Australia and Vanuatu for punitive action. Aid to Vanuatu was slashed by ten percent while ministerial visits between Canberra and Paris were suspended. The most bewildering of French acts towards Australia was the expulsion of consul-general John Dauth. Unfounded allegations were made that he had disbursed sums of money in New Caledonia in 'inappropriate' ways and that he had gone too far in his contacts with the FLNKS.

Former Tahitian President Gaston Flosse began using his Papeete-based role as France's State Secretary for Pacific Affairs to further the aims of France. He had already predicted that some French aid would be distributed differently, and that countries like Vanuatu would suffer while they 'are doing all they can to chase France out of the Pacific'. Flosse was accused by several Pacific politicians of buying French influence in the region by dispensing aid. As veteran Pacific writer Stuart Inder described the tactics:

> It is probably robbing Peter to pay Paul. It is seen as significant that France has given generous help to the Cook Islands following recent cyclone damage there. There is a close blood relationship between the Polynesians of French Polynesia and the Cooks, but Cooks Prime Minister Sir Tom Davis was also the only Forum leader to give full support to France's New Caledonia politics at the historic Suva meeting of the Forum which has launched France on its present confrontation in the South Pacific.[8]

Accusing Bernard Pons of rampant colonialism, the influential French ecumenical weekly *Témoin Chrétien* noted that the minister had stepped up his optimistic statements about the future. 'But,' the newspaper said, 'every day, he puts into practice some new aspect of his anti-Kanak policy.' In fact, *Témoin* added, Pons was in reality only the minister of Europeans in New Caledonia, or, more precisely, 'of his friends of the RPCR.'[9] President Mitterrand was also critical, saying that to reduce the debate to a 'mere electoral confrontation' would be to make a serious historical mistake. 'The democratic process,' he said, 'has no chance of succeeding except in a society which is itself democratic, where citizens are equally respected and communities are equally heard.'

Pons launched a fierce attack against the most potent political lever of the Kanak independence movement: its control of three out of the four regional governments. While the four regions set up under the 1985 Fabius plan remained in force, Pons prepared legislation which would redefine the boundaries. They would be gerrymandered to guarantee at least two regions under the control of anti-independence white governments. Both regions would control most of the territory's economic resources. The Kanak regions had their budget funds slashed by 80 percent, development banks had credit cut off and seconded French civil servants were ordered to cease work for the regional administrations and return to their civil service posts. Kanak development plans were left in chaos.

'The truth,' said Tjibaou, 'is that France is creating a system of apartheid here. The struggle for our people over the next year or two is going to be very hard.' He explained:

> French rule is based on delusions; it fosters the illusion that there is no problem here yet it turns our country into an armed camp with 8000 troops. It spread the illusion that tourists are welcome yet stops them from coming to Kanak areas on the pretext that they aren't 'safe'. It has the illusion that there is no reason why it cannot have normal relations with other South Pacific nations yet it refuses visas and expels the Australian consul. And it pushes the illusion that the economy is recovering yet strangles the economic initiatives of the Kanak-run regions by cutting off our funds and depriving us of technicians.[10]

Early in August 1987, French government decrees banned a week-long 'great march of the people' planned by the FLNKS to involve about 10,000 Kanaks. It would have been a peaceful, cultural celebration in protest against the terms of the referendum. The film *Gandhi* was shown to Kanak 'struggle committee' activists and plans made for civil disobedience acts reminiscent of the Indian leader's classic struggle for independence. But in the first protest, local police and paramilitary gendarmes staged a baton and teargas charge against 300 Kanak men and women sitting cross-legged in Nouméa's Place des Cocotières. Kanak officials said 23 people were injured in the assault. Although the French administration tried to play down the incident, an Australian television crew filmed brutal scenes which sparked an international outcry.

The *'non'* referendum

When it was finally held on 13 September, the referendum was an anti-climax providing no solutions. With the FLNKS deciding to boycott the poll, the result was predictable. Chirac insisted that all French citizens with more than three years' residence in the territory be entitled to vote, and posed them two simple questions: *Do you wish New Caledonia to become independent?* and *Do you wish New Caledonia to remain in the bosom of the French Republic?* But the FLNKS refused to contest the ballot on such an 'unjust' basis. Why should short-term French residents by given as much say on the territory's future as the indigenous people? The FLNKS wanted the vote limited to Kanaks and the 'victims of history' — those people who were born in the territory with one parent also of Caledonian birth.*

French loyalists distorted the results. In the Belep Islands, for example, where only two people (one Kanak and one Frenchman) out of 557 on the roll voted, a 100 percent vote for France was declared on the local radio. The claim that the ballot was a 'great victory for France' was not borne out in a closer analysis of the figures. Official results showed a 58.9 percent turnout, in spite of the boycott. Of these voters, 48,611, or 98.3 percent, voted to remain tied to France, while only 842 supported independence. But 58.78 percent of the roll was non-Kanak. Of the Kanak electorate 83.2 percent chose to boycott the ballot — indicating slightly stronger support than in past elections or ballots. Only 16.8 percent of Kanaks voted for French rule.

This result was remarkable in view of the enormous campaign of publicity and influence which attempted to persuade people to vote for France. In contrast, the pro-independence parties were shut out of the state-run radio and television and anti-independence daily newspaper *Les Nouvelles Calédoniennes*. (Radio Djiido and two other Kanak radio stations were subjected to sabotage and jamming by right-wing extremists, with no protection from French authorities.)

Allegations were made of 'vote buying' through the abuse of a controversial proxy voting system whereby voters can vote for up to five other people; electoral roll anomalies (about 2000 Wallis and Futuna Islanders were on the roll in both New Caledonia and Wallis and Futuna); the bribing of Kanak villages by financial and material 'gifts'; and coercion involving threats against Kanaks who held jobs in the French administration.

Even the 'nomad' troops and paramilitary gendarmes maintaining 'law and order' in the territory were accused of blatant involvement in the referendum campaign on the side of the anti-independence parties. According to one account, General Franceschi and fellow officers hosted a party for Kanak customary chiefs at Tougourou village. The Kanaks were served alcohol in defiance of a ban outside of Nouméa and the Isle of Pines. Franceschi reportedly told the chiefs why they should vote for France. When Kanak militants tried to take photographs they were barred from doing so until bottles were cleared away.[11] 'It smacked of the Wild West with the "bluecoats" buying support from the Cheyennes with booze,' said a French journalist.

In another incident, near Yaté, Kanak militants were ordered to lower the Kanaky flag — when they refused they were charged by troops. Soldiers also tried to persuade Kanaks to sell proxy votes.

---

* Although French officials and anti-independence *Caldoches* denounced this request as 'undemocratic,' there is in fact a little-known precedent in French constitutional law: in 1947, a referendum was held in the valleys of Roya, Tinée and Vesubie to decide their future after they were regained from Italy after the Second World War. Anybody with a parent born in the region or who had lived there for 25 years was eligible to vote.

Kanak leader Jean-Marie Tjibaou at a custom ceremony in Nouméa. He was assassinated on 4 May 1989.

Roger Holièndre, a former paratrooper, *Paris-Match* journalist and now deputy in the French National Assembly, called for massive migration* from France to turn the territory into a new *frontier* in an Anglo-Saxon lake, the Pacific. He called for the construction of a second large 'white' city, this one on the mainly Kanak northern end of Grande Terre, to join the capital, Nouméa. A passionate speaker who challenges people that he attacks to sue him for libel, Holièndre packed out meetings wherever he talked during the campaign.

'I fought like a dog to keep Indochina from falling under the communists,' he said. 'I fought right to the end to keep Algeria French — I'm not going to allow us to be kicked out of New Caledonia.'

In contrast to the 'racist' myth portrayed by the right-wing parties, the FLNKS actually pledges a multiracial state. Article 1 of the draft constitution states: 'The Kanak people constitute a national and multiracial community, free, united and sovereign, founded on solidarity and diversity. The Kanak Republic is a democratic, secular and socialist republic.'

While anti-independence leaders like Jacques Lafleur claimed the referendum had settled the independence issue 'once and for all' and the FLNKS no longer had any legitimate constituency, the conservative *Pacific Islands Monthly* was more conciliatory. Politicians on both sides, the magazine said, had spent the previous two years engaged in sterile debate, putting forward absolutist demands, secure in the knowledge that the territory's future was uncertain. 'The referendum.' it added, 'has now cleared the way for a more constructive dialogue between the communities that must learn not only to cohabit but to develop together, and devise their own common solution to a range of political problems.'

The FLNKS rejected the ballot outright and called for a referendum organised under the United Nations Charter formula which grants colonised people the right to self-determination. France's 'rubbish referendum', as Tjibaou branded it, was designed to perpetuate 134 years of colonial rule. The only vote that concerned the FLNKS was the Kanak vote: French people had already had their chance to decide their own independence, now it was time for the indigenous people to decide on their own destiny.

---

* His views echoed a former French Prime Minister, Pierre Messmer, who declared on 19 January 1972: 'In the immediate future, a massive immigration of French nationals from metropolitan France and such an overseas territory as Réunion should avert this danger [of Kanak nationalism] by preserving the present demographic imbalance in New Caledonia. In the long run, the native aspirations will be neutralised . . .

'The necessary conditions exist thus for transforming New Caledonia in 20 years time into a small, prosperous French territory comparable to Luxemburg, but, of course, of a much greater relative importance in the empty Pacific than Luxemburg has in Europe. The success of such an undertaking, which is necessary for the maintenance of French positions east of Suez, depends on our strong will to realise, at long last, after so many historical failures, a French settlement beyond the seas.'

'One must not forget the Kanaks are here,' he said, a few days before the ballot. 'They will always be here and they will give the French *merde* [shit] until independence. On the evening after the vote many French people will drink champagne, but the next day we'll still be here to say, *merde!*'

Less than a month after the referendum, Pons announced that he would press for a bill granting New Caledonia a large decree of autonomy. But the 'anti-Kanak' changes were shelved until after the French presidential election in April 1988. By the end of October 1987, however, an event was to happen in Tahiti which severely embarrassed Pons and damaged French credibility in the eyes of Pacific nations. It was to have far-reaching implications for the *indépendantistes*.

15

The Siege of Ouvéa

During the French presidential elections in May 1988, 28 people were killed in a bloody military assault on Ouvéa Island and in other clashes in New Caledonia. The re-election of President Mitterrand cleared the way for a new political formula — the so-called Matignon accord — but a paradox remained. Elsewhere in the South Pacific, French troops were used to quell rioting in Polynesia where a 'palace coup' against Gaston Flosse ousted the conservative Tahitian Government, and Vanuatu also faced uncertainty with rioting and an abortive constitutional coup.

On Friday, 23 October 1987, Tahitian slum-dwellers and poor youths went on a rampage of looting, smashing and burning in the business and tourist quarter of the capital, Papeete. Overnight French Polynesia's image as an affluent, problem-free corner of the South Pacific was shattered. The riot peaked by 8 p.m.: at that time blazing shops and offices seared the tropical night high above the city; more than 1000 Tahitians were in control; and about 100 families could be found fleeing their downtown apartments clutching bundles of clothes.

As devastated French and Chinese businessmen picked their way through the charred, twisted, and still smouldering remains of their premises next morning, French and Tahitian government officials were quick to blame the so-called Black Friday on the 'terrorism' of striking Polynesian dockers. But as the demands grew for the resignation of President Jacky Teuira's government and the establishment of a commission of inquiry, it was clear the real causes lay in a serious social and economic malaise.[1]

French Foreign Legion troops were flown from Moruroa Atoll, setting up barbed-wire barricades between the city, the industrial zone of Fare Ute and port area of Motu Uta where a strike had triggered the riots. Military guards were posted at Faaa International Airport, the city's power plant, the Territorial Assembly and other strategic points. More than 1000 paramilitary and troop reinforcements, including three squadrons of *gendarmes mobiles* from New Caledonia, were also dispatched to Tahiti. A state of emergency — the first ever in French Polynesia — and a dusk-to-dawn curfew were declared. Police made 77 arrests, mainly of women and teenagers, and cracked down on trade unions. Four union leaders, including Dockers Union president Felix Rara, were arrested without charge.

A leading Tahiti journalist and most opposition politicians — who collectively had won 54 percent of the vote in the March 1986 elections — bitterly attacked French policies. 'The disastrous combination of Gaston Flosse and [High Commissioner] Pierre Angéli has led Tahiti to the brink of a precipice,' reported former *Les Nouvelles de Tahiti* director Lucien Maillard from Paris. 'Their policies have created this climate of insurrection.'[2] While some commentators suggested Angéli's retirement after the riot was a 'sacking', Pons denied it. He said the departure of Angéli, aged 66, who was also the last governor of French Polynesia, from 1969 to 1973, had been considered three months earlier.

When High Commissioner Jean Montpezat left Nouméa to take up his new post at the residency in Papeete his job was regarded by some as a sinecure after the referendum in New Caledonia. 'I'm here to listen,' he told Papeete television after his arrival, 'and to maintain political peace.' As it turned out he had no choice but to watch over the funeral rites of the five-year Flosse reign in Tahiti.

Faced with mounting criticism over his administration's handling of the social issues that had led to the rioting, the defection of three cabinet ministers, and a demand for his resignation by 28 MPs in the 41-seat Territorial Assembly, Teuira finally stepped down. His reputation was dealt a final blow when it was revealed the *gendarmes mobiles* and troops had been called in to crush the port strike at his request. Until then, the blame for the military 'overkill' had been levelled at the French High Commission.

The collapse of the government was also a severe blow to the personal credibility of Flosse, leader of the ruling *Tahoeraa Huiraatira* party. In a widely publicised *Le Figaro* interview, Flosse accused Australia and New Zealand of being responsible for the riot. The pro-Flosse weekly magazine *Maito* cited the presence in Papeete of an official from the Australian consulate in Nouméa in the days before the disturbance, claiming this was not a simple coincidence.

French authorities also unsuccessfully tried to pin the blame on *indépendantiste* politicians such as the mayor of Faaa, Oscar Temaru, leader of *Tavini Huiraatira*. Angéli told journalists before he departed 'the arsonists were well prepared, well organised and acted in a determined and not at all spontaneous manner'. But the territory's two most influential religious leaders, chairman Jacques Ihorai, of the Evangelical Church, and Catholic bishop Michel Coopenrath, said such accusations diverted attention from the real causes of the social unrest that Tahiti had experienced since the nuclear tests programme began in 1966.[3]

The cabinet revolt began while Flosse was safely out of Tahiti. When the resignation came of Economy Minister Alexandre Leontieff, and two other ministers — part-Rarotongan Georges Kelly and Huguette Kiou — Flosse flew back immediately from Paris to Papeete in a desperate effort to save the reeling Teuira government. He failed.

Leontieff, a 39-year-old technocrat, and his 15 rebel Tahoeraa members forged a new 'government of unity' coalition with the opposition parties *Here Aia* (led by Papeete Mayor Jean Juventin), *Aia Api*, *Maohi Nui* and the socialist pro-independence party *Ia Mana Te Nunaa*. Teuira was replaced by Leontieff with 28 votes. Among Leontieff's new cabinet was *Ia Mana's* Jacqui Drollet, who became Health and Environment Minister. Drollet's appointment was crucial in view of his party's strong anti-nuclear sentiments, and revelations by a British television documentary, *Tahiti Witness*, about serious health problems from fallout from the French atmospheric nuclear tests before 1974.

Crisis in Vanuatu

France had its problems in Vanuatu, too. Prime Minister Walter Lini's government expelled ambassador Henri Crepin-Leblond shortly before the election on 30 November 1987, claiming France was funding the Union of Moderate Parties opposition. Paris predictably denied the allegations and withdrew almost all its diplomatic staff in Port Vila.

Lini's *Vanuaaku Pati* was returned to power, but with its majority of 26 sharply reduced from 26 seats to 20 in the expanded 46-seat Parliament. It was a difficult time for Lini, now aged 44. He had been partially crippled nine months earlier by a stroke suffered while he was visiting the United States. His biggest hurdle turned out not to be the pro-French UPM, which fostered rumours that the *Vanuaaka Pati* would stage a coup to retain power if it lost the election. Rather, it was party secretary-general Barak Sope, long a close ally of Lini during the independence struggle and the mastermind of the non-aligned strategy. Announcing that Lini's poor health had made it time for him to go, the 35-year-old Sope said he wanted the prime minister's job for himself.

Declaring that the stroke — which left him with a crippled right arm, awkward limp, and other disabilities — was no handicap, Lini made it perfectly clear he intended to retain the prime ministership. He out-manoeuvred Sope and his leadership was endorsed by a 59 to 29 vote of confidence at a special party congress a week after the election. A month later, while speculation continued over his health, Lini moved to heal the rift by including Sope in his cabinet, as Tourism and Transport Minister.

If Sope, who had pushed hardest for stronger ties with Libya, had succeeded it was conceivable but unlikely that Vanuatu would take a more radical stance in foreign affairs. And, in spite of a pledge to restore full diplomatic links with Paris, there was never any possibility as suggested by the Western press that Vanuatu might take a more low-key attitude over the Melanesian independence struggles in East Timor, West Papua and New Caledonia.

Vanuatu's priorities, cautioned the conservative *Pacific Islands Monthly*, should be clear: it needed more education, more foreign aid, more investment and a careful meshing of traditional and modern values as the difficult transition was made from independence to development. 'Seen in this light, the *Vanuaaku Pati* government's running diplomatic war with the French is a quixotic struggle, covertly and ruinously directed at Vanuatu's own large Francophone minority and the UPM.'[4]

Less than six months later, in May 1988, the leadership issue finally erupted again. When Lands Minister William Mahit abolished the Vila Urban Land Corporation (Vulcan) — and its sister land company in Luganville — on 10 May, freezing its funds and records, evicting its staff and posting a police guard on its premises, the move was widely interpreted as an attempt by Lini to curb Sope's power. Sope had been a board director, representing Ifira Island, since it had been established in 1981. The corporation's investments were regarded as a cornerstone of Sope's powerbase, and there were widespread allegations of misappropriation of funds totalling up to 750 million vatu ($NZ1 million) — accusations denied by Sope.

Although the government claimed it was an 'administrative' move in line with the first and second national development plans and insisted there was no change in land policy, Sope branded the sudden seizure of the corporation a 'surprise commando attack'. He claimed the shutdown was an assault on party policy and the nation's constitution which guarantees that all land belongs to customary owners.

'*Vanuaaka* means "our land",' he said. 'Before independence the land issue was the foundation for the *Vanuaaku Pati* — take away that and you're destroying the party.'

Sope launched a counter-attack by organising meetings of the three villages which have customary land in the capital — Ifira, Erakor and Pango — and his militants set up a protest march on the Prime Minister's office on 16 May. Supposed to be non-political and peaceful, the 3000 marchers soon unfurled banners claiming *Lini hemi wan kommunist* ('Lini is a communist') and denounced the Prime Minister in the next breath as a 'fascist'.

Ifira militants armed with iron bars and clubs attacked Vietnamese-owned businesses and wrecked a police truck. Marchers chanted: 'We want a revolution like in Fiji.' Outer islanders, who comprise most of the town's 20,000 population, felt threatened by the demonstration.

After the petition seeking the repeal of the closure of Vulcan was presented to William Mahit, most of the demonstrators disbanded peacefully. But a hardcore group of 150 militants, after a drunken barbecue on the port foreshore, went on a rampage of destruction through the town's Kumul Highway shopping district. Vanuatu Mobile Force soldiers were called in to quell the rioters with teargas. They battled the militants in scenes of violence never previously witnessed in Vanuatu, even during the struggle for independence.

'The people who caused the disturbance failed to respect their chiefs and custom,' Lini lamented. 'The *namele* leaves [a traditional symbol of peace] were abused by the rioters.'[5]

Backed by pledges of help — including riot police if needed — from Australia, New Zealand and Papua New Guinea (assistance that was withheld from Bavadra's government in Fiji), Lini now retaliated. After a week of seeking a consensus with his ministerial and party colleagues, he first sacked Sope from the cabinet as Minister of Tourism, Immigration and Transport. Later, Sope was also stripped of the secretary-generalship of the party, a position he had held since 1977.

Finally, at the end of July, Sope, four rebel government MPs, and 18 opposition UPM parliamentarians were expelled from Parliament. Accusing Lini of 'dictatorship', Sope and Opposition Leader Maxime Carlot challenged the legality of the expulsions in the Supreme Court. The chief justice upheld the actions of the parliamentary Speaker against the UPM while reinstating Sope's 'gang of five'. Sope and his new political group, the Melanesian Progressive Pati, and the UPM boycotted the byelections for 18 seats in December 1988.

Speculation that Sope planned a constitutional coup to emulate his Fiji mentor, Sitiveni Rabuka, were borne out when he persuaded President Ati George Sokomanu to 'dissolve' Parliament and call for a new general election in February 1989. In a Supreme Court challenge by the Lini government, Sokomanu's dissolution attempt and swearing in of Sope as caretaker 'prime minister' was judged unconstitutional and illegal. Sope and his four rebel 'cabinet' ministers were arrested and charged with sedition; Sokomanu was stripped of the presidency and faced charges of incitement to mutiny. After a two-week trial in February 1989, the disgraced Sokomanu was sentenced to a six-year prison term while Sope and former Opposition Leader Maxime Carlot received five years. Another rebel minister, former MP Willie Jimmy, was jailed for two years.

In April, a three-judge Court of Appeal freed all four and quashed the convictions against them after finding the trial judge had 'erred' in his summing up and that the case against them 'lacked evidence'.

Pastor Fred Timakata, a former health minister and parliamentary speaker, was elected to the largely ceremonial office of president. He pledged to keep out of politics.

The Ouvéa uprising

The New Caledonian fuse, meanwhile, had come close to being ignited at the end of 1987 when the Loyalty Islands regional government president, Yéiwene Yéiwene, was jailed two days before Christmas. Like Tjibaou, he had been charged with 'incitment to violence' by appealing to Kanaks to take up arms to defend themselves. Yéiwene was freed on probation by an appeals court a week after being imprisoned and he declared French policy in New Caledonia bankrupt. 'They have no other argument than locking people up,' he said, comparing the repression for Kanaks to 'that facing the French under the Nazi occupation when people were arrested in the middle of the night and locked away.'

On 22 February 1988 a 'commando' group of about 100 Kanak militants from the Tieti tribe attacked gendarmes with stones and clubs in the north-east township of Poindimié, where New Caledonia's second 'white' city was being developed under the Pons plan. Fifteen gendarmes were injured and ten taken hostage; four military vehicles and two civilian cars were firebombed. The militants were protesting against traditional Tieti tribal land being prepared as a construction site for a regional hospital.

The attack came on the eve of the FLNKS congress at Tibarama *tribu* on the other side of Poindimié. Although criticised by the Kanak leadership, it reflected the new strategy of 'muscular mobilisation', as Tjibaou described it. The congress confirmed it would boycott and disrupt the presidential and regional elections of 24 April which would implement the 'colonial' Pons statute (enacted in January 1988). Endorsing Mitterrand as President for a second term, Tjibaou declared:

> I hope, Mr President, that you will return in strength at the head of the state to offer to our people, and to France, of course, a new era of liberty. French and Kanaks are considered as adversaries. More and more, they have become enemies. At least you would accept to return with us to a path of liberty for the Kanak people and for all those who live in New Caledonia.[6]

Mounting tension as the French security forces were built up to 9500 for the elections finally erupted on Friday, 22 April, two days before the poll. Hooded Kanak militants, arguably the first real guerrilla force in the territory, seized a heavily armed Fayaoué gendarme post on Ouvéa, in the Loyalty Islands. Armed with machetes, axes and a handful of sporting guns hidden under their clothes, they killed four gendarmes who resisted, injured five others, and seized 27 as hostages. They abducted most of their prisoners to a three-tiered cave in rugged bush country near Gossanah in the north-east of the island; the rest were taken to Mouly in the south. As almost 300 gendarmes flown to Ouvéa searched for them, the militants demanded that the regional elections be abandoned and that a mediator be flown from France to negotiate for a *real* referendum on self-determination under United Nations supervision. They threatened to kill their hostages if their demands were not met.

Declaring on Radio Djiido that he was dismayed by the attack, Tjibaou blamed it on the 'politics of violence' adopted by the Chirac government against the Kanak people. 'The [colonial] plunderers refuse to recognise their subversive lead,' he said. 'From the moment they stole our country, they have tried to eliminate everybody who denounces their evil deeds. It has been like that since colonialism began.'[7] Mitterrand appealed for calm and a halt to the spiral of violence; Chirac condemned the 'savage brutality' of the attack, claiming the guerrillas were 'probably full of drugs and alcohol'.

Despite the Ouvéa uprising and shootouts on Grande Terre, the elections went ahead. The guerrillas freed 11 hostages but remained hidden in their cave with the others. Another hostage, who was ill, was later released. But the French authorities suffered further humiliation six days after the kidnapping. Captain Philippe Legorjus, head of France's élite anti-terrorist GIGN squad, approached the nationalists and, embarrassingly, was seized hostage along with five of his men, a Melanesian gendarme and a Nouméa magistrate. Pons portrayed the guerrilla leader, Alphonse Dianou, as a 'Libyan-trained religious fanatic'. In fact, he had trained at a Roman Catholic seminary in Fiji and was regarded by people who knew him as 'a reflective man, fond of books and non-violent'.[8] He spent hours explaining to his captives why they had been seized.

In other clashes, an 18-year-old Kanak woman was shot in crossfire between militants and gendarmes near Canala; a mixed-race youth was killed in shooting near Houailou; and one of the Hienghène massacre killers, José Lapetite, was shot by snipers on his farm near Voh. The presidential candidates traded on the New Caledonian violence to enhance their electoral hopes. Mitterrand appealed to the Constitutional Council to annul the elections in New Caledonia, a step enabling the Kanaks to make a face-saving ceasefire and begin a fresh round of negotiations.

But the Chirac government was in no mood to conduct negotiations with 'terrorists'. Extreme right-wing National Front leader Jean-Marie Le Pen called for the 'extermination' of the Kanaks, and Pons declared: 'The barbarism of these men is such that they will get what they deserve.' Chirac and Pons gave the green light to Operation Victor, an assault plan aimed at freeing the hostages and killing all the Kanak nationalists.[9] Many regarded it as a cynical plan designed to gain the maximum political advantage for Chirac before the second and decisive round of the French presidential election the following Sunday.

At dawn on Thursday, 5 May, French military and secret service forces launched their attack on the Ouvéa cave and killed 19 Kanaks in what was reported by the authorities to be a fierce battle. The hostages were freed for the loss of only two French soldiers. If the military authorities were to be believed, their casualties were from the 11th Shock Unit of the DGSE. (This unit was formerly the Service Action squad, used to sabotage the *Rainbow Warrior*.) The assault came just three days before the crucial presidential vote, and hours after three French hostages had been freed in Lebanon following the Chirac government's reported payment of a massive ransom. To top it off, convicted *Rainbow Warrior* bomber Dominique Prieur, now pregnant, was repatriated back from Hao Atoll to France.

Leaders of the FLNKS immediately challenged the official version of the attack. Léopold Jorédie issued a statement in which he questioned how the 'Ouvéa massacre left 19 dead among the nationalists and no one injured' and the 'absence of bullet marks on the trees and empty cartridges on the ground at the site'. Yéiwene insisted that at no time did the kidnappers intend to kill the hostages — 'this whole massacre was engineered by Pons who knew very well there was never any question of killing the hostages'. Nidoish Naisseline also condemned the action. 'Pons and Chirac have behaved like assassins,' he said. 'I accuse them of murder. They could have avoided the butchery. They preferred to buy the votes of Le Pen's friends with Kanak blood.'

But the political gamble backfired for Chirac. Although he gained a predictable 90 percent of the vote in New Caledonia, he was decisively beaten by Mitterrand overall for an unprecedented second term. The new socialist Prime Minister, Michel Rocard, took office and immediately embarked on a policy of conciliation. He sent a six-member political mission to Nouméa amid mounting allegations of a massacre at the cave by French troops. A *Le Monde* journalist, Frédéric Bobin, beat the French media blockade on Ouvéa to record the testimony of the 'tea boys' who had taken food to the hostages in the cave.

One old man from the Wadrilla tribe described the brutal treatment dealt out to Dianou and the only survivors. Dianou's body along with two others who had come out of the cave alive was 'found' next day.*

> One soldier who was outside [the cave] again ordered Dianou to give himself up, Alphonse refused, shouting back: 'I'd rather die on my land'.
> Then I told Alphonse: 'You're fighting for the land, but you must also think of us. We want to get out alive, because if not there'll be no one left to till the earth.'

---

* The victims of the Ouvéa massacre were: Bouama Dao, Samuel Dao, Vincent Daoume, Alphonse Dianou, Martin Haiwe, Patrick Esekia Ihili, Zephirin Safo Kella, Edouard Lavellois, Jean Lavellois, Wenceslas Lavellois, Jean-Luc Madjele, Nicolas Nine, Philippo Nine, Seraphin Ouckewen, Nicodeme Teinbouone, Donatien Wadjeno, Michel Wadjeno, Patrick Amossa Wain and Samuel Wamo.

Just then, the soldier again ordered him to surrender and come out with the hostages. This time, Alphonse accepted. 'Right, we're coming out'. He said. The soldier answered: 'If you're coming out, drop your weapons and come out empty-handed'. Alphonse dropped his weapons and we all got out together . . .

Once out of the cave, the soldiers got us to lie down on the ground. Then a soldier fired a shot into Alphonse's leg. Injured, Alphonse was taken away in a stretcher where an Army doctor attended to him. He fixed tubes to put him on a drip. But then other soldiers came up and wrenched the tubes away and turned the stretcher over. Alphonse rolled on to the stones and was kicked and hit with rifle butts.[10]

What followed was even more disturbing: Amossa Wain, a 19-year-old youth who just six months earlier had been campaigning for the *Vanuaaku Pati* in Vanuatu, was one of the 'tea boys', not a militant. His friends described how he got up when ordered by a soldier. As he stood up the soldiers shot him in cold blood. There was evidence of at least six other summary executions.

Two weeks after the cave attack, the new Defence Minister, Jean-Pierre Chevènement, ordered an inquiry, saying that Pons had not used 'all possible means' of negotiation with the nationalists. Autopsies were ordered for the dead militants. But increasingly the political debate centred on what the socialists planned for the territory. With Rocard again appointed Prime Minister after the socialists failed to gain an outright mandate in the June general election, he favoured an experimental period of self-rule.

The Matignon Accord

After the first talks in five years between Jean-Marie Tjibaou and Jacques Lafleur and delegations of their supporters a consensus emerged marking a diplomatic triumph for Rocard's government. While the FLNKS had called for a 'real' vote on self-determination in five years' time, to be limited to Kanaks and first-generation settlers, the RPCR wanted the vote put off until 1998 and kept open to all residents with French nationality. Rocard's Matignon agreement established direct rule from Paris until July 1989, granted an amnesty to many political prisoners and offered a limited form of self-rule with a federation of three autonomous provinces to govern the territory until the referendum in 1998. A national referendum, marked by wide-spread abstention, endorsed the Matignon Accord. But the 81 percent vote in favour, of the 37 percent of the electorate who cast a vote, was hardly a victory for Rocard.

The developments emphasised yet again how the future of New Caledonia was at the mercy of French metropolitan politics. But the peace was rather fragile and questions remained about the Matignon Accord. Although the Kanaks had the demographic edge (Europeans have 1.5 children per women of fertile age, the Kanak 5.5) and the *Caldoches* were slowly drifting out of the territory, the undeclared war of attrition was likely to continue.[11] And the sporadic incidents and deaths could flare into a major conflict at any time.

Although the nomadisation strategy was shelved by the socialists, the aggression displayed by both the military and the gendarmerie failed to cool the tension. Military repression in villages, confiscations of Kanak legally owned guns — but no seizures of the thousands of illegal guns smuggled in for the settlers — only increased Kanak bitterness. However, while some commentators and politicians speculated about a possible civil war in New Caledonia, it seemed unlikely. The huge military presence would probably prevent it and the French Government could not allow it to happen. Likewise, the news media attention focused on New Caledonia made it unlikely that the heavily-armed *Caldoche* would attempt a massacre of Kanaks.

After less than three years of destructive confrontational policies under the Chirac government, the Rocard strategy had offered fresh hope for a peaceful solution. But the personalities of Tjibaou and Lafleur were crucial to the achievement of the Matignon Accord. As president of the FLNKS, Tjibaou felt some personal responsibility for the bloody Ouvéa killings. And with the memory of the deaths of his two brothers in the 1984 Hienghène massacre he was strongly influenced into opting for a peaceful plan to independence.

For his part, Lafleur, who had suffered a heart attack two years earlier, was apparently also determined to find a peaceful solution after the Ouvéa tragedy. He certainly did not want to go down in history as the man who pushed New Caledonia into civil war and, with his mentors Chirac and Pons defeated, he could also no longer count on partisan support from the French Government.

However, although Tjibaou was established in a power-sharing role with Lafleur, he could not control the spontaneous actions of young Kanak militants who regarded the accord as a sell-out and sought guarantees of independence. There were also serious doubts that Lafleur could rein in the more extremist groups among the settlers. While the National Front had lost ground in metropolitan France, it had gained support in New Caledonia.

On 4 May 1989, the eve of the anniversary of the Ouvéa massacre, a tragic event shook the unity of the FLNKS and jeopardised the Matignon Accord. At a custom ceremony in the chiefdom of Wadrilla, close to where the cave victims were buried, Tjibaou and Yéiwene were assassinated — gunned down by assassins from their own movement. Shouting '*Vive l'independence*', former Protestant pastor Djoubelly Wea shot Yéiwene point-blank with a machine pistol. He was in turn shot fatally by one of Tjibaou's bodyguards; Andre Tangopi, wounded in the knee, was charged with murder and attempted murder.

Wea, a respected political leader of the militants of Gossanah and long an advocate of non-violence, believed the independence struggle had been betrayed by Tjibaou and Yéiwene. His followers were bitter that the FLNKS had failed to support their call for an international inquiry into the allegations of French atrocities on Ouvéa.

Epilogue

The death of democracy in Fiji was a blow to many nationalists in the South Pacific, putting the struggle of the Kanaks and other liberation movements in jeopardy. Major-General Sitiveni Rabuka's *coup d'états* were a hijack of military power by an oligarchy that refused to recognise and accept the winds of social change in Fiji. In fact, Fiji's traditional way of life and indigenous Fijian land rights were secure under the 1970 constitution. But because they had not been allowed to know their rights, Fijians were readily manipulated and swayed by demagogues.

Rabuka's military-led régime sought close links with French military forces occupying New Caledonia and Tahiti, as well as the military dictatorships in Indonesia, South Korea and Taiwan, régimes with little respect for human and democratic rights and which have suppressed movements for democracy and justice.

Indonesia offered military and development assistance and France provided helicopters and military vehicles as well as military training, including naval exercises between French naval frigates and ships of Fiji's navy. Israel — an expert in pre-emptive military strikes and skilled in the use of proxy forces to promote its interests — established an increasing presence. There was strong circumstantial evidence for CIA support of the first coup in particular. And the United States Government indicated it would recognise the new republic when it agreed to 'assure the United States that its security interests in the region would be strengthened under the Rabuka régime.'

France and the United States expected the Rabuka régime to support their nuclear expansion in the Pacific, and the suppression of progressive movements for independence, self-determination, denuclearisation and demilitarisation. A foreign affairs spokesman for the regime, Filipe Bole, outlined its attitude towards nationalist movements in East Timor, New Caledonia, Tahiti and West Papua: they were 'internal problems' for the French and Indonesian military to deal with. Fiji, he implied, would turn a blind eye to any repression. The Taukei Movement only identified with other Melanesians when it had self-interest at stake.

The fact that the Taukei and the military-backed regime in Fiji are indigenous, argue some Pacific analysts, should not blind the rest of the South Pacific region from seeing clearly whose interests they are serving. 'For this reason the military regime in Fiji must be opposed and condemned,' researcher Jone Dakuvula, a Fiji Anti-Nuclear Group (FANG) campaigner and a cousin of General Rabuka, told the Nuclear-Free and Independent Pacific movement at Manila in November 1987. '[Otherwise] the movement as we have known it will divide just at a time when it is most needed by those progressive movements at the forefront of the struggle for a more just and humane world.'

'If we acquiesce to government by the gun in Fiji,' said Maori academic Dr Ranginui Walker, 'then how can we condemn it in New Caledonia and elsewhere?'[1] On the other hand, reactionary Maori nationalists manipulated news media and the Fiji coups to support their own agenda over Maori sovereignty in New Zealand. Many of the nationalists 'cared little about the real causes of the coups, even less about the abuse of human rights in Fiji. They saw the Fiji crisis as the perfect opportunity to threaten the uneasy calm of the guilt-ridden *pakeha*'.[2] The coups were alternatively defended or attacked not because of whether what was happening in Fiji was 'seen as evil or good' but because it had significant implications for the struggles in New Zealand.

During a meeting with Bavadra in May 1989, Matiu Rata, leader of the Maori party *Mana Motuhake* (Power to the People), described initial expressions of support for the Rabuka régime by some Maori nationalists as 'kneejerk reactions' based on misunderstanding. 'They assumed the coup was indigenous Fijians reasserting themselves,' he said, 'when in fact it was the military acting on behalf of the leaders who believed they had the God-given right to govern.' Rata, who as Maori Affairs Minister represented New Zealand at Fiji's Deed of Cession centenary celebrations in 1974, described the Fijian politicians supporting the coup as 'political rogues'. He added that he was satisfied Ratu Mara either knew of or endorsed the plans for the coup.

Rabuka's seizure of power in Fiji also posed a dilemma for the Kanak leadership. How should it respond? At first, like most Melanesian governments — and indeed virtually all Pacific island nations — the FLNKS saw the issue in simplistic terms as the indigenous people of Fiji reasserting their supremacy. It was reluctant to debate the issue and its initial response was ambiguous. Kanak leader Jean-Marie Tjibaou suggested after the initial coup that a similar seizure of power might happen in New Caledonia if the Chirac government persisted with its provocative policies. Kanaks and Fijians had both been turned into minorities in their homeland by the actions of their colonial rulers. Condeming the coup, he said, would be like Kanaks condeming their own 1984 insurrection which could have turned into a coup if Kanaks had been sufficiently armed and had supported the militancy of Éloi Machoro.

'I'm sorry about the Indians,' Tjibaou confided on the eve of the September 1987 referendum, 'but Melanesians must support Melanesians.' He said that if the FLNKS had failed to resist the repressive measures of French Overseas Territories Minister Bernard Pons then the Kanak people would have faced what he understood to be the same problem that Fiji was confronting. Fijians wanted what the coup makers claimed would be a 'Fijian' constitution — 'exactly what we are seeking' — for *their* house of the future. 'The colonial government can build a house to live in. But when it goes then the house will fall down.'[3]

An influential faction of the FLNKS, however, recognised the implications of the coup for nationalist movements seeking independence. Gradually, as the extent of French collaboration with the coup leadership became apparent, the front's attitude hardened towards Rabuka. After all, were not the Indo-Fijians also 'victims of history' who had been exploited by colonialism? During his visit to Suva in mid-August 1987, then French Pacific Affairs Secretary Gaston Flosse made an offer of aid to the Fiji military, including weapons and finance to build a new naval base at Uduya Point, near Lami. Rabuka also sought training by an elite team of *gendarmes mobiles* — the very force being used to repress the Kanaks. (It was later claimed that the military were using part of an $18 million French soft-loan development aid package signed in April 1988.)

Noting the 'cynical and opportunistic' offer, even the right-wing *Australian* was able to point out that France was extending support for the same indigenous forces in Fiji that it opposed in New Caledonia.[4]

Back home, however, Flosse and other French officials appeared delighted while they stressed that the events in Fiji were a warning of the fate that would befall New Caledonia and Tahiti if they became independent. French interests, backed by right-wing television and newspaper magnate Robert Hersant, owner of *Les Nouvelles Calédoniennes*, unsuccessfully tried to buy the closed *Fiji Sun*. The newspaper would have been an ideal springboard for influencing English-speaking Pacific nations — and perhaps undermining the consensus of the South Pacific Forum backing Kanak independence and opposing nuclear tests.[5]

At the Manila NFIP conference Louis Kotra Uregei, a trade unionist and senior FLNKS political bureau member, denounced Rabuka's military takeover as a setback for the region's independence movements. He blamed the Fiji military and the Taukei Movement for undermining the FLNKS in the crucial weeks leading to the referendum. In spite of attempts by Maori and Hawaiian delegates to seek a resolution supporting Rabuka's 'indigenous revolution', the conference condemned any military coups in the region and called for respect for human rights in Fiji.

It also accused the French, Indonesian and United States governments of destabilising regional security through their efforts to strengthen the military capabilities of South Pacific countries. (But there was little discussion of the Chilean military control over another colony — Rapanui [Easter Island] which became a 'province' of Chile in 1966. The islanders became 'full citizens' then after being virtual slaves since annexation on 9 September 1888. Since the incorporation a secret US Air Force base has been built on the island and the settler population has been increased tenfold to 500. Although a Rapanui islander is governor, virtually all other colonial officials are Chilean.)

The former Fiji Army's chief-of-staff, Lieutenant-Colonel Jim Sanday, now a regional defence analyst at the Australian National University's Strategic and Defence Studies Centre, warned in early 1989 that Rabuka, facing a loss of credibility in Fiji, might feel compelled to divert public attention away from the country's ills by some form of military adventurism in a neighbouring state. 'This would give him the opportunity to cast himself as the undisputed leader of a wider "nativistic" movement within the South Pacific,' said Sanday, 'including Australia and New Zealand where he is likely to receive support from elements within the indigenous societies of these two countries.'[6]

While the Methodist Church of Fiji, which claims three-quarters of Fijians as its supporters, tried to provide religious justification for the Taukei Movement and the coups, several church leaders spoke out bravely against the excesses. One clergyman, the Church's communications secretary, the Rev Akuila Yabaki, went so far as to liken the situation to that of the Nazi era and warned of the dangers of a climate of 'terror' in Fiji.

'By strange coincidence, in the past eight weeks two dramas have been unfolding on opposite sides of the world,' he declared in an open letter to the *Fiji Times*. 'In Lyons, France, the trial of perhaps the last Nazi war criminal to be prosecuted — Klaus Barbie, "the Butcher of Lyons". And this side of the world our Fiji coup . . . and its aftermath.'[7]

Yabaki argued that the two apparently unrelated events had some disturbing points in common. His criticism came in response to the scores of arrests, the detention and harassment of deposed government members, supporters, trade unionists and other critics of the military régime. The link, he said, was uncomfortably close: a pseudo-nationalist ideology and a disregard for world opinion; a convenient scapegoat in another racial group and culture which have often done better economically than the indigenous inhabitants; simplistic intepretations and expectations; a new fundamentalism without much regard for the complexity of human and international relationships; a thirst for power; a group of ill-trained but uniformed and armed soldiers who can harass people without explanation: a real depression in economic and human terms; and, most strikingly, more than a few in the Church (more than in Hitler's Germany) willing to back the ideology with dubious theological argument.

Many indigenous Fijians have begun to see the crisis in their country in a context of traditional tribal alignments. They view the Rabuka-Ganilau-

Mara triumvirate as confirming their suspicions of a conspiracy by the eastern Tovata élite (led by Ganilau and Mara) to hold on to the reins of power in Fiji in order to entrench their dominance in all aspects of Fiji's political and economic life. Fijians supporting the once powerful and predominant Kubuna confederacy fear their relegation to a lower social ranking. Hence the abortive attempt in January 1988 to restore the social order represented by Ratu Cakobau, the *Vunivalu* (warlord) of Bau, the head of the Kubuna and regarded by many as the paramount chief of Fiji. In November 1988, western chiefs tried to break the Tovata dominance by declaring a fourth confederacy, Vasayasa Vakara, but this was shunned by the eastern elite.

By contrast, Dr Timoci Bavadra's 'new nationalism' represents a new generation of post-independence political leadership which is genuinely concerned with the welfare of the disadvantaged and working classes of Pacific peoples. The rise of the Fiji Labour Party represented the emergence of development and political options which inevitably challenged the privileged élites. This phenomenon is now being reflected in the emergence of 'labour' or 'peoples movements' such as the Leba Pati in Vanuatu, the Solomon Islands' Labour Party, and a new commoner movement in Tonga rallying around crusading MP Akilisi Pohiva and his investigative Tongan-language newspaper, the *Kele'a* (conch shell, the bearer of tidings).

The Fiji upheaval leaves vital questions about political principles and beliefs for Pacific Islanders. Do they subscribe to the colonialist notion that nations must be organised and developed along ideologies of racial, political and economic supremacy over other races and cultures? Is the solution to colonial racism the substitution of indigenous chauvinist supremacy? If nationalist movements in the South Pacific are concerned with the development of more just, equal and democratic nations, can they achieve this by means that are unjust to other communities in the same territory in which they live?

'In the Solomons, Papua New Guinea, Western Samoa, the Cook Islands and elsewhere in the South Pacific, there have been many changes of government through elections and other democratic devices, and without guns,' says Dakuvula. 'We indigenous Fijians faced the first real test of our political discipline and civilisation in 1987 — and we blew it.' He adds:

> We have set a cancerous precedent for other countries in the South Pacific with still viable democratic systems . . . We have sent a message to a colonial power such as France which enables it now to assume the moral high ground over indigenous people struggling for political independence in Kanaky and Tahiti . . .
>
> Our reactionary nationalism has gravely damaged the progressive nationalism of other indigenous Pacific people. If military oppression is 'legitimised' in Fiji then military oppression in Kanaky and Tahiti must also be 'legitimate'. There is a notable similarity between the Royal Fiji Military Forces propaganda

against Dr Bavadra's government and that of the French military against indigenous political movements. They both paint them as having Libyan or communist connections, habouring alien ideas that are dangerous to the people they rule.[8]

Taukei extremists in Fiji have pushed the argument that democracy does not sit comfortably with Fijian culture, or for that matter most Pacific cultures. But these apologists for authoritarian rule must face the challenge of change, not turn their backs on it. Christianity was introduced to Fiji only 150 years ago; now it is a deeply embedded part of Fijian culture. Can it seriously be suggested that democracy cannot be a part of it as well?

Many people in the region see the conflict as an indigenous people's struggle that deserves their support. But, as former *Fiji Times* journalist Richard Naidu says, 'They must not allow their justifiable concern for indigenous rights in the Pacific to cloud their judgement on Fiji. If they cannot make the distinction between justice and hypocrisy, they cannot hope to advocate the cause of any disadvantaged group, anywhere.'[9]

Nationalism invokes the sovereignty of the political nation and not just the sectional interests of one island, one tribe, one clan or one culture. In the post-colonial age the greatest test which faces the islands of the South Pacific is the legacy of traumatic colonialism. Withdrawal into self-absorbed ethnocentric isolation provides no solution; instead it creates new dilemmas.

And what of the destabilisation created by colonial strategies of France, Indonesia and the United States in the Pacific? Are there alternative policies available to these powers in the region? There are, but they need to be based on the acceptance that the South Pacific peoples and nations do form an entity in their own right. They must endorse the validity of 'nuclear-free and independent' aspirations in Oceania. Their present colonial and military emphasis would need to be replaced by a contribution based on mutual respect and on equal terms. The future of South Pacific countries belongs primarily to their own people.

Glossary

ABRI	*Angkatan Bersenjata Republik Indonesia* (Indonesian Armed Forces).
brousse	bush in New Caledonia.
broussard	bush farmer; often poor white.
Caldoche	New Caledonian-born European settler.
CAP	*Comité d'Action Patriotique de Nouvelle Calédonie* (Patriotic Action Committee). Extremist right-wing group.
CEA	*Commissariat à l'Energie Atomique* (Atomic Energy Commission).
CEP	*Centre d'Expérimentation du Pacifique* (Pacific Nuclear Testing Centre).
CSRC	Colonial Sugar Refining Company of Fiji.
DGSE	*Directorate Générale des Services Extérieur* (French external secret service).
EPK	*Écoles Populaires Kanakes* (Kanak people's schools).
FN	*Front National* (New Caledonian offshoot of Jean-Marie le Pen's extreme right-wing party in France).
Foulards rouges	Red Scarves. Radical left-wing group which spawned new generation of Kanak pro-independence parties.
FULK	*Front Uni pour la Libération Kanak* (left-wing Kanak United Liberation Front).
FLNKS	*Front de Libération Nationale Kanak et Socialiste* (Kanak Socialist National Liberation Front). Major pro-independence coalition of parties and progressive people's movements.
FLP	The multiracial Fiji Labour Party.
GFKEL	*Groupe des Femmes Kanakes et Exploitées en Lutte* (Kanak and Exploited Women's Struggle Group).
GIGN	*Groupe d'Intervention de la Gendarmerie Nationale* (National Gendarmerie Intervention Group).

Kopassandha	Indonesian red beret paratrooper force.
Kopkamtib	Command for the Restoration of Security and Order. Indonesian military intelligence body.
LKS	*Libération Kanake Socialiste* (Kanak Socialist Liberation party).
machochos	Young Kanak militants supporting Machoro. The word was borrowed from the Nicaraguan term *muchachos* — youthful guerrillas.
mataqali	Fijian tribal land-owning clan.
MOP	*Mouvement pour l'Ordre et la Paix* (Peace and Order Movement). Extremist right-wing group in New Caledonia.
NFP	National Federation Party. Indian-dominated party which joined coalition with multiracial FLP.
NFIP	Nuclear-Free and Independent Pacific movement, a coalition of Pacific grassroots movements.
OPM	*Organisasi Papua Merdeka* (Free Papua Movement). De facto government formed by PEMKA faction of OPM. Provisional revolutionary government formed by *Victoria* faction.
PALIKA	*Parti de Libération Kanak* (radical left-wing Kanak Liberation Party).
pakeha	Maori term for white New Zealander.
PEMKA	*Pemulihan Keadilan.* Command for the Restoration of Justice — one of OPM's two main factions.
PSC	*Parti Socialiste Calédonien* (Caledonian Socialist Party).
RFMF	Royal Fiji Military Forces; later becoming the republican FMF.
RPCR	*Rassemblement pour la Calédonie dans la Républic* (Caledonian Republican Rally Party). Major anti-independence settler party; affiliated to the conservative RPR (*Rassemblement pour la Républic*) party in metropolitan France.
tribu	Kanak tribe or tribal village.
taukei	indigenous Fijian.
Taukei Movement	Right-wing Fijian group claiming 'indigenous rights' which backed 1987 *coup d'états*.
UNHCR	United Nations High Commissioner for Refugees.
UPM	*Union Progressiste Melanésienne* Melanesian Progressive Union).
SLN	Societé le Nickel of New Caledonia.
Vanuaaku Pati	Formerly the National Party in pre-independence Vanuatu. Now the ruling party, it is the strongest

	supporter among Pacific political parties of nationalist movements.
Victoria	For 'Victory' — OPM group launched by Seth Rumkorem.
wantok	Pidjin meaning literally member of the same Melanesian language group, but in more general usage, 'friend'.

Names and terms

Nationalist and indigenous spellings of names and peoples crucial to the subject of this book have generally been used in preference to the style of post-colonial maps and texts. Hence Kanaky is frequently used in preference to New Caledonia, and Kanaks rather than pro-independence Melanesians; Belau is retained rather than Palau; Maubere for Timorese; West Papua (*Irian Barat*) rather than Irian Jaya; and Moruroa, not Mururoa.

Notes

Introduction

1. John Connell, *New Caledonia or Kanaky? The Political History of a French Colony*, Australian National University, Canberra, 1987, p.377.
2. *Pacific Islands Monthly*, March 1981.
3. *Les Nouvelles Calédoniennes*, 18 April 1985.
4. Peter Worsley & Kofi Buenor Hadjor (eds), *On the Brink: Nuclear Proliferation and the Third World*, Third World Communications, London, 1987, p. 136.
5. Owen Wilkes, 'US Involvement in the Fiji *Coup d'État*', article published by *Wellington Confidential*, June 1987.
6. Peter Hayes et al, *American Lake: Nuclear Peril in the Pacific*, Penguin, Melbourne, 1986. p. x.
7. F. West et al, 'Toward the year 1985; The Relationship between US Policy and Naval Forces in the Pacific,' Appendix C, in Institute for Foreign Policy Analysis, *Environments for US Naval Strategy in the Pacific Ocean—Indian Ocean Area, 1985-1995* (mimeo), Conference Report for Centre for Advanced Research, US Naval War College, Cambridge, Mass., June 1977, p. 138.
8. Luncheon address by William Bodde, Honolulu, 10 February 1982.
9. *East Timor: Violations of Human Rights*, Amnesty International, London, 1985, p. 6.
10. José Ramos-Horta, *Funu: The Unfinished Saga of East Timor*, Red Sea Press, Trenton, New Jersey, 1987, p. 191.
11. David Robie, *Eyes of Fire: The Last Voyage of the Rainbow Warrior*, Lindon Publishing, Auckland, 1986, p. 156.
12. Ibid., p. viii.
13. Interview with Éloi Machoro, 6 December 1984.

1. Atoll of Great Secrets

1. Bengt and Marie-Thérèse Danielsson, *Poisoned Reign*, Penguin Australia, Melbourne, 1987, p. 24.

1. Atoll of Great Secrets

1. Bengt and Marie-Thérèse Danielsson, *Poisoned Reign,* Penguin Australia, Melbourne, 1987, p. 24.
2. Ron Crocombe et al, *Politics in Polynesia,* Institute of Pacific Studies, University of the South Pacific, 1983, p. 198.
3. Danielsson, p. 27.
4. Crocombe, p. 200.
5. Danielsson, p. 39.
6. Giff Johnson, *Collision Course at Kwajalein: Marshall Islanders in the Shadow of the Bomb,* Pacific Concerns Resource Centre, Honolulu, 1984, p. 11.
7. Bengt Danielsson, 'Under a Cloud of Secrecy,' *Ambio,* vol. 13, no. 5-6, 1984.
8. Danielsson, *Poisoned Reign,* pp. 97-100.
9. Ibid., pp. 102-103.
10. David McTaggart, *Greenpeace III: Journey into the Bomb,* Collins, London, 1978, pp. 280-281.
11. David Robie, 'French Piracy Charges: Skipper Sues Navy', *Nation Review,* Melbourne, 9-15 May 1975, p. 776.
12. Danielsson, *Poisoned Reign,* pp. 188-189.
13. Robie, 'What Happened on Moruroa?' *Auckland Star,* 27 October 1979, pp. 5-16.

2. The Forgotten Wars

1. Jill Jolliffe, *East Timor: Nationalism and Colonialism.* University of Queensland Press, St Lucia, 1978, p. 3.
2. José Ramos-Horta, *Funu: The Unfinished Saga of East Timor,* Red Sea Press, Trenton, New Jersey, 1987, p. 2.
3. *East Timor: Violations of Human Rights,* Amnesty International Publications, London, 1985, p. 24.
4. Ibid., p. 26.
5. Ibid., p. 28.
6. James Dunn, *Timor: A People Betrayed,* Jacaranda Press, Brisbane, 1983, p. 24.
7. Carmel Budiardjo & Liem Soei Liong, *The War Against East Timor,* Zed Books, London, 1984, p. 9.
8. Budiardjo & Liem, p. 5.
9. Ibid., p. 20.
10. Dunn, p. 348.
11. Budiardjo & Liem, p. 20.
12. James Dunn, 'East Timor, Notes on the Humanitarian Situation',

Parliamentary Legislative Research Service, Canberra, 26 September 1979, pp. 2-3.

13. Amnesty *Timor* report, p. 10.
14. Ramos-Horta, p. xi.
15. *Sydney Morning Herald*, 5 April 1977.
16. Budiardjo & Liem, p. 37.
17. Sydney *National Times*, 'The Timor Papers', 6-12 June 1982.
18. David Robie, 'Blood on Our Hands', *New Outlook*, October 1983, p. 14.
19. Budiardjo & Liem, 'The Indonesian Army's Secret Instructions for Counter-insurgency Operations in East Timor', appendix, p. 237.
20. Amnesty *Timor* report, p. 54.
21. Dunn, *Timor: A People Betrayed*, p. xiii.
22. Robie, p. 14.
23. *Sydney Morning Herald*, 10 September 1984.
24. Radio New Zealand *Checkpoint*, 12 December 1984.
25. Robie, *New Zealand Times*, 7 April 1985.
26. Ramos-Horta, p. 206.
27. Robin Osborne, *Indonesia's Secret War*, Allen & Unwin, Sydney, 1985, p. 44.
28. *Sydney Morning Herald*, 14 July 1969.
29. Osborne, p. 50.
30. Ibid., p. 62.
31. *Pacific Islands Monthly*, July 1984.
32. *Ecologist*, London, May 1986.
33. *Times of Papua New Guinea*, 10-16 November 1988.
34. *Pacific Islands Monthly*, November 1988.

3. Vanuatu: Beyond Pandemonium

1. John Beasant, *The Santo Rebellion*, University of Hawaii Press/Heinemann, Melbourne, 1984, p. 94.
2. Ahmed Ali & Ron Crocombe, *Politics in Melanesia*, University of the South Pacific, Suva, 1982, p. 84.
3. Beasant, p. 1.
4. Richard Shears, *The Coconut War*, Cassell, Melbourne, 1980, p. 22.
5. Brian Macdonald-Milne & Pamela Thomas, *Yumi Stanup: Leaders and Leadership in a New Nation*, University of the South Pacific, Suva, 1981, p. 7.
6. Walter Lini, *Beyond Pandemonium: From the New Hebrides to Vanuatu*, University of the South Pacific, Suva, 1980, p. 13.
7. Macdonald-Milne, p. 8.
8. Lini., p. 15.

9. Ibid., p. 27.
10. Beasant, p. 45
11. Ali & Crocombe, p. 88.
12. Lini, p. 50.
13. Shears, p. 43.
14. Lini, p. 53.
15. London *Daily Express*, 2 June 1980.
16. Beasant, p. 98.
17. Ibid., p. 103.
18. Lini, p. 62.
19. Details in *Pacific Islands Monthly*, April, July, August, September 1982.

4. From Atai to Tjibaou

1. Myriam Dornoy, *Politics in New Caledonia*, Sydney University Press, 1984, p. 14.
2. Martyn Lyons, *The Totem and the Tricolour*, New South Wales University Press, Sydney, 1986, p. 16.
3. Alan Ward, *Land and Politics in New Caledonia*, Australian National University, Canberra, 1982, p. 2.
4. Maurice Lenormand, *L'Evolution Politique des Autochtones de la Nouvelle Calédonie*, Société des Océanists, Paris, 1954, p. 262.
5. Lyons, p. 54.
6. Ibid., p. 56.
7. Dornoy, p. 29.
8. Lyons, p. 61.
9. Ibid, p. 63.
10. Ingrid Kircher, *The Kanaks of New Caledonia*, Minority Rights Group, London, 1986, p. 6.
11. Donna Winslow, 'Independence and Ethnicity in New Caledonia', unpublished article, University of Montréal, November 1986, p. 12.
12. Ibid., p. 14.
13. Lyons, p. 101.
14. Ibid., p. 102.
15. Winslow, p. 20.
16. *Le Calédonien*, 27 February 1953, as quoted by Dorney, p. 164.
17. John Connell, *New Caledonia or Kanaky? The Political History of a French Colony*, Research School of Pacific Studies, Australian National University, Canberra, 1987, p. 251.
18. Lyons, p. 119.
19. Dornoy, p. 170.
20. Kircher, p. 7.
21. Appollinaire Anova Ataba, *D'Atai à l'Indépendance*, Edipop, Nouméa,

1965-1984; Marc Coulon, *l'Irruption Kanak: de Calédonie à Kanaky*, Messidor, Paris, 1985, pp. 45-52.

22. Nidoish Naisseline, in *Réveil Canaque*, 1970, 1973, as quoted by Lyons, p. 125.
23. Dornoy, p. 207.
24. FLNKS document, tabled by deputy Roch Pidjot in the French National Assembly, May 1984.
25. *Le Matin* magazine, 3 October 1981.
26. Winslow, p. 28.
27. An Independence Front statement, quoted by Kircher.
28. David Robie, 'Blood on Their Banner', *NZ Listener*, 27 October 1984, pp. 14-15.
29. Robie ' Election Fury Splits a Nation', *Islands Business*, December 1984, p. 11.
30. Ibid, pp. 10-17.
31. Ibid, p. 11.

5. The Massacre of Hienghène

The reconstruction of the massacre in this chapter is based mainly on interviews with the survivors and transcripts of sworn testimony in the Pierre Declercq Committee report 'Attempt to Reconstruct the Crime', 8 October 1986.

1. Declercq committee report.
2. Ibid.
3. Ibid.
4. Ibid.
5. Ibid.
6. *La rivière pleure* is a poem dedicated to the victims of the Hienghène massacre; from a collection of revolutionary poetry by Kanak activist Déwé Gorode, *Sous les cendres des conques*, Edipop, Nouméa, 1985.
7. David Robie, 'Slaughter in the Moonlight', *Islands Business*, January 1985, p. 12.
8. Declercq committee report.
9. *Les Nouvelles Calédoniennes*, 8 October 1986.
10. *NZ Listener*, 15 November 1986.
11. Robie, 'Mockery of Justice', *Islands Business*, November 1986, p. 37.
12. Robie, 'Slaughter in the Moonlight'.
13. Robie, 'Aftermath of Hienghène', *Islands Business*, December 1986, p. 31.
14. Robie, 'Massacre Accused in Dock', *Dominion*, 19 October 1987.
15. *The Dominion*, 31 October 1987.

6. Martyrdom of Machoro

1. 'Testament' of Éloi Machoro, *Bulletin de l'USTKE*, 18 November 1984 anniversary edition.
2. *Amnesty International Report 1986*, p. 282.
3. *NZ Listener*, 'The Waiting War', 26 January 1985, p. 13.
4. David Robie, 'Police Kill Machoro', *Islands Business*, February 1985, p. 6.
5. *Rouge*, 14-20 December 1984.
6. Donna Winslow, 'State Crime in New Caledonia?' The Death of Éloi Machoro,' *South Pacific Forum* pamphlet, 2 (2): 93-105.
7. *Pacific Islands Monthly*, March 1986.
8. Ibid.
9. *L'Avenir Calédonien*, No. 929, 7 February 1985.
10. Robie, *Islands Business*, February 1985.
11. *L'Avenir Calédonien*, No. 929, 7 February 1985.
12. Robie, *Islands Business*, February 1985.
13. 'Machoro', from cassette album *Taim Mi Mitim Yu*, by Black September, recorded with Studio Vanuwespa, August 1985.
14. *Les Nouvelles Calédoniennes*, 3 December 1986.
15. *Pacific Islands Monthly*, March 1986.
16. Ibid.
17. Robie, 'Amnesty Probes Death', *Islands Business*, April 1987. p. 23.
18. Ibid.

7. Dien Bien Thio

1. *Afrique-Asie*, No. 341, 11 February 1985.
2. *Le Figaro*, 29-30 November 1984.
3. *Minute*, 1-7 December 1984.
4. *Valuers Actuelles*, 28 December 1984.
5. *Les Nouvelles Calédoniennes*, 14 January 1985.
6. *Le Quotidien de Paris*, 24 January 1985.
7. Ingrid Kircher, *The Kanaks of New Caledonia*, Minority Rights Group, Report 71, June 1986, p. 11.
8. *Pacific Islands Monthly*, April 1985, p. 25.
9. David Robie, 'Picnic Turns Violent', *Islands Business*, March 1985, p. 14.
10. Kircher report, p. 11.
11. Ibid, p. 12.
12. Ibid, p. 12.
13. Robie, 'Hunting Recognition', *Islands Business*, July 1985, p. 25.
14. *Pacific Islands Monthly*, October 1985, p. 27.
15. Kircher report, p. 12.

16. Robie, 'Upset after the Poll', *Islands Business*, November 1985, p. 21.
17. Free Caledonian Forces (FCL) document, *Liste des Enemis de la Nouvelle Calédonie de la Liberté et de la Republique*, 1985.

8. Niuklia Fri Pasifik

1. See Glenn Alcalay, 'US Nuclear Imperialism in Micronesia', *On the Brink: Nuclear Proliferation & the Third World*, Third World Communications, 1987; and Giff Johnson, *Collision Course at Kwajalein: Marshall Islanders in the Shadow of the Bomb*, Pacific Concerns Resource Centre, Honolulu, 1984.
2. Donald McHenry, *Micronesia: Trust Betrayed*, Carnegie Endowment for International Peace, Washington DC, 1975, p. 54.
3. Robert Kiste, *The Bikinians: A Study of Forced Migration*, Cummings Publishing, Menlo Park, CA, 1974, p. 27.
4. Johnson, p. 7.
5. Alcalay, p. 121.
6. Ibid, p. 132.
7. Pierre Mauroy, speech, 20 September 1982.
8. William Arkin, *Nuclear Battlefields: Global Links in the Arms Race*, Ballinger, 1985, p. 226.
9. Vijay Naidu, 'The Fiji Anti-nuclear Movement: Problems and Prospects', papers to the United Nations University Conference, Auckland, April 1986, p. 5.
10. Preamble to the People's Charter for a Nuclear-Free and Independent Pacific, NFIP Conference, 10-20 July 1983, Port Vila.
11. Stewart Firth, *Nuclear Playground*, Allen & Unwin, Sydney, 1987, p. 134.
12. David Robie, 'Where Was the Aroha?', *New Outlook*, August 1983, p. 33.
13. Ibid., p. 34.
14. *The Economist*, quoted by *Fiji Sun*, 23 January 1987.
15. *Islands Business*, November 1986.
16. *Pacific Islands Monthly*, July 1986.
17. *The Economist*, quoted by *Fiji Sun*, 23 January 1987.
18. Owen Wilkes, 'The Rarotonga Treaty and the Movement for a Nuclear-Free and Independent Pacific', unpublished discussion paper, September 1985.
19. Ibid.
20. 'Report by the Chairman of the Working Group on a South Pacific Nuclear-Free Zone (SPNFZ)', South Pacific Forum, 14 June 1985.
21. Ibid.
22. Fiji *Sunday Times*, 10 August 1986.

23. NZ *Sunday Times*, 31 August 1986.
24. Walter Lini, from the foreword to David Robie's *Eyes of Fire: The Last Voyage of the Rainbow Warrior*, Lindon Publishing, Auckland, 1986, p. viii.
25. *Islands Business*, September 1986.
26. Sydney *Times on Sunday*, 17 August 1986.
27. *Fiji Sun*, 13 May 1986.

9. Belau: Trust Betrayed

1. *New York Times*, 27 November 1986.
2. *New York Times*, 21 July 1987.
3. *Rengel Belau*, 2-16 September 1984.
4. Robert Aldridge and Ched Myers, *Will Palau Survive? A Story of Covert Imperialism in the Pacific*, mimeographed book, Pasadena, 1988, pp. 3-14.
5. *Philadelphia Inquirer*, 22 July 1985.
6. 'Assassination of President Remeliik of Palau; Subsequent Conviction of Three Defendants and Related Events,' ACLU briefing paper by David G. Richenthal, New York, 1 September 1986, p. 10.
7. *Philadelphia Inquirer*, 22 July 1985.
8. Pheroze Jagoze, 'Denial of Democracy: An Investigation into the US Administration of the Republic of Belau as part of the Trust Territory of the Pacific Islands', School of Law, Auckland University, 1985, p. 56.
9. *New York Times*, 27 November 1986.
10. *Republic of Belau vs. Tmetuchl, Tewid and Sabino*, Belau Supreme Court Crim. No. 388-85, App. No. 2-86 (July 1987).
11. Richenthal.
12. Richenthal.
13. Ibid.
14. *San Jose Mercury News*, 29 November 1987.
15. *Auckland Star*, 30 April 1987.
16. David Robie, 'Belauans Face Dilemma over Nuclear Stand', *Dominion*, 2 December 1986.
17. Aldridge & Myers, pp. 1-13.
18. Robie, 'Belau: The Mouse that Roared', *Cue*, Auckland, 27 Oct-2 Nov, 1984.
19. Republic of Belau Constitution, 1979, Art. XIII, Sect. 6.
20. *Ground Zero*, Winter 1986.
21. 'Report of Belau Visit 1981', unpublished paper, by Jim Douglass and Robert Aldridge, 28 October-6 November 1981.
22. Aldridge & Myers, pp. 3-4.
23. Ibid., pp. 3-6.

23. Ibid., pp. 3-6.
24. Ibid., pp. 3-7.
25. Ibid.
26. Robie, 'Belau in Ferment over Pact with US', *Dominion*, 19 July 1987.
27. Statement by Belauan House of Delegates Speaker Santon Olikong before US Congress Interior and Insular Affairs Committee, 23 July 1987.
28. Ibid.
29. Roger Clark, 'Statement Submitted for the Record on S. J. Res. 231, Senate Committee on Energy and Natural Resources,' Rutgers University, New Jersey, 4 February 1988.
30. Robie, 'The Bizarre Riddle of Belau', *Dominion Sunday Times*, 28 August 1988.
31. Aldridge & Myers, pp. 5-25.

10. Barbouzes and Bombs

1. David Robie, *Eyes of Fire: The Voyage of the Rainbow Warrior*, Lindon Publishing, Auckland, 1986, pp. 21-22.
2. Ibid., p. 28.
3. Ibid, see details of evacuation, pp. 47-63.
4. *Les Nouvelles de Tahiti*, 31 December 1986.
5. NZ *Sunday Star*, 19 July 1987.
6. *Michael King, Death of the Rainbow Warrior*, Penguin, 1986, p. 197.
7. *New Zealand Herald*, 13 August 1985.
8. Robie, 'White Men and Coups', *Islands Business*, February 1985, p. 24.
9. Robie, *Eyes of Fire*, p. 127.
10. Cited by Robie, 'Anger over Spy Deal', *Islands Business*, August 1986, p. 19.
11. Robie, 'Ching in the Slammer', *Islands Business*, August 1986, p. 24.
12. *New Zealand Times*, 9 March 1986.
13. Robie, 'Mafart "Smuggled Out before NZ Told" ', *Dominion*, 21 December 1987; *Les Nouvelles de Tahiti*, 19 December 1987.
14. Robie, 'Spectre of the CIA', *Islands Business*, September 1986, p. 54.
15. *Sydney Morning Herald*, 3 January 1986.
16. *Islands Business*, May 1986.
17. Robert Robertson, 'The People Stand Up: Vanuatu's Foreign Policies in the 1980s', SSED Working Paper No. 9, University of the South Pacific, Suva, 1987.
18. *Vanuatu Weekly*, 25 August 1984.
19. Owen Wilkes, 'US Involvement in the Fiji Coup d'État', Wellington Confidential, June 1987.

21. *New Zealand Times,* 30 October 1983.
22. *Sydney Morning Herald,* 17 May 1986.
23. *NZ Monthly Review,* October 1986.
24. As cited in Robie, 'A Grenada in the Pacific?', *Dominion Sunday Times,* 1 May 1987.
25. See Wilkes, 'Sir Papadoc and the CIA: Dirty Work in the Cook Islands', *NZ Monthly Review,* September 1987.
26. Christchurch *Star*, 7 May 1987.

11. The Rise of Bavadra

1. David Routledge, *Matanitu: The Struggle for Power in Early Fiji,* University of the South Pacific, Suva, 1985, p. 41.
2. Everett Frost, 'Fiji', in Jesse Jennings (ed), *The Prehistory of Polynesia,* Australian National University, Canberra, 1979, pp. 79-80.
3. Routledge, p. 54.
4. Ibid., p. 74
5. G. Kerr and T. Donnelly, *Fiji in the Pacific*, Jacaranda Press, Brisbane, 1976, p. 38.
6. Vijay Naidu, *The Violence of Indenture in Fiji,* World University Service (in association with USP), Suva, 1980, p. 3.
7. Ibid., p. 35.
8. Hugh Tinker, Naresha Duruaiswamy, Yash Ghai and Martin Ennals, *Fiji,* Minority Rights Group, London, 1987, p. 3.
9. Simioni Durutalo, 'Internal Colonialism and Unequal Regional Development: The Case of Western Viti Levu, Fiji', MA thesis, University of the South Pacific, 1985, p. 199.
10. Robert Robertson and Akosita Tamanisau, *Fiji: Shattered Coups,* Pluto Press, Sydney, 1988, p. 11.
11. Derryck Scarr (ed.), *The Three-legged Stool: Selected Writings of Ratu Sir Lala Sukuna,* Macmillan, London, 1983, p. 58.
12. Tinker et al., p. 3.
13. Robertson, 'Fiji: Political Background to the Coup', *South Pacific Forum,* 4:1, Suva, August, 1987, pp. 49-56.
14. Minority Rights report, *Fiji,* p. 6.
15. Robertson, 'Political Background'.
16. Owen Wilkes, 'US Involvement in the Fiji Coup d'État', *Wellington Confidential,* June 1987.
17. Report of the Royal Commission of Inquiry into the 1982 Fiji General Election by Sir John White, November 1983, Fiji Parliamentary Paper No. 74 of 1983.
18. *Pacific Islands Monthly,* February 1985.
19. *Pacific Islands Monthly,* May 1986.

20. David Robie, 'Ailing Fiji Turns to the "Doc" for a Cure', *Dominion Sunday Times,* 19 April 1987.
21. Robertson and Tamanisau, p. 39.
22. Robie, *Dominion,* 10 April 1987.
23. Robie, 'Ailing Fiji . . .'.
24. Robie, 'Fiji: Countdown to a Coup', *NZ Outlook,* June 1987, p. 29.

12. 'Out of the Barrel of a Gun'

1. Fiji Parliament *Hansard,* 14 May 1987.
2. Sitiveni Rabuka, *Rabuka: No Other Way,* Doubleday, Sydney, 1988, p. 72. Only the coup leader has made this claim; other versions contradict this.
3. *India Today,* 30 November, 1987.
4. Radio FM96, Suva, 14 May 1987.
5. *Fiji Sun,* 15 May 1987.
6. Lieutenant-Colonel Jim Sanday, 'Truths Rabuka Left Out', *Islands Business,* March 1988, p. 62.
7. *The Australian,* 19 May 1987.
8. *Fiji Times,* 21 May 1987.
9. *Bulletin,* 26 May 1987.
10. Address by Jone Dakuvula to the NZ Institute of International Affairs, 16 October 1987.
11. Radio Fiji, 10 April 1987.
12. *Sydney Morning Herald,* 19 May 1987.
13. *Times on Sunday,* 24 May 1987.
14. See the author's detailed account 'Why the Fijian plot theory is gaining ground', *Times on Sunday,* 12 July 1987, p. 12. A shorter version was translated into the Fiji language and distributed widely in Fiji. Later, other journalists and authors explored the theme, notably Robert Robertson and Akosita Tamanisau, *Fiji: Shattered Coups,* Pluto Press, Sydney, 1988, pp. 96-99.
15. This version reprinted in *Fiji Times,* 28 May 1987.
16. Rabuka, p. 42.
17. Sanday, 'The Soldier', *Islands Business,* May 1988, p. 16
18. *NZ Listener,* 6 June 1987.
19. *Islands Business,* June 1987.
20. *Sunday Sun,* 19 July 1987.
21. Taukei draft constitution document, unpublished.

13. The Rabuka Regime

1. *Islands Business*, July 1987.
2. *Pacific Islands Monthly*, November 1987.
3. *Fiji Times*, 28 May 1987.
4. David Robie, 'Suva, Mon Amour! (Except Sundays)', *Islands Business*, March 1988, p. 48.
5. London *Times*, 21 October 1987.
6. For details of news media distortion see Robie, 'The Muzzling of the Pacific Press', *NZ Monthly Review*, December 1988, pp. 20-22; Shaista Shameen, 'The Fiji Coups: Media Distortion', *NZ Monthly Review*, February 1989, pp. 13-19.
7. Robie, 'Troops Aim Propaganda at Fijians', *NZ Sunday Times*, 12 July 1987.
8. Robie, 'Life After Black Thursday', *NZ Outlook*, July 1987, p. 43.
9. *Sunday Star*, 6 December 1987.
10. Unpublished report to Amnesty International, 8 October 1987.
11. *Bulletin*, 23 October 1987.
12. Wendy Bacon, 'Somebody's Man in Fiji', *NZ Listener*, 26 December 1987, pp. 18-21; see also articles by Wendy Bacon in *The Eye* (Sydney), January 1988, March 1988.
13. Bacon, *Listener*.
14. For details of CIA and other alleged foreign involvement in the coups see Owen Wilkes, 'US Involvement in the Fiji Coup d'État,' *Wellington Confidential* and *Wellington Pacific Report*, July 1987; Wendy Bacon, SBS *Dateline*, screened on ABC *Four Corners*, 17 November 1987; and Jo Ann Wypijewski, 'The Fiji Coup: Was the US behind It?', *The Nation*, New York, 15-22 August 1987, reprinted in *Pacific Islands Monthly*, October 1987.
15. *Sydney Morning Herald*, 26 March 1988; *Wellington Pacific Report* No. 11, May 1988, pp. 1-3.
16. Wilkes, p. 6.
17. Karen Mangnall, 'Blueprint for Supremacy', Auckland *Sunday Star*, 15 May 1988.
18. Interview with Owen Wilkes, 30 August 1988.
19. Robie, 'Spectre of the CIA', *Islands Business*, September 1986.
20. *Sydney Morning Herald*, 18 May 1987.
21. John Cameron, 'Aid, Trade, the Multinationals, and Foreign Policy', unpublished paper at Coalition for Democracy in Fiji conference, Wellington, 27 August 1988.
22. *The Australian*, 7 December 1987.
23. Christopher Harder, *The Guns of Lautoka*, Sunshine Press, Auckland, 1988.
24. *The Dominion*, 24 June 1988.

25. Address by Jone Dakuvula to the NZ Institute of International Affairs, 16 October 1987.
26. Professor Yash Ghai et al, *Fiji*, Report 75, Minority Rights Group, London, 1987, p.12.
27. Robert Robertson and Akosita Tamanisau, *Fiji: Shattered Coups,* Sydney, Pluto Press, 1988, pp. 142-153.

14. 'Nomads' and Delusions

1. David Robie, 'Occupation or Protection?', *Islands Business*, March 1987, p. 28.
2. *Le Monde,* 14 May 1986.
3. Robie, p. 29.
4. Robie, 'Kanaks Take Case to the UN', *Dominion*, 17 March 1987.
5. *International Herald Tribune*, 13 October 1986.
6. Robie, 'A "Subversive" in Kanaky', *Islands Business*, February 1987, pp. 22-23.
7. Robie, 'Occupation or Protection?', *Islands Business*, March 1987, p. 29.
8. *Bulletin*, 27 January 1987.
9. *Témoin Chrétien*, 29 December 1986-4 January 1987.
10. Robie, 'Pons' Recipe for Trouble', *Islands Business*, March 1987, p. 28.
11. *Le Point*, 14 September 1987.

15. The Siege of Ouvéa

1. David Robie, 'Tahiti's Night of the Inferno', *Islands Business*, December 1987, p. 14.
2. *Les Nouvelles de Tahiti*, 26 October 1987.
3. Robie, 'Fallout from the Inferno Hurts Flosse', *Islands Business*, January 1988, p. 18.
4. *Pacific Islands Monthly*, January 1988.
5. Robie, 'The Ifira Challenge', *NZ Listener*, 25 June 1988, p. 47.
6. *Politis*, 31 March 1988.
7. Jean-Marie Tjibaou in a statement on Radio Djiido, 23 April 1988.
8. Robie, 'The Bullet and the Ballot', *NZ Listener*, 11 June 1988, p. 16.
9. Ibid., p. 17.
10. Frédéric Bobin, *Le Monde*, 10 May 1988.
11. Jean Guiart, 'The Truth about Jean-Marie Tjibaou', *Islands Business*, September 1988, p. 29.

Epilogue

1. *NZ Listener,* 27 June 1987.
2. Shaista Shameen, 'The Fiji Coups: Media Distortion', *NZ Monthly Review,* January 1989, p. 19.
3. Interview with Jean-Marie Tjibaou, Nouméa, 11 September 1987.
4. *The Australian,* 2 September 1987.
5. See David Robie, 'The Muzzling of the Pacific Press', *NZ Monthly Review,* December 1988, pp. 20-22.
6. Lieutenant-Colonel Jim Sanday, 'Setting the Scene for a Pacific War', *Australian Financial Review,* 30 January 1989, p. 9.
7. Robie, *Accent,* 'Chosen by God: Fiji's Rabuka', September 1987.
8. *Fiji Sun,* 17 August 1987.
9. Interview with Richard Naidu, Auckland, 8 January 1988.

Bibliography

Aldridge, Robert and Ched Myers, *Will Palau Survive? A Story of Covert Imperialism in the Pacific*, unpublished manuscript, Pasadena, 1988.

Ali, Ahmed and Ron Crocombe (eds), *Foreign Forces in Pacific Politics*, Institute of Pacific Studies, University of the South Pacific, Suva, 1983.

Ali, Ahmed and Ron Crocombe (eds), *Politics in Melanesia*, Institute of Pacific Studies, University of the South Pacific, Suva, 1982.

Ali, Ahmed and Ron Crocombe (eds), *Politics in Polynesia*, Institute of Pacific Studies, University of the South Pacific, Suva, 1982.

Amnesty International Report 1988. Amnesty International Publications, London, 1988.

Association pour la foundation d'un Institut Kanak d'Histoire Moderne. *L'Histoire du Pays Kanak*. Edition IKS, Nouméa, 1985.

Ataba, Apollinaire, *D'Atai à l'indépendence*, Édipop, Noumèa, 1983.

Barry, Alister and Philip Shingler, script research notes for Pacific Stories Partnership television documentary, *Niuklia Fri Pasifik*, Wellington, 1989.

Beasant, John, *The Santo Rebellion*, University of Hawaii Press/ Heinemann, Melbourne, 1984.

Bello, Walden, Peter Hayes and Lyuba Zarsky, *American Lake: Nuclear Peril in the Pacific*, Penguin Books, Melbourne, 1986.

Budiardjo, Carmel and Liem Soei Liong, *West Papua: The Obliteration of a People*, Tapol Human Rights Campaign, London, 1988.

Chomsky, Noam and Edward Herman, *The Washington Connection and Third World Facism*, Spokesman, Nottingham, 1979.

Connell, John, *New Caledonia or Kanaky? The Political History of a French Colony*, Australian National University, Canberra, 1987.

Connell, John, Michael Spencer and Alan Ward (eds), *New Caledonia: Essays in Nationalism and Dependency*, Queensland University Press, Brisbane, 1988.

Coulon, Marc, *L'Irruption Kanak: de Calédonie à Kanaky*, Messidor, Paris, 1985.

Crocombe, Ron, *The South Pacific: An Introduction*, University of the South Pacific, Suva, 1973 (revised fifth edition 1989).

Danielsson, Bengt and Marie-Thérèse, *Moruroa, Mon Amour: The French Nuclear Tests in the Pacific*, Penguin, Melbourne, 1977.

Danielsson and Danielsson, *Poisoned Reign: French Nuclear Colonialism in the Pacific* (revised and updated edition of *Moruroa, Mon Amour*), Penguin, Melbourne, 1986.

Dibblin, Jane, *Day of Two Suns: US Nuclear Testing and the Pacific Islanders*, Virago, London, 1988.

Dornoy, Myriam, *Politics in New Caledonia*, Sydney University Press, Sydney, 1984.

Dean, Eddie and Stan Ritova, *Rabuka: No Other Way*, Doubleday Books, Sydney, 1988.

Dunn, James, *Timor: A People Betrayed*, Jacaranda Press, Brisbane, 1983.

East Timor: Violations of Human Rights, Amnesty International Publications, London, 1985.

Firth, Stewart, *Nuclear Playground*, South Sea Books/Allen & Unwin, Honolulu and Sydney, 1987.

Fraser, Helen, *New Caledonia: Anti-colonialism in a Pacific Territory*, Peace Research Centre, Research School of Pacific Studies, Australian National University, Canberra, 1988.

Gabriel, Claude and Vincent Kermel, *Nouvelle-Calédonie: La Révolte Kanake*, La Brèche, Paris, 1985.

Guiart, Jean, *La Terre est le Sang des Morts*, Éditions Anthropos, Paris, 1983.

Harder, Christopher, *The Guns of Lautoka: The Defence of Kahan*, Sunshine Press, Auckland, 1988.

Heine, Carl, *Micronesia at the Crossroads*, University of Hawaii Press, Honolulu, 1974.

Hempenstall, P. and N. Rutherford, *Protest and Dissent in the Colonial Pacific*, University of the South Pacific, Suva, 1984.

Johnson, Giff, *Collision Course at Kwajalein: Marshall Islanders in the Shadow of the Bomb*, Pacific Concerns Resource Centre, Honolulu, 1984.

Jolliffe, Jill, *East Timor: Nationalism and Colonialism*, University of Queensland Press, Queensland, 1978.

King, Michael, *Death of the Rainbow Warrior*, Penguin, Auckland, 1986.

Kircher, Ingrid, *The Kanaks of New Caledonia*, Minority Rights Group, Report 71, London, 1986.

Kohler, Jean-Marie, *Colonie ou Democratie: Élements de Sociologie Politique sur la Nouvelle-Calédonie*, Édipop, Nouméa, 1987.

Lal, Brij. V., *Politics in Fiji: Studies in Contemporary History*, Allen &

Unwin, Sydney, 1986.

Lecompte, Claude, *Coulez le Rainbow Warrior!*, Messidor, Paris, 1985.

Les Temps Modernes, Paris, No. 464, March 1985.

Lyons, Martin, *The Totem and the Tricolour: A Short History of New Caledonia since 1774*, New South Wales University Press, Sydney, 1986.

Liliuokalani, *Hawaii's Story: By Hawaii's Queen*, Tuttle, Rutland, Vermont, 1964.

McIntosh, Malcolm, *Arms Across the Pacific*, Pinter, London, 1987.

McTaggart, David, *Greenpeace III: Journey into the Bomb*, Collins, London, 1978.

Minority Rights Group, Reports 42 *East Timor & West Irian*; 63 *Micronesia: The Problem of Palau*; 71 *The Kanaks of New Caledonia*; 75 *Fiji*, London.

Naidu, Vijay, *The Violence of Indenture in Fiji*, World University Service (in association with USP), Suva, 1980.

Nicol, Bill, *East Timor: The Stillborn Nation*, Visa Books, Melbourne, 1978.

Osborne, Robin, *Indonesia's Secret War: The Guerilla Struggle in Irian Jaya*, Allen and Unwin, Sydney, 1985.

Ounei, Susanna, 'For Kanak Independence: The Fight Against French Rule in New Caledonia', Labour Publishing Cooperative Society and Corso pamphlet, Auckland, 1985.

Plant, Chris, Walter Lini et al., *New Hebrides: The Road to Independence*, University of the South Pacific, Suva, 1977.

Prasad, Satendra (ed.), *Coup and Crisis: Fiji, a Year Later*, clandestine publisher, Suva, 1988; revised and republished by Arena Publications, Melbourne, 1989.

Ramos-Horta, José, *Funu: The Unfinished Saga*, Red Sea Press, New York, 1987.

Robertson, Robert and Akosita Tamanisau, *Fiji: Shattered Coups*, Pluto Press, Sydney, 1988.

Robie, David, *Eyes of Fire: The Last Voyage of the Rainbow Warrior*, Lindon Publishing, Auckland, 1986.

Routledge, David, *Matanitu: The Struggle for Power in Early Fiji*, University of the South Pacific, Suva, 1985.

Shears, Richard, *The Coconut War: The Crisis on Espiritu Santo*, Cassell, Australia, Melbourne, 1980.

Tjibaou, Jean-Marie et al, *Kanaké: The Melanesian Way*, Éditions du Pacifique, Papeete, 1978.

Toyosaki, Hiromitsu, *Goodbye Rongelap!*, Tsukijishokan, Tokyo, 1986.

Ward, Alan, *Land and Politics in New Caledonia*, Australian National University, Canberra, 1982.

Wilkes, Owen, 'US Involvement in the Fiji *Coup d'État*,' article published by *Wellington Confidential and Wellington Pacific Report*, Wellington, June 1987.

Worsley, Peter and Kofi Buenor Hadjor (eds), *On the Brink: Nuclear Proliferation and the Third World*. Third World Communications, London, 1987.

Index